W9-CVS-260

ENGINEERING

for

POTATOES

B. F. (Burt) Cargill, Professor
Research and Extension
Michigan State University
Editor and Coordinator
for development of the
"Engineering for Potatoes" Program

Joint Publishers:

 Michigan State University and
American Society
of Agricultural Engineers

Library of Congress Catalog Card Number: 86-71269

International Standard Book Number: 916150-79-8

Additional Copies of this book
"Engineering for Potatoes" may be
purchased from
American Society of Agricultural Engineers
St. Joseph, MI   49085

PREFACE

The five sections of this book are the result of the development of an Engineering for Potatoes program in conjunction with the 1985 ASAE summer meeting at Michigan State University.

Four ASAE committees were responsible for putting together five one-half day sessions. The committees were as follows:

1. PM-48 - Fruit and Vegetable Harvesting Committee

2. FE-706 - Fruit and Vegetable Packinghouse Operations Committee

3. FE-705 - Transportation, Handling and Warehousing of Agricultural Products Committee

4. SE-304 - Environment of Stored Products Committee

These five sessions were held in June 1985 in the McDonel Kiva on the MSU campus. The following four committee members with their committee were responsible for their programs:

D.B. Churchill, USDA-ARS, Lake Alfred FL, PM-48; D.E. Hammett, Ross Industries, Midland, VA, FE-706; S.E. Prussia, Agricultural Engineering, University of Georgia, Athens, GA, FE-705; and K.J. Hellevang, Agricultural Engineering, North Dakota State University, Fargo, ND, SE-304; B.F. (Burt) Cargill served as the Engineering for Potatoes program coordinator.

The combined efforts of the above group resulted in 36 scientific papers by key authors from ten countries and ten major potato production regions of the United States. Your editor recognized that this material represents very valuable information for the potato industry,however, only a handful of potato industry people knew about and attended the meetings. This is not unusual because the potato industry people have their own meetings and organizations and the tendency for the potato industry people to attend ASAE meetings is slim.

For this reason it was decided to edit these important scientific contributions about the potato industry and make same available through the normal channels used by the potato industry. This edited information involves harvesting, potato handling, mechanization, utilization, quality, storage design, storage environment, air handling, processing, etc.

Your editor has reworked the information into common terminology for people stateside and abroad. Engineering journals require metric units, however, our stateside potato people use English units (feet, pounds, hundredweight (cwt), cubic feet, etc.). Most of these contributions have been reedited into dual units for our stateside potato industry people.

Some important potato conversions that you need when you read information are as follows:*

1 hectar	= 2.47 acres
1 meter	= 3.28 ft^3
1 cubic meter (m^3)	= 35.28 ft
1 $meter^3$ potatoes	= 14.1 cwt
1 $meter^3$ potatoes	= 0.74 short tons
1 $meter^3$ potatoes	= 0.67 metric tons
1 meter per minute	= 3.28 feet/minute
1 meter per minute	= 0.0546 feet/second

There are about 12,000 worldwide members of ASAE but only a handful of the ASAE membership serve as scientists for the potato industry. For this reason a more consciousness effort is needed to make contributions like "Engineering for Potatoes" available to the potato industry. Your editor hopes his personal contacts with the potato industry will help distribute this scientific information to the worldwide potato industry.

----

*For additional conversion units consult the conversion table at the end of this book.

iv

TABLE OF CONTENTS

v

INTRODUCTION

ENGINEERING FOR POTATOES

B.F. (Burt) Cargill

INTRODUCTION

ENGINEERING FOR POTATOES

by

B.F. (Burt) Cargill, Professor, Research and
Extension, Department of Agricultural Engineering,
Michigan State University and Fellow Member ASAE

In the "preface" I described how this book was
made possible. Normally at ASAE meetings relevant
scientific papers are presented but rarely in impact
themes such as this "Engineering for Potatoes."

There are relatively speaking few agricultural
engineers, other engineers, potato scientists, etc.
working on mechanization for potatoes. With
considerable involvement it was possible to pull a
group of these scientists together to make this
impact session. We called it Engineering for
Potatoes. The oral meeting was held in June 1985 in
connection with the 1985 ASAE meeting at Michigan
State University.

ASAE Paper No. 85-1069

Input by key scientists from ten countries and ten potato growing regions makes this Engineering for Potatoes publication a valuable asset to your library of potato knowledge. These key scientists met and presented 36 scientific papers during five one-half day sessions.

ASAE (The American Society of Agricultural Engineers) realize that very few members of the potato industry had an opportunity to hear the original presentations. In fact the intent of these 36 10- to 12-minute oral presentation is to expose the pertinent subject matter to others concerned but not give the entire paper.

For this reason and my personal and deep involvement in the potato industry I have collected all 36 papers and edited same to make them easier for the non-engineering and potato industry people to understand and comprehend the information. We must be aware of the tremendous variations in potato mechanization throughout the world. These variations may be due to production environments, soils, harvesting, utilization, processing, marketing. etc.

The Potato as a food source is a key staple and the world food supply. As one travels about the potato production regions of the world one becomes aware of the dire need for potato industry people and other concerned scientists to expose these world-wide variations.

I hope this compilation of knowledge by scientists gives you a new vision on facts and people. Note at the end of each paper that a list of reference material is inserted. These references give you an additional resource of people involved in the potato industry.

I hope you feel it worth while for us to have made this book conveniently available to you through your potato industry media.

The following figures also provide relevant information on the U.S. potato industry. I do not have same for the world but some of the world information is presented in this book by Robert Booth from the International Potato Center in Lima, Peru.

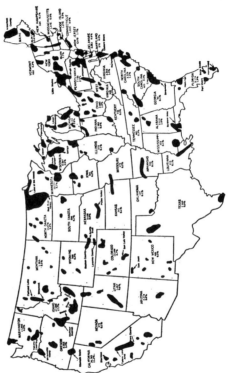

Figure 2. Potato Acreage.

Acres/Farm	Farms	Percentage of Total Acreage
*5 - 9.9	4,366	2.4
10 - 24.9	7,668	10.0
25 - 49.9	5,828	17.1
50 or more	6,492	64.1

*Under 5, 6.4 percent of total acres.

Season	Percent of U.S. Crop
Winter	1.6
Early Spring	1.5
Late Spring	9.2
Early Summer	5.3
Late Summer	13.1
Fall	69.3

Figures under state names indicate the production of that state in percentage of the U.S. crop (1958-62 average). From *Agricultural Handbook 267*, U.S. Dept. of Agriculture

Figure 1. U.S. Potato Acreage Distribution Map.

Fall Production

Six-year comparison of production (in 1,000 cwt). Underlined areas indicate a state's top production within the period (USDA).

state	1980	1981	1982	1983	1984	1985
			1,000 cwt.			
California	6,438	6,919	7,585	7,790	7,280	7,878
Colorado	10,950	11,600	12,825	13,950	17,225	17,920
Connecticut	405	486	369	266	315	350
Idaho-10 sw Co.	7,820	8,040	8,625	8,500	9,380	10,875
-Other Co.	72,020	76,500	83,160	77,490	77,220	91,640
Indiana	726	615	924	600	750	624
Maine	24,960	26,520	27,030	22,560	21,360	27,160
Massachusetts	748	743	779	646	580	825
Michigan	8,160	8,575	10,530	9,840	12,540	12,100
Minnesota	9,920	13,300	11,520	10,313	13,775	14,145
Montana	1,725	1,739	1,924	1,800	1,924	1,890
Nebraska	1,876	2,252	2,332	2,025	2,480	2,173
Nevada	4,420	3,480	4,095	3,720	3,300	3,105
N.Y. Long Island	4,794	5,365	5,130	4,075	3,577	3,870
-Upstate	6,250	6,875	6,500	5,635	6,630	6,125
N. Dakota	15,680	20,125	17,250	20,480	20,615	23,630
Ohio	1,995	1,890	2,205	1,886	2,418	2,465
Oreg-Malheur	3,650	3,450	3,885	3,330	3,960	4,066
-Other Co.	16,095	18,260	17,220	17,380	19,565	22,635
Pennsylvania	4,180	5,250	4,935	4,300	5,160	5,720
Rhode Island	736	832	720	630	598	700
S. Dakota	1,072	702	1,550	2,310	1,820	1,920
Utah	1,170	1,276	1,440	1,357	1,728	1,658
Vermont	120	154	92	88	63	66
Washington	43,935	52,920	52,800	54,080	56,925	62,370
Wisconsin	16,000	18,190	22,575	18,910	21,350	24,130
Wyoming	1,340	1,060	1,134	718	550	245
Total	266,428	295,593	309,134	294,679	313,088	350,285

Figure 2. U.S. Fall Production Figures by Key Potato Growing States or Regions for 1980-1985.

Harvested Acreage

		acres
1.	Idaho	345,000
2.	N. Dakota	139,000
3.	Washington	126,000
4.	Maine	97,000
5.	Minnesota	75,500
6.	Wisconsin	63,500
7.	Colorado	63,400
8.	California	61,300
9.	Oregon	61,000
10.	Michigan	57,800
	U.S.	1,358,000

Yield Per Acre

		cwt
1.	Washington	495
2.	Oregon	438
3.	Wisconsin	380
4.	California	374
5.	Nevada	345
6.	Colorado	318
7.	Idaho	297
8.	Illinois	285
9. & 10.	Delaware, Maine, New Jersey, Rhode Island	280
	U.S.	298

By Production

		cwt
1.	Idaho	102,515,000
2.	Washington	62,370,000
3.	Maine	27,160,000
4.	Oregon	26,701,000
5.	Wisconsin	24,130,000
6.	N. Dakota	23,630,000
7.	California	22,945,000
8.	Colorado	20,140,000
9.	Minnesota	15,933,000
10.	Michigan	15,136,000
	U.S.	404,131,000

USDA Annual Crop Summary

Figure 3. Top Ten Ranking of U.S. States in Potato Acreage Harvested, Yield, and Production, 1985 (all seasons).

7

Acreage and Production, United States

CROP	Acreage Harvested (1,000 Acres)		Unit	Yield per Acre		Production (1,000)	
	1983	1982		1983	1982	1983	1982
Corn, for grain	51,537	73,030	Bu.	81.6	114.5	4,203,777	8,359,364
Corn, silage	7,722	7,879	Ton	12.3	14.3	95,046	112,627
Oats	9,098	10,618	Bu.	52.5	58.4	477,303	620,509
Barley	9,902	9,113	Bu.	52.4	57.3	519,026	522,387
Wheat, all	61,492	78,981	Bu.	39.4	35.6	2,425,408	2,812,297
Winter	47,686	58,487	Bu.	41.8	36.1	1,993,888	2,111,806
Durum	2,492	4,217	Bu.	29.3	35.0	72,979	147,503
Other Spring	11,314	16,277	Bu.	31.7	34.0	358,541	552,988
Rye	923	721	Bu.	30.5	29.1	28,152	20,954
Soybeans	62,163	69,821	Bu.	25.7	31.9	1,595,437	2,229,486
Hay, all	60,461	60,679	Ton	2.36	2.51	142,979	152,534
Hay, Alfalfa	25,937	26,598	Ton	3.22	3.41	83,522	90,678
Dry Beans	1,105.7	1,748.4	Cwt.	13.80	14.33	15,254	25,049
Potatoes, all	1,239.1	1,273.9	Cwt.	263.0	276.0	325,721	351,822
Sugarbeets	1,055.0	1,026.8	Ton	20.0	20.3	21,111	20,894
Peppermint, for oil	59.3	58.2	Lb.	62.0	60.0	3,703	3,482
Spearmint, for oil	25.4	22.5	Lb.	55.0	60.0	1,398	1,343

Figure 4. U.S. Crop Acreage and Production Including Potatoes for the Years 1982–83.

I. HARVESTING AND MECHANIZATION

POTATO HARVESTER PERFORMANCE WITH
ROTARY DISK BLADES

by

Gary M. Hyde, Associate Professor/Department of
Agricultural Engineering, and Robert E. Thornton,
Extension Horticulturist, Washington State
University, Pullman, Washington

ABSTRACT

Field experiments were conducted to compare the
draft force (drawbar pull) required for a rotary disk
blade system to that for a conventional, fixed-blade
potato harvester in sandy and silt-loam soils; to
evaluate blade performance and tuber damage for the
rotary blade system; and to survey the depth vs.
draft relationship for the fixed blade. The results
show that in silt-loam soil the 0.91 m (36-inch)
diameter disk blades required 76 percent less draft
than the fixed blade in one case and 57 percent less
overall. The 1.04 m (41-inch) disks required 43
percent less draft than the fixed blade in silt-loam
soil. In fine sand soil, however, draft forces among
the three blade systems were not significantly

ASAE Paper No. 85-1070

11

different. The fixed blade used in the experiments was of low profile and the primary chain had all down links. These factors may have resulted in less draft for it than for more typical fixed blades. However, even with this efficient fixed-blade design, the draft force required increased very significantly with deep blade depth setting. With proper adjustment of attack angle and lateral tilt angle, tuber damage caused by the rotary blade was 1 to 3 percent and blade cuts were nil.

INTRODUCTION

The first United States trials of the Scottish-invented rotary disk potato harvester blade confirmed its potential for improving both efficiency and quality in potato production. The new blade system substantially reduced tractor draft (drawbar pulling force) required to operate the harvester even in deep, difficult harvesting conditions. At the same time it delivered 97 percent or better damage--free tubers to the harvester.

The concept of the rotary disk system is that rather than using tractor draft to force a fixed, flat blade under the tubers and using sliding motion to lift them onto the primary chain, a pto-powered rotating blade uses more efficient rotary motion to lift and place the tubers on the chain. In experiments at the Scottish Institute of Agricultural Engineering where the disk system was invented, the tractor draft requirement for the disk blade was as much as 80 percent less than that required for a conventional harvester blade (Hutchison and Fleming 1980). Also, since the disks lifted the material as much as 15 inches, the front of the primary chain ran well above the soil level. Such positioning reduced stress, wear, and power requirement for that chain to the point that rubber-covered chain could be economically used for the primary as well as other chains on the harvester.

This paper describes the disk blade system and discusses Washington field experiments, blade adjustment effects on performance, relative power and draft requirements, tuber damage, effects of soil texture, and suggested design modifications.

MATERIAL AND METHODS

Thanks to Stetner Brothers, Blue Ribbon Produce, the Washington State Potato Commission, Braco Mfg., and cooperating growers, the rotary disk harvester blade system was tested extensively. The experiments included comparisons of two sizes of disk blades to a fixed-blade Braco harvester in both Quincy fine sand and Shano silt loam soils. The harvesters were instrumented to measure true ground speed, draft force, and blade position; and a portable computer was used to record draft, true ground speed and blade postion. Tuber samples were taken from the rear third of the primary chain and evaluated for mechanical damage.

The Disk System

The disk blade system (Figure 1) consisted of two 0.91 m (3-foot) diameter or two 1.04 m (41-inch) diameter concave main disks mounted side-by-side with their concave sides upward. The disks were attached to shafts which were hydraulically powered to rotate toward each other. The blades were tilted leading edge downward at an attack angle of about 25 degrees, and sideways (inward toward each other) at a lateral tilt angle of 5 to 10 degrees. Thus they cut sideways into the potato hill, moved the soil and tubers toward the center of the two-row swath, and lifted them up and back onto the primary chain. Each blade dug one row. The soil, tubers, and vines from each row were lifted from the main disk onto the primary chain by a smaller, powered cleaning disk mounted concave-side-down and positioned above the rear half of each main disk.

Field Conditions

The intent of our experiments was to investigate the operation of the disk blade system under Washington's potato harvesting conditions. The initial trials emphasized some of the differences between potato harvesting conditions in Scotland and in Washington. These differences include the following:

13

1. In the U.K. potatoes are ridged higher than in Washington, but the harvester blade depth is only 2/3 of the way down to the bottom of the furrow. The U.K. soils hold the ridge shape over the growing season, and generally no irrigation is used. In Washington, the potato ridges are lower, the sprinkler irrigation tends to flatten them in the sandy soil, and the potatoes are planted deeper so that the harvester blade must dig to a depth that is below the furrow bottom.

2. Vines are chopped before harvest in the U.K., but left intact until harvest in Washington.

Because we must dig deeper and handle more soil and vines than is done in the U.K., mounting the disk blades on the harvester in the same way as for Scottish conditions resulted in insufficient capacity for soil, vines, and tubers to flow through the blade assembly. The sandy soil tended to flow toward the outside edges of the main disks and to spill out, along with some tubers, at the edge of the swath. The vines tended to bunch up at the throat of the blade assembly between the two main blade shafts and eventually plugged the assembly.

Blade Modification and Adjustment

Adjustments made to improve blade performance included blade rotational speed, attack angle, lateral tilt angle, blade depth, blade lateral separation, the addition (and subsequent removal) of shielding to stop spillout at the outer edges of the blades, deletion of shielding between the main and cleaning disk mounting shafts, and the addition of angle irons welded along the main disk shafts to act as paddles (later replaced) to help move vines and soil through the assembly.

Widening the spacing of the disks was the best solution to all of the problems, particularly the plugging and spillout problems. The main disks were initially spaced with their inner edges less than 25 mm (1 in.) apart. Information supplied from Scotland cautioned that spacing them more than approximately 100 mm (4 in.) apart may result in spillout BETWEEN the blades. But note, that problem occurred where blade depth was less than the depth of the furrows.

14

Spillout between the blades did not occur in our field trials because blade depth was below the bottom of the furrow. The lateral spacing of the blades was gradually increased in our trials until there were 230 mm (9 inches) between blades at a lateral tilt of 15 degrees. The result was elimination of machine plugging with no spillout between blades. Subsequent reduction of lateral tilt to 9 degrees resulted in a lateral spacing of 220 mm (8.75 inches) with the blades equally spaced to either side of the center of the harvester. The 220 mm (8.75 in.) lateral spacing resulted in good blade performance.

Addition of angle iron paddles to the disk shafts improved flow of material through the blade assembly and worked well in light vines. In heavy vines the paddles worked well when the blade was running at depth, but when it was lifted while running, the paddles quickly wrapped with vines and cleanout became necessary. The paddles were replaced with round smooth extensions of the rotating hub which facilitated soil flow without the vine wrap problems.

Increasing the attack angle decreased the torque required to rotate the blades slightly, as also occurred in Scottish experiments. However, greater attack angle seemed to cause the soil to pile up and plug the blade assembly more, and it increased spillout at the outer edges of the disks. Decreasing the attack angle to less than 25 degrees greatly increased the torque required to turn the disks because the curved, undersurface of the blade was then forced into the soil below the cutting edge. The optimum attack angle for the .91 m (36-inch) blades used appeared to be 25 degrees (Figure 2).

Increasing the lateral tilt of the blades from 9 to 15 degrees did not reduce the spillout problem, but it resulted in the outer edges of the disks running shallower which caused more tuber slicing. Increasing blade depth reduced slicing somewhat, but reducing the lateral tilt back to 9 degrees was the best solution to the slicing problem, and resulted in less spillout at the outer edges of the blades rather than more.

Increasing blade rotational speed appeared to improve throughput early in the trials before the lateral spacing had been increased to 220 mm (8.75 inches). However, after full width was reached, trials at varying engine speeds (and corresponding blade speeds) showed that small speed changed did not have a significant effect on flow of material through the blade system. Removal of bottom support bearings on the main disk shafts improved reliability and caused no difficulty. (Each shaft is supported with two additional bearings mounted above the disk.)

In very heavy vines, the conventional straight colters on the harvester were replaced with dual concave angled colters (hilling disks) (Johnson et al. 1974) with good success. The dual colters cut cleanly through the vines and reduced plugging and wrap problems.

RESULTS AND DISCUSSION

Draft Comparisons

The results showed considerable draft reduction for heavier soil, and indicate that with some blade configuration changes, similar reductions could occur in sandy soil as well. For a blade depth such that approximately 200 to 230 mm (8 to 9 inches) of loose soil were left behind the harvester, the average draft forces for the three blades in the two soil types were as shown in Table 1.

In the silt-loam soil, the fixed blade averaged 2.3 times draft force of the smaller disks over several tractor gears and 1.7 times that for the larger disks. This amounted to a draft reduction of the disk blades compared to the fixed blade of 43 percent for the large disks and 57 percent for the small ones. In third gear the differences were more dramatic, where the draft for the smaller disks was 76 percent less than that required for the fixed blade. Draft in the sandy soil did not vary significantly with blade types at the 200 mm (8-inch) loose soil depth; however, observations indicate that a change in blade shape, spacing and angle could make a marked improvement in performance in that soil as well. Main disk rotational speed was approximately 160 rpm, which gave peripheral disk speeds 8 to 9 times the ground speed.

16

The power required to rotate both blades varied with field conditions and forward speed, but ranged from 15 to 37 kW (20 to 50 hp). The drawbar power requirements vary directly with ground speed as well as with draft force. In third gear (Table 1) the ground speed was 3.39 km/h (2.11 mph), and the corresponding draft horsepower for fixed blade, the large disks, and the small disks are 15, 9.7, and 3.7 kW (20, 13, and 5 hp), respectively. Power required to drive the primary chain for each blade type was not measured; but it was sufficiently less with the disk blades that the chain sagged between support rollers during harvesting. Thus, the primary chain tension was considerably reduced, with resultant reduced power requirement and improved chain life.

The variation of draft with tractor gear (ground speed in this case) is shown in more detail in Figure 3. At 2200 engine rpm, ground speed ranged from 3.4 km/h (2.1 mph) in third gear to 5.6 km/h (3.5 mph) in sixth gear for the John Deere 4450 tractor with 15-speed power shift transmission.

Draft (Figure 3) increased moderately with ground speed for the fixed blade. The draft for the small disks was much smaller, but had a much steeper increase with ground speed than for the fixed blade draft. The draft-speed relationship for the large disks lay between that for the fixed blade and the small disks, but the slope of the curve was somewhat irregular. In general, these data indicate that the ground speed may be more critical for the disk blades than for a fixed blade.

The blade attack angle was increased from 25 to 27 degrees during the trials to accommodate the slightly smaller radius of curvature (deeper dish) of the larger disks. As with the small disks, too small an attack angle resulted in excessive disk torque because the rounded portion of the disk was forced into the undug soil by the forward motion of the machine. The increased angle tended to slightly restrict flow of material through the blade system and slightly reduced machine capacity. The lateral tilt angle was kept at 9 degrees.

The fixed blade harvester was operated at several blade depths in the fine sand soil to estimate relationship between blade depth and draft.

The data indicate that going from a 200 to 230 mm blade depth requires about 2kN more draft, but going from 250 to 280 mm depth requires about 4.2 kN more (going from 8 to 9 inch blade requires about 450 lb more draft, but going from 10 to 11 inches requires a 900 to 1000 lb increase in pull) (Figure 4).

Bruise Data Analysis Results

Analysis of tuber samples taken before the blades were properly adjusted showed that 7 out of 15 samples contained tubers with blade cuts. Cut tuber weight was 4.8 percent of total sample weight. The bruise-free percentages were approximately 96.5 from the primary chain.

The sampling after readjusting the blade lateral tilt from 15 to 9 degrees was more extensive. The experimental factors were two engine speeds and two tractor gears. Measurements included tuber bruise damage, cut tubers, and tuber size. These trials were made in fine sand soil. The tubers in that field were very deep and required that the blades go deep enough to leave 10 inches of loose soil behind the harvester. The results are shown in Table 2.

Blade Cut Tubers:

Blade cuts were 0.74 percent in this trial. Comments from operators of conventional machines in the same field indicated that their machines were cutting more tubers.

Tuber Size:

The tubers in that field were often very large, but tuber damage proved to have no correlation with tuber size. Mean tuber weight in the samples ranged from 204 to 381 grams (7.2 to 13.4 ounces).

Black Spot and Shatter Bruise:

Averages for combined blade and primary chain damage (Table 1) show 96.5 to 99 percent damage-free tubers. The data indicate that engine speed had more to do with tuber damage than did tractor gear at this point in the harvester. This may have been because the primary chain was running a little fast for sandy

18

soil (chain speed-to-ground speed ratios of 1.17 at 4 mph and 1.46 at 3 mph) and was thus very lightly loaded. The reduction of engine speed then reduced bruise by reducing chain speed and giving less bounce to the tubers.

CONCLUSIONS

We were able to operate the harvester with a 120 hp, 2-wheel drive John Deere 4250 tractor with 16.9 x 38 inch rear tires on moderately rolling terrain in fine sand soil at up to 3.5 mph with no traction problems.

The combined results for the tuber sampling showed that the tubers on the primary chain were 96.5 to 97.9 percent bruise-free; hence, tuber damage caused by the blades was nil. With the reduction in lateral tilt from 15 to 9 degrees, the blade cuts also became nil, so the conclusion is that with these adjustments the rotary disk blades operate essentially bruise-free, even in difficult, deep digging.

We now know much more about how the disk blade system works and can work with the soil in potato harvesting. Under certain conditions, such as in third gear with the 36-inch disks in heavy soil (Table 1), the rotating blades nearly pulled the harvester through the field. Observations of the flow of soil around and over the blades in both heavy and sandy soils convinced us that the two soils act quite differently under these conditions. We are now beginning to understand why the different shape of the potato ridge here, compared to that in the U.K., has such a large influence on rotary blade performance.

With the new knowledge gained in the field experiments, we are now ready to undertake a series of blade and blade substitute experiments to find the best configurations for our harvesting conditions. the proper rotary blade shape, attack angle, and tilt angle to match our soils and ridge shapes can result in significantly reduced harvester draft using less than the 50 horsepower needed to drive the disk blades in their present configuration.

REFERENCES

Hutchinson, P.S. and J. Fleming. 1980. An investigation into the performance of a twin disk share for potato harvesters. Departmental Note SIN 286, SIAE, Bush Estate, Penicuik, Midlothian, Scotland, U.K.

Johnson, L.F., C.L. Peterson, J.P. Gentry and E.M. Bailey. Design and field testing of a low damage potato harvester. ASAE Paper No. 74-1509, ASAE, St. Joseph, MI.

Table 1. Potato Harvester Draft Force for Three Blade Types in Quincy
Fine Sand and Shano Silt-Loam Soils.

| Blade Type | Draft force, KN (lb)* | | |
	Fine Sand	Silt-loam	Draft reduction**
Average over several tractor gears:			
Fixed	12.06 (2722)a*	19.32 (4344)a	0%
Large disks	13.26 (2981)a	11.08 (2490)b	43%
Small disks	13.16 (2959)a	8.35 (1877)c	57%
Tractor in third gear:			
Fixed	-----	15.66 (3520)a	0%
Large disks	-----	10.08 (2267)b	36%
Small disks	-----	3.72 (836)c	76%

* Means with same letter are not different at the 5% level of significance
** Compared to fixed-blade draft in heavy soil.

Table 2. Bruise-free percentages for the primary chain related to rpm and
gear.

| Bruise-free means by gear: | | |
Gear	Mean	Grouping*
3	97.734	A
4	97.929	A
Bruise-free means by rpm:		
Rpm	Mean	Grouping*
1900	99.204	A
2150	96.508	B

* Means with same letter are not significantly different at the 5% level.

21

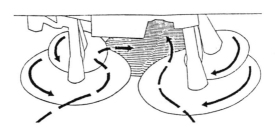

Figure 1.   Rotary disk potato harvester blade.   (Drawing courtesy
of the Scottish Institute of Agricultural Engineering.)

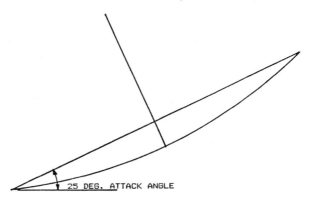

25 DEG. ATTACK ANGLE

Figure 2.   Disk blade profile.

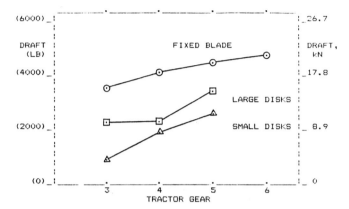

Figure 3. Potato harvester draft force for three blade types over four tractor gears for a blade depth that produced approximately 8 inches of loose soil behind the harvester (Shano silt-loam soil).

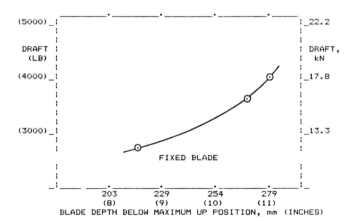

Figure 4. Draft force variation with blade depth for the fixed-blade potato harvester in fine sand soil.

23

CHAIN SPEED ADJUSTMENT TO OBTAIN LOW
TUBER DAMAGE AT HARVEST

by

Robert E. Thornton, Extension Horticulturist,
Horticulture Department; G.W. Hyde, Associate
Professor, Agricultural Engineering Department,
Washington State University, Pullman, Washington,
R.K. Thornton, Horticulturist, UI Group, Inc.
M.W. Hammond, Cenex Corporation

ABSTRACT

The concept of operating potato harvesters so
that the volume of material on a given chain is equal
to capacity of that chain will result in tuber damage
reduction and can lead to increased grower returns.
The further modification of harvester primary chain
speed to ground speed ratios to maximize soil
separation will allow further refinement in ratios of
the subsequent chains within the harvester to assure
minimum tuber damage.

Commercial application of the concepts have been
shown to result in an increase in grower returns and
an increase in machine capacity.

ASAE Paper No. 85-1141

Rapid access to the effect of harvester
adjustments is also an economical consideration.
Using the contract values discussed and comparing the
values of potatoes from properly adjusted equipment
vs. non-adjusted equipment will show this.

ORIGINAL CONCEPT

The original concept for low damage harvester
operation based on chain speed to forward speed
ratios was developed from data obtained when variable
harvester forward speeds were used in attempts to
identify optimum harvester operational parameters.
The initial set of data was obtained as a result of
various harvesters operating at harvester field days
in the early 1970's. These results are summarized in
Figure 1.

At subsequent harvester operation field
demonstrations of the use of forward speed chain
speed ratios additional confirming data has been
obtained. An example of these type of results is
given in Table 1.

Close observation and subsequent measurements
showed that tuber damage reduction on any chain
within the harvester was closely associated with an
increase in forward speed or a decrease in chain
speed which resulted in the volume of material on
that chain being equal to the capacity of that chain.
When all chains were operated in this manner minimum
tuber damage resulted. Since volume of material is
the factor in this concept the forward speed and the
tuber yield need to be known. Examples of ratios
that result in the desired chain load are given in
Table 2.

However when forward speed of the harvester is
increased to obtain a more desirable ratio the volume
of material on any given chain becomes predominantly
soil or other non-tuber material (Figure 2).
Although this is an effective way to reduce tuber
damage, it can and often does lead to an excessive
amount of soil being placed into the truck. Unless
some arrangement is made to remove this soil before
the potatoes are placed into storage serious storage
management problems can result. The removal of the
soil from tubers once they are in the truck becomes

25

an additional expense to the producer (Table 3). To optimize returns to the grower and maximize the value of the tubers to the user the harvester operation must achieve maximum soil separation while minimizing tuber damage.

Maximizing Soil Separation

The results of additional research on soil separation and tuber damage showed that when the primary chain speed was increased to as much as 50 percent faster than the original ratios would indicate soil elimination was increased without a comparable increase in tuber damage (Figure 3).

Although there is a slight increase in tuber damage when the primary chain speed is increased the absence or reduction in soil load on the subsequent chain results in a substantial reduction in total tuber damage (Figure 4).

An additional advantage of soil elimination by the primary chain is that much less soil is dumped onto the secondary chain, i.e., down through the override deviner allowing more complete vine elimination because the soil doesn't force vines through the deviner onto the secondary chain. An example of the ratios which have been used by a large corporate farm in Washington State is given in Table 4.

Commercial Application of the Concept

In the 1970's growers began utilizing the forward speed to chain speed ratios to manage potato harvesting operations. To fully comprehend the value for harvester changes to reduce tuber damage it is important to understand that most, if not all, potatoes purchased for processing in Washington are subject to bruise incentives and penalties. A general interpretation of this concept follows:

incentive = 50 cents/Ton (20 cwt) for each 1%
above 50% bruise free up to 75%

penalty = 50 cents/Ton for each 1% below 50%
bruise free down to 27% at which
point delivery can be refused.

26

The out of field value at the time this example was
calculated was $54.00/Short Ton ($59.40 per 1000 Kg
or $2.70/cwt). The effect of tuber damage on gross
returns on a 25 ton (500 cwt) crop is as follows:

50% bruise free. Gross Return = $54.00/T x 25T =
$1,350.00/A

27% bruise free. Penalty = 50% - 27% = 23% x
$.50/T x 25T = $287.00/A
Gross Return = $1,350 - 287 =
$1,106.00/A

75% bruise free. Incentive = 75% - 50% = 25% x
$.50/T = $312.00/A
Gross Return = $1,350.00 +
$312.00 = $1,662.00/A

The difference in value in harvesting 27 percent vs.
75 percent bruise free potatoes would be $556.00/A
($1662.00 - $1,106.00 = $556.00/A).

To be able to obtain maximum bruise incentives
from the processor an incentive plan for harvester
operators was utilized. This program is outlined
below.

Incentive base: $.11/load gain for each 1% gain
above 60-% bruise free to an
upper limit of 90% bruise free.

Per load maximum incentive =

$$\underline{load} \text{ \% } \underline{B.F.} - \underline{60\%} = \$3.30$$
$$\overline{30\%}$$

Daily Maximum Incentive (30 loads/day):

30 x $3.30 = $99.00/day

To make this work, a system of rapid bruise analysis
was employed. Using the combination of operator
incentives and rapid bruise detection the average
bruise free for one operation was 70 percent. The
return per acre for 70 percent bruise free compared
to the base level of 50 percent was $250.00/A. A 500
acre grower would return to this program $125,000.
The cost of this program is as follows:

Cost of Operator Incentives:

500 Acres x 25T/A x $\frac{\text{load}}{12.5}$ x 1.10/load of

70% bruise free = $1,100.00

Labor for bruise analysis =   1,500.00

Equipment for bruise analysis =   3,200.00

        Total $5,800.00

The net gain in return to a grower on the 500 acre operation for obtaining a 20 percent increase in bruise free level is:

$125,000.00 (gross gain) — $5,880.00 (incentive costs) = $119,120.00 or $238.00/A at 25T/A.

The value of harvester adjustment to minimize tuber damage and rapid knowledge of the damage level associated with any harvester operation adjustment can be seen to be very important.

One of the options to place a harvester into the desired ratio is to increase the forward speed, assuming the internal chain speed is too fast for the previously selected speed. The influence of this management alternative is as follows:

90% bruise free @ 1.2 MPH = 10-15 loads/day

90% bruise free @ 2.1 MPH = 20+ loads/day

An increase of at least 5 loads per day per machine. A load is 10-12.5 T (200 to 250 cwt.) if the yield/A is 25 T/A (Washington State average yield) this would amount to an increase in capacity of 50 to 62.5 T per harvester per day. If a producer has a 500 acre operation and one harvester this harvest season would be reduced from 33 days to 25 days. Each additional harvester would reduce the time required proportionately. The difference between a 25 day harvest season and a 33 day harvest season if harvest began on September 15 would be a completion date of October 10 vs. October 18, often the difference between frost free harvest and serious difficulties. To obtain accurate values for damage level, potatoes

28

are held at least 48 hours following harvest. If a harvester is operating during this 48 hour period a large number of tubers will be harvested at that level of damage before the performance level is known to the operator. As an example, assume that the percent bruise free can be increased from the base level of 50 percent to 70 percent with harvester adjustments involving chain speed ratios, tractor gears, truck belt speeds and piler adjustments. The changes needed are identified by bruise analysis either by traditional 48 hour holding or by some rapid bruise method that provides results in 24 hours. If it requires five sets of equipment analysis and subsequent change to increase the bruise free from 50 percent to 70 percent, holding the tubers for 48 hours between sampling and machine adjustment would require a total time of two weeks from beginning to final adjustment. Using a 24 hours analysis method would cut the time delay in half, to one week. If the harvester is able to harvest 90 A/week, the change in value of 50 percent bruise free to 70 percent bruise free in the week difference in analysis and adjustment time would net $250.00/A or $22,500.00 for the increased speed of damage detection.

CONCLUSION

Harvester chain speed to ground speed ratios can be used by commercial potato producers to increase economic returns. These increased returns result from a reduction in level of tuber damage and an increase in capacity of individual machines.

REFERENCES

Dwelle, R.B. and G.F. Stallnecht. 1976. Rates of internal blackspot bruise development in potato tubers under conditions of elevated temperatures and gas pressures. Am. Pot. Jr. 53:235-245.

Hammond, M.W. 1978. Bruise Detection and Incentive Program - A Growers Application. Washington Potato Conference and Trade Fair Proceedings, pp. 57-74.

Iritani, W.M. 1985. Enhancement of Blackspot Development by Hot Water Soak Method. Washington Potato Conference Proceedings, pp. 1-6.

Thornton, Rob. 1982. A Rapid Method of Bruise
    Analysis and Its Usefulness. Washington Potato
    Conference and Trade Fair Proceedings, pp. 133-
    138.

Table 1. Effect of harvester forward speed and windrower on tuber damage.

| | | % Tubers by Number | | |
FORWARD SPEED	SERIOUS	SLIGHT	SKINNED	UNDAMAGED
4.5 Windrower alone	0	4	50	46
4.5 Windrower 2.6 Harvester	14	19	62	5
4.5 Windrower 3.6 Harvester	5	0	55	40

Table 2. Harvester Chain-to-forward Speed Ratios.

| | Yield, ton/acre | | | | | |
| | For Sandy Soil | | | For Heavy Soil | | |
Chain	20	25	30	20	25	30
Primary	.90	.90	.90	1.05	1.05	1.05
Secondary	.62	.62	.62	.68	.68	.68
Rear cross	.47	.56	.67	.47	.56	.67
Elevator	.45	.54	.63	.45	.54	.63
Boom	.38	.45	.53	.38	.45	.53

Table 3. Estimated soil hauling and handling costs.

Item	Cost per Ton of Soil Soil Type		Annual Cost for 7,000-ton (140,000 cwt) Storage Soil Type	
	Heavy	Sandy	Heavy	Sandy
Haul to storage	$3.69	$3.69	$2,583	$1,033
Collect & stockpile	1.45	3.62	711	710
Disposal	2.75	2.75	1,348	539
			$4,642	$2,282

Table 4. Example of ratio of chain to ground speed ratios used in Washington.

Chain speed to Ground Speed Ratios

Primary = 1.2 X Ground Speed

Secondary = .65 X Ground Speed

Deviner = .65 X Ground Speed

Rear Cross = .55 X Ground Speed

Side Elevator = .50 X Ground Speed

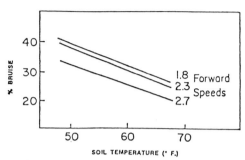

Figure 1. Effects of forward speed (MPH) and soil temperature on potato tuber damage.

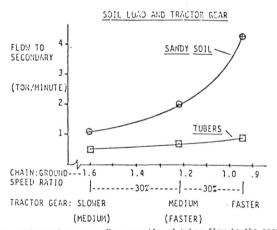

Figure 2. Effect of tractor gear on soil and tuber flow to the secondary chain at constant primary chain speed.

33

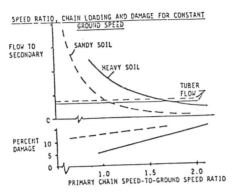

Figure 3. Effect of primary chain-to-ground speed ratio on tuber damage and soil elimination at constant ground speed.

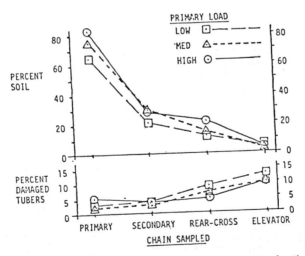

Figure 4. Soil and damage levels through the potato parvester for three primary chain load level.

34

SIEVING CONTROL AND HORIZONTAL AGITATION OF POTATO HARVESTER CHAINS

by

D.C. McRae, P.S. Hutchinson, J. Carruthers
Scottish Institute of Agricultural Engineering,
Penicuik, Midlothian, Scotland

ABSTRACT

The performances of two types of prototype potato harvesters were investigated. One was fitted with a primary web (chain) delivering to a secondary web which was agitated horizontally, either parallel or perpendicular to the direction of travel.

The other machine embodied a variable area primary web, agitated vertically or horizontally. Field tests indicated that horizontal agitation can improve sieving and reduce potato damage by 17 to 30 percent. Varying the effective sieving area can improve efficiency of clod break-up and soil loss, without the need to change from the optimum web/forward speed ratio.

ASAE Paper No. 85-1071

INTRODUCTION

At present the accepted method of removing soil and breaking up soft clods on a potato harvester chain (or web as it is referred to in Europe) is to agitate it vertically. The agitators are mounted in such a way that the primary web adopts an approximately sinusoidal motion as it progresses from the nose cones behind the share to the point of transfer to the secondary web. Sieving occurs over the entire area of the web.

A second function of the web is to convey the material to the next stage of the harvester. This combination of sieving and conveying poses problems, particularly in sandy soils and if the harvester forward speed is varied. In the former situation, soil cushioning is lost near the front of the primary web and potato damage may then occur on the bare web rods further up the web. Any alteration of the harvester forward speed without altering the web drive upsets the ratio of web speed to forward speed, which has been shown by Thornton et al. (1973) in USA and Butson et al. (1978) in UK, to have a marked effect on tuber damage.

Apart from considerations of web speed, the method of agitation of the web used universally at present has drawbacks. The application of vigorous vertical agitation creates potato damage in the presence of stones, if there is roll back, where there is binding organic material, or on sticky soil. The efficiency of sieving is impaired probably by the tendency for soil and debris to cone on top of the vertically agitated rods, or bridge between them.

The application of horizontal agitation to soil riddling has been shown by McGechan (1977) to be beneficial in several ways. In a series of riddling experiments, he examined the soil removal rate and potato damage levels when sample lengths of undisturbed ridge were subjected to a variety of riddling motions. It was found that to achieve the same soil sieving rate, the riddle had to impart twice the acceleration in a vertical direction compared with the acceleration required to riddle in a horizontal plane. At a peak acceleration of 2 g, horizontal acceleration perpendicular to the direction of travel of the web led to only about one third of the damage caused by the same value of acceleration applied in a vertical plane. When the horizontal acceleration was applied parallel to the direction of travel of the web, potato damage was halved compared with vertical acceleration.

For the above reasons it was considered worthwhile to evaluate the application of horizontal agitation to harvester webs in the field.

DESIGN CONSIDERATIONS

Description of Field Machines

Two field machines were constructed--a horizontally agitated web harvester and a variable area web harvester. Both were fitted with power driven double disc shares (Hutchison et al. 1980).

Horizontally Agitated Web Harvester

The harvester was initially designed for digging only, but with provision for fitting a delivery conveyor to up-grade it to a full harvester. A primary web was designed to deliver the crop to a secondary web mounted on hangers to enable it to be oscillated in a horizontal plane parallel or perpendicular to the direction of travel of the web rods (Figure 1). The secondary conveyor was driven by a hydraulic motor to simplify the drive system and was agitated by a variable throw crank attached to a heavy flywheel to accommodate load fluctuations. Frequency of agitation could be altered by changing sprockets. An amplitude of 25 mm (1 in.) was chosen for the web oscillations and a frequency of 4.5 Hz for much of the field work. The rear part of the machine is shown in Figure 2 with secondary conveyors mounted for agitation either parallel or perpendicular to the direction of travel of the web. During the tests only one secondary conveyor was agitated. The machine has now been made into a full unmanned harvester with provision for pickers in difficult conditions. A series of concurrent tests were run to evaluate an improved design of web rod fitted to the secondary web. This will be the subject of another paper.

Variable Area Web Harvester

This machine differed from the other in having a single long web (Figure 3) fitted with a step. The step served as the demarcation point between the agitated area starting at the share and terminating at the rear idler rollers in the step, and the remaining area which was free from agitation. The step could be moved by means of a small electric winch capable of shifting a carriage containng the step up or down the length of the harvester chassis.

A quick release for a connecting rod linking the rear step rollers with the nose cone rollers was designed. Though the amplitude of the oscillation of the connecting rod was set at 25 mm (1 in.), the frequency selected was 2 Hz. Drive to the connecting rods was from a variable throw crank driven by a small hydraulic motor. The machine, with two settings of the step for light and heavy soils, is shown in Figures 4a and 4b. The connecting links for the horizontal agitation system are not shown.

The objective for future development is to use sensors to automatically adjust the position of the carriage and the agitation characteristics (amplitude and frequency) to control the effective sieving area and the rate of soil loss required for the field conditions prevailing.

FIELD TESTS

1. Horizontally Agitated Web Harvester

Tests were carried out in stone-placed soil in which stones had been previously mechanically buried (the potato ridges then being almost stone free) and in untreated soil which contained stones. Two agitation modes were compared. In the first mode the secondary or transfer web was agitated horizontally in the direction of translation of the web, while in the second mode the web was agitatd in a direction perpendicular to its direction of travel, i.e. parallel to the web rods. Tuber samples were taken from the delivery point of the secondary web and analysed to find the severity of potato damage. The number of clods >30-60 mm (1.2-2.4 in.) and >60 mm

(2.4 in.) in size and the weight of loose soil
carried over the end of the secondary web were
recorded.

2.   Variable Area Web Harvester

The harvester was tested in two soil types (a
sandy loam and a sandy clay loam). In 1983, the
objective was to determine the effect on sieving and
potato damage of altering the sieving area. The
season proved very wet and in the heavier soil,
sieving became difficult. For the 1984 harvest the
vertical agitators were removed and a horizontal
agitation system fitted, capable of confining the
agitation to the part of the web between the nose
cones and the rear rollers of the web step.

It was considered important to establish whether
or not the horizontal agitation was largely confined
to the area of web between the share and the step.
Though the use of accelerometers mounted on web rods
and appropriate radio telemetry was considered, a
simpler approach was adopted to use a stroboscope
technique. The harvester was operated after dark. A
Dawe 1203B Strobo Sun Unit was used to provide
illumination of the web in the region of the step,
where it was hoped there would be a sharp transition
from oscillation to non-oscillation. The flash rate
of the strobe was set to the frequency of the passage
of the web rods of around 35 Hz. A Sony single tube
colour video camera (type DXC1800P) recorded the
operation and playback was arranged through a Hitachi
SV340 U-matic videocassette recorder.

Examination of the video record showed clearly
that almost all oscillation was confined to the web
area from the nose cone to the rear rollers on the
web step. Since the recording was carried out at
full harvesting speed, with the soil burden on the
web, it was evident that the oscillations were being
maintained and not damped by either web stretch or
soil loading.

Similar field tests were carried out in the same
two soil types selected for the 1983 test, but using
a frequency of horizontal agitation of 1.7 and 3.3
Hz. Due to adverse weather conditions only limited
time was available for testing and difficulties arose

through faulty weed control in the light soil area. Sampling was limited to 5 row lengths per treatment.

In order to obtain some indication of the relative merits of horizontal versus vertical agitation in terms of propensity to cause damage, static tests were run with half and full web lengths agitated both vertically and horizontally at 1.7 Hz.

The damage indices used throughout the tests were calculated from the following formula which is based on losses incurred by the consumer in preparing the potatoes by peeling: Damage index (weight base) = % scuffed + 3 x % Peeler (damage <3 mm deep) (0.12 in.) + 7 x % Severe damage (damage >3 mm depth) (0.12 in.).

RESULTS AND DISCUSSION

Results of the tests carried out with the horizontally agitated web harvester are shown in Table 1. The virtual absence of stones in the stone-placed land insured improved sieving and lower damage levels than in the untreated land, where damage to potatoes was higher.

In both types of land, the secondary conveyor gave lower potato damage if it was agitated parallel to the direction of travel, rather than when oscillated sideways (perpendicular to the direction of travel of the web rods). More clod appeared to break-up with a sideways shaking motion but due to the relative shortness of the conveyor, the loose soil thereby created was not quite removed, though the quantity remaining was small for the sample length of 2 m (6.56 ft.). A similar situation appeared to apply to the untreated land where there were significant reductions in clod and weight of soil for the horizontal agitation perpendicular to the direction of travel of the web, compared with horizontal agitation parallel to the direction of travel and highly significant in comparison with vertical agitation of the primary web. A significantly higher level of potato damage was obtained when the primary web, which is much longer than the secondary web, was agitated vertically--the other results were obtained without agitation of the primary web.

The results of field work carried out in autumn 1983 with the variable area web harvester fitted with a vertical agitation system are shown in Table 2. As the web speed was increased, there appeared to be little change in the combined weight of loose soil and clod carried over the end of the web. On the sandy loam, the full area web compared with half the area reduced the amount of loose soil significantly and also reduced the clod. The difference at the higher web speed was small.

On the sandy clay loam which was very wet and sticky it did not prove possible to separate clods and loose soil so only a combined weight could be recorded. At the lower speed there was a gain in moving from the half web to full web. At the higher speed the quantity of soil carried over with the full web was greater than for the half web. It would appear that the explanation for this lies in the relatively short length of the unagitated web prior to the delivery point on which material from the agitated part of the web lands, having passed over the step. The step causes a large increase in removal of loose soil due to the re-positioning of material on to an area of web virtually free of soil burden. The sieving of loose soil at this point requires time. Had the web step carriage been positioned to enable say 0.75 of the sieving area to be used, the total weight delivered would probably then have been consistent with the increased sieving area from the half web setting. The effect on tuber damage of the two web area settings in two soil types is also shown in the table. The damage indices are very low, but the full web gives significantly higher damage levels in the sandy soil. The increased damage to some extent relates to the thinness of the soil cushion, though it does not explain the added damage when the full web is run at the maximum speed where there was an increase in the weight of soil passing over the web. It is more probable that the extra damage is related to impacts occurring on transfer to the cross conveyor at higher speeds.

When horizontal agitation is substituted for vertical agitation, the effect of different frequencies of agitation can be seen. The results of further field trials in 1984 are indicated in Table

3. The general trend is for the higher frequency to improve sieving by reducing clod and soil carried over the end of the web, but at the expense of increasing potato damage. With the exception of the damage level sustained at a frequency of 3.3 Hz with a full web in the clay loam, the damage indices are quite low. The anomaly of increased clod and soil carried over when the half web was operated at the higher frequency in sandy loam may have been related to the presence of weeds which impaired the sieve effect of the web during part of the test.

An indication of the difference in severity of damage in conditions of nil soil cushioning between horizontally and vertically agitated webs is shown in Table 4. The longer period spent on the web at its maximum area setting by the potatoes while being agitated, is reflected in the higher damage index for each method of agitation when the full web is used, compared with the half web. For each web setting there is a gain for horizontal agitation over vertical agitation in terms of reduced potato damage, this is highly significant in the case of the full web.

CONCLUSIONS

1. It is feasible to apply horizontal agitation, either perpendicular or parallel to the direction of travel of a secondary sieving web and achieve acceptable cleaning rates at lower damage levels than for the conventional agitated primary web system.

2. Horizontal agitation of a web conveyor parallel to the direction of travel appears to cause slightly less damage but at a lower sieving rate than horizontal agitation perpendicular to the direction of travel of the web rods.

3. A variable area web can be operated in such a way, that without altering the web speed it is possible to effect worthwhile changes in effective sieving rates with low potato damage levels.

4. Horizontal agitation can be imparted to a variable area primary web in such a manner as to confine most of the agitation to the required portion of the web.

5.   The effect of tuber damage and sieving rates of altering the effective sieving area and frequency of oscillation suggests the need for automatic control of these adjustments.

6.   There is need for further evaluation of these new agitation systems and the variable area concept and they need to be tested in a wider range of soil types and conditions.

ACKNOWLEDGEMENTS

The authors wish to record their thanks to J. Fleming and H. Melrose for their work of data collection and damage evaluation, and C.A. Carlow and M. Faulds[1] for assistance with the stroboscope and video work.

REFERENCES

Butson, M.J., Hamilton, A.J. 1978. How potato harvester speed settings influence primary web damage. Abstracts of 7th Trienn. Conf. of Eur. Assoc. Pot. Res., p. 113.

Hutchison, P.S., Fleming, J. 1980. An investigation into the performance of a twin disc share for potato harvesters. Dep. Note SIN/286, Scot. Inat. Agric. Eng., Penicuik, (unpubl.)

McGechan, M.B. 1977. An investigation into the relative effectiveness of various riddling motions for removal of soil from potatoes. J. Agric. Engng. Res. 22:229-245.

Thornton, R.E., Smittle, D.A., Peterson, C.L. 1973. Reducing potato damage. Proc. 12th Annual Washington Potato Conf:1-11.

----

[1]Scottish Institute of Agricultual Engineering, Penicuik, Midlothian, Scotland.

Table 1. Effect of different methods of agitation on sieving rate and potato damage with a horizontally agitated web harvester.*

| Land Treatment | Method of Agitation | Clod Numbers | | Wt. of Soil | Damage |
		>60 mm	30-60 mm	kg	Index
	HORIZONTAL				
Stone Placed	Parallel to direction of travel of web	1.0	21.0	0.9	97
	Perpendicular to direction of travel of web	0.3	15.0	1.4	126[1]
	HORIZONTAL				
Untreated	Parallel to direction of travel of web	6.8[2](4)	14.8	8.5[4]	109
	Perpendicular to direction of travel of web	1.6	12.2	5.5	125
	VERTICAL				
	Agitation of primary web	3.1[4]	177[0]	8.0[2]	133[4]

*mean of 8 runs

Note:

0   P = 0.005
1   P = 0.01
2   P = 0.025
3   P = 0.05
4   P = 0.10

Figures with suffix are significantly larger than the lowest in the group without a suffix. Suffix in brackets denotes figure is significantly larger than next lower in group.

44

Table 2. The effect of altering agitated area on weight of soil carried over the end of the web and on potato damage index with a variable area web harvester.*

Soil type	Web speed m/s	Portion of Web agitated	Wt. of loose soil kg	Wt. of Clod over 30 mm kg	Total Wt. kg	Damage Index
Sandy loam	1.02	Half	16.9[2]	8.9	25.8[3]	45
		Full	9.0	7.3	16.3	54[4]
	2.03	Half	17.1	10.2	27.3	68
		Full	13.6	8.1	21.7	71
Sandy Clay Loam	1.02	Half	-+	-	133	32
		Full	-	-	107	35
	2.03	Half	-	-	123	43
		Full	-	-	140.4	57[4]

*mean of 25 lengths of 3.5 m
+conditions too wet to obtain figures for loose soil and clod separately.

2 P = 0.025
3 P = 0.05
4 P = 0.10

Table 3. The effect of two frequencies of horizontal agitation on clod reduction, soil sieving and potato damage using a variable area web harvester.*

Soil type	Proportion of web agitated	Frequency of agitation Hz	Clod over 33 mm kg	Soil Wt. kg	Total Wt. kg	Damage Index
Sandy loam	Half	1.7	6.4	9.2	15.6	26
		3.3	9.4[4]	11.1	20.5	42[3]
	Full	1.7	29.7[1]	29.0[1]	58.7[0]	43
		3.3	9.6	11.6	21.2	66
Sandy clay loam	Half	1.7	22.4	74.8	97.2	59
		3.3	14.0	49.1	63.1	62
	Full	1.7	11.3	77.3[2]	88.6[2]	49
		3.3	7.8	25.3	33.1	80[4]

*mean of 5 samples 3.5 m

0 P = 0.005
1 P = 0.01
2 P = 0.025
3 P = 0.05
4 P = 0.10

46

Table 4. Comparison of damage indices of samples of potatoes passed over horizontally and vertically agitated webs on a variable area web harvester.

Proportion of web agitated	Method of Agitation	Damage Index
Half	Vertical	85
	Horizontal	71
Full	Vertical	184[1]
	Horizontal	125

[1] P = 0.025

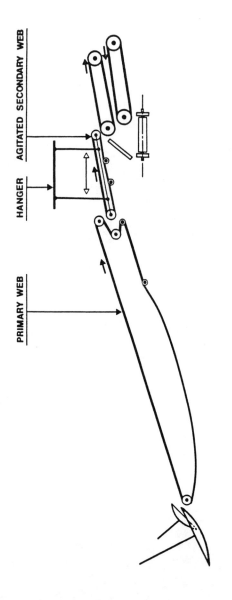

PRIMARY WEB

HANGER

AGITATED SECONDARY WEB

FIG. 1

Layout of horizontally agitated web harvester

48

FIG. 2

HORIZONTALLY AGITATED WEB HARVESTER SHOWING
SECONDARY CONVEYORS

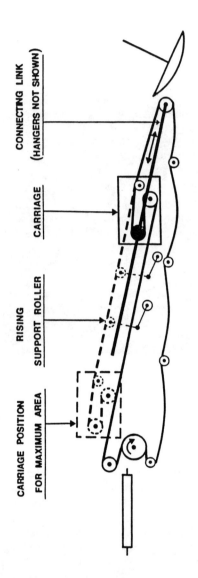

CONNECTING LINK
(HANGERS NOT SHOWN)

CARRIAGE

RISING

SUPPORT ROLLER

CARRIAGE POSITION

FOR MAXIMUM AREA

FIG. 3

Layout of variable area web harvester

50

FIG. 4a

VARIABLE AREA WEB HARVESTER SET FOR LIGHT SOILS

FIG. 4b

VARIABLE AREA WEB HARVESTER SET FOR HEAVY SOILS

COMPRESSION TESTS FOR MEASURING THE
FIRMNESS OF POTATOES

by

V.K. Jindal, Associate Professor; On-Rawee Techasena,
Former Graduate Student, Division of Agricultural &
Food Engineering, Asian Institute of Technology.
G.P.O. Box 2754, Bangkok 10501, Thailand

ABSTRACT

The changes of firmness of potatoes during
storage at 5, 10, 20 and 30°C (41, 50, 68 and 86° F)
were studied for 8 weeks in terms of elasticity
modulus based on axial compression, radial
compression and Hertz analysis using an Instron
testing machine. Each test method showed an
exponential decrease in firmness during storage at
any given temperature. However, the radial
compression test appeared to be most sensitive for
monitoring potato firmness.

ASAE Paper No. 85-1072

INTRODUCTION

The quality changes in potatoes during storage may be tissue softening, wilting, rotting, sprout growth or their various combinations. Adverse storage conditions exaggerate the softening of potato tissues and thus produce undesirable changes in its firmness. In practice, the assessment of potato firmness is qualitative and there is the need for instrumental methods for the objective evaluation of firmness paramters.

Objective measurements involve the determination of the mechanical properties of the material linked with its quality. Among the several mechanical properties used for this purpose, the modulus of elasticity has been widely used and claimed to be related to the firmness of potatoes (Finney and Hall, 1967; Matthews and Hall, 1968). The elasticity modulus can be determined from simplest compression tests by using the Instron testing machine.

Intact potatoes and their specimen, like other food materials, present inherent difficulties in the evaluation of elasticity modulus based on the standard ASTM techniques. As a result, other test techniques involving radial compression of the specimen as well as the point loading have also been suggested (Sherif et al., 1967; Timbers et al., 1965; Bourne and Mondy, 1967; Fluck et al., 1968). There appears to be a wide variation in the values of the elasticity modulus reported due to the use of different test techniques and their limitations. In this study, various methods for determining the elasticity modulus of potatoes have been investigated experimentally and compared for their relative merits in describing potato firmness.

OBJECTIVES

The objectives of this study were:

1. To investigate the applicability of axial, radial and Hertz compression test techniques to determine the elasticity modulus of potato specimens and the influence of experimental conditions on such determinations.

53

2. To compare the experimental value of the modulus of elasticity determined from different compression tests.

3. To study the changes in the firmness of potatoes during storage at various temperatures in terms of elasticity modulus based on each test technique.

RELATED STUDIES

Potato Storage in General

A potato tuber is a living organism consisting of 80 percent water. During storage, tubers lose weight and quality. In general, quality changes can be minimized by keeping the storage temperature low. The softening of potato tissue during storage takes place due to the degradation of insoluble protopectins to the more soluble pectic acid and pectin and the reduction in starch content by respiration. At a low temperature, below 6°C (42.8 °F) the conversion of starch into sugar proceeds at a fast rate. Therefore, potatoes for processing industries are stored at a higher temperature than those for immediate consumption (fresh market). The choice of storage temperature is greatly influenced by the duration of the storage period, end use of the tubers and the varieties involved (Booth and Shaw, 1981). It is usually recommended to keep freshly harvested potatoes for one to two weeks at 15 to 20°C (59 to 68 °F) at air humidity above 85 percent to stimulate skin setting and wound healing (suberization) before storage. This is called the "curing" period.

Mechanical Testing of Potatoes and Other Similar Materials

Tensile testing: Huff (1967) measured the tensile stength of potato tissues and found wide variation in its values depending primarily upon the structural zone from which the tissues were taken. The tensile strength and failure modulus increased with an increase in the loading rate. However, no significant change in failure modulus was observed during storage.

54

Compression testing: Bourne and Mondy (1967) measured the deformation of a cylinder of potato tissue and of whole potatoes under a metal punch, using a constant force, as an indication of the firmness of whole potatoes. They found that measuring deformation under a punch is preferred over measuring the deformation of a cylinder because of its simplicity, non-destructive nature and a better correlation with sensory evaluation. Both methods of measuring deformation gave a useful objective index of potato firmness. Finney and Hall (1967) studied the elastic properties of potatoes by using the Instron testing machine. The apparent elastic constants of the potato were estimated based on the elastic modulus under uniaxial compression and the bulk elastic modulus under hydrostatic stress. The stress-strain relationship for cylindrical specimens was linear during the first loading cycle. The ratio of stress to strain (elastic modulus) of potato tissue was significantly influenced by its previous load history. Matthews and Hall (1968) found that the thermal diffusivity and elastic modulus of potatoes were increased by a small amount and then decreased when the heat exposure was increased. Fluck et al. (1968) studied compression plunger tests of sweet potatoes during a normal harvest-curing-storage sequence and reported that there were significant mechanical changes with curing, cooling and storage as well as varieties.

Snobar (1973), while working on the hardness determination of carrots, performed some tests on the axial and radial compressions of cylindrical specimens of the potato flesh. He reported that there was no difference in the modulus of elasticity values calculated from axial and radial compression tests. Later, radial compression of cylindrical samples was studied in detail by Sherif et al. (1976) for determining the modulus of elasticity.

Wright and Splinter (1968) found that the rupture parameter values of sweet potatoes were sensitive to the rate at which the tissue was deformed; in general, these values decreased as the rate of deformation increased.

Relationship between elasticity modulus and texture: Even though the modulus of elasticity may be directly related to the moisture content and turgor within fruits and vegetables, its relationship to texture is not clear. Finney (1972) suggested that the modulus of elasticity should be related to the "firmness" attribute of texture, arguing that firmness should be closely allied with those characteristics of materials which physicists call "stiffness" and "rigidity." Mohsenin and Mittal (1977) have suggested that the term "modulus of deformability" should be substituted in research with food materials for the term "modulus of elasticity" in order to maintain the purity of the well-established and precise meaning of the latter term. They also suggested that in fresh fruits, 1.5 to 3.0 percent strains can be tolerated and the appropriate rheological concepts valid for small deformations can be used as the first approximation. Bourne (1979) suggested using the term "small compression" in place of "small strain" and stated that small compression means less than 25 percent absolute compression or less than 50 percent of the rupture compression, whichever is the lesser. Peleg (1977) reported that mechanical measurements of foods may not be theoretically comparable if the tests are performed under distinctly different conditions with regard to the specimen dimensions, the level of the deformation, and its application rate.

BACKGROUND INFORMATION

The elasticity modulus of potatoes can be determined by axial compression, radial compression, and Hertz contact stress analysis.

Axial Compression Test

For a cylindrical specimen, the modulus of elasticity (E) can be calculated by the equation:

$$E = (F/A)/(\Delta/L)$$

where   F = compression force
        A = cross sectional area
        Δ = change in length under compression
        L = original length   ...(1)

Radial Compression Test

The elasticity modulus (E) of cylindrical food materials under radial compression between two rigid planes can be calculated by the equation (Sherif et al., 1976):

$$E = \frac{8(1 - \mu^2)Z^2 F}{\pi DL} \qquad \ldots (2)$$

where
$$\mu = \text{Poisson's ratio}$$
$$Z = R/b$$
$$R = \text{radius of cylindrical specimen}$$
$$b = \text{half-contact width}$$
$$F = \text{compression force}$$
$$D = \text{diameter of specimen}$$
$$L = \text{length of specimen}$$

The value of Z is determined by the equation

$$\frac{\Delta}{D} = \frac{1}{2Z^2} [\ln(2Z) + 1/2] \qquad \ldots (3)$$

The configuration of a radially compressed cylindrical sample is shown in Figure 1 for clarity.

Compression Tests Based on Hertz Analysis

Rigid spherical indenter upon a flat surface: In this case, the elasticity modulus is calculated by the equation (Mohsenin, 1971):

$$E = \frac{0.531F(1 - \mu^2)}{\Delta^{3/2}} [\frac{4}{d}]^{\frac{1}{2}}$$

where d is the diameter of spherical indenter. ... (4)

57

Whole potato between two parallel rigid plates:
The elasticity modulus of a convex body compressed
between two parallel planes is calculated by the
equation (Mohsenin, 1971):

$$E = \frac{0.531F \ (1 - \mu^2)}{\Delta^{3/2}} \ [\ (\ \frac{1}{R_1} + \frac{1}{R_1'} \ )^{1/3} \ +$$

$$(\ \frac{1}{R_2} + \frac{1}{R_2'} \ )^{1/3} \ ]^{3/2}$$

where R_1, R_1', R_2, R_2' are radii of curvature of convex
body at the points of contact.   ...(5)

EXPERIMENTAL INVESTIGATION

Potatoes

Potatoes of the Spunta variety and grown in
Changwat Chiangmai (northern Thailand) were used in
this study. Though potatoes had been transported to
Bangkok the same day after digging, the potatoes were
three to four days old when received in the market.
After initial testing, the potatoes were placed in
perforated plastic bags and stored at different
temperatures.

Potato Storage Conditions

Potatoes were stored at the temperatures of 5,
10, 20, and 30°C (41,50,68 and 86°F). The ambient
conditions in the room were 30 C temperature and 67-
70 percent relative humidity. The storage periods of
1, 2, 4, and 8 weeks were arbitrarily selected for
testing schedule. After each storage period, potato
samples were drawn and conditioned at room
temperature for at least 24 hours before preparing
the cylindrical test specimens.

Preparation of Test Specimens

To obtain cylindrical specimens with different
diameters and lengths, stainless steel sample corers

with inside diameters of 1.0, 1.5, 2.0 and 2.5 cm
(0.394, 0.591, 0.787, and 0.984 in.) were fabricated.
A knife fixed with a square steel plate was used to
trim the ends of the samples to proper length for
axial and radial compression tests.

Experimental Conditions

Loading rate: The loading rates of 50, 100, 200
and 500 mm/min (1.97, 3.94, 7.87, and 19.69 in/min)
available with the Instron testing machine (Model
1140) were used to study the variation in elasticity
modulus values based on different compression test
methods.

Specimen dimensions: Test specimens with length
to diameter (L/D) ratios of 1:1, 2:1, 3:1 were used
to investigate the influence of (L/D) ratio on
elasticity modulus determination.

Diameter of spherical indenters: Stainless
steel balls of 1.430, 1.587, 1.746 and 1.900 cm
(0.563, 0.625, 0.687, and 0.748 in.) diameter were
fixed at one end of the 6 cm (2.36 in.) long rods and
used as spherical indenters to compress the flat
surface of potato specimens.

Poisson's Ratio Determination

An overhead projector was used to determine the
change in lateral dimension of the test specimens.
Cylindrical specimens, 2.0 cm (0.787 in.) in diameter
and of different lengths, were removed lengthwise
from the individual potatoes. The overhead projector
was positioned with the Instron testing machine in
such a way that the diameter of the specimen produced
an enlarged image on a screen. The magnification
ratio of image to actual specimen dimensions was
about 20. The diameter of specimen prior to and
following the compression could be measured on the
screen. The initial length of specimen was measured
by a micrometer. The change of length during
compression was recorded on the chart of the Instron
testing machine. Finally, the Poisson's ratio could
be calculated as the ratio of the experimental values
of lateral to longitudinal strain.

Force-Deformation Plots

The compression force and the corresponding deformation in any given test could be determined from the chart of the Instron the testing machine and analyzed. The elasticity modulus values were calculated using equations given in the preceding section.

RESULTS AND DISCUSSION

Poisson's Ratio

The Poisson's ratio of fresh potatoes was determined based on the direct measurement of longitudinal and lateral strain for 15 test specimens. The average value of Poisson's ratio was found to be 0.48 with a coefficient of variation of about two percent. Finney and Hall (1967) reported Poisson's ratio of potatoes to be 0.492 which is close to the value determined in this study.

Experimental Validation of Test Techniques

It was necessary to verify the applicability of each test method to the experimental data in order to calculate the elasticity modulus values. This verification was essentially based on the theoretical relationships for different test methods.

Axial compression: A typical force-deformation plot for potato specimen is shown in Figure 2. These plots exhibited non-linear relationships and could be adequately represented by three-degree polynomial equations. The differentiation of fitted equations yielded the tangent modulus at different values of percent compression (Figure 3). For potato samples, the tangent modulus gradually increased with percent compression and then levelled off. Thus it may be concluded that potato samples deviate considerably from ideal elastic behavior under axial compression. Therefore, the values of percent compression must be stated when reporting the tangent modulus.

Radial compression: The relationship between Z, which is the ratio of sample radius to half contact width, and deformation is complex (Equation 3). This necessitates a trial and error approach for

60

calculating first the value of Z and then
substituting in Equation 2 to determine the modulus
of elasticity. In this study, the relationship
between Z and (Δ/D) was redefined in an alternate
form as follows:

$$Z = 0.87 (\Delta/D)^{-0.60} \qquad \ldots (6)$$

A log-log plot of Equation 6 presented in Figure 4
clearly depicts the usefulness of a direct and
simplified relationship between Z and (Δ /D).
Equation 6 when substituted in Equation 2 yielded the
following relationship:

$$E = [\frac{1.927 \ (1 - \mu^2) D^{0.2}}{L}] \ \frac{F}{\Delta^{1.2}} \qquad \ldots (7)$$

Equation 7 was used for calculating the elasticity
modulus based on experimental force-deformation
relationships and thus checking the applicability of
radial compression test. Theoretically, a plot of
log F versus log should yield a straight line with
a slope of 1.2. The experimental values of these
slopes for potato specimen varied from 1.3 to 1.6
depending upon percent compression.

As a result, the calculated values of elasticity
modulus from Equation 7 were expressed as a function
of percent compression (Figure 3).

Hertz contact stress analysis: The log-log
plots of force versus deformation for whole potato
and flat surface compression yielded a slope close to
1.5 in most cases and thus validated the
applicability of Hertz theory. In cases where a
slight deviation existed, a line with a slope of 1.5
was drawn to coincide with as much of the initial
part of the force-deformation curve as possible
(Arnold and Mohsenin, 1971). The force-deformation
values corresponding to the fitted line were used to
calculate the elasticity modulus.

61

Influence of Experimental Conditions on Elasticity Modulus Values

The elasticity modulus values in both axial and radial compression tests depended upon the percent compression due to nonlinear force-deformation behavior. Spot checks on a number of loading and unloading curves revealed that percent recovered deformation was about three percent in both axial and radial compression tests. Therefore, the force and deformation values corresponding to three percent compression were used in calculation of elasticity modulus.

Specimen dimensions: For any given length to diameter (L/D) ratio, the dimensions of the test specimens influenced the modulus of elasticity determinations in axial as well as radial compresion tests. Higher (L/D) ratios resulted in decreased values of elasticity modulus in axial compression. Likewise, an increase in the specimen diameter apparently led to lower elasticity modulus values in radial compression. In absence of any consistent trends, specimens 1.5 cm (0.59 in.) in diameter and 3.0 cm (1.18 in.) long were used in quality evaluation tests.

Loading rates: Potato specimens 1.5 cm in diameter and 3.0 cm long were subjected to the loading rates of 50, 100, 200 and 500 mm/min. Table 1 shows the tangent and elasticity modulus values calculated at three percent compression in axial and radial compression tests, respectively. It appears that the radial compression test is relatively more sensitive to loading rates, showing an increase in modulus values up to 200 mm/min loading rate but followed by a sudden drop at 500 mm/min loading rate. The tangent modulus values decreased progressively with increasing compression rates. However, very high loading rates resulted in a sharp decrease in respective modulus values in each test.

Table 2 presents the elasticity modulus values based on Hertz analysis as influenced by the different loading rates in whole potato and flat surface compression tests. It appears that whole potato compression between parallel plates results in consistent values at higher loading rates between 100

62

and 500 mm/min.   In case of compression of spherical
indenters on flat surface of potato specimens, the
magnitude of elasticity modulus values was about 50
percent less than in whole potato compression and
with a suddden drop at 500 mm/min loading rate.

Changes in Firmness of Potatoes During Storage

       Potatoes were tested initially after receiving
from the market and subsequently stored at 5, 10, 20
and 30°C (41 , 50 , 68 , 74°F). After 1, 2, 4 and 8
weeks of storage, potatoes were randomly drawn and
evaluated for their firmness in terms of the
elasticity modulus based on different compression
tests. A loading rate of 50 mm/min (1.97 in/min) was
used throughout.   The experimental results are
summarized in Table 3.

       The storage temperature and time both
contributed to a decrease in the firmness of
potatoes.   There was a wide variation in the
elasticity modulus values determined by different
test methods. However, the elasticity modulus values
decreased in magnitude with storage time at all
temperatures. This reduction in the firmness of
potatoes during storage could be represented by an
exponential function of storage time at any given
temperature in all compression tests:

$$E = E_o \, e^{-A\theta^B}$$

where E_o = elasticity modulus of fresh potato, MPa
         θ = storage time, weeks
         A,B = constants   ...(8)

The parameters of fitted equations relating time-
temperature dependence of eleasticity modulus on
various compression tests are given in Table 4 along
with their respective correlation coefficients.

Comparison of Testing Methods

       The elasticity modulus based on whole potato
compression was highest in comparison with other

tests. Axial compression, flat surface identation and radial compression followed next to yield the elasticity modulus values in decreasing order. Since different test methods resulted in widely varying values of elasticity modulus at the start or during the storage of potatoes, a direct comparison cannot be made to evaluate their relative merits. Therefore, a change in the elasticity modulus of potatoes during storage at various temperatures relative to initial modulus was expressed in terms of the elasticity modulus ratio (E/E_0). At the start of storage, this ratio was unity in all testing methods and decreased exponentially during storage (Figure 5). A rapid decline in the value of elasticity modulus ratio with storage time should be indicative of the sensitivity of the test method in monitoring the firmness. The plots presented in Figure 5 clearly indicate that the radial compression test was consistently more sensitive in reflecting the changes in potato firmness. It is interesting to note that whole potato and flat surface compression led to a somewhat similar relative change in elasticity modulus values despite the difference in their individual values.

In axial compression, the initial curvature of experimental force-deformation curves increased with the storage time at all temperatues. For example, in the case of fresh potatoes, the initial curvature was confined up to the deformation of about 0.6 mm or 2 percent strain. But after 8 weeks of storage at 30°C (86°F), the initial curved part increased up to the deformation of about 2.0 mm or 6 percent strain. This was perhaps because of the decrease in the elasticity of potatoes during storage. In radial compression tests, the change in the experimental force-deformation curves was not so evident.

In this study, the elasticity modulus determinations made at the start of the storage period should only be considered in relative sense. The basic objective in compression testing of potatoes stored at various temperatures was to study the relative change in their firmness based on selected approaches. Thus, various compression testing methods could be compared for their effectivenesss and used for an accurate characterization of changes in the material properties.

64

CONCLUSIONS

Potatoes exhibited nonlinear force-deformation behavior in axial compression tests requiring the calculation of tangent elasticity modulus values as a function of percent compression. In radial compression tests, there was marked deviation of experimental force-deformation relationships from the theory. Therefore, the computed values of elasticity modulus were expressed as a function of percent compression. In compression tests with whole potatoes and their flat surface, the force-deformation relationship conformed to Hertz analysis only at low compression values and could be used to calculate elasticity modulus independent of percent compression. The experimental elasticity modulus values showed a wide variation in their magnitudes primarily due to the characterization of each test method used.

The firmness of potatoes appeared to decrease exponentially with storage period at all temperatures. Since the elasticity modulus values as determined in various compression tests were different, it was necessary to express the change in their magnitude during storage in terms of elasticity modulus ratio for making relative comparisons. The radial compression test showed maximum decrease in the elasticity modulus ratio with storage time. The axial compression test values were next. The compression of whole potatoes and their flat surface followed very closely to each other and showed minimum decrease in the elasticity modulus values during the storage at all temperatures.

REFERENCES

Arnold, P.C. and N.N. Mohsenin. 1971. Proposed techniques for axial compression tests on intact agricultural products of convex shape. Transactions of ASAE, 14(1):78-84.

Booth, R.H. and R.L. Shaw. 1981. Principles of Potato Storage. International Potato Center, Lima, Peru. 105 p.

Bourne, M.C. and N. Mondy. 1967. Measurement of whole potato firmness with a universal testing machine. Food Technology, 21, 97-100.

Bourne, M.C.   1979.   Rupture tests vs. small-strain
    tests   in   predicting   consumer   response   to
    texture. Food Technology, 33(10):67-76.

Finney, E.E.   1972.   Elementary concepts of rheology
    relevant   to   food   texture   studies.   Food
    Technology, 26(2):67-76.

Finney,   E.E.   and   C.W.   Hall.   1967.   Elastic
    properties   of   potatoes.   Transactions of ASAE,
    10(1):4-8.

Fluck, R.C., F.S. Wright and W.E. Splinter. 1968.
    Compession   plunger,   skinning   and   friction
    properties of sweet potatoes.   Transactions of
    ASAE, 11(2):167-170, 174.

Huff,   E.R.   1967.   Tensile   properties of Kennebec
    potatoes. Transactions of ASAE,   10(3):414-419.

Matthew, F.V. and C.W. Hall. 1968. Method of finite
    differences   used to relate changes   in   thermal
    and   physical   properties   of   potatoes.
    Transactions of ASAE, 11(4):558-562.

Mohsenin,   N.N.   1970.   Physical Properties of Plant
    and   Animal   Materials.   Vol.   I.   Gorden   and
    Breach Science Publishers, New York.

Mohsenin,   N.N.   and   J.R.   Mittal.   1977.   Use   of
    rheological terms and correlation of compatible
    measurements in food texture research.   Journal
    of Texture Studies, 8(5):395-408.

Peleg, M. 1977. The role of the specimen dimensions
    in   uniaxial   compression   of   food   materials.
    Journal of Food Science, 42(3):649-651, 659.

Sherif,   S.M.,   L.J. Segerlind and J.S. Frame.   1976.
    An   equation for the modulus of elasticity of   a
    radially compressed cylinder.   Transactions of
    ASAE, 19(4):782-785.

Snobar, B. 1973. Engineering parameters related to
    the   hardness   of   carrots.   Unpublished   Ph.D.
    dissertation,   Michigan State   University,   East
    Lansing, MI.

Timbers, G.E., L.M. Staley and E.L. Watson. 1965. Determining modulus of elasticity in agricultural products by loaded plungers. <u>Agricultural Engineering</u>, 46(5):274-275.

Wright, F.S. and W.E. Splinter. 1968. Mechanical behaviour of sweet potatoes under slow loading and impact loading. Transactions of ASAE, 11(6):765-770.

Table 1. Effect of loading rate in axial and radial testing at 3 percent compression of potato specimens 1.5 cm in diameter and 3.0 cm long

Rate of loading (mm/min)	Tangent modulus[*] (MPa)	Elasticity modulus[*] (MPa)
50	2.79	1.04
100	2.42	1.39
200	2.24	1.51
500	1.68	0.70

[*] Average of three tests.

Table 2. Effect of loading rate on elasticity modulus based on Hertz analysis of whole potato and flat surface compression

Rate of loading (mm/min)	Elasticity modulus[*] (MPa)				
	Whole potato	Flat compression with indenters of different diameters (cm)			
		1.43	1.59	1.75	1.90
50	4.57	1.22	1.16	1.42	1.29
100	2.17	1.43	1.29	1.23	1.08
200	2.61	1.35	1.53	1.08	0.95
500	2.31	0.75	0.92	0.83	1.05

[*] Average of three tests.

68

Table 3. Elasticity modulus of potatoes during storage based on different compression tests

Storage temperature (°C)	Storage period (weeks)	Elasticity modulus[1] (MPa)			
		Axial[2]	Radial[2]	Hertz analysis	
				Flat surface	Whole potato
5	0	2.93	2.11	2.58	5.76
	1	2.29	1.94	2.31	4.60
	2	2.15	1.33	1.86	4.29
	4	1.36	1.00	1.68	3.49
	8	1.14	0.47	1.31	1.75
10	0	2.93	2.11	2.58	5.76
	1	2.11	1.18	1.85	3.77
	2	1.89	1.15	1.51	3.24
	4	1.14	0.76	1.47	2.06
	8	0.56	0.22	0.85	1.57
20	0	2.93	2.11	2.58	5.76
	1	1.77	1.10	1.51	3.52
	2	1.47	0.76	1.29	2.97
	4	0.64	0.39	1.13	1.86
	8	0.41	0.08	0.76	1.43
30	0	2.93	2.11	2.58	5.76
	1	1.64	0.59	1.56	2.94
	2	1.25	0.58	1.06	2.91
	4	0.64	0.33	0.78	1.79
	8	0.32	0.04	0.52	1.04

[1] Average of three tests.

[2] Based on 3 percent compression of cylindrical specimens 1.5 cm in diameter and 3.0 cm long.

69

Table 4. Parameters of fitted equations representing time-temperature dependence of elasticity modulus values based on different compression tests

Compression test	Storage temperature (°C)	A	B	Correlation coefficient
Axial	5	0.23	0.70	0.961
	10	0.30	0.81	0.986
	20	0.49	0.70	0.979
	30	0.57	0.67	0.997
Radial	5	0.12	1.32	0.959
	10	0.47	0.67	0.939
	20	0.63	0.77	0.996
	30	1.00	0.55	0.916
Hertz (Flat surface)	5	0.15	0.75	0.969
	10	0.33	0.54	0.988
	20	0.52	0.38	0.987
	30	0.70	0.39	0.998
Hertz (Whole potato)	5	0.20	0.80	0.972
	10	0.42	0.57	0.987
	20	0.49	0.53	0.987
	30	0.59	0.48	0.952

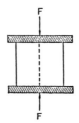

F

F

Axial Test

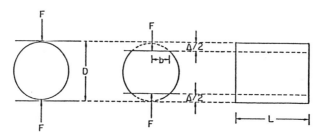

Radial Test

Fig. I   Test sample configurations in axial and radial compression

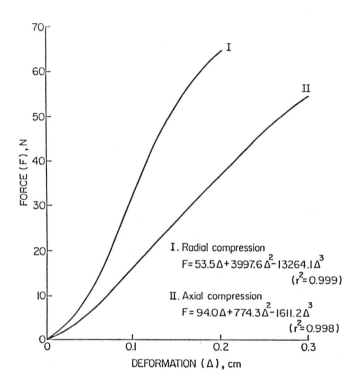

Fig. 2 Typical force – deformation relationships for axial and radial compression of a cylindrical potato specimen (1.5 cm dia , 3.0 cm long)

72

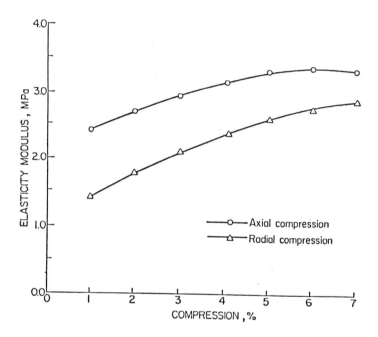

Fig. 3   Elasticity modulus of cylindrical sample of fresh potato
(1.5 cm dia , 3 cm long) as a function of percent compression

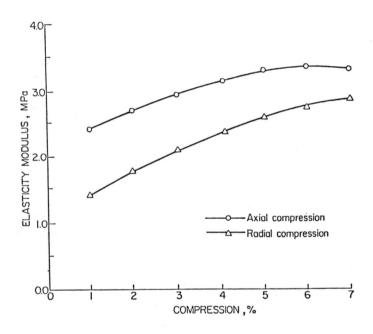

Fig. 3   Elasticity modulus of cylindrical sample of fresh potato
(1.5 cm dia , 3 cm long) as a function of percent compression

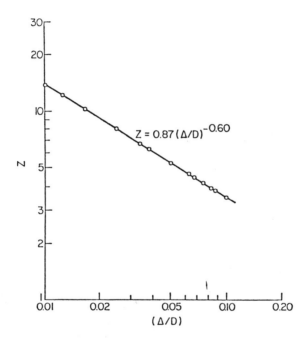

Fig. 4   Z as a function of (Δ/D) based on Sherif
et al. equation (1976)

75

I – Axial compression ; 2 – Radial compression ; 3 – Hertz (Flat surface) ; 4 – Hertz (Whole potato)

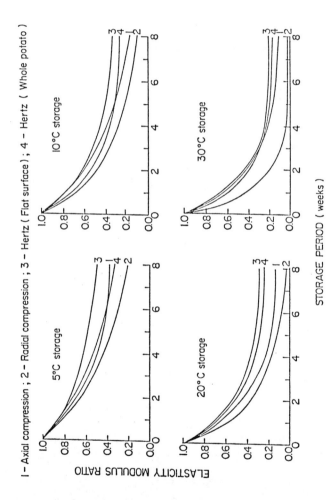

Fig.5   Elasticity modulus ratio of potatoes during storage at different temperatures

76

MECHANICAL KILLING OF POTATO VINES

by

J.L. Halderson, Agricultural Engineer, and
L.C. Haderlie, Weed Scientist, University of Idaho
Research and Extension Center, Aberdeen, Idaho

ABSTRACT

Potato vine killing is a widely used practice in the U.S.A. Reasons for vine killing vary considerably between production areas. The period for tuber maturation after vine killing ranges from approximately 10-21 days, primarily affected by soil temperatures. Most potato production specialists recommend slow vine killing methods but recent University of Idaho research shows the most rapid methods to be preferable on Russet Burbank. Mechanical vine killing methods, such as flails and pullers, are used very little nationally but are frequently used in seed production areas and sometimes used in commercial production areas with high elevations and cool nights. Vine rollers are sometimes used alone to kill vines and close soil cracks. University of Idaho researchers recommend vine rolling before application of chemical vine killers.

ASAE Paper No. 85-1073

Key words: vine desiccation, specific gravity, stem-end discoloration, vine killing, vine rolling, flails, tuber quality, yield.

INTRODUCTION

Potato vine killing in the U.S.A. is primarily a practice in commercial production areas where vines are still green and vigorous when harvesting must begin. Vines are killed in this situation to cause tuber skin to set before harvest. Fresh market harvesting of early potatoes also necessitates killing of vines in most instances. Seed potato producers will often kill vines to control tuber size or to reduce transmission of disease organisms from the plant to the tuber in addition to reducing vine volume before harvest.

Where some form of vine killing is practiced, chemicals account for the vast majority of acreage and dinoseb is the major chemical being used. Mechanical devices, such as rollers, flails and pullers, account for a relatively small percent of the acreage on a national basis, but can become quite important in certain production areas.

A three-year study has recently been completed at the University of Idaho to examine the tuber quality and yield effects of various vine killing methods. Subsequently, research on vine killing at Aberdeen and other southern Idaho sites has been concentrated on mechanical killing and placement of detached vines to preclude pickup by harvesting machines. Mechanical treatments in the current research have been with a flail, a roller, or a puller. Comparisons also continue between mechanical and chemical methods. The major conclusion of the three-year study was that vines should be killed as rapidly as possible to maximize benefits. Sulfuric acid and dinoseb achieved the most rapid killing but flails appeared to do equally as well. Pullers tended to lower yields more when killed on the same date but maintained higher specific gravity in the tests which were all confined to the Russet Burbank variety.

OBJECTIVE

Reduced Vine Volume at Harvest

Killing with chemicals produces a great reduction in vine volume and weight so that devining chains on harvesters readily convey vines away from tubers. Some fragmentation of vines leads to small vine pieces in the pile of potatoes. Hand picking on the harvester is a common practice to reduce the amount of vine pieces going into the bulk truck. Wet weather during harvest can produce very tough vines which hairpin around digger blades and supporting frames to cause interference and delay.

Flails cut the aerial portion of the vine into small pieces but leave the lower stem and root in one piece. The latter factor can result in vine pieces small enough to fall through the deviner chain but large enough to be retained on the secondary and subsequent chains. To give the best performance with flails, the conformation of the hill should closely correspond to that of the cutting blades. Pullers offer the possibility of positioning the vines or chopping them such that deviner chains can be removed from harvesters. However, the economics of killing vines with pullers would not seem to permit the addition of chopping equipment onto pullers. This matter is part of the current research effort on vine killing at Aberdeen.

Set Tuber Skin

Vines are normally killed 10-21 days prior to harvest to permit sufficient maturation of the skin to reduce skin slip. There apparently are no objective devices for measurement of the force required to slip the skin. Normally this measurement is subjective and done by applying pressure and lateral force to the skin with the thumb. Research has suggested that the rate of skin maturation is probably affected by the type of vine killing methods which are used. There is promise of shortening the maturation period if objective measurement devices could be developed to measure skin slip differences due to different vine killing methods. Higher soil temperatures have been shown to reduce the tuber maturation period. Areas such as Wisconsin tend to allow slightly less than two weeks for maturation.

Control Disease

Diseases, such as leafroll, are transmitted by aphids as they move through the field and feed on potato plant leaves. The virus is subsequently relocated throughout the plant by the vascular system so vine killing methods can be effective in preventing the movement to tubers. Vine pullers are potentially the most effective means of disease reduction in tubers because they remove roots also. However, vine pullers are generally not as thorough in killing all plants and are presently not economically advantageous compared to other killing methods. A small improvement in disease control in seed potato production could potentially be of great economic importance. Sulfuric acid has been shown to be faster than dinoseb but the economic implications of these two methods, compared to puller or flails, has not been explored for seed production usage.

Control Tuber Size

Vine killing for control of tuber size is of primary importance in some production areas for potato seed. There appears to be a number of factors which are applicable other than direct size control by vine killing. Several of these factors include variety and the predominance of single drop seed usage. Colorado uses vine kill in the San Luis Valley predominately on the Centennial Russet for limiting seed size. Idaho most often uses vine kill in the seed-producing areas to reduce vine volume before harvest.

Reduce Dehydration in Storage

Tubers with proper periderm maturity lose less moisture during storage and vine killing can be used to initiate rapid periderm maturity. Studies have shown that vine killing can reduce dehydration of approximately 50 percent during a storage duration of approximately ten months. The reasons for a decrease in the periderm permeability have not been completely investigated. Reduced skinning and reduced permeability to moisture movement are two closely related factors that are affected by vine kill.

Facilitate Harvest Scheduling

Vine killing prior to harvest permits a more predictable harvesting rate per day because vines are reduced in volume or entirely removed prior to harvesting. The actual harvesting rate is usually somewhat increasd because skinning is greatly reduced and there is reduced sensitivity toward bruising. Since yield and specific gravity are both generally reduced due to vine killing, this operation should not be done any earlier than necessary to achieve sufficient tuber maturity before harvest. Measurements in Russet Burbank in Idaho have shown yield changes of approximately 560 kg/ha/day (500 lbs/ac/day) and specific gravity changes of approximately 0.0006/day at the normal vine killing time of early-to-mid September.

Reduce Bruising

The generally held perception is that vine killing causes a reduction in tuber bruise sensitivity during subsequent harvesting. However, some test show mature tubers to be considerably more sensitive to impact damage than immature tubers. Relatively little quantitative information exists for direct cause-and-effect relationships between these two parameters because so many factors appear to be involved in determining the bruise sensitivity of potatoes. Some production areas employ windrowing and harvest. In both instances, bruise reduction appears to result from dehydration of the cells near the tuber surface while the type of bruise is shifted from shatter to black spot.

VINE KILLING PRACTICES

Nationally

Less than half of the total potato acreage on a national basis is subject to some form of vine killing. Of the various methods of killing, chemicals account for well over three-fourths of the acres that are killed. The most popular chemical is dinoseb, which accounts for approximately 90 percent of the chemically-killed acres. Most of the remaining vines are chemically-killed with paraquat.

Sulfuric acid is of little national importance. Mechanical methods of vine kill are used on less than ten percent of the acreage which is killed. Rolling, in combination with chemical killing, is the most often used mechanical method but some production areas use two applications of chemicals in preference to rolling prior to a single application of chemicals. Tuber maturation, after vine killing, is allocated slightly less than two weeks on a national basis.

Idaho

Approximately 55 percent of Idaho producers use chemicals to kill vines and approximately 25 percent use some mechanical method. Dinoseb accounts for around two-thirds of the chemically-killed acres while sulfuric acid is second in importance with about one-fourth of the chemically-killed acres. Sulfuric acid usage is rapidly increasing despite not being directly labeled for potato vine killing. Most of the mechanical killing is confined to rolling before chemical application. However, rolling is sometimes used alone to seal soil cracks. Rolling alone is not recommended for vine killing. Idaho producers use a slightly longer maturation period than is done nationally, possibly because of the higher elevation and cool nights.

IDAHO RESEARCH RESULTS

The following factors are the major points of interest as a result of potato vine killing studies on Russet Burbank potato vines in Idaho.

1. The most rapid means of vine killing is recommended to maintain high tuber quality and yield (Table 1).

2. Rolling (Figure 1), followed by sulfuric acid application, achieved the highest rate of chemical desiccation (Table 2).

3. Rapid vine killing did not increase stem-end discoloration when recommended production practices for higher yield and quality were followed (Table 3).

4.   Tuber specific gravity was highest for vines
killed by hand pulling (Table 4).

Table 1. Total yield and percent No. 1's following several vine killing
treatments on full-season Russet Burbank in 1983.

Killing Treatment**	Not Rolled		Rolled	
	Total Yield Mt/Ha*	% No. 1's	Total Yield Mt/ha	% No. 1's
Control	38.6	66	43.1	65
Dinoseb	39.3	65	41.9	67
Diquat	35.7	61	41.4	66
Sulfuric acid	38.1	66	41.9	66
Pulled	34.2	64	.	.
LSD (P - 0.05)	4.8	n.s.	n.s.	n.s.

. No reading

*Metric tonnes per hectare - one metric Tonne - 22 cwt

**From February 7, 1986 letter, James L. Helderson.
 Spray application was with a tractor-mounted boom of 3.7 m wide delivering
 164 L/ha at 193 KPa. Nozzles were Tee Jet 8002's. Sulfuric acid was
 applied as 93% concentrate at a rate of 88 Kg (sulfur equivalent)/ha, dinoseb
 at 2.5 Kg/ha, diquat at 0.28 Kg/ha, and endothall at 1.1 Kg/ha. Herbimax oil
 (Loveland Industries crop oil concentrate) was used with dinoseb and X-77
 (Chevron Chemical non-ionic surfactant) with diquat at approximately 1%
 by volume.

Table 2. Rate of vine desiccation following chemical application and rolling treatments.

Killing Treatment*	n[2]	% Desiccation[1] Days After Treatment**		
		4	11	20
Control	24	11	21	62
Endothall	16	50	79	92
Diquat	8	55	79	92
Dinoseb	24	64	85	92
Sulfuric acid	24	79	89	95

[1] Combined over rolling treatments and two vine maturities.

[2] n = number of observations

*See Table 1

**From February 7, 1986 letter, James L. Helderson.
Desiccation values on the day of vine killing were 5% overall. We tried to apply vine killing treatments when vines were mature but with no more than 10% natural drying. We observed that our activity in the plots accelerated "natural" drying so the 11% desiccation value for the control on day four should be considered typical. We did not attempt to separately measure the accelerated desiccation rate due to our activity in the plots.

Table 3. The effect of vine kill method on stem–end
discoloration (SED) on Russet Burbank.

Killing Treatment*	% Total SED[1]
Hand Pulled	12
Sulfuric Acid	12
Slow Chemical[2]	13
Natural Death	14
Dinoseb	15
LSD (P = 0.05)	n.s.

[1]Over 12 location-years.

[2]Endothall or Diquat

*See Table 1

Table 4. Specific gravity of tubers following several
vine killing treatments on Russet Burbank.

Killing Treatment**	1981	1982	1983
Control	1.086	1.085	1.082
Dinoseb	1.082	1.082	.
Diquat	1.083*	1.083	.
Sulfuric acid	1.081	1.082	1.076
Pulled	1.084	1.082	1.073
Cut	1.081	.	1.073[T]
LDS (P = 0.05)	0.002	0.002	0.007

.No reading

*Endothall

**See Table 1

Figure 1. The typicl potato vine roller used in Idaho prior to chemical application or some times alone to close cracks in the soil. The roller shown is 5 m (18 ft). The rollers are custom made to many different sizes.

PRACTICAL AND SEASONAL PERFORMANCE OF ONE-ROW POTATO HARVESTERS ON PRIVATE FARMS IN POLAND

by

T. Karwowski, Professor, Institute for Buildings,
Mechanization, and Electrification in Agriculture,
Warsaw, Poland

ABSTRACT

Potato harvesting with combine harvesters on private farms has been increasingly popular in Poland since 1972. The annual depreciation cost of a potato harvester is a fixed cost and is one of the major costs of harvesting. These investigations were conducted to determine the total costs for harvesting and harvester performance over a six-year period.

ASAE Paper No. 85-1074

INTRODUCTION

In 1985, the potato cultivation area in Poland was 2.1 million hectars (5.2 million acres), of this total 150 thousand hectars (370 million acres) were in big state owned farms (PGR). The remainder of the potato cultivation area was in small private family farms. The average potato crop on these farms in 1985 was estimated at about 20T/ha (178 cwt/acre). The distribution of potato production in Poland in 1985 is shown in Table 1.

Potato harvesters were first utilized in Poland in the beginning of the sixties. In the period of 1961-72 potato harvesters were used almost exclusively on state farms. The machines were two-row harvesters imported from the GDR. The use of potato harvesters on family farms was started in the period of 1973-74 when the home industry began to produce the one-row harvester, Figure 1.

Since 1975 about 3.0 to 4.0 thousand of these machines have been put on the market each year. At the present production level, these harvesters are capable of harvesting not more than 15-20 percent of the potato area. The rest of the potato acreage is harvested as follows:

    two-row diggers 65%
    one-row spinners 15%

The average area harvested by one-row harvesters has been rapidly declining the past few years. The reason for this is the increase of the share of these harvesters bought by individual farms. Since the introduction of combine harvesting two serious problems have been gaining importance:

    - the seasonal efficiency of the harvester and the cost of the operation

    - the increase in damaged tubers.

SEASONAL EFFICIENCY OF ONE-ROW HARVESTER

The efficiency of one and two-row harvesters working on state farms is satisfactory since the large field areas on these state farms ensures the

appropriate   utilization   of   machines.   What
constitutes a problem is the utilization of the   one-
row harvester on family farms, Table 1.

These   one-row harvesters are those provided   to
the   small farms by the agricultural service stations
and machines purchased by the private farms.

Research   was initiated during 1982-84   to   help
understand   the problem of harvester   utilization   on
small farms.   For this research 36 one-row harvesters
were studied;   12 harvesters in each of three country
districts.   The 36 harvesters consisted of four each
produced   in 1977,   1979,   and 1981 in each district.
This   cross   section   of   harvesters   enabled   the
determination   of   areas   harvested   by   particular
machines over the six-year study period.   The results
are shown in Table 2.

The   research   data showed that   the   harvesters
were   utilized 10-36 days during the season on   small
private   farms.   The   area harvested by one   machine
ranged   from 11.1 to 48.6 ha (27.4 to 120 acres)   per
season.

Table   2   also shows that the   average   seasonal
efficiency   per harvester declined over the   six-year
study period.   The basic reason for this is harvester
breakdowns due to the aging machines.

The   seasonal efficiency of a harvester   depends
also upon the user.   For example,   the efficiency of
harvesters   utilized on the   14-state   farms   (large
acreages)   is   35   to 48 ha (86.4 to 110   acres)   per
season   whereas   the efficiency of   the   Agricultural
Service Stations harvesters utilized on family   farms
is 15-20 ha (37-50 acres) per season.

Season   efficiency   of   a   harvester   is   also
influenced by two factors: the dead time to repairs
and   the   operator.   Table   2   shows   that   hourly
efficiency the sixth year (0.108 ha [0.267 acres] per
hour)   was only 76 percent of the second year   (0.141
ha   [0.348 acres] per hour).   Based on conversations
with   the harvester operators it was   concluded   that
due   to breakdowns the operator became more   cautious
over   the seasons and basically slowed down operating
speeds   in   hopes to reduce breakdowns on   the   aging
harvesters.

90

The researchers studied the first and second year seasonal efficiency in relationship to the harvester and the operator. The researchers concluded that the least number of breakdowns were in the first and second seasons. In order to maintain a satisfactory hourly efficiency in the third and fourth year the operation depended upon the psychology of the operator. The operator that studies and determines the harvester features and capabilities the first year is able to maintain a higher seasonal efficiency the third and fourth seasons.

Table 2 shows that hourly efficiency of the harvesting operation in years 2, 3, and 4 appears to remain about the same in spite of the increasing number of breakdowns. The apparent observed answer is "operator experience." The unfamiliarity of the machines and the operation the first year was off set byoperator experience in following years. For example the operator was able to reduce minor breakdown time due to his experience in making these repairs. The declining efficiency over years 5 and 6 may be due to the nature of repairs; as the machines age, the nature of the repairs become more serious and complicated and breakdowns take longer to repair.

The Argicultural Service which provides many harvesters for the small family farm operation initially estimated the seasonal harvesting operation at 30 ha/(74 acres) season. This study shows that the real seasonal efficiency is less than 20 ha/(49 acres) season. Two factors enter into the estimated seasonal efficiency: the relationship of the harvester operation on large areas of the state farm (35-48 ha/(86.4-110 acres) season) and the experience of the state farm operators. The real small farm efficiency is influenced by area harvested per farm, number of farms, number of operators and the experience of these operators. These factors continue to reduce the seasonal efficiency from our estimated 30 to a real 20 ha/[74-49.4 acres) season efficiency.

Initially the Agricultural Service provided the one-row harvester for the small family farm, however, an increasingly greater portion of these harvesters are owned by the family farms. This new role of harvester ownership may reduce or limit the service to these small farm operators by the Agricultural Service Stations. A major factor that will influence the role of the Service Stations is the increasing extent of tuber damage.

TUBER DAMAGE IN POLAND

The average tuber damage in Poland over the past ten years amounted to 20-30 percent[1] of the crop. Tuber damage is highly influenced by tuber pulp temperature during harvesting and handling (Specht, 1981). If tuber damage in Poland is to be reduced, harvesting and handling must be limited to days and pulp temperatures above 10 °C (50°F).

For Poland this can be done in two ways: introducing early varieties and by limiting the days of harvest during the season. Earlier in this paper seasonal harvester efficiency was discussed; if harvest days are reduced then the seasonal efficiency will be reduced (contrary to the original concept of the Agricultural Service Research).

Harvesting efficiency of the small family private farms cultivating 1-5 ha (2.47-12.3 acres) of potatoes is less important than the quality of crop (less damaged tubers). Private farms rely upon family member and neighbors for their harvesting crews so altering the number of harvesting days to improve quality is of greater importance to the small farmer than the efficiency of the operation.

The Classical Potato harvester is too expensive for the small farm due to the manner of his work crew and product quality emphasis. These factors have forced the home industry to design and produce a simplified harvester, Figure 2. The capacity of this machine is less than the classical machine, Figure 1.

Mechanical down time for the simplified harvester should be less and repairs should be easier

----

[1]Percent damage = Severe damage + 0.3 medium damaged tubers (damages determined three days after harvest).

to perform by the small farmer. The less expensive simplified harvester may increase the trend for the private farms to own their own harvester. Private harvester ownership will enable the small farmer to select good harvesting weather for harvesting tubers with minimum damage.

Research on the simplified harvester marked Z642 shows encouraging results. The harvester has less weight (3520 lb/1600 kg) in comparison to the classical harvester. The Z642 is less expensive. Potato quality during harvest with the Z642 was studied, see Table 3.

Data shows that the Z642 harvester on a working efficiency of 0.06 to 0.13 ha/hr (0.15-0.2 acres/hr) has less tuber damage. This data along with the other desirable characteristics of less weight and lower cost can make the Z642 better suited for the small private Polish farmer. The Z642 has stimulated further interest in developing a more simplified less weight (1200 kg) less expensive harvester. The classic harvester Z644 (Figure 1) has been produced in Poland for ten years; the Z642 can be produced on the same assembly lines. The harvesting capacity of the two machines is similar to the Z644's 0.1 to 0.15 ha/hr (0.247-0.37 acres /hr) whereas the smaller Z642 is 0.06 to 0.13 (0.15-0.32 acres/hr); for this reason the smaller less expensive harvester is better suited for the small family farm requirements.

Introducing the simplified harvester or mini-harvester into world practice can bring about more profits for the small farmer. Private ownership can decline harvester and harvesting costs; the mini-harvester is one half the cost of the classic Z644 harvester.

One can predict that due to only the slight decrease in harvesting capacity (0.06 to 0.13 vs. 0.1 to 0.15 ha/hr) that the Z642 harvester will be used on two out of four small Polish farms (0.5 to 5.0 ha [1.2 to 12.3 acre]). These are the farms with family or neighbor crews and a number one emphasis for quality (non-damaged) tubers. For this group quality is more important than harvester efficiency.

In conclusion it appears the privately owned low cost simplified harvester is the answer for the small and scattered Polish farmer; it should make the mechanized harvest of quality potatoes affordable for the small farmer.

REFERENCES

Pawlik, A. 1985. Operational tests on reliability of Z644 potato harvester. IBMER. Warsaw (typescript).

Specht, A. 1981. Beschadigungen an der Kartoffel vermeiden. ADJ No. 78, Bonn.

Table 1. Distribution of Cultivated Potato Areas in Poland in 1985

Farm area ha	The number of farms culti- vating potatoes thousands	The area of potato culti- vation thousands of ha	Production Million tóns
over 15	104	275	5.5
10-15	210	420	8.4
5-10	616	715	14.3
under 5	1500	540	10.0
state farms	3	150	3.0
TOTAL	2433	2100	41.2

Table 2. Research results of the Z-644 Potato Harvester operations on small family farms in Poland over a six-year period*

Name of characteristic	Average value per harvester in following years of operation						Total average value
	I	II	III	IV	V	VI	
Number of working days in season	19.2	23.7	16.6	22.8	21.3	20.9	20.74
Number of working hours in season	126.5	158.2	114.4	154.1	143.9	153.7	141.75
Daily efficiency ha/day	.95	.94	.92	.92	.79	.80	.88
Hour efficiency ha/day	.146	.141	.134	.136	.116	.108	.129
Season efficiency ha/season	18.5	22.3	15.3	21.0	16.8	16.7	18.4
t/ season	343.0	420.6	250.1	384.7	334.0	311.3	340.6
Potato crop q/ha	187.8	189.0	162.8	183.4	198.4	185.9	186.2
Number of harvesters used in tests	14	12	11	11	13	13	----

*Data by Pavlik, 1985.

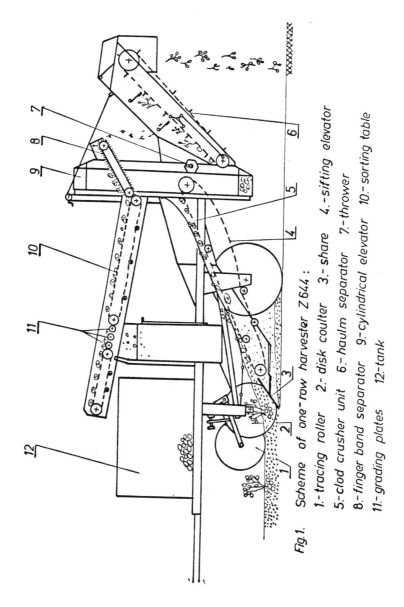

Fig.1. Scheme of one-row harvester Z644 :

1.- tracing roller   2.- disk coulter   3.- share   4.- sifting elevator
5.- clod crusher unit   6.- haulm separator   7.- thrower
8.- finger band separator   9.- cylindrical elevator   10.- sorting table
11.- grading plates   12.- tank

97

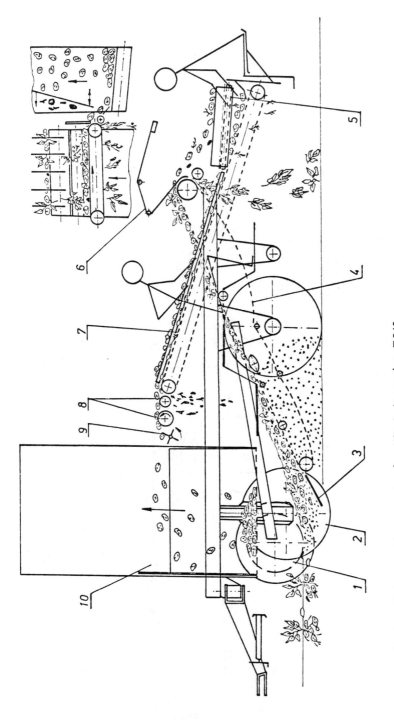

Fig. 2 Scheme of one-row simplified harvester Z 642:

1.- tracing roller 2.- disk coulter 3.- share 4.- sifting elevator
5.- elevator 6.- haulm separator 7.- sorting table
8.- grading plates 9.- paddle thrower 10.- tank

98

POSSIBILITIES FOR DECREASING TUBER DAMAGE CAUSED BY MECHANIZATION

by

Sander Horvath, University of Agricultural Sciences
Hungary

ABSTRACT

In Hungary the production and storage of potatoes on the large state and cooperative farms was highly mechanized between 1974 and 1978. As a consequence, the extent of tuber damages caused by mechanical handling has greatly increased. Of the volume of potatoes produced, 15-20 percent do not meet the requirements due to wounds and discoloration of flesh. For some years we have therefore paid increased attention to the question of how to decrease the mechanical damages and improve market quality.

ASAE Paper No. 85-1075

In 1981 after filling the storages we studied the damages caused to potatoes on ten farms and in commercial storages. A large proportion of the 34 lots examined had been graded and sorted before storing. The distribution of tuber damage is shown in Table 1.

The proportion of damaged tubers ranged between 6.6 and 36.1 percent when only wounds deeper than 1.7 mm (approximately 1/16 in.) were taken into account. On the average, tubers larger than 60 mm (2.36 in.) in diameter were damaged 80 percent. Apart from these investigations in some storages we have encountered rates of damage much higher than the above values. The results of these surveys induced us to carry on thorough investigations into the causes of damages and the possibilities of lessening them.

The results of an experiment started in the autumn of 1983 on the susceptibility of varieties to damages are shown in Table 2 (12 commercial varieties and 39 variety candidates). As shown in Table 2 the varieties, and even more so the variety candidates, greatly vary as to their response to the same stress, which means that tuber damage is a genetically determined characteristic.

Mechanical damage is a further source of damages and losses; the grey discoloration of the tuber is the most characteristic. The relationship between damage and grey color is shown in Figure 1 (based on examinations in autumn and spring). It can be seen that in autumn the proportion of wounds exceeds the rate of grey discoloration; in spring after storage the damage to tubers is less, while their grey color increases.

In the 51 varieties examined no correlation was found between damage, grey discoloration and the dry matter or starch content of the tubers. The higher rate of grey discoloration and moderate damage in spring are unambigously connected with the evaporation of water from the tubers. The starch content of the tuber increases in proportion to the evaporation of water. It is a rather widely held

100

opinion that the grey discoloration of the tuber is a more frequent phenomenon with the higher starch content varieties.

The effects of tuber size and temperature on the extent of tuber damages are shown in Table 3.

The characteristics of potatoes as to mechanical damage was examined. The type of harvesting system and the method used were studied. The E 671 lifter generally used on the Hungarian farms is of rather complicated construction, therefore, a two-row machine of higher capacity to remove trash was compared to the simple three-row machine which requires better working conditions. Under equivalent operating conditions 6.74 percent of the tubers showed mild damage and 13.36 percent showed severe damage. With the latter machine the corresponding values were 4.41 and 3.62 percent, respectively.

According to our investigations most damages are caused by inadequate soil preparation and the consequent overworking of the soil. More tubers are damaged in the course of loading and preparations for market than by harvesting due basically to poor management and improper use of machines. On the basis of experiments and surveys made on farms, using existing types of machines, we studied the possible systems of loading (see Figure 2). At present the Scheme I is used: the fresh potatoes highly susceptible to damage arriving from the field are sorted and graded before placing in storage. The different solutions speak for themselves. The most important advantage of the development is that the more careful methods are more productive, less damaging and at the same time less expensive.

From our investigations we have concluded that the wounds and the grey color of the flesh of the tuber are genetically closely related to varietal features but are also largely modified by the growing conditions and the condition of the potatoes at harvest. Tuber damage depends upon the impacts and forces exerted on the tuber during mechanical handling, the construction of the equipment, and the method of operation. Owing to the diversity of the causes of damage, a coordinated activity of many special disciplines is necessary if the damages are to be decreased.

REFERENCES

Gall H. - Truckenbrodt M. /1974/:
Beschadigungsminderung bei Kartoffeln ein
Komplexes Problem von der Zuchtung bis zur
Einlagerung Feldwirtschaft. 8. 351-356.

Horvath S. - Kutassy B. /1984/: Moglichkeiten
zur senkung von Knollenbeschadigungen.
EAPR Abstracts of Conference Papers.
Interlaken 174-175.

Hunnius W. - Munzert M. /1976/: Der Einfluss des
Jahres und Erntewitterung auf die Knollen-
beschadigungen von Kartoffelsorten.
Zeitschrift fur Acker- und Pflanzenbau.
Berlin. 3. 237-245.

Psetsenkov K.A. - Demirtsiev P.F. /1977/: Fiziko-
mechanitseskie swojstwa i prowredzdenija
kartofelja. Mechanizacija i. elektrifikacija
socialistitseskowoselskowo hozjajstwa. 9.
10-12.

Speckt A. /1981/: Beschadigungen an der Kartoffel
vermeiden.
A.I.D. Landwirtschaft und Forsten. 1-28.

Table 1. Distribution of the damages in 34 lots in the different potato storages.

Index of damage percent	Number of lots examined	Percentage Distribution
0 - 5	8	23.5
10.1 - 15	18	52.9
15.1 - 20	4	11.8
above 20.1	4	11.8
Total:	34	100.0

Table 2. Mechanical Injuries to tubers of selected potato varieties and variety candidates.

variety	Number of variety candidates	Damaged tubers	Number of wounds	Index of Damage
		per 100 tubers		
2	1	8-14	14-18	5-10
-	2	18-20	32	10-15
4	2	18-34	24-44	15-20
3	6	26-34	34-48	10-25
2	4	28-40	34-50	25-30
1	3	36-44	54-70	30-35
-	5	42-50	47-80	35-40
-	4	50-60	66-80	40-45
-	2	52-58	74-78	45-50
-	2	56-60	70-90	50-55
-	5	62-76	72-130	55-60
-	3	76-82	118-156	60
12	39	41.1	60.61	37.74

103

Table 3. Effect of tuber size and temperature on the extent of tuber damage

Tuber size mm/in.	Tuber temperature °C	°F	Damage index
below 40 (1.6")	9.5	49	22.0
40 - 60 (1.6-2.36")	9.5	49	35.1
above 60 (2.36")	9.5	49	49.7
AVERAGE	9.5	49	35.6
below 40	14.5	58	10.3
40 - 60	14.5	58	21.5
above 60	14.5	58	40.9
AVERAGE	14.5	58	24.2

104

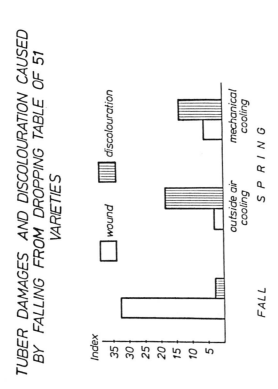

Fig. 1

TUBER DAMAGES AND DISCOLOURATION CAUSED
BY FALLING FROM DROPPING TABLE OF 51
VARIETIES

APPLIED MACHINE SYSTEMS IN THE STORE HOUSES

Fig. 2

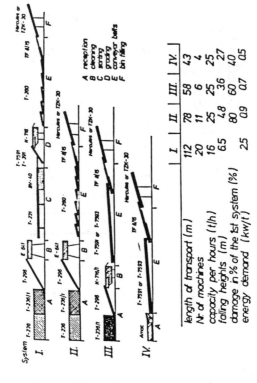

	I.	II.	III.	IV.
length of transport (m)	112	78	58	43
Nr of machines	20	11	6	4
capacity per hours (t/h)	16	25	25	25
falling heights (m)	65	48	36	27
damage in % of the 1st system (%)		80	60	40
energy demand (kw/t)	25	09	07	05

A reception
B cleaning
C sorting
D grading
E conveyor belts
F bin filling

106

FIELD COMPARISON OF THE EFFECTIVENESS OF AIR
ASSISTED ROTARY ATOMIZERS VS. CONVENTIONAL HYDRAULIC
NOZZLES FOR DISEASE CONTROL AND VINE KILL IN POTATOES

by

Richard L. Ledebuhr, Specialist; Gary R. Van Ee,
Assistant Professor; Randy Resmer, Research
Assistant; Todd Forbush, Research Assistant;
Agricultural Engineering Department and Howard S.
Potter, Professor Emeritus, Department of Botany
and Plant Pathology, Michigan State University,
East Lansing, Michigan

ABSTRACT

Air assisted rotary atomizers using turbulent
and straight steam air flow were field tested for
disease control and vine kill in potatoes. Their
performance indicated an increased efficiency in
coverage as compared to conventional hydraulic
nozzles. The addition of a drift retardant increased
the effectiveness of application with a conventional
hydraulic nozzle sprayer.

ASAE Paper No. 85-1076

INTRODUCTION

The use of rotary atomizers may improve the application of pesticide sprays. Conventional nozzles tend to shear spray liquid into droplets of widely varying sizes. Many droplets are larger than required thus resulting in inefficient deposition of spray materials. Large droplets also increase runoff and waste chemical. Because these oversized droplets contain a disproportionately higher percentage of the liquid sprayed, the total number of effective droplets is reduced. Hydraulic nozzles also produce a great number of small droplets many of which are so fine that they fail to impact on the crop and evaporate or drift away. With a rotary atomizer, the droplets are concentrated into a relatively narrow size spectrum, the range of which can be conveniently altered by varying the speed of rotation.

During the 1984 growing season, field trials were conducted to determine the effectiveness of various chemical application methods for disease control and vine kill in potatoes. These studies compared air assisted (turbulent and straight stream air flow) rotary atomization with conventional hydraulic nozzles. There were two experiments for disease control. One dealing with the control of early blight (Alternaria solani), at the Keilen Farms, Inc. Lansing, Michigan. The other dealing with the control of early blight and late blight (Phytophthora infestans), at the MSU Muck Farm near Bath, Michigan. A third study investigated potato vine kill and was conducted at Sandyland Farms, Howard City, Michigan.

APPLICATION METHOD

In all three of these tests, the spray systems used, and the volumes of application remained the same, they were:

1. Brush Type Boom sprayer with hollow- cone (D4-25) nozzles applying 50 gal/a (468 l/ha) at 40 psi (276 kPa),

2. Micronair AU3000 turbulent air sprayer applying 5 gal/A (46.8 l/ha) and 2.5 gal/A (23.4 l/ha),

rotating at 4200-4500 rpm, [1] and

3. Air Curtain with Micronair AU7000 straight stream air sprayer applying 5 gal/A (46.8 1 liter/ha) and 2.5 gal/A (23.4 1 liter/ha) rotating at 6500-7000 rpm.[1]

CHEMICAL TREATMENTS

All chemical treatments included standard herbicide and insecticide materials applied at label rates as needed before and after planting. Dithio Carbamate fungicide was the basic compound used for control of diseases. Fungicide[2] treatments were applied on a weekly basis over seven weeks from mid-summer through early fall. In late August and again in mid-September, potatoes at the MSU Muck Farm were artificially inoculated with the late blight fungus (Phytophthora infestans). There was no significant increase of disease after the inoculations.

In the vine kill experiment, Chevron Diquat at 1 pt/A (1.17 1 liter/ha) plus spreader (Chevron X-77) at 4 oz/A (292 ml/ha) was applied approximately one week before harvest. A drift retardant, STA-PUT, was added to one of the boom application treatments at a rate of 0.75 gal/100 gal (2.84 1/379 1), the other boom application received no drift retardant.

EXPERIMENTAL DESIGNS

A completely randomized design was used on all experiments. Trials at the Keilen Farms consisted of

----

[1]MSU research sprayer and Micronair AU3000, all applications at 2.5 gal/A (23.4 1/ha) included one quart of soybean oil with emulsifier as a partial carrier.

[2]At the MSU Muck Farm only Dithane M-45 80W at a 2.0 lb/a (2.24 kg/ha) was used. At the Keilen Farms Manex 4F applied at 1.5 qts/A (3.5 1/ha) was alternated with Dithane M-45 80W at 2 lb/A (2.24 kg/ha). One application of copper (Kocide 101 at 2 lb/A (2.24 kg/ha) was added to the regular fungicide treatment, and one application of Bravo 500 at 2 pts/A (2.33 1/ha) was substituted for the regular treatment.

two replicates.   Plots were 0.825 A (0.334 ha).   At
the MSU Muck Farm three 0.007 A (0.00283 ha)
replicates were used.   Sprayer plots were 0.017 A
(0.00283 ha) except for the boom and check plots,
which   were   0.34 A (0.1377ha).   The vine kill
experiment on Sandyland Farms used four sampling
areas within each 1.25 A (0.506 ha) sprayer plot.

EVALUATION METHODS

     Data was compiled by means of subjective panel
evaluations.   The disease index, in disease control
tests; and the desiccation index, in the vine kill
tests, were both based on a scale from 0-10.   In
disease control trials, data on disease index was
collected approximately one week before kill down,
and was an average of 10 readings per plot area.   In
the vine kill trial, the desiccation index was
evaluated at two and four day observations after
spraying.   This index represents an average of 10
readings taken in each replication.   Occurrence of
frost on the fifth day following treatment prevented
further vine kill evaluations.

RESULTS AND DISCUSSIONS

     The   results and dicussions of   the   field
comparison of air assisted rotary atomizers and
conventional hydraulic nozzle boom sprayer will be
addressed as follows:

1.   Effectiveness of vine kill,

2.   Control of early and late blight in potatoes, and

3.   Potato yields.

Effectiveness of Vine Kill

     Table 1 and Figure 1 show the desiccation   index
of each of the vine kill treatments. Applications by
both rotary atomizer systems and by boom with drift
retardant, resulted in highly signficant increase in
foliar desiccation over the boom without drift
retardant.   Micronair at 2.5 gal/A (23.4 l/ha), and
both Air Curtain applications, significantly (1%
level) increased desiccation over either boom
application, and over the Micronair at 5 gal/A (46.8
l/ha).

110

Deposition studies performed on mature tomatoes, with much the same foliar form and density as potatoes, may explain the improved performance of the Micronair and Air Curtain sprayers. The volume of application of these tests was 5 gal/A (46.8 l/ha) and the tracer material was metallic copper. Deposition of metallic copper (ppm) was collected on horizontally-placed mylar targets located at the top and in the middle of the plant canopy. Two targets were held in a rigid frame to provide an upper and lower surface. The frames were supported by upright iron rods, (See Figure 2). Table 2 shows the deposition recorded on both sides of the target. [3] Similar tests were performed on celery, their results are reported in Table 3. These deposition tests show that the Micronair and Air Curtain sprayers consistently deposited more copper, particularly on the under surface of the targets. In the potato vine kill study the improvement of the Micronair and Air Curtain desiccation, correlates to increased deposition, particularly underside coverage.

Disease Index

In the Keilen Farms study fungicide treatments applied with all spraying systems were highly effective in reducing foliar early blight infection, (see Table 4 and Figure 3). The most effective control resulted from applications with the Air Curtain. Treatments applied with the boom with hydraulic nozzles resulted in significantly more foliar infection than those applied with rotary atomizers.

In the MSU Muck Farm studies the Air Curtain provided the most effective disease control, and at both spray volumes, the disease index was significantly lower (1% level) than any of the other systems, (see Table 5 and Figure 4). The boom with hydraulic nozzles was the least effective system of application.

----

[3] The values of Table 2 should be used for comparison between sprayers only, the volumes represented are relative to the amount of copper applied.

<u>Yield</u>

In both disease control studies, the yields of US #1 potatoes from all spraying systems were significantly higher than the check, (see Tables 4 & 5 and Figures 3 & 4). Yield between spray systems did not differ significantly. Yields of B-Grade potatoes were significantly higher in the check sample than in the treated samples at the MSU Muck Farm. There was no significance in the B-Grade yield differences at the Keilen Farms. A likely explanation for the lack of signficant yield differences between methods of application is that the disease infection occurred late in the growing season. At that time tubers were already set and in the process of maturing. Consequently these potatoes were not affected as much as if the disease had occurred earlier.

CONCLUSIONS

1. For the potato vine kill studies, the use of air assisted rotary atomizers greatly increases the rate of "kill down" and percent desiccation over the conventional hydraulic nozzle spray equipment.

2. The addition of a drift retardant with conventional hydraulic nozzles significantly increases the efficiency of the vine kill treatment as compared with no drift retardant.

3. The Air Curtain method of application provided the best foliar protection against early blight (<u>Alternari solani</u>) and late blight (<u>Phytophthora infestans</u>) infection in potatoes.

4. The Micronair AU3000 atomizer provided better disease protection than the conventional hydraulic nozzle boom sprayer.

TABLE 1. Effect of Application Method on Vine Kill of Potatoes

Sprayer	Appl. Vol. (Gal/A)	Desiccation Index* (Days after treatment)	
		2	4
BOOM (-) (No Drift Retardant)	60.0 (561 1/ha)	4.50	6.38
Boom (+) (Drift Retardant)**	60.0 (561 1/ha)	5.25	7.25
Micronair AU3000	5.0 (46.8 1/ha)	5.38	6.75
Micronair AU3000	2.5 (23.4 1/ha)	6.50	7.88
Air Curtain	5.0 (46.8 1/ha)	6.13	7.13
Air Curtain	2.5 (23.4 1/ha)	6.75	8.13
Check	--	0.00	0.00
L.S.D. (.05)		0.54	0.62
L.S.D. (.01)		0.74	0.85

*   Index: 0 = No Kill; 10 = 100% Desiccation.
** Drift Retardant: Sta-Put (Nalco Chemical Co.) + Spreader
    (Chevron X-77).

TABLE 2. Copper Deposition of Tomatoes, 1984.

Target Position	Boom D4-25	Micronair AU3000	MSU Air Curtain
Upper Top	0.39	0.48	0.60
Bot.	0.04	0.30	0.33
Lower Top	0.18	0.34	0.65
Bot.	0.00	0.21	0.35
Grand Means	0.15	0.33	0.48

TABLE 3. Copper Deposition on Celery, 1984.

Target Position	Boom D4-25	Micronair AU3000	MSU Air Curtain
Upper Top	0.35	0.39	0.45
Bot.	0.05	0.25	0.35
Lower Top	0.13	0.22	0.48
Bot.	0.01	0.18	0.21
Grand Means	0.13	0.26	0.37

TABLE 4. Effect of Application Method on Disease Control and Yield in Potatoes. (Keilen Farm)

Sprayer	Appl. Vol. (1/ha)	Disease Index*	Est. Yield (Kg/ha) U.S. #1	B-Grade
Boom	468	3.25	334.49	79.73
Micronair AU3000	46.8	2.83	371.88	45.35
Micronair AU3000	23.4	2.83	346.46	71.33
Air Curtain (w/AU7000)	46.8	2.13	339.38	59.97
Air Curtain (w/AU7000)	23.4	2.10	386.98	95.29
Check	--	5.90	281.97	84.94
L.S.D. (.05)		0.31	56.86	15.87
L.S.D. (.01)		0.41	75.92	21.16

* Disease Index: 0 = No Disease Index; 10 = 100% Infection

TABLE 5. MSU Muck Farm Effect of Application Method on Disease Control and Yield of Potatoes.

Sprayer	Appl. Vol. (1/ha)	Disease Index*	Est. Yield (Kg/ha) U.S. #1	Est. Yield (Kg/ha) B-Grade
Boom	468	3.15	792.81	80.88
Micronair AU3000	46.8	2.40	826.20	69.79
Micronair AU3000	23.4	2.28	748.34	49.09
Air Curtain (w/AU7000)	46.8	1.76	774.01	58.70
Air Curtain (w/AU7000)	23.4	1.88	760.56	68.01
Check	--	6.16	468.10	103.05
L.S.D. (.05)		0.26	96.99	19.96
L.S.D. (.01)				

* Disease Index: 0 = No Disease;   10 = 100% Infection

115

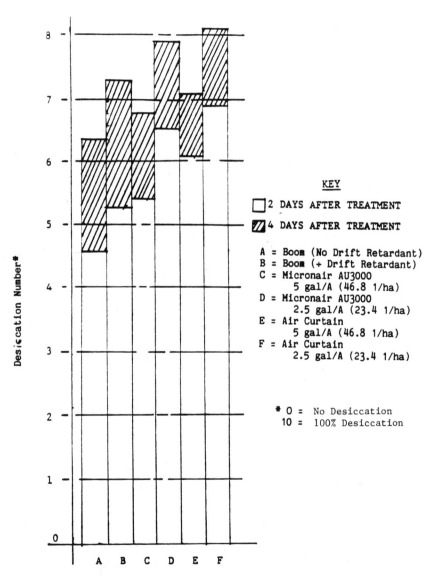

FIGURE 1. Effect of Application Methods on Vine Kill of Potatoes.

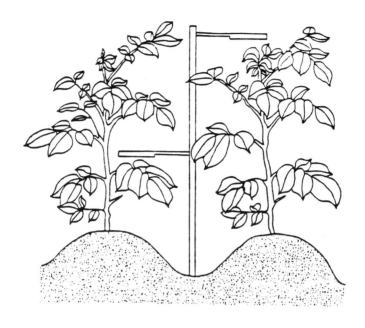

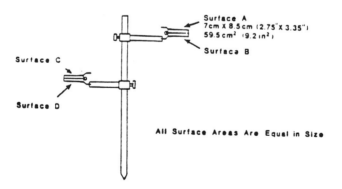

Surface A
7cm X 8.5cm (2.75"X 3.35")
59.5cm² (9.2 in²)

Surface B

Surface C

Surface D

All Surface Areas Are Equal in Size

FIGURE 2. Upper and lower horizontally-placed mylar
targets were placed in the canopy as shown.

117

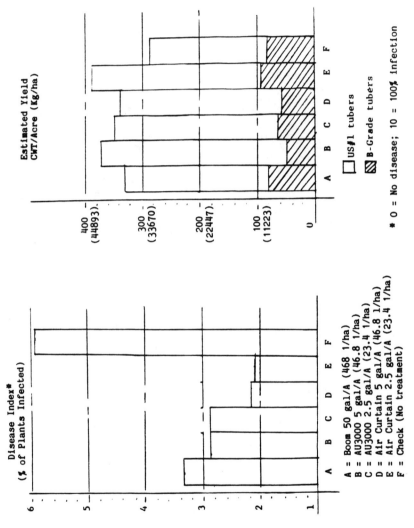

FIGURE 3. Effect of Application Method on Disease Control and Yield in Potatoes. (Keilen Farms)

A = Boom 50 gal/A (468 l/ha)
B = AU3000 5 gal/A (46.8 l/ha)
C = AU3000 2.5 gal/A (23.4 l/ha)
D = Air Curtain 5 gal/A (46.8 l/ha)
E = Air Curtain 2.5 gal/A (23.4 l/ha)
F = Check (No treatment)

* 0 = No disease; 10 = 100% infection

Disease Index*
(% of Plants Infected)

Estimated Yield
CWT/Acre (Kg/ha)

☐ US#1 tubers
▨ B-Grade tubers

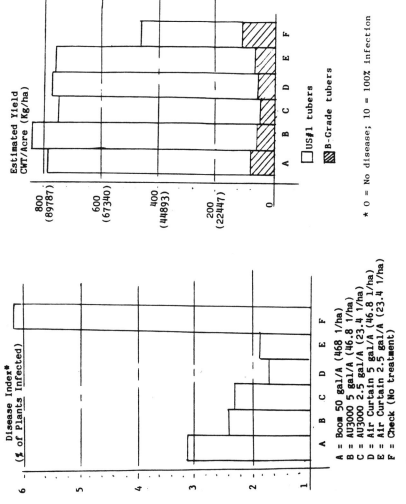

Disease Index*
(% of Plants Infected)

A = Boom 50 gal/A (468 1/ha)
B = AU3000 5 gal/A (46.8 1/ha)
C = AU3000 2.5 gal/A (23.4 1/ha)
D = Air Curtain 5 gal/A (46.8 1/ha)
E = Air Curtain 2.5 gal/A (23.4 1/ha)
F = Check (No treatment)

Estimated Yield
CWT/Acre (Kg/ha)

☐ US#1 tubers
▨ B-Grade tubers

* 0 = No disease; 10 = 100% infection

FIGURE 4. MSU Muck Farm Effect of Application Method on
Disease Control and Yield of Potatoes.

119

II. HANDLING POTATOES

Mechanical Properties and Bruise Susceptibility
of Potatoes - A. Wouters

Spectral Analysis of Acoustical Signal for
Damage Detection - B.L. Upchurch

Rapid Identification of Bruising in Potatoes -
Gary Beaver

An Evolution of the Potato Fluidized Bed Medium
Separator - A. Zaltzman

The Size and Shape of Typical Sweet Potatoes -
Malcolm E. Wright

Algorithms for Determining Tuber Shape and
Cutting Potato Seed Pieces - Marvin J.
Pitts

Potato Production From True Seed in Warm
Climate - Casimer A. Jaworski

Engineering Needs for Potato Production From
True Seed - Suhas R. Ghate

MECHANICAL PROPERTIES AND BRUISE
SUSCEPTIBILITY OF POTATOES

by

A. Wouters, Graduate Assistant, F. Vervaeke, Research
Assistant (NFWO), J. De Baerdemaeker, Associate
Professor, Agricultural Engineering,
Leuven, Belgium

ABSTRACT

The work was aimed at exploring the
possibilities of measuring and controlling bruise
susceptibility of potatoes. Experiments showed that--
on light soils--K and P fertilizer application can
have beneficial effects.

Bruise susceptibility was related to dry matter
content. It showed a very good correlation with a
puncture force which could lead to a damage
susceptibility-test in the field.

INTRODUCTION

The suitability of potatoes for industrial
processing depends on several quality criteria:

ASAE Paper No. 85-6013

. size and shape of the tuber
. dry matter content
. maturity and reducing sugars content
. presence of diseases
. (external) mechanical tuber damage
. (internal) bruise damage

In practice it appears that the reducing sugars content and bruise damage are the main factors determining suitability for processing. Research in the Netherlands has revealed that about 90 percent of all assessed departures from threshold quality, which is set more and more stringent by industry, is due to bruise damage, i.e. blue discoloration and hypodermic damage (KVIV 1985). From this it is clear that over the entire production chain every possible precaution to minimize bruise damage should be taken. Therefore it is important to know which factors determine bruise damage and how these factors contribute. Damage limiting measures can be taken at cultivation time and/or at handling time.

At cultivation time the control actions can be seen as "batch" operations for which the output (potatoes with a certain inherent bruise susceptibility) of a given input (variety, fertilizer application soil type, weather conditions,...) is more or less known. Here, the choice of variety and/or fertilizer application can be seen as the most important control action.

At handling time (harvest & storage) the extent of damage is determined both by the susceptibility of the tuber to damage and by the manner of handling. As a consequence, a means for "on line" monitoring of the bruise susceptibility along the handling line should prove useful for an efficient bruise damage control.

The choice of harvest time, the adjustment of machine operating conditions and the careful setting of transport circumstances (e.g. limitation of height and number of drops, adjustment of the belt-speed/ground-speed ratio, use of padding,...) may be based on these data.

During storage, pressure spots should be avoided and the storage atmosphere (gas composition, temperature, and relative humidity) should be controlled accordingly.

PREVIOUS WORK

Factors contributing to bruise damage (i.e., internal damage to plant tissue by external forces causing physical change in texture and/or chemical alteration of color, flavor are fairly well documented (KVIV 1985; Visserij, et al, 1980; Mohsenin 1970; Nivert 1980; Noble 1985; Rastovski, et al. 1981; and van Loon, et al. 1980). Assuming constant susceptibility, the extent to which a tuber is damaged (black spot damage/blue discoloration) is determined by the mechanical force exerted on the tuber or alternatively by the amount of mechanical energy the tuber absorbs due to static or impact loading. Several technical determinants of the extent of bruise damage are given by Rastovski, et al. 1981. Most of this research, however, has been directed toward the design of harvesting and handling machinery, not to control the machinery operating conditions.

Bruise susceptibility is an inherent characteristic of the potato tuber which depends on many factors. All of these can (must) be looked at in the context of two necessary and sufficient conditions for blue discoloration (black spot) to occur:

1. tuber tissue (i.e. cell walls and cell membranes) must be ruptured.

2. oxygen is required to react enzymatically with chemical compounds of the cytoplasm.

Cell rupture is needed to free certain phenols of the cell cytoplasm (e.g. tyrosine, chlorogenic acid, caffeic acid) (Rastovski, et al. 1981 and van Loon, et al. 1980) which are then oxidized by the enzyme phenol oxydase. In these reactions, the blue-black pigment melanine is formed via the red-colored intermediate dopachrome.

It can be concluded that influencing factors act on the mechanical resistance of the tuber tissue and/or on the enzymatic reaction.

An overview of several of these interrelated and interacting factors - together with their effect on the bruise susceptibility (as given in Mohsenin 1970; Rastovksi, et al. 1981 and van Loon, et al. 1980) is given in Table 1. For some factors, the presumable operation mode is also given. The same authors also report on further investigations of the association between bruise susceptibility and mechanical properties.

OBJECTIVES

The main objectives of the work reported here are:

- Determine the bruise susceptibility of available lots of potatoes and point out how it is related to their mechanical properties.

- Compare the influence of several factors on both bruise susceptibility and mechanical properties. These factors include soil texture, fertilizer application, temperature, storage time and variety.

- Investigate the predictive power of some "easy-to-determine" parameters to assess bruise susceptibility ("on line").

PROCEDURES

Experimental Set-up

To accomplish the objectives, two different series of experiments were conducted. Bruise susceptibility was determined at storage temperature (4°C, 39°F) whereas the mechanical properties were determined at ambient temperature (18°C, 64.4°F).

The first series of experiments was carried out on nine lots of potatoes of the same variety i.c. Bintje. The factors under investigation were soil texture and fertilizer application.

According to C.V.B. (Belgian Soil Mapping Center) classification, the soil texture classes were sandy loam (L), loam (A), sandy clay (E), loamy clay (A-E) and heavy clay (U) but for sake of this analysis they were classified into "light" soils (L) and "heavy" soils (A,E,A-E,U). Organic matter content (%C) was also determined.

The fertilizer application is given in terms of concentrations of the individual elements (P, K, Mg, Ca) in the soil as determined from a chemical soil test. During these experiments the evaluation of bruise susceptibility was also done at the ambient temperature of 18°C.

All measurements took place in October 1984, immediately after harvesting.

The second series of experiments included nine lots of potatoes but of five different varieties (i.c. Bintje, Corine, Erntestolz, Mona Lisa and Saturna) which were to be compared with each other.

Bruise susceptibility and mechanical properties were determined respectively at 4 °C and 18 °C. All measurements were done in March 1985, thus after a storage period of six months (at 5 °C, 41 °F).

Testing Procedure and Parameter Calculation

Mechanical Properties:

Mechanical properties were obtained from quasi-static tests on a WOLPERT testing machine at a displacement rate of 25mm/min (0.98 in./min.). Force and displacement readings were recorded directly by a micro-computer. The computing of the necessary parameters from these data is discussed below. Two classes of mechanical properties are distinguished.

Elastic and Visco-elastic parameters

Apparent Elastic Modulus (E_a), Rupture Stress (α_r), Rupture Strain (ε_r) and Rupture Volumetric Work (W_r) were determined in uniaxial compression rates on cylindrical samples of size 18 mm x 18 mm (diameter x length).

A conventional stress-strain curve (Figure 1) was obtained from the force-displacement data and the following parameters were derived:

The Apparent Elastic Modulus (E_a) was defined as the slope of the middle third part of the stress-

strain curve (i.e. a "chord"-modulus) and was
calculated from the expression

$$E_a = \frac{\frac{2}{3} \cdot \sigma_r - \frac{1}{3} \cdot \sigma_r}{\varepsilon_{2/3} - \varepsilon_{1/3}}$$

where A_o is the initial cross-section area of the
test-sample.

Rupture Stress (α_r) and Rupture Strain
(ε_r) were calculated respectively as

$$\sigma_r = \frac{F_r}{A_o} \qquad \text{and} \qquad \varepsilon_r = \frac{d_r}{l_o}$$

where F_r and d_r are respectively the (measured)
rupture force and rupture displacement.

The Rupture Volumetric Work (w_r) represents
the area under the stress-strain curve and is given
by

$$w_r = \int_0^\varepsilon \sigma(\varepsilon) \cdot d\varepsilon$$

Relaxation Time (τ) was derived from Uniaxial
Stress-Relaxation Tests. Conventional Stess vs. time
curves were recorded after stressing the samples by
uniaxial compression up to about 60 percent (range
56-64%) of their rupture stress' (i.c. at a load of
200 N). After stopping the displacement, stress
relaxation was recorded for a duration of 20 seconds.

It was found that, at these relatively low
initial stresses, the stress in these curves always
leveled off quite fast with time and well within the
measuring period (Figure 2).

The stress-relaxation curves could be
represented very well by a two term exponential
equation (Maxwell model with a spring in parallel)

$$\sigma(t) = \sigma(\infty) + \sigma_{rel} \cdot e^{-\frac{t}{\tau}}$$

128

so that relaxation time could be determined easily by a least squares linear regression after performing a log transformation. In all cases, the correlation coefficient of the regression was equal to 0.999.

Empirical parameters

Rupture Force ($F_{r,s}$), Relative Skin Strength (RSS) and Stiffness (S_s) were obtained from Puncture Tests on whole potatoes. The circular cross-section of the sharp-edged plunger had a diameter of 8 mm (0.3 in.) Force-displacement curves as shown in Figure 3 were recorded and the empirical parameters calculated as follows:

Rupture Force ($F_{r,s}$) – which is the rupture force measured on the whole potato with skin – is measured directly.

Relative Skin Strength (RSS) is defined as the ratio of the rupture force of the whole potato with skin ($F_{r,s}$) to the rupture force of the same potato without skin ($F_{r,\bar{s}}$).

$$ RSS = \frac{F_{r,s}}{F_{r,\bar{s}}} $$

The Stiffness (S_s) was determined as the slope of the middle third part of the force-displacement curve

$$ S_s = \frac{\frac{2}{3} \cdot F_{r,s} - \frac{1}{3} \cdot F_{r,s}}{d_{2/3} - d_{1/3}} $$

Bruise Susceptibility

Bruise Susceptibility (BS) was determined after giving the different lots a comparable treatment. At a temperature of 4°C samples of approximately 5 kg (11 lb) were impacted during 40 seconds in a metal, horizontal drum with a diameter of 0.45 m (1.5 ft.) and rotating at 58 rpm. Then the potatoes were kept for 24 hours at a temperature of 38° C (100 °F) and a relative humidity of 95 percent. This was done to accelerate the blue discoloration. Subsequently, the potatoes were peeled for 45 seconds in an industrial peeling machine, which resulted in an average removal of about 20 percent of the total mass. Finally, the potatoes were classified according to the number of black spots (i) they presented. Up to 6 black spots could be discerned acccurately and relative frequency counts were done on number basis (nf_i)

$$nf_i = \frac{n_i}{n_{tot}} \qquad \sum_0 nf_i = 1$$

as well as on mass basis (mf_i)

$$mf_i = \frac{m_i}{m_{tot}} \qquad \sum_0 mf_i = 1$$

From the resulting relative frequency histograms, (Figure 4), two parameters were calculated as indicators of the degree of susceptibility to blue discoloration.

Black Spot Probability (BSprob) was defined as the probability of the condition occurring, no matter the number of black spots. This thus represents the fraction of potatoes exhibiting blue discoloration. It can be calculated from the relative frequency histogram as follows

$$BSprob_n = \sum_{i=1} nf_i = 1 - nf_0$$

$$BSprob_m = \sum_{i=1} mf_i = 1 - mf_0$$

It seems that in the potato processing industry, this criterion is considered as most important since once blue discoloration has occurred, it is only a matter of time for the discoloration to become more intense.

Black Spot Intensity (BSint) was defined as the centroid of the relative frequency-histogram and thus represents the average number of blue spots per potato exhibiting blue discoloration ($BSint_n$), if based on number counts

$$BSint_n = \frac{\sum nf_i \cdot i}{(1 - nf_0)}$$

130

It can also be expressed, based on mass fractions
($BSint_m$)

$$BSint_m = \frac{\sum mf_i \cdot i}{(1 - mf_0)}$$

Other Physical Properties

Other relevant physical properties that were
determined are Density (ρ), Dry Matter Content (DM)
and Average Mass per Potato ($\overline{m}_\rho$).

Density (ρ) for each lot was obtained from an
underwater weighing of samples of approximately 5 kg
and was calcualted by

$$\rho = \frac{1}{(1 - r)} \cdot \rho_w$$

where ρ_w is the temperature dependent mass density of
water and r is as dimensionless weight-ratio given by

$$r = \frac{W}{UWW}$$

with W, the weight of the sample (in air) and UWW,
the underwater weight of the sample.

Dry Matter Content (DM) was determined by the
gravimetric method, based on drying potato samples in
an oven for 48 hours at 70°C (158° F).

RESULTS AND DISCUSSION

First Series of Experiments

The descriptive statistics for all data are
given in Table 2. The potato lots (of the same
variety but of soils with different texture and
fertilizer application) are identified "A" through
"I" by soil texture and in order of increasing dry
matter content.

Mean value (MEAN) and coefficient of variation
(CV) are given for all the mechanical parameters.

From Table 2 it can be seen that the variability of the mechanical parameters within lots is relatively small. Also the values agree well with values given in literature. Between the different lots, significant differences for these parameters were found ($p < 0.001$). Table 3 gives the results of a Duncan multiple comparison test with level 0.05.

For the other parameters, mean values are given, with an experimental error well within five percent. From the Table it can be seen that potatoes cultivated on heavy soils were more susceptible to bruise damage (average BSprob = 0.921) than potatoes from light soils (average BSprob = 0.886). (The overall average BSprob = 0.909.)

The average black spot intensity is practically the same in both cases (2.693 for "heavy" vs. 2.728 for "light"). (The overall average BSint = 2.705). A similar result holds for the bruise susceptibility based on mass fractions.

In Table 4 the linear correlation coefficients between bruise susceptibility parameters and fertilizer application are given for both distinghished soil texture classes. It appears that fertilizer application has a higher impact on bruise susceptibility for the light soils than for the heavy soils. Also the organic matter content (humus) plays an important role in case of a light soil. From this table we may conclude that there is no real possibility for controlling bruise susceptibility on heavy soils through fertilizer application (correlation coefficients almost zero).

On the other hand, a fertilizer application on light soils may be a feasible way of (partially) controlling bruise susceptibility and must be taken into consideration. For these soils and especially those with a higher organic matter content, bruise susceptibility will be reduced by lowering the Mg and Ca doses and by supplying more P and K to the soil.

Figure 5 shows that the black spot probability increases with increasing dry matter content whereas the black spot intensity is a negative function of dry matter content. The single non-conforming point (Figure 5) for the light soils is probably due to the low Ca and Mg applications. Furthermore, it can be seen in Figure 6 that the rupture force from the puncture tests is highly correlated with the dry matter content. Linear correlation coefficients as high as 0.990 for the light soils and 0.971 for the heavy soils were found (overall correlation coefficient = 0.955; p<0.001). This suggests that the rupture force could be used as a proper indicator for bruise susceptibility.

A comparison of the bruise susceptibility parameters at 4 C (see Table 2) and at 18 C (Table 5) shows that the the potato lots were less susceptible at the higher temperature [all differences 'BS(t=4) – BS(t=18)' are positive]. This temperature effect is more pronounced at low dry matter contents.

Second Series of Experiments

Similar descriptive statistics as for the first series of experiments are given in Table 6. The potato lots are identified "1" through "9" by the name of the variety and in order of increasing dry matter content within each variety.

Here again there is low variability of the mechanical properties within lots. Between lots, significant differences were found (p < 0.001). The results of a Duncan multiple comparison test (level 0.05) are given in Table 7.

The lower level of bruise susceptibility, found in the second series of experiments as opposed to the first series, indicates a significant influence of storage time.

For comparison, bruise susceptibility parameters are plotted against dry matter content in Figure 7, where each variety is separately indicated. As in the previous case, a high dry matter content increases bruise susceptibility. It also appears that ERNTESTOLZ is most resistant to bruise damage and MONA LISA shows the highest bruise susceptibility. Also SATURNA seems less sensitive to a change in dry matter content than f.i. ERNTESTOLZ or BINTJE. As a consequence these varieties would react differently on an evaporation-loss during storage.

CONCLUSIONS

Establishing bruise susceptibility for potatoes, two indicators (black spot probability and black spot intensity) were determined after giving potato lots a comparable treatment. Different factors were found to have a well established influence on these susceptibility parameters. On light soils, a fertilizer application (i.c. low Mg and Ca doses and more P and K) could be used to reduce the black spot susceptibility of potatoes, especially in soils with a high organic matter content. For heavy soils, this does not seem a good solution. A choice of the right variety would seem more appropriate. From the five varieites tested, ERNTESTOLA showed the lowest bruise susceptibility and MONA LISA the highest. A warming of potato tubers before handling appears to be an efficient way of reducing bruise susceptibility (and thus damage), especially when dry matter content of the tubers is low.

By correlating the bruise susceptibility parameters to the mechanical parameters, it was found that the rupture force obtained from a puncturing test could be used as a good indicator for bruise susceptibility. Such a rapid way of assessing bruise susceptibility can be useful during handling to control the machinery operating conditions.

Acknowledgement

The authors would like to thank Mr. G. Ampe (Beitem-Roeselare) and Mr. L. Vande Ginste for their help in contacting potato growers and obtaining the samples.

REFERENCES

Ampe, G., Bockstaele, L. (1982).
Aardappel: Overzinct van het onderzoek in 1981. Publikatie van het Onderzoek - en Voorlichting- scentrum voor Land-en Tuinbouw, Beitem- Roeselare, November 1982.

KVIV Genootschap Plantenproduktie en Ekosfeer (1985). Teelt van Kwaliteitsaardappelen voor Verse Konsumptie en Industriele Verwerking. Publikatie Studie- en Vervolmakingsdag, April, 1985.

Ministerie van Landbouw en Visserij (1980).
Mechanisatie en Kwaliteit bij de aardappeloogst.
Vlugschrift voor de Landbouw nr. 295.

Mohsenin, N.N. (1970).
Physical Properties of Plant and Animal
Materials, Vol. 1. Gordon and Breach Science
Publishers, New York.

Nivert, C. (1980).
De Beschadiging van Aardappelknollen.
Publikatie Institut Technique de la Pomme de
Terre, November 1980.

Noble, R. (1985).
Kartoffelverluste durch innere Beschadigung.
Landtechnik 40 (3), 135-137.

Rastovski, A., van Es, A. et al. (1981).
Storage of Potatoes.
(Post-harvest behaviour, store design, storage
practice, handling). Centre for Agricultural
Publishing and Documentation, Wageningen.

van Loon, C.D., Meijers, C.P. (1980).
Blauw in Aardappelen.
Stichting Aardappel Studiecentum, Wageningen.
Publikatie Nr. 00327.

Table 1. Summary of factors affecting bruise susceptibility of potatoes

FACTOR	(1)	(2)	EFFECT	PRESUMABLE OPERATION MODE
ENVIRONMENTAL CONDITIONS				
.soil type	x		- / +	
.temperature	x	x	- -	change of cell wall strength and stiffness
.water supply	x	x	- - 0 +	via turgidity
.turgidity	x		- 0 +	
CULTIVATION PRACTICE				
.fertilizer			- / +	depending on type of element
N, Cl	x	x	- - -	via dry matter decrease and lowered cell wall stiffness
K	x		- - -	via dry matter decrease
Cu	x			via cell size reduction
.maturity	x	x	- / -	via skin toughening by suberization (-) or via increasing cell size (+)
.storage time	x	x	-	via dry matter decrease (evaporation loss)
.ethylene				
VARIETY & PLANT PROPERTIES				
.dry matter content	x		+	
.bulk density	x		+	contact stresses depending on radius of curvature
.tuber shape	x		- /	
.tuber size	x		+ +	impact forces depending on tuber mass
.size of intercellular spaces	x		+	
.cell wall strength	x		- -	
.cell wall stiffness	x		-	
.cell size	x		+	
.phenol content		x	+	
.starch kernel size	x		+	

(1) = acts on mechanical tuber tissue resistance
(2) = acts on enzymatic reaction

effect = sign of d(Bruise Susceptibility) / d(FACTOR)

-     = reduction of Bruise Susceptibility
/ +   = increase of Bruise Susceptibility
-     = reduction or increase (depending on other factors)
- 0 + = exhibits a maximum Bruise Susceptibility

Table 2. Descriptive statistics for the series of experiments on Bintje

Lot	SOIL PARAMETERS					FERTILIZER APPLICATION				PHYSICAL PROPERTIES			BRUISE SUSCEPTABILITY			
	TEXTURE	CLASS	pH	C (%)	P	K	Mg	Ca	DM (1)	ρ (kg/m**3)	$\bar{m}_p$ (kg)	BSprob (1) n	BSint n	BSprob (1) m	BSint m
					(mg / 100 g soil)										
A	sandy loam	LIGHT	7.6	1.5	41	28	10.	325	0.274	1078	0.226	0.889	2.949	0.908	3.119
B	sandy loam	LIGHT	7.4	1.3	21	21	13.	265	0.288	1076	0.159	0.906	2.950	0.928	3.036
C	sandy loam	LIGHT	7.4	1.1	37	28	6.	250	0.334	1075	0.195	0.865	2.287	0.899	2.485
D	heavy clay	HEAVY	7.2	1.3	18	27	11.5	350	0.263	1076	0.211	0.896	2.791	0.925	2.885
E	loam	HEAVY	7.3	1.2	30	23	6.	280	0.278	1081	0.209	0.918	2.577	0.918	2.840
F	sandy clay	HEAVY	7.8	1.8	38	31	55.	1000	0.291	1086	0.140	0.917	2.744	0.936	2.954
G	loamy clay	HEAVY	7.4	1.1	17	24	8.	335	0.291	1081	0.185	0.964	2.924	0.968	3.023
H	loam	HEAVY	7.6	1.3	27	20	9.	325	0.305	1077	0.192	0.906	2.628	0.928	2.665
I	loam	HEAVY	7.4	2.1	12	25	14.5	360	0.307	1081	0.148	0.926	2.496	0.939	2.630

Lot	ELASTIC AND VISCO - ELASTIC PARAMETERS										EMPIRICAL PARAMETERS					
	E (MPa) MEAN	CV	σ_r (MPa) MEAN	CV	ε_r (1) MEAN	CV	Wr (MJ/m**3) MEAN	CV	τ (s) MEAN	CV	$F_{r,s}$ (N) MEAN	CV	RSS (1) MEAN	CV	s (N/mm) MEAN	CV
A	3.612	0.088	1.356	0.089	0.342	0.054	0.219	0.104	1.398	0.034	104.6	0.043	1.169	0.111	16.95	0.108
B	3.389	0.078	1.230	0.086	0.322	0.065	0.192	0.118	1.406	0.034	105.7	0.084	1.171	0.148	19.29	0.089
C	3.634	0.101	1.357	0.116	0.349	0.079	0.220	0.140	1.421	0.031	117.1	0.085	1.183	0.143	19.16	0.116
D	3.375	0.076	1.263	0.087	0.329	0.066	0.202	0.116	1.436	0.036	99.6	0.044	1.083	0.095	20.41	0.068
E	3.351	0.091	1.367	0.102	0.355	0.071	0.228	0.139	1.403	0.028	105.2	0.074	1.144	0.084	18.20	0.045
F	3.758	0.077	1.410	0.092	0.352	0.072	0.231	0.139	1.445	0.030	104.3	0.069	1.048	0.064	18.55	0.037
G	3.373	0.091	1.284	0.105	0.348	0.068	0.212	0.137	1.433	0.030	105.1	0.038	1.232	0.077	18.33	0.037
H	3.466	0.097	1.295	0.111	0.339	0.071	0.208	0.140	1.416	0.029	106.7	0.045	1.148	0.107	18.33	0.059
I	3.491	0.083	1.230	0.108	0.329	0.081	0.190	0.147	1.443	0.042	116.3	0.091	1.289	0.071	19.51	0.080

Table 3. Duncan multiple comparisons test results   (level 0.05)
for the mechanical properties   (Bintje experiments)

Table 4.   Linear correlation coefficients between
bruise susceptability parameters and
fertilizer application

	LIGHT SOILS				HEAVY SOILS			
	BSprob n	BSint n	BSprob m	BSint m	BSprob n	BSint n	BSprob m	BSint m
C	0.56	0.86	0.30	0.92	0.05	-0.43	0.14	-0.36
P	-0.69	-0.33	-0.87	-0.21	-0.01	0.20	-0.14	0.59
K	-0.81	-0.50	-0.95	-0.39	-0.08	0.28	0.06	0.49
MG	0.99	0.90	0.95	0.84	-0.09	0.13	0.04	0.32
CA	0.28	0.65	-0.02	0.74	-0.08	0.17	0.05	0.36

Table 5.   Bruise susceptability parameters at 18°C
and the difference with those at 4°C

lot	BRUISE SUSCEPTABILITY (t = 18°C)				DIFFERENCE [BS(t=4) - BS(t=18)]			
	BSprob n	BSint n	BSprob m	BSint m	dBSprob n	dBSint n	dBSprob m	dBSint m
A	0.367	1.177	0.474	1.169	0.522	1.712	0.434	1.950
B	0.100	2.000	0.093	2.000	0.806	0.950	0.835	1.036
C	0.295	1.461	0.278	1.401	0.570	0.826	0.621	1.082
D	0.083	1.349	0.081	1.358	0.813	1.442	0.844	1.527
E	0.000	0.000	0.000	0.000	0.918	2.577	0.918	2.840
F	0.196	1.102	0.199	1.070	0.721	1.642	0.737	1.884
G	0.024	2.000	0.023	2.000	0.940	0.924	0.945	1.023
H	0.143	1.405	0.161	1.366	0.763	1.223	0.767	1.299
I	0.173	1.219	0.174	1.327	0.753	1.277	0.765	1.303

Table 6. Descriptive statistics
           for the experiment on varieties

Lot	VARIETY	PHYSICAL PROPERTIES			BRUISE SUSCEPTABILITY			
		DM (1)	ρ (kg/m**3)	$\bar{m}_p$ (kg)	BSprob n (1)	BSint n	BSprob m (1)	BSint m
1	BINTJE	0.201	1066	0.118	0.311	1.429	0.340	1.438
2	BINTJE	0.291	1079	0.108	0.425	1.647	0.486	1.588
3	CORINE	0.267	1066	0.150	0.615	1.313	0.664	1.315
4	ERNTESTOLZ	0.222	1073	0.111	0.188	1.441	0.201	1.463
5	ERNTESTOLZ	0.315	1091	0.123	0.441	1.000	0.489	1.000
6	MONA LISA	0.178	1056	0.167	0.267	1.124	0.229	1.249
7	MONA LISA	0.193	1061	0.156	0.579	2.273	0.609	2.207
8	SATURNA	0.214	1085	0.099	0.449	1.409	0.499	1.351
9	SATURNA	0.313	1092	0.093	0.413	1.221	0.527	1.228

Lot	ELASTIC AND VISCO - ELASTIC PARAMETERS														EMPIRICAL PARAMETERS					
	E_a (MPa)		σ_r (MPa)		ϵ_r (1)		W_r (MJ/m**3)		T (s)		$F_{r,s}$ (N)		RSS (1)		S_s (N/mm)	
	MEAN	CV	MEAN	CV	MEAN	CV	MEAN	CV	MEAN	CV	MEAN	CV	MEAN	CV	MEAN	CV
1	3.451	0.071	1.271	0.084	0.354	0.059	0.205	0.111	1.679	0.022	104.6	0.070	1.168	0.056	17.14	0.134
2	3.712	0.089	1.442	0.114	0.395	0.098	0.248	0.165	1.722	0.030	108.9	0.081	1.043	0.075	16.15	0.136
3	3.658	0.164	1.503	0.147	0.387	0.105	0.272	0.195	1.705	0.024	111.6	0.088	1.079	0.099	15.65	0.054
4	3.760	0.110	1.279	0.140	0.330	0.078	0.194	0.183	1.703	0.039	99.5	0.078	1.053	0.106	17.53	0.091
5	3.704	0.102	1.379	0.080	0.355	0.097	0.232	0.129	1.702	0.036	124.9	0.050	1.038	0.081	12.54	0.134
6	3.414	0.168	1.183	0.156	0.340	0.137	0.185	0.220	1.652	0.018	99.6	0.075	1.155	0.119	16.47	0.139
7	3.092	0.099	1.016	0.080	0.339	0.056	0.160	0.087	1.662	0.019	86.3	0.121	1.208	0.128	14.06	0.163
8	3.180	0.074	1.120	0.098	0.321	0.082	0.163	0.154	1.718	0.030	90.7	0.094	1.106	0.127	15.91	0.112
9	3.742	0.137	1.288	0.130	0.365	0.127	0.204	0.241	1.745	0.025	105.2	0.080	1.064	0.129	15.22	0.120

Table 7. Duncan multiple comparisons test results   (level 0.05)
           for the mechanical properties   (variety experiments)

139

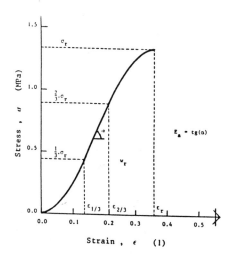

Fig. 1. Stress vs. Strain for cylindrical potato-samples with derived parameters

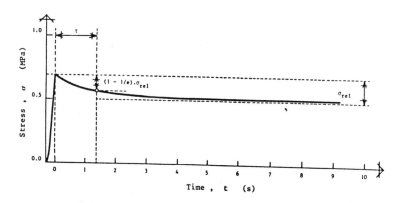

Fig. 2. Stress-relaxation curve for cylindrical potato-samples with derived parameters

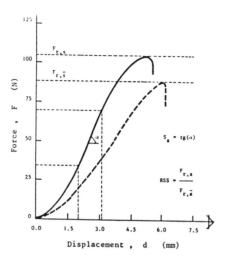

Fig. 3. Force-displacement curve from puncture test on whole potatoes

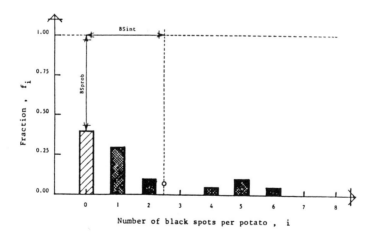

Fig. 4. Black Spot Distribution and Bruise Susceptability parameters derived from it

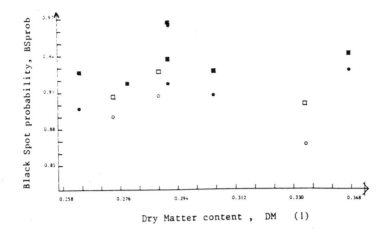

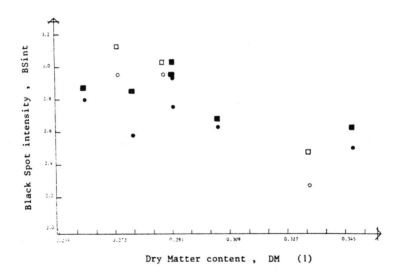

Fig. 5. (a) Black Spot probability vs. Dry Matter content
        (b) Black Spot intensity   vs. Dry Matter content

        o = for light soil, on number basis
        • = for heavy soil, on number basis
        □ = for light soil, on mass basis
        ■ = for heavy soil, on mass basis

142

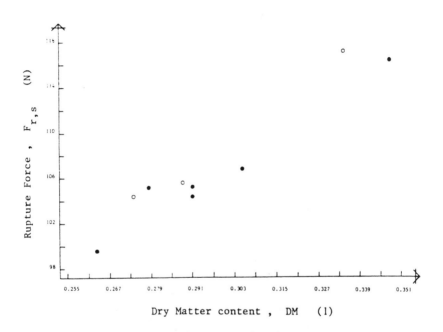

Fig. 6. Rupture Force from puncture test
vs. Dry Matter content

o = for light soil
• = for heavy soil

143

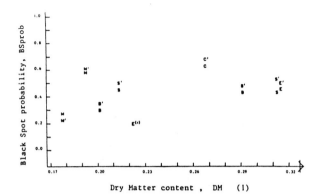

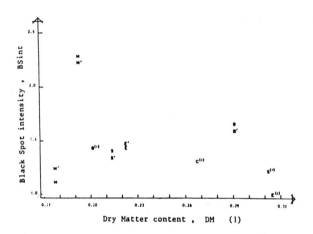

Fig. 7. (a) Black Spot probability vs. Dry Matter content
(b) Black Spot intensity vs. Dry Matter content

```
B  =  Bintje          M  =  Mona Lisa
C  =  Corine          S  =  Saturna
E  =  Erntestolz

( X : number basis   ;   X' : mass basis )
```

SPECTRAL ANALYSIS OF ACOUSTICAL SIGNAL FOR DAMAGE DETECTION

by

B.L. Upchurch, USDA-ARS, Department of Agricultural Engineering; E.S. Furgason, Associate Professor, Department of Electrical Engineering; G.E. Miles, Associate Professor, Department of Agricultural Engineering, Purdue University, West Lafayette, Indiana 47907

ABSTRACT

Bruised apple tissue is very difficult to detect immediately after being damaged; however, ultrasonic measurements may provide a method for detecting damaged tissue. In tests with peeled apples, the composition of the power spectrum offers a potential for distinguishing between undamaged and damaged tissue.

INTRODUCTION

Fruit quality depends on several characteristics that indicate the acceptance of the product to

ASAE Paper No. 85-6014

the consumer. These characteristics can be classified
as appearance, firmness, and flavor. The consumer
evaluates the appearance and firmness of the fruit at
the market, while flavor is evaluated after
purchasing.

Evaluation of appearance is a very complex task.
The consumer considers color, shape, size, mechanical
damage and evidence of diseases. Research has shown
the lack of bruises and blemishes to be very
important in the selection of apples (Solverson,
1969). The procedure for grading apples is described
in "United States Standards for Grading Apples"
published by the USDA. The grading standards specify
tolerances for maturity, shape, disease, damage, and
color. Although all defects are of interest,
bruising is of primary concern, because the amount of
bruised fruit will increase with the use of
mechanical harvesters.

The methods employed by the human graders for
detecting bruises suggest two nondestructive
techniques for detecting bruises. Visual inspection
involves detecting changes in the diffuse reflectance
caused by discoloration in the bruised tissue.
Firmness testing suggests detecting firmness
differences between the damaged and undamaged
tissues.

LITERATURE REVIEW

Bruising is defined as damage to plant tissue by
external forces causing a physical change in texture,
and/or eventual chemical alteration of color, flavor,
and texture (Mohsenin, 1970). Changes in the apple's
physical properties due to bruising provide a means
of classifying the methods which could be used to
detect bruises.

The change or damage to the plant tissues is
caused by the rupturing of cells beneath the loading
point (Mohsenin and Goehlich, 1962). Researchers
(Holt and Schoorl, 1977) observed cells bursting when
the apple flesh was compressed. The cells near the
compression distort, resulting in cell wall
distention; however, when the elastic limit of the
cell wall has been exceeded, the cell walls burst,

releasing their contents into the air-filled interstitial spaces. The force at which the cell walls fail has been referred to as the bio-yield point (Mohsenin and Goehlich, 1962). The physical changes which occur are: (1) tissue rigidity is lost (Holt and Schoorl, 1982); and (2) cell sap is liberated into the intercellular air spaces (Mohsenin, 1977). The chemical changes which occur are: (1) initation of phenolic production which causes tissue browning (Ingle and Hyde, 1968); (2) decline in ethylene production (Robitaille and Janick, 1973; Klein, 1982); and (3) increase in carbon dioxide production (Klein, 1982). In addition to the above changes, the surface geometry may be altered (Rehkugler et al., 1971).

Past research in nondestructive bruise detection involved either transmission or reflection of electromagnetic radiation such as gamma rays, X-rays, visible light, infrared radiation, or microwaves. Diener, et al. (1970) reported transmission of "soft" X-rays through bruised tissue was less than that for good tissue; however, problems occurred in (1) masking the fruit to give good resolution and (2) orienting the fruit. Most of the effort in seeking a technique for bruising detection involved either transmission or reflection of visible or infrared light. Decreases in the body reflectance of near infrared light after burising were observed by Brown, et al. (1974), Rehkugler, et al. (1976), and Reid (1976). Holcomb, et al. (1977) considered using microwave reflectivity to detect the inferface between damaged and undamaged tissue; however, the method was unacceptable because the reflection coefficient at the bruised/unbruised tissue interface was small.

The use of acoustics to detect damage such as bruises on fruit has not been attempted; however, acoustics have been used successfully to measure the texture or firmness of fruits and vegetables. Finney and Abbott (1978) and Morrow and Mohsenin (1968) reported that the velocity of propagation of acoustic waves through solid foods is a measure of the firmness of the food. By using sonic techniques, Abbott, et al. (1968) correlated resonance frequency with Young's modulus for apple tissue. Garrett and

Furry (1972) used the velocity of sonic pulses through intact and sectioned apples as a measure of the tissue's modulus of elasticity. With sonic techniques, Finney, et al. (1968) detected changes in the firmness of ripening bananas by correlating Young's modulus with the resonance frequency for the specimen.

Medical researchers are using feature characteristics of ultrasonic waves as a means for discriminating between normal and abnormal tissue. Ultrasonic feature characteristics which might be useful include velocity of propagation through the tissue, amplitude of the reflected wave, and attenuation of the transmitted wave through the tissue (Rose and Goldberg, 1979). The first two feature characteristics are affected by the density and modulus of elasticity of the tissues. The attenuation of an ultrasonic is affected by the chemical composition within the tissues. Ultrasound has been used to measure differences as small as 1 ppm for different tissues (von Ramm and Smith, 1979).

OBJECTIVES

The purpose of this research project is to investigate the use of ultrasonic measurement techniques as means for distinguishing between undamaged and damaged apple tissue.

THEORY

Ultrasonic energy is transmitted through a medium by wave motion of particles within the medium. If the wave propagation is in the same direction as particle motion, the wave is described as a longitudinal or compressional wave. A transverse or shear wave occurs when the direction of energy flow is perpendicular to the particle motion. The transmission of a wave through a medium is the result of the combined effects of elastic forces between particles and inertia of the particles (Auld, 1973).

Velocity of Propagation:

The velocity of propagation depends upon the density of the medium and its elastic constants.

Since fluids do not exhibit shear rigidity and only support longitudinal waves, the velocity of propagation, v, of a longitudinal wave in a fluid is given by the equation

$$v = (k/\rho)^{\frac{1}{2}} \qquad [1]$$

where k = adiabatic bulk modulus, and
ρ = density of the medium (Wells, 1969).

The expression for wave velocity in a solid medium is not as simple, because the shear rigidity of the solid converts some of the compressional wave energy into a shear wave. The formula for the wave velocity (Wells, 1969) becomes:

$$v = \frac{Y(1-\sigma)}{(1-2\sigma)(1+\sigma)\rho} \qquad [2]$$

where Y = Young's modulus of elasticity,
σ = poisson's ratio, and
ρ = density of the medium.

The above equation is valid only when the diameter of the solid is larger than the length of the wave being propagated, otherwise the velocity equation is identical to the equation describing the velocity of propagation in a fluid (Kolsky, 1963). Estimating the velocity of propagation through biological tissues is very difficult. The Young's modulus is difficult to measure due to the complexity of the tissues and the variation of the elastic constants between particles. Therefore, the velocity of propagation of ultrasonic energy through biological tissues is usually obtained by direct measurements.

Reflection and Refraction:

When a wave reaches a boundary between two different media, part of the wave energy will be reflected and part will be refracted or transmitted into the second medium. The amplitude of the reflected and refracted waves is dependent upon the difference in the acoustic impedances of the two media at a boundary.

A boundary is the point at which two dissimilar media meet. The acoustic impedance for a particular medium is given by Wells (1969).

$$Z = \rho v. \qquad [3]$$

Using the acoustic impedances for the two media at a boundary, the reflection coefficient for a wave at normal incidence can be calculated from

$$\Gamma = \frac{Z_t - Z_i}{Z_t + Z_i} \qquad [4]$$

where Z_i = acoustic impedance for the initial medium, and
Z_t = acoustic impedance for the second medium (Wells, 1969).

The amplitude of the reflected wave can now be determined by

$$A_r = \Gamma A_i \qquad [5]$$

where A_i = amplitude of the incidence wave, and
A_r = amplitude of the reflected wave (Wells, 1969).

The acoustic impedance for biological tissues is very difficult to determine theoretically, because the value of the elastic constants are needed. In biological tissues, the elastic constants can vary with turgor pressure (Mohsenin, 1970), geometry (Finney and Abbott, 1978; Morrow and Mohsenin, 1968), and size (Cooke, 1972; Abbott, et al., 1968).

150

Attenuation:

    The amplitude of the ultrasound wave can be attenuated as it travels through the medium due to scattering or absorption of the wave energy. Scattering of the energy is due to inhomogenities within the medium, while absorption is the result of the wave energy being converted to an alternate form of energy such as heat (Nicholas, 1977). The attenuation (α) for a medium is a function of the wave frequency (f) and is expressed as

$$\alpha = af^b \qquad [6]$$

where the factors, a and b, depend upon characteristics of a particular tissue (Wells, 1975).

    For detecting the difference between damaged and undamaged fruit tissue, measuring the attenuation of the wave energy at different frequencies is preferable to amplitude measurements. Amplitude measurements are difficult to achieve because of large variations within and between seemingly identical tissues (Abbott, et al., 1968). For example, the firmness of flesh within a single apple varies with the location of the sample (Table 1). The mean and standard deviation for each apple is calculated from a set of eight fruit pressure test readings which were taken at different locations on the fruit.

    An alternative to the amplitude is a root mean square (rms) measurement; however, signal caused by nonplanar reflective surfaces, angle of incidence changes, and varying distances from the focal point contribute to the variability in the rms value. The variability of the reflected signal due to geometry changes in the apple are shown in Table 2 and Table 3. The data in Table 2 were taken from undamaged locations on the apple.

    After bruising 3 of the 4 locations, another set of data were obtained and is reported in Table 3.

    From the data in Table 3 and 4, the separability

151

of the two classes, damaged and undamaged tissues, is not large enough to use the time signal as a method for distinguishing between damaged and undamaged tissues.

An alternative analysis is to utilize the spectral composition of the reflected signal. Apple tissue is approximately 23 percent air (Mohsenin, 1970), which will cause most of the incident wave energy to be reflected at the surface due to the large acoustic mismatch at the boundary (Eqn. 4 and Eqn. 5). The acoustic impedance mismatch refers to the difference between the acoustic impedances of the coupling medium and the reflective surface. Water is usually selected as a coupling medium, because of its property to transmit ultrasonic energy with little attenuation. When the tissue is damaged, the cell walls burst releasing their contents into the air-filled interstitial spaces. Damaged tissue contains a lower proportion of air-space, and thus has a lower acoustic impedance than undamaged tissue. Because of this, the acoustic impedance mismatch at the water and damaged tissue interface is small, and more of the wave energy penetrates the tissue. However, the acoustic impedance is large and most of the wave is reflected at that boundary. The signal received contains a reflection from the outer surface, and a second reflection from the back surface of the damaged area. If the transmit signal is represented by s(t), the received signal from undamaged tissue is

$$r(t) = \Gamma_o s(t + \tau_1); \qquad [7]$$

whereas, the reflected signal from damaged tissue is given by

$$r(t) = \Gamma_1 s(t + \tau_1) + \Gamma_2 s(t + \tau_2) \qquad [8]$$

where r(t) = received signal,
$s(t + \tau_1)$ = signal reflected from the outer surface of the fruit,
$s(t + \tau_2)$ = signal reflected from a second surface,
Γ_o = reflection coefficient for water-damaged tissue interface,
Γ_1 = reflection coefficient for the water-damaged tissue interface,
Γ_2 = reflection coefficient for the damaged-undamaged tissue interface.

Since both signals must travel through the medium, the attenuation effects due to the coupling medium have been omitted. The time delays, and is the time required for the wave to travel to the reflecting boundary and back to the receiving transducer after the transmit pulse. For a single frequency in a lossless, isotropic, and homogeneous medium, the wave equation is given by Hayt (1974) as

$$s(t) = A_o Re(e^{-i\omega_o t}) \qquad [9]$$

where A_o = peak acoustic pressure,
ω_o = transmitted frequency,
t = time.

Only the real part is needed to describe a cosine waveform. The single sided Fourier transform of the transmitted signal is:

$$S(\omega) = A_o(2\pi\delta(\omega-\omega_o)) \qquad [10]$$

where $\delta(\omega)$ is the dirac delta function (Oppenheim and Willsky, 1983). The delta function is defined as

$$\delta(\omega) = 1 \quad \omega = 0 \qquad [11]$$

$$\delta(\omega) = 0 \quad \omega \neq 0 \qquad [12]$$

The spectrum of the signal reflected from undamaged tissue is equal to the spectrum of the transmitted signal except for a phase shift and a scale factor. To show the similarity, consider Eqn. 7 which shows that the reflected signal from undamaged tissue is only a time delay of the transmitted signal. Applying the time shift theorem to the Fourier transform (Oppenheim and Willsky, 1983) yields

$$R(\omega) = \Gamma_o A_o e^{-i\omega_o T} 2\pi\delta(\omega-\omega_o) \qquad [13]$$

153

as the transform for the signal reflected from the undamaged area. The term $e^{-iw_0T_1}$ is the phase shift due to the location of the reflecting surface. On the other hand, the spectrum of the signal from damaged tissue is different from the transmitted spectrum. An additional time delay causes a superposition of two waves. Depending upon τ_1 and τ_2, the two waves may either produce constructive (in phase) or destructive (out-of-phase) interference. The Fourier transform of the signal from damaged tissue (Eqn. 8) is represented by

$$R(\omega) = \Gamma_1 A_o e^{-i\omega_o \tau_1} 2\pi\delta(\omega-\omega_o) +$$

$$\Gamma_2 A_1 e^{-i\omega_o \tau_2} 2\pi\delta(\omega-\omega_o). \qquad [14]$$

In the previous equation, the term A_1 is the amplitude of the wave energy which was transmitted into the damaged tissue.

The broadband signal can be represented as a Fourier series (Oppenheim and Willsky, 1983); therefore, the frequency spectrum for a broadband signal is the sum of delta functions over the bandwidth of the transducer. The interference caused by the superposition of the two signals occurs between the same frequency components of the signals. The magnitude of determines which frequencies are 180 out-of-phase. As a result, the frequency spectrum would exhibit a decrease in signal power at those frequencies.

Procedure:

The instrumentation for recording the tissue data is shown in Figure 1. A 5 MHz broadband, 1.77 cm diameter, ultrasonic transducer with a 3 cm focal length was used in the pulse-echo mode. To improve the signal-to-noise ratio, a digital noise correlator system was used to supply the excitation to the transducer and to amplify the reflected signal. The correlator system applied a sequence of coded pulses to the transducer. Upon the return of the reflected

154

signal, the correlator compared the received signal with the transmitted code. The output of this comparison is the cross-correlation between the transmitted and received signals. When the reflected signal is identical to the transmitted signal, the output of the system is the autocorrelation function which is equivalent to the impulse response of the transducer (Lee and Furgason, 1981).

The apple was placed in a holding unit which allowed the apple to be rotated to a desired location. The apple could be removed from the tank, damaged at a specific position, and placed back into the tank. Position data was acquired from an indicator on the rotation disc to which the apple was attached. To keep the apple stationary on the unit, the rotation disc had two 2.54 cm spikes to which the apple was attached. The rotation disc was attached to a holding unit which had markings at 4 degree increments. When the apple was inserted in the holder, the position of the apple could be determined by aligning the indicator on the rotation disc with the holding unit marking.

After recording the reflected waveform from an undamaged area, the apple was removed from the water tank and was damaged by dropping a weight onto the fruit. The apple was placed under the drop tube of the damaging apparatus. The location to be damaged was placed under the tube such that the centerline of the tube was aligned with the spot. The area was damaged by dropping a 2.9 cm diameter 184 gram mass a distance of 30.5 cm. A foam pad was placed under the fruit to prevent the back surface from being damaged. After damaging, the apple was placed back into the water tank, and the reflected waveform from the damaged area was recorded.

The power spectrum was estimated for reflections from undamaged and damaged tissues. Since the output signal is the correlation function, the power spectrum is estimated by taking the FFT of the signal (Bendat and Piersol, 1971). This method is known as the Blackman-Tukey. An assumption made when taking the FFT of a signal is equal to the sampling window. To prevent errors from this assumption, a Hamming window of length 70 data points is used to window the

155

data. The data is multiplied by a window function
which is 1 at the middle of the data and decays to 0
at the boundaries. The decay or roll-off reduces the
sharp discontinuities in the data which reduces
leakage effects (Bendat and Piersol, 1971).

Results:

A comparison between the reflected signals from
a high acoustic impedance material (brass) and a low
acoustic impedance material (plexiglass) is shown in
Figures 2 and 3 respectively. The high acoustic
impedance material results in a high reflection
coefficient (Eqn. 4) at the boundary causing more of
the wave energy to be reflected at the surface
(Figure 2). When a lower impedance material is used
at the boundary, most of the wave energy is refracted
into the material (Figure 3).

A parallel comparison can be made between
undamaged and damaged apple tissue as shown in
Figures 4 and 5. Undamaged apple tissue has a very
high acoustic impedance causing most of the wave
energy to be reflected at the surface (Figure 4). In
addition to the initial reflection, some scattering
also occurs due to surface roughness as indicated by
the additional low amplitude reflections. The
reflected signal for the damaged tissue (Figure 5)
shows a very low amplitude reflection at the surface
while the reflection from the back side of the
damaged area contains more energy. A reflection from
the back of the damaged area occurs due to the high
acoustic mismatch at the damaged-undamaged tissue
boundary.

The spectral composition of the two signals
shows a difference in the signal power distribution
at different frequencies (Figure 6). Although the
power spectrums of the two signals differ, the
composition will vary with surface geometry which
causes secondary reflections due to scattering and
bruise depth.

Conclusions:

An acoustic impedance difference between
undamaged and damaged apple tissue was observed. By

comparing the reflected signals from the two tissue
types, the acoustic impedance for damaged tissue is
less than the impedance for undamaged tissue. This
difference in the acoustic impedance results in a
reflection coefficient difference. By reducing the
acoustic impedance mismatch, more of the wave energy
penetrates the tissue and is reflected from
boundaries inside the fruit. These boundaries can
include fragmented cell walls as well as an undamaged
tissue boundary. As a result of tests with peeled
apples, the power spectrum compositions of undamaged
and damaged tissue were substantially different.

Analysis of the power spectrum composition or
power at a given frequency offers potential for
distinguishing undamaged and damaged tissue.

REFERENCES

Abbott, J.A., G.S. Bachman, R.F. Childers, J.V.
Fitzgerald, and F.J. Matusik. 1968. Sonic
techniques for measuring texture of fruits and
vegetables. Food Technology 22(5)101-112.

Auld, B.A. 1973. Acoustic Fields and Waves in
Solids. John Wiley and Sons, Inc., New York,
New York.

Bendat, Julius S. and Allan G. Piersol. 1971.
Random Data: Analysis and Measurement
Procedures. Wiley-Interscience, New York, New
York.

Brown, G.K., L.J. Segerlind, and Robert Summitt,
1974. Near-infrared reflectance of bruised
apples. Transactions of ASAE 17(1):17-19.

Cooke, J.R. 1972. An interpretation of the resonant
behavior of inact fruits and vegetables.
Transactions of ASAE 15(6):1075-1080.

Diener, R.G., J.P. Mitchell, and M.L. Rhoten. 1970.
Using an X-ray image scan to sort bruised apples.
Agricultural Engineering, 51(6):356-361.

Finney, E.E., and J.A. Abbott. 1978. Methods for
Testing the dynamic mechanical response of solid
foods. Journal of Food Quality 2:55-74.

Finney, E.E., I. Ben-Gera, and D.R. Massie. 1968. An objective evaluation of changes in firmness of ripening bananas using a sonic technique. Journal of Food Science 32(6):642-646.

Garrett, R.E., and R.B. Furry. 1972. Velocity of sonic pulses in apples. Transactions of ASAE 15(4):770-774.

Hayt, W.H. 1974. Engineering Electromagnetics. McGraw-Hill Book Co., New York, New York.

Holcomb, D.P., J.R. Cooke, and P.O. Hartman. 1977. A study of electrical, thermal, and mechanical properties of apples in relation to bruise detection. ASAE paper No. 77-3512, American Society of Agricultural Engineers, St. Joseph, MI, 49805.

Holt, J.E., and D. Schoorl. 1977. Bruising and energy dissipation in apples. Journal of Texture Studies, 7:421-432.

Holt, J.E., and D. Schoorl. 1982. Mechanics of failure of fruits and vegetables. Journal of Texture Stuides, 13:83-97.

Ingle, M., and J.F. Hyde. 1968. The Effect of bruising on discoloration and concentration of phenolic compounds in apple tissue. Proceedings of the American Society of Horticultural Science, 93:38-738-745.

Klein, J.D. 1983. Physiological causes for changes in carbon dioxide and ethylene production by bruised apple fruit tissues. Unpublished Ph.D. Dissertation, Michigan State University, East Lansing, Michigan.

Kolsky, H. 1963. Stress Waves in Solids. Dover Publications, Inc., New York, New York.

Lee, B.B., and E.S. Furgason. 1981. A new digital correlation flaw detection system. Journal of Nondestructive Evaluation, 2(1):57-63.

Mohsenin, N.N. 1970. Physical Properties of Plant and Animal Materials. Gordon and Breach Science Publishers, New York, New York.

Mohsenin, N.N. 1977. Characterization and failure in solid foods with particular reference to fruits and vegetables. Journal of Texture Studies, 8(1977):169-193.

Mohsenin, N.N., H. Goehlich, and L.D. Tukey. 1962. Mechanical behaviour of apple fruits as related to bruising. Proceedings of the American Society of Horticultural Science 81:67-77.

Morrow, C.T., and N.N. Mohsenin. 1968. Dynamic viscoelastic characterization of solid food materials. Journal of Food Science 33(6)646-651.

Nicholas, D. 1977. Orientation and frequency dependence of backscatter energy and its clinical application. Recent Advances in Ultrasound in Biomedicine, Vol. 1., White, D.N. ed., Research Studies Press, Forest Grove, Oregon 97116.

Oppenheim, A.V., and A.S. Willsky. 1983. Signals and Systems. Prentice-Hall, Inc. Englewood Cliffs, New Jersey.

Rehkugler, G.E., T.L. Stiefvater, and J.A. Throop. 1971. An optical bruise detection technique. Transactions of ASAE, 14(6):1189-1194.

Rehkugler, G.E., W.F. Millier, R.A. Pellerin, and J.A. Throop. 1976. Design criteria for apple bruise detection by infrared radiation. Paper presented at the 1st International Congress on Engineering and Food, Boston, MA.

Reid, W.S. 1976. Optical detection of apple skin, bruise, flesh, stem, and calyx. Journal of Agricultural Engineering Research, 21(3):291-295.

Robitaille, H.A., and Jules Janick. 1973. Ethylene production and bruise injury in apple. Journal of the American Society of Horticultural Science, 98(4):411-413.

Rose, J.L., and B.B. Goldberg. 1979. Basic Physics in Diagnostic Ultrasound. John Wiley and Sons, Inc., New York, New York.

Solverson, L. 1969. Consumer knowledge for Sovereignty apples. American Journal of Agricultural Economics, 51(5):1247-1250.

Wells, P.N.T. 1969. Physical Principles of Ultrasonic Diagnosis. Academic Press, New York, New York.

Wells, P.N.T. 1975. Review: absorbtion and dispersion of ultrasound in biological tissue. Ultrasound in Medicine and Biology 1:369-376.

von Ramm, O.T., and S.W. Smith. 1979. Prospects and limitations of diagnostic ultrasound. SPIE: Recent and Future Developments in Medical Imaging II.

Table 1. The variance of measurements to be expected within an apple. The mean and variance were calculated from 8 fruit pressure test readings from the same apple.

apple #	Mean Pressure kPa	(lb/in^2)	Standard Deviation	
1	106.0	(15.3)	4.3	(0.63)
2	104.0	(15.1)	6.8	(0.98)
3	108.9	(15.8)	9.7	(1.40)
4	101.4	(14.7)	4.7	(0.68)

Table 2. Readings from different locations around the fruit. The variability in the readings are attributed to the changes in the angle of incidence and to the varying distance to the transducer.

Location	Peak Voltage Max	Min	Power (RMS)
apple # 1			
a	1.7265	-1.9100	0.2653
b	1.9692	-1.5855	0.2685
c	1.7341	-1.8315	0.2234
d	1.4121	-1.3674	0.2058
apple #2			
a	1.9306	-2.3406	0.2722
b	1.9445	-1.4503	0.2705
c	2.0190	-2.3010	0.2326
d	1.8022	-1.7012	0.2069
mean	1.8173	-1.8109	0.2432
stddev	0.1973	0.3627	0.0291

161

Table 3. Variability of the reflected signal for damaged locations on the fruit. The locations, a,b,c, are the damaged areas of the same locations reported in the previous table.

| Location | Peak Voltage | | Power |
	Max	Min	(RMS)
apple # 1			
a	2.0410	-2.4732	0.2817
b	2.1645	-2.0994	0.2494
c	1.4348	-2.1162	0.2348
apple # 2			
a	2.2210	-2.3151	0.2738
b	2.4504	-2.2371	0.2640
c	1.9142	-2.3180	0.2389
mean	2.0377	-2.2700	0.2571
stddev	0.3460	0.1478	0.0191

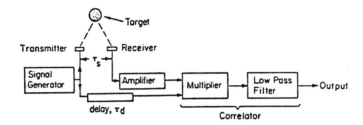

Figure 1. Schematic of a flaw detection system using a correlator receiver.

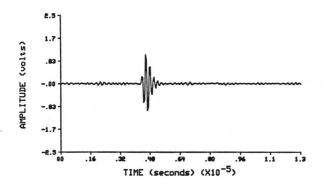

Figure 2. Reflected signal from a water-brass interface. The brass represents a high acoustic impedance medium.

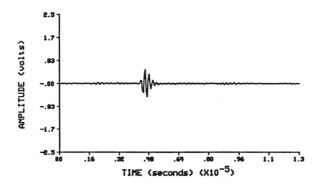

Figure 3. Reflected signal from a water-plexiglass interface. The acoustic impedance mismatch for this boundary is smaller than the water-brass one.

164

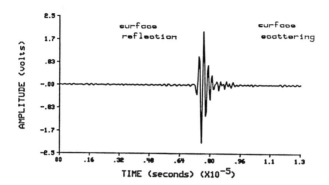

Figure 4. Signal reflected from undamaged apple tissue.

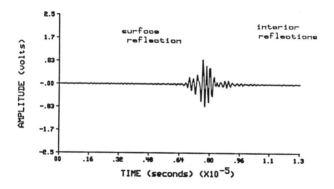

Figure 5. Signal reflected from a damaged area on the apple. The data were taken from the same location as the above undamaged data.

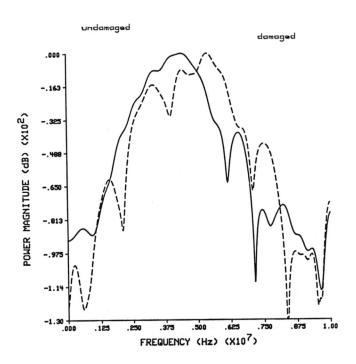

Figure 6. Power spectrum of the reflected signals from undamaged and damaged apple tissue.

166

RAPID INDENTIFICATION OF BRUISING IN POTATOES

by

Gary Beaver, Extension Potato Specialist, and
Mary DeVoy, Technical Aide
Department of Plant, Soil and Entomological Sciences,
University of Idaho

ABSTRACT

Two methods for identifying blackspot bruise in potatoes were compared: (1) standard incubation for 48 hours and (2) the tetrazolium chloride test. A high positive correlation was obtained between the reactions of the two tests.

The weight dropping method was used to bruise Russet Burbank variety tubers. Black spots developed after 30 hours in the standard test while pink spots developed after 45 minutes with the tetrazolim chloride test.

Because of the simplicity and rapid rate of color development with the tetrazolium chloride test, it can be effectively used under field conditions to quickly identify bruising at various locations on potato harvesters.

ASAE Paper No. 85-6015

INTRODUCTION

Bruise and bruise detection in potatoes has long been a problem for growers, handlers, processors and the fresh pack industry. An ongoing search for bruise resistance in potatoes has resulted in various methods for testing for bruise susceptibility (Gall 1967, Johnson 1972, Kunkel 1959, Maas 1956, Pavek 1982 and 1985, Schippers 1971). In addition several methods for identifying bruised areas on impacted susceptibility tubers have been developed (Dwell 1976, Hammond 1978, Iritani 1985, O'Leary 1969, and Thornton 1982). Efforts have all been directed toward reducing bruise losses in potatoes. These losses are estimated to cost the U.S. potato producers 150 million dollars annually (Stiles 1983). Although these procedures are accurate and effective in identifying bruised areas on potatoes they also require from 6 to 48 or more hours to complete. This poses a problem when modifications are necesary in equipment or methods of operation during potato harvest. Examples of the costs of delay in correcting equipment faults are given by Thornton, Beaver and DeVoy (1985).

The need for a more rapid test to identify blackspot bruising has been expressed by the National Potato Antibruise Committee (Stiles 1983). This paper describes a rapid technique for identifying blackspot bruise in potatoes.

METHOD

A variety of chemical strains were evaluated for their effectiveness to detect fresh bruising in Russet Burbank potatoes including 2,3,5-triphenyl-tetrazolium chloride (tetrazolium red) as used by Rocstacher, Klotz and Eaks (1956) to detect surface injuries to citrus fruits. None of the chemicals tested except tetrazolium red were found to be effective (Table 1).

Solutions of 0.1 to 5.0 percent tetrazolium red in tap water were prepared. Tubers of the variety Russet Burbank were artifically bruised by dropping steel balls weighing 32 or 67 grams (1.13 or 2.4 oz.) through lengths of 2.5 cm (1 in.) diameter PVC tubes

(15, 30, 45, 60, 90, 120, 150, and 180 cm or 6, 12, 18, 24, 36, 48, 60 and 71 in. in length) onto their surface of known points. The tubers were subsequently placed into the solution for varying periods of time. The unpeeled tubers were then peeled and evaluated along with the peeled tubers. Test solution temperatures were maintained at ambient temperature (approximately 22°C, 72°F).

Russet Burbank variety tubers were artificially bruised with different impact levels at known points on opposite sides and sliced longitudinally. One half of each tuber was peeled and placed in the tetrazolium red solution. The second half was placed on a shelf for 48 hours to allow normal blackspot bruise to develop. A visual comparison was then made between the tetrazolium red test and normal blackspot development.

Russet Burbank variety tubers were also removed from a peel line at a potato processing plant. The tubers had been lye peeled. The peeled tubers were placed in the tetrazolium red test solution and evaluated for fresh bruise. A comparison was made with hand peeled tubers from the same lot.

Subsequent to the laboratory trials, field trials were conducted using a 0.1 percent tetrazolium red solution. Both clean tap water and irrigation ditch water were used. Solution temperatures ranged from 4.5 ° C to 27°C (40 to 80 °F). Tubers of the varieties Russet Burbank, Lemhi Russet, Norgold Russet, Butte, and Norchip were selected from harvesters operating in the field. Tubers were also selected from storages after storage periods of one to nine months. Tubers selected from harvesters were immediately peeled and placed in the test solution. Tubers selected from storage were mechanically bruised, peeled and placed in the test solution.

Peeling of the tubers was carried out using a hand held kitchen potato peeler or an electric "Dazy" vegetable stripper.

RESULTS

Only tetrazolium red gave a pigmented reaction to freshly bruised potato tissue. Concentrations of

0.1 percent or greater in water gave a light-to-dark color to freshly bruised tissues beneath the periderm. It was necessary to remove the periderm prior to placing the tuber in the test solution. Unpeeled tubers would not react. The solution strength did not appear to affect the reaction as long as the strength was 0.1 percent or greater. The source of water had no effect on the activity of the test solution except that chlorinated water may interfere by slowing the reaction time or making the reaction less intense. Water temperatures between 4.5 °C and 27 °C permitted the reaction to occur although colder temperature required an additional 15 to 30 minutes for the pink color to develop. There was a perfect correlation between the tetrazolim red test and normal blackspot development for all bruise levels tested.

There were no consistent differences in reaction between the varieties of potatoes tested. There was some variation between tubers within a variety or between lots of tubers selected from different fields and/or storages. The variations ranged in reaction from a light pink to a dark pink color within the bruised areas.

All tests performed on fresh tubers selected from harvesters gave positive reaction to bruising. Tubers selected from storage also gave a positive reaction to fresh bruises. However, in one instance tubers selected from a storage where they had been held for seven months did not give any reaction to the tetrazolium test. In addition these tubers also did not develop blackspot after mechanical injury and incubation for 48 hours at 22°C (72 F).

The method of peeling did have an influence on the time required for the reaction to occur and on the intensity of the reaction. Hand peeling gave satisfactory results when the tubers were lightly peeled although it was difficult to evenly peel the tubers. It was found that using an electric "Dazy" peeler gave more uniform peeling and the reaction was more defined and took slightly less time (5-10 minutes). The amount of peel removed with the Dazy peeler ranged from 8 to 11 percent. This is comparable to lye or steam peeling.

170

The tetrazolium test was run on lye peeled potatoes with positive results. The bruised tissue did stain but the color was fainter, and the incubation period was extended to two hours or more. Steam peeled potatoes have not been tested.

In addition to identifying fresh bruised tissues the tetrazolium test will also stain fresh shatter bruise. The injury appears as fine pink lines on the peeled tuber. In most cases, however, fresh shatter bruises can be seen on peeled tubers without the aid of staining.

DISCUSSION

The tetrazolium red test for fresh bruise can be used any time potato tubers are being handled, e.g. in the field, during handling to and from storage, in processing plants, on the fresh pack line or during shipping. The test is rapid and accurate and permits timely adjustments to equipment or equipment operation that can result in lower impact damage to the tubers.

The tetrazolium red solution has a shelf life of about six days. Its use life depends on the number of tubers being tested. Tests have been conducted on a continuous basis during a 12 hour period with no noticeable reduction in reaction. It is advisable, however, to use a fresh solution each day.

There was excellent correlation between the tetrazolium red test and normal blackspot development on mechanical bruised potatoes. Therefore, a high level of confidence may be placed in the accuracy of the tetrazolium red procedure.

The test procedures are as follows:

1. Select tubers to be tested--usually 8-10 tubers.

2. Lightly peel the tuber. Remove only enough skin to expose the white flesh beneath. Do not rinse the tuber after peeling.

3. Place the peeled tuber in the test solution. Completely submerge the tubers and leave them there until the bruised areas are visible-- usually 45 minutes to 1 hour.

171

4. Remove the tubers and examine. The bruised areas will appear as light pink spots. If the tuber is left in the solution four to six hours or more, the entire tuber will turn a dark pink and the bruised areas will no longer be visible. It may be necessary to leave tubers in the test solution up to two hours if the temperature of the test solution and tubers is very cold (5-8° C, 41-46°F or colder) or if the tubers have been in storage for more than four to six months.

The test solution is made as follows:

Mix a solution of 0.1 to 1.0 percent 2,3,5-triphenyltetrazolium chloride in water (most any water source will work). This solution is equivalent to four grams of material in one gallon of water. The solution will be slightly colored when mixed but will turn dark pink if exposed to sunlight. This will not affect the test and may even speed the reaction slightly.

REFERENCES

Dwelle, R.B. and G.F. Stallknecht. 1976. Rates of internal blackspot bruise development in potato tubers under conditions of elevated temperatures and gas pressures. Am. Pot. J. 53:235-245.

Gall, H., P. Lamprecht, and E. Fechter. 1967. Erste ergebnisse mit dem ruckschlagpendel zur bestimmung der beschadigungsempfindlichkeit von kartoffeln. Eur. Potato J. 10:272-285.

Hammond, M.W. 1978. Bruised detection and incentive program--a grower's application. Wash. Pot. Conf. and Trade Fair Proc., pp. 67-75.

Iritani, W.M. 1985. Enhancement of blackspot development by hot water soak method. Wash. Pot. Conf. Proc., pp. 1-6.

Johnson, Lynn F. 1972. A simple field device to measure potato tuber susceptibility to bruise. Am. Potato J., 49:359 (Abstr.).

Kunkel, R. and W.H. Gardner. 1959. Blackspot of Russet Burbank potatoes. Proc. Am. Soc. Hort. Sci., 73:436-444.

Maas, E.F. 1956. A simplified potato bruising device. Am. Potato J., 43:424-426.

O'Leary, A.G. and W.M. Iritani. 1969. Potato bruise detection. Amer. Potato J. 46(9):352-354.

Pavek, J.J. and D.L. Corsini. 1982. An improved method for screening potato clones for blackspot reaction. Amer. Potato J., 59(10):481-482.

Pavek, J.J., D. L. Corsini and F. Nissley. 1985. A rapid method for determining blackspot suscepti-bility of potato clones. Id. Ag. Exp. Sta. Res-earch Paper No. 84740 (In press).

Raistacher, C.N., L.J. Klotz, and I.L. Eaks. 1956. Effective color indicator for detecting surface injuries to citrus fruits. Citrus Leaves, June 1976.

Schippers, P.A. 1971. Measurement of blackspot susceptibility of potatoes. Am. Potato J. 48:71-87.

Stiles, D.G. 1983. The National Potato Anti-Bruise Committee. Am. Potato J., 60:821-822.

Thornton, Rob. 1982. A rapid method of bruise analysis and its usefulness. Wash. Pot. Conf. and Trade Fair Proc., pp. 133-138.

Thornton, R., G. Beaver and M. DeVoy. 1985. Rapid detection of potato tuber damage. Spudman, July/August 1985.

Table 1. Effect of selected stains on fresh bruised potato tuber tissues.

Stain	Effective Results on Bruised Tissue
2,3,5-Triphenyltetrazolium chloride	Pink color
2,3,5-Triphenyltetrazolium formazan	None
Neotetrazolium chloride	None
Tetrazolium blue	None
Tetrazolium violet	None
Tetranitro blue tetrazolium	None
Crystal violet	None
Eosin Y	None
Orange G	None
Floxine B	None
Analine violet	None

AN EVOLUTION OF THE POTATO FLUIDIZED BED
MEDIUM SEPARATOR*

by

A. Zaltzman, Visiting Research Scientist,
Agricultural Engineering Department, Georgia
Experiment Station, University of Georgia,
Experiment, Georgia; Z. Schmilovitch, Research
Agricultural Research Organization, The Volcani
Center, Bet-Dagan, Israel

ABSTRACT

An evolution of a potato fluidized bed medium
(FBM) separator is described. Two schemes of introducing a potato-clod-stone mixture in the FBM were
theoretically evaluated and experimentally examined
under field conditions. Three experimental potato
FBM separators were developed and tested in the
framework of these schemes.

----
*Contribution from the Agricultural Research
Organization, The Volcani Center, Bet Dagan, Israel.
No. 1412-E, 1985 Series.

ASAE Paper No. 85-6016

INTRODUCTION

One of the basic problems not yet solved satisfactorily in the mechanical harvesting and processing of potatoes is the separation of potatoes from clods and stones. This process until presently consumed much manual labor.

Numerous methods have been investigated for solving the problem over the past three or four decades. They can be classified in the following groups:

1. Based on differences in shape and coefficient of friction as well as rolling resistance of stones and clods compared with potatoes. Most of them were realized on sloped conveyors or even horizontal conveyors but under forces produced by an air blast or rotating brushes (Maack, 1957a, 1957b; Schafer, 1959, 1960a, 1960b; Krasheninnikov, 1962; Kusov, 1964; Rohrs, 1964).

2. Used different mass properties of potatoes and stones. This was materialized on various elastic supporters or brushes through which stones passed more easily than potatoes (Schafer, 1959, 1961; Rosel, 1963; Eaton and Hanson, 1969; Misener et al., 1984).

3. Based on a difference of air terminal velocity of potatoes and stones (Kolchin, 1957; Avtukhov, 1960, 1961; Gilfillan and Grother, 1959; Hallee, 1970; Sides and Smith, 1970; Sides et al., 1974).

4. Utilized difference in density of potatoes and clods and stones (Farm Mechanization, 1953; Pflug et al., 1955; Zinnovev, 1959; Zabeltitz, 1967; Elliott and Diener, 1970).

5. Used difference in response to electro-magnetic waves – optical, gamma or x-ray, electrical conductance, etc. (Gilmour, 1960; Slight, 1961, 1966; Palmer, 1961; Srapenyants and Said-Khodzhaev, 1963, 1964a, 1964b; Krashennikov, 1964; Batyaev, 1965, 1966; Story and Raghavan, 1973).

6.   Based on firmness of products being separated (Koch, 1964; Gray and Ellis, 1970).

Most of the works quoted above were performed in the laboratory and at other experimental levels. The separation effectiveness in many cases was not high and only some of the methods have dealt with a clod separation just as the majority of the work was aimed for stone separation. The first commercially practical devices were tilted conveyors. Later on they were superceded by air stream devices which lacked in capacity to separate clods and consumed large amounts of power. In some types of potato harvesters separation methods based on elastic supporters or brushes were used. A suspension of small soil particles in water was used to separate potatoes from clods in a potato harvester (Farm Mechanization, 1953), but this method was not acceptable because of contamination of the potatoes that caused spoilage during storage. The above also prevented a "water harvester," developed in Idaho (Story and Raghavan, 1973). An x-ray potato-clod separator was produced commercially for a long time in Europe. Today its production is broken off and most European countries have ended its usage.

Theoretically, the strongest and distinguished difference in properties between potatoes and clods and stones is the density difference. But in practice, in various methods where this difference is used for separation it is shaded by other properties. This decreases its separation potential. One of the potentially best separating methods for realizing this potential is the use of a fluidized bed medium (FBM) formed by particles considerably smaller than the particles of the products to be separated. In practice, this reduces the influence of other factors and separation is done according to density only.

In previous work (Zaltzman et al., 1983) the research of using a sand FBM for separating potatoes from clods and stones was reported. The first experimental model was developed and tested in laboratory and field conditions. The tests confirmed a good separation effectiveness and showed the directions for further development. Additionally, an analytical model of a separation process in FBM was developed (Zaltzman et al., 1985a) and checked in

177

laboratory conditions (Mizrach et al., 1984) and during observed phenomena in actual practice. The method was expanded by separating flower bulbs (Zaltzman et al., 1985b).

The goal of this work was a further development of a potato-clod-stone separating device and its examination under field conditions.

THE METHOD OF POTATO SEPARATION WITH INITIAL VELOCITY OF INTRODUCING A POTATO-CLOD-STONE MIXTURE IN A FBM

Preliminary Consideration

In separation processes the product being separated often falls down into the separation media from a feeding conveyor. It appears that the value of the drop height is affected only by design considerations. In the case of a FBM separation, this parameter has a direct influence on the process results. In previous work (Zaltzman et al., 1985a) it was reported that increasing the drop height of the mixture introduced into FBM resulted in an increasing of the efficiency of a separation process. It was a main reason of the choice of this feeding method for the first experimental model (Zaltzman, et al., 1983). Additional argument for this method of application could be explained by considerations of the possibility of using the similar schemes of the FBM separator for both potatoes and flower bulbs. In the case of flower bulbs, such feeding has advantage that promotes disconnection of clods from bulbs when they are engaged.

Tests of the first experimental model showed some of its inadequacies resulted from the machine design principle. Most important was free potato movement in the separation chamber and using a drum as a clod-stone output conveyor. These prevented increasing of the machine capacity.

The second prototype of the potato separator was designed also with a feeding system, based on an initial velocity of introducing the mixture into the FBM. By means of theoretical predictions based on the developed analytical model of the FBM separation process, the data sufficient for the choice of a form

178

and design of separation chamber were obtained. The
major parameters calculated in this way concerned
depth of the FBM and the machine capacity.

Depth of the fluidized bed is one of the import-
tant design characteristics of the FBM separator.
From the one hand, it is directly linked with a power
requirement for the air supply and it is desirable to
use the minimum bed depth. On the other hand, the
depth has to be sufficient to provide successful
completion of the separation process.

From the design considerations the drop height
of the mixture in the second prototype was chosen as
0.5 m (19.7 in.). The typical size of potatoes and
clods, (on which can be based calculations) was taken
as 0.1 m (3.9 in.). By means of the analytical model
of FBM separation processes (Zaltzman et al., 1985a)
the potato and clod trajectories were calculated and
showed in Figure 1. It is necessary to note that the
theoretical considerations were carried out only for
clods because in the case of stones being separated
requirements of the process parameters for successful
separation were much easier. From the trajectories
it is clear that the clods have only a sinking movement, at the same time the potato has a diving movement up to the specific depth and an ascending movement to the fluidized bed surface. The depth of the
FBM which provides the separation conditions without
interactions between potatoes and clods can be obtained from the Figure 1 as 0.4-0.45 m (16-18 in.).
On the basis of the above considerations the FBM
effective depth was chosen as 0.5 m (20 in.) for the
second prototype.

The drum which was used in the first
experimental model as a clod and stone lifting
conveyor and contained an internal separation zone
was not an effective appartus for usage of optimum
depth and width of a FBM. In Figure 2 are presented
the schemes and comparative characteristics of drum
and rectangular conveyors as clod-stone lifting
mechanisms. Their performance is characterized by
the coefficients of the effective usage of FBM width
K and depth n.

where

$$K = \frac{B_{ef}}{B} \qquad (1)$$

and

$$n = \frac{H_{ef}}{H} \qquad (2)$$

In Equations (1) and (2) B_{ef} and H_{ef} — effective width and depth; B and H — the whole width and depth. By considering Figure 2a and 2b relationships can be s ... for drum and rectangular conveyor respectively:

$$K_1 = \frac{2 \; [0.5 \; (B-2B_0)]^2 - H_{ef}^2}{B} \qquad (3)$$

$$n_1 = \frac{H_{ef}}{0.5 \; (B-2B_0) + H_0} \qquad (4)$$

$$K_2 = \cdot \frac{B-2B_0}{B} \qquad (5)$$

$$n_2 = \frac{H_{ef}}{H_{ef} + H_0} \qquad (6)$$

From the experience, th minimal values of B_0 and H_0 can be taken as 0.1 m. For these values and H_0 and $H_{ef} = 0.5$ m coefficients k and n versus width B are plotted in Figure 2c. From graphic presentation of the above relationships it is obvious that coefficients of the effective usage of FBM width and depth for the rectangular lifting conveyor are much larger than for the drum. According to this a rectangular conveyor was chosen as clod-stone lifting mechanism for the second prototype of a potato FBM separator.

From the theory of the separation processes it is known that duration of separation (which is

proportional to a length of a separation chamber)
regularly influences (up to a specific limit) quality
of separation. The capacity of the separation system
depends on the width of a separation chamber. The
theoretical capacity of the separation chamber was
determined on the basis of assuming that every next
potato cannot be immersed in the FBM until the
previous potato completes its ascending movement,
i.e., the potato stream in a separation chamber
consists of only a single layer of potatoes. From
Figure 1, it can be seen that for a typical potato
time of diving in a FBM and ascending to the surface
for chosen specific conditions is approximately equal
0.89 s. From this and a coefficient of FBM area
usage (assumed to be 0.5) the maximum theoretical
capacity of the separation chamber for potatoes was
taken as 28.95 $B_{ef}m^3$/h or 14.47 $B_{ef}t$/h (bulk
density of potatoes was taken as $0.5t/m^3$.

The Second Experimental Separator Design

Considering the data presented above and the
results of tests with an experimental flower bulb
separator (Zaltzman et al., 1985b) the second prototype of the potato FBM separator was developed and
built by "Pachtaas" Co., Ashkelon, Israel. Its
principal scheme is shown in Figure 3 (Zaltzman et
al., 1982) and it is similar to that of the flower
bulb separator. Adjusting to potato sizes and
properties respectively were made. Also, an
additional horizontal potato output conveyor was
added transverse to the longitudinal axle of the
machine. Special arrangements were included in the
machine design to make it easier to replace sand and
improve the fluidizing air distribution.

The fluidized bed is created by air supplied
from blowers through air inlets to the separation
chamber. A potato-clod-stone mixture is fed by
feeder conveyor into the separation zone enclosed by
the lifting conveyor which drops them onto the clod
and stone output conveyor. The output conveyor
removes clods and stones from the machine.

The potatoes float on the surface of the same
FBM in the separation zone and are raked by the
fingers of a potato extraction conveyor to the sloped
potato output conveyor which delivers them from the

FBM to the second horizontal potato output conveyor.
The purpose of the ladder is to separate potatoes
from medium particles handled with potatoes and
remove potatoes from the separator. The lifting,
clod and stone output, and the second potato output
conveyor are perforated to permit the medium
particles to be returned to the bed. The first
sloped potato output conveyor is comprised of a
conveyor belt of the "Brukema" type (two rubber
straps with a rubber covered steel rod between them)
with rubber fingers. The potatoes are constrained to
move to the rectangular lifting conveyor by a pair of
side baffles.

Pertinent dimensions of the separator are:
length of the separation chamber, 2500 mm (98 in.);
width of the separation chamber, 2200 mm (87 in.);
depth of the fluidized bed, 600 mm (24 in.). The
blowers delivered 2200 m^3/h (86 cfm) air at a
pressure of 10 kPa. All conveyors are driven by
variable speed electric motors.

Test Results

The machine was tested under field conditions in
the packinghouse at "Shar a Negev." A special line
was built (Figure 4) for preliminary mechanical
processing potato-clod-stone mixture as it is usually
done in a packinghouse and for feeding the separator.
It includes a hopper for track unloading, vibrational
cleaner for separating the small clod fraction, a
separation table for hand separating foliage, stems,
roots and other plant residues and also supplying the
mixture into the machine and accessory conveyors for
removing clods and potatoes.

The tests were carried out as follows: the
trucks with the mixture from a field were unloaded in
the hopper. The weighing was made before and after
unloading. The mixture from the hopper was
transferred to the vibrating cleaner, where small
clod fractions were separated, and then passed to the
hand separation table, where two workers picked out
the foliage and plant residues. From the separation
table the mixture was fed into the FBM separator.
After separating potatoes by means of conveyors and
elevators they were loaded on a truck. At the same
time, clods and stones separated from potatoes were

transferred into special containers. The time for a separation of the mixture entrained in every truck was registered. Weight of potatoes obtained after separation in the potato exit of the machine was determined by weighing the truck conveyed potatoes before and after its loading. In every test two samples of the mixture were taken for determination of clod and potato contents distribution.

Results of the tests are shown in Table 1. Every test relates to a specific truck with a potato-clod-stone mixture from a field. Effectiveness of a separation (not shown in Table 1) was high, very close to 100 percent. Product in the potato exit of the machine was completely free from the clods and stones. In the clod-stone exit was 0.01-0.02 percent of small potatoes (< 60g). The maximum capacity of the machine achieved was 20-22 t/h (440-484 cwt/h) of the mixture from the field. Capacity depends on the percentage of potatoes in the mixture. From Table 1 it is clear that increasing percent of potatoes in the mixture resulted in decreasing capacity of the machine. This was due to limited capacity of the first potato output conveyor (15 t/h [330 cwt/h] of potatoes). Whenever the feeding rate exceeded the output conveyor capacity, potatoes rolled down above the rubber fingers and were not conveyed. Thus, the maximum capacity of the separation zone (determined in theoretical calculations as 26 t/h [572 cwt/h] of potatoes) was not used completely.

The machine was set in operation in the end of a summer season. Approximately 220t (4840 cwt) of mixture (or 150 t potatoes) were separated in the prototype. During this short period of its testing no special problems were revealed. The common note can be related to its size, which resulted in a large amount of sand as a medium and high power requirements for sand fluidizing. It was planned to continue the tests in the winter season but circumstances and obstacles not concerned to technical problems prevented this. Meanwhile a new prototype with better operational characteristics was developed and the tests of the described separator were not resumed.

THE METHOD OF POTATO SEPARATION WITH ZERO-ORDER
INITIAL VELOCITY OF INTRODUCING POTATO-CLOD-STONE
MIXTURE IN A FBM

Preliminary Consideration

Continual search for improving technical characteristics of FBM potato separators resulted in
revision of the concept of introducing the mixture in
FMB with initial velocity. This was fair for flower
bulbs when it was necessary to disconnect clods from
bulb roots. Also, this is fair in the case when the
products being separated have a small difference in
densities. In this case, introducing the products
with initial velocity in FBM would result in
increasing the process efficiency. However, potatoes
and clods have a sufficient difference in their
densities and previous arguments are not applied for
them.

In the case when the mixture is supplied to a
FBM without sufficient initial velocity (example of
sufficient initial velocity is dropping from any
height) movement of potatoes immersed in the FBM is
floating only as clods and stones sink. Most proper
mechanical means for this is a sloping, perforated
conveyor allowing the FBM to pass through it. In the
point of the conveyor contact with the FBM potatoes
start to flow. Clods and stones remained on the conveyor, submerged in a FBM and transferred by the
conveyor to the projected destination. In this case,
depth of the FBM is not influenced by mutual potato
and clod movement as in the previous prototype but
can be chosen on the basis of their physical
dimensions only with consideration to prevent interference between potato and clod layers. On the above
basis the effective and whole depths of the FBM for
the new experimental model were chosen respectively
as H = 0.2m and H = 0.3m.

The capacity of the separation zone depends on
the velocity of the potato layer when it moves after
being fed by a sloped, perforated conveyor. The
layer velocity is equal to a horizontal component of
the conveyor velocity. The last one has to be chosen
in the limits that the vertical component of the
conveyor velocity will be less or equal to a sinking
velocity of clods, i.e., by this way it will prevent

separation of clods from the conveyor. The average
sinking velocity of clods for the chosen depth can be
determined from Figure 5, which represented a
trajectory of typical clod introduced in a sand FBM
with a zero-order initial velocity. Considering data
presented in Figure 5, the slope of the perforated
conveyor of 120 to the direction of the potato
stream and coefficient of FBM area usage assumed 0.5,
the maximum theoretical capacity of this separation
zone can be obtained as 65.4 B_{ef} m^3 /h or 32.7 B_{ef}t/h.
In this case, B_{ef} = B, i.e., the whole width is used
effectively. The above method was realized in the
third FBM separator.

The Third Experimental Separator Design

Schematic drawing of the third experimental
model is shown in Figure 6. A view of the model from
the feeding side is presented in Figure 7.

The central part of the model is a FBM
container, which contains sand used as a medium. The
upper part of the clod and stone output conveyor and
bottom parts of the potato extraction and output
conveyors are disposed in the container. The clod
and stone output conveyor is comprised of a conveyor
belt of the "brukema" type covered by netting. The
potato extraction and output conveyors include the
conveyor belts of the "Brukema" type also. The first
one is equipped with steel fingers covered by rubber,
the second has rubber covered steel rods of the
"Brukema" conveyor. Compressed air is supplied from
the blower to an air chamber and further through an
air distributor to a FBM container. By this way,
sand is fluidized.

The upper input slope portion of the clod and
stone output conveyor is outside the bed, the middle
portion is submerged in the bed and constitutes the
bottom of the separation zone, the slope output
portion is partially in the bed and horizontal output
portion is outside the bed. The lower portion of
this conveyor is outside the FBM container and
constitutes with the whole upper portion a loop round
the FBM container. The slope portion of the potato
output conveyor has submerged and outside parts. The
rubber covered fingers of the potato extraction
conveyors are partially immersed in a FBM.

The separator operates as follows: the mixture of materials to be separated is supplied to the upper input sloped portion of the clod and stone output conveyor, which is used also as a feeding mechanism for introducing the mixture in a FBM with zero-order initial velocity, and by this way the mixture is fed into the FBM. The potatoes float on the FBM surface and are raked out of the separation zone by fingers of potato extraction conveyors partially immersed in a FBM. By means of this, potatoes are transferred to a submerged part of the potato output conveyor. Sloped parts of the potato extraction and output conveyor constitute the enclosed departments and by this way potatoes are taken out from the FBM. Furthermore, a horizontal portion of a potato output conveyor removes them out of the device.

The clods and stones continue to stay on a sloped portion of the clod-stone output conveyor after it is immersed in FBM and transferred by it through an FBM container out of the machine. To prevent their sliding, this conveyor is provided with low steps.

All conveyors are made permeable for sand to allow it to be passed back into the FBM container when it is lifted out from the bed by products or conveyors. For this purpose special air cleaners were assembled and supplied with air from the same blower which delivers air for FBM.

Pertinent dimensions and details of the separator are: length of the FBM container, 2500 mm, width of the container, 640 mm, depth of the fluidized bed, 300 mm. The model requires an airflow of 650 m^3/h at a pressure of 5 kPa. All conveyors are driven by variable speed electric motors with a total power of 3 HP.

The Test Results

The separator was included in the processing line of the packinghouse "Shar a Negev" parallel to the x-ray separator to separate mixtures containing small potatoes (with weights less than 120 g) and clods and stones of corresponding size. Accessory conveyors are arranged to enable the flow of materials to the machine or to the x-ray separator or to both of them simultaneously.

The separator was tested during continuous operation. In every test, two samples were taken from the mixture entrance and potato and clod exists. The typical results are shown in Table 2 in comparison with the result of separation in the x-ray device. Separation effectiveness was evaluated by remultiplication of potato recovery by clod and stone rejection (Brown, 1951). Feed rate was changed from 1 to 7 t/h. Anaylsis of the data shows that a good effectiveness was achieved in all tests. The data indicate also a slight decreasing in the separation effectiveness with increasing feed rate. Comparison of separation in the FBM machine and x-ray device clearly evidences the better quality of separation in the FBM separator that was achieved in both potato and clod-stone exits.

The machine was working continuously through winter and summer seasons as much as 500 actual hours. Approximately 3000 t of the mixture was separated in the device. The maximum capacity achieved during stable continuous operation of the separator was 8 t/h. No special mechanical problems were revealed through the work. Enough stable work was achieved also in the winter season when very wet potatoes and clods were transferred through the separator. This caused only increased losses of sand which stuck to wet products. The regular losses of sand were approximately 0.06 m^3 per 10 hours of operation.

The single problem of partial clogging of the air distributor by dust prevented stable continuous work of the machine. Unfortunately, the machine was located near the conveyor that discharged the ground and small clod fraction from the processing system and increased dust intake to the machine. Figure 8 shows increased resistance of the air distributor in 250 hours of operation. When resistance of the air distributor periodically achieved the limit of the air supplied by the blower the quality of FBM rapidly decreased which caused a breaking off of FBM separation. This required stopping the machine and cleaning the distributor.

187

Special tests were performed to determine the
contamination of sand by clods during the continuous
operation. It was found that no special techniques
were required to separate clods and stone from sand.
Small clod particles of the size of sand became a
part of the sand medium which did not cause any loss
in the separation efficiency.

DISCUSSION

Comparative characteristics of FBM experimental
separators are shown in Table 3. It presents some
data obtained from theoretical considerations as well
as actual characteristics revealed in practice during
the tests of the separators. Comparison of the
coefficients of effective usage of FBM indicates that
they are better for the third experimental separator.
Small decreases of coefficient of effective depth
usage for this separator compared with the second
prototype is explained by sufficiently decreasing
this depth and the necessity to use part of the depth
for design purposes. Considering the small width of
the third separator it has also a maximum relative
theoretical capacity of FBM according to potato,
i.e., the best usage of the FBM area. The
theoretical prediction of its best operation characteristics was confirmed by actual data received
during the tests. Relative power expense for air
supply in the third model was 4.7 times less than in
the first separator and 2.5 times less than in the
second one.

Relative amount of medium (sand) in the third
separator was 9 and 2.5 times less than in the first
and second ones, respectively. This sufficiently
lightens the maintenance of the separator. Actual
usage of the FBM area calculated as ratio of the
actual capacity to area of FBM was largest for the
third separator. It is important to note that this
model has a considerable potential of decreasing FBM
area, i.e. for sufficiently improving its technical
characteristics.

Comparison of maximum theoretical capacities of
FBM for potatoes with actual capacities for the
mixture for all separators indicates that in all
cases FBM area is not used completely. It is
explained by insufficient capacity of the accessory

conveyors and mechanisms as potato extraction and output conveyors and clod and stone output conveyors. Also, a good preparation of a potato-clod-stone mixture and its feeding is very essential for increasing the capacity of a FBM separator. Realizing the above conditions will allow developing a 1 meter wide potato FBM separator with a capacity of 33 t/h of potatoes or 66 t/h of mixture with potato-clod ratio of 1:1.

The third FBM potato experimental separator was subjected to a severe evaluation in the commercial conditions. Its tests did not reveal special mechanical problems. Partial clogging of the air distributor by dust can be overcome by using special filters for air cleaning, location of the separator in an area with small contents of dust in the air or developing a device which would allow easy cleaning or replacing of an air distributor. In spite of these shortcomings, this model is very close to its full commerical application.

SUMMARY AND CONCLUSION

1. Two schemes of introducing a potato-clod-stone mixture in FBM were theoretically evaluated and experimentally examined under field conditions.

2. Three experimental potato FBM separators were developed and tested in the framework of these schemes.

3. The first scheme with initial velocity of introducing the mixture in FBM passed designing evolution from drum for clod-stone lifting to rectangular conveyor for this purpose. That sufficiently improved its technical characteristics.

4. The second scheme which introduced the mixture with zero-order initial velocity has the largest potential in the case of potato separation. This was realized in the third experimental model, which has the best technical characteristics among the three experimental FBM separators.

5. Continuous examination of the third model and carried out under commercial conditions. It revealed a good separation effectiveness and mechanical reliability. Some shortcomings were discovered through the tests (such as sand losses) can be overcome or decreased in the further development.

6. The potential capacity of FBM separators is large. Improving accessory mechanism for moving and lifting potatoes and clods would allow realization of the potential capacity of the FBM in full and develop the future FBM separators with very large capacity under relatively small dimensions of the separator.

REFERENCES

Avtukhov, I.V. 1960. Separating potato tubers from hard clods and stones in an air stream. Trakt. i Selkhomash. 30(6):22-24. (In Russian)

Avtukhov, I.V. 1961. The effect of an air stream on the operation of a vibrating sieve in separating potatoes from clods. Trakt. i Selkhomash. 31 (5):21-23. (In Russian)

Baganz, K. 1959. Removal of rubbish in a complete potato harvester. Tag Ber. 22:47-59. dtsch. Akad. Landw Wiss.

Bartu, J. 1955. The results of Czechoslovak research on new components for potato harvesters. Tagungsber. Sect. Landtech. dtsch. Akad. Landw Wiss. Bad. Schandau. Dec.:53.

Batyaev, F.I. 1965. Separating potatoes by the photoelectric methods. Trakt. i Selkhomash. 35(3):23-26. (In Russian)

Batyaev, F.I. 1966. Investigation of operation of photoelectric separator of potatoes from clods, stones, and other trash. Trakt. i Selkhomash, 36(9):34-37. (In Russian)

Brown, G.G., D. Kate and A.S. Foust. 1951. Unit Operations. J. Wiley & Sons, New York., p. 15.

Eaton, F.E. and R.W. Hansen. 1970. Mechanical separation of stones from potatoes by means of rotary brushes. Transactions of ASAE 13(5): 591-593.

Elliott, K.C. and R.G. Diener. 1970. Fluid screen for rapid separation of potatoes and stones. ASAE Paper No. 70-813, ASAE, St. Joseph, MI. 49085.

Farm Mechanization. 1953. No. 4.

Gilfillan, G. and A.T. Growther. 1959. The behavior of potatoes, stones, and clods in a vertical air stream. Journal of Agricultural Engineering Research 4(1):9.

Gilmour, W.D. 1960. Electronic potato screener. Journal of Agricultural Engineering Research 5(1):437.

Gray, G.L. and W.R. Ellis. 1972. Individual separation of stones and potatoes. A progress report. Transactions of ASAE 15(3):406-408, 413.

Hallee, N.D. 1970. Aerodynamic properties of potatoes and associated soil material. ASAE Paper No. 70-813, ASAE, St. Joseph, MI 49085.

Koch, M. 1964. A new method, using sound impulses for separating stones from potatoes. Grundl Landtech. 21:56-65.

Kolchin, N.N. 1957. Combined pneumatic and mechanical separation of potato tubers from clods. Selkhozmaschina 1957 (3) 19. English translation, Journal of Agricultural Engineering Research 2(3):230.

Krasheninnikov, S.N. 1962. Investigation of the separation of potato tubers from soil clods and stones using an air blast. Mech Elektrif. selkhoz. 20(6):38-40. (In Russian)

Krasheninnikov, S.N. 1964. The automation of separating potato tubers from clods and stones. Problemy avtomatizatsii skh. proizvodstva, kolos 349-362. (In Russian)

Kusov, T.T. 1964. Fundamentals of the theory and investigation of the separation of potatoes from clods and stones. Trakt. i Selkhomash. 34(5): 31-34. (In Russian)

Maack, O. 1957a. Die mechanische Trennung von Kartoffeln und Steinen. Landtechnische Forschung 7(3):71, Munch.

Maack, O. 1957b. Trennung von Kartoffeln und Steinen nach Ruckprallvermogen und Rollwiderstand Landtechnische Forschung 7(4):106, Munch.

McRae, D.C. 1973. Recent development of potato harvesting machinery. The Agricultural Engineer. 28(1).

Misener, G.C., C.D. McLeod and L.P. McMillan. 1984. Evaluation of a prototype potato harvester. Transactons of the ASAE 27(1):24-28.

Mizrach, A., A. Zaltzman, G. Manor and Z. Nir. 1984. Gravitational motion of spheres in a fluidized bed. Transactions of the ASAE 27(6):1674-1678.

Palmer, J. 1961. Electronic sorting of potatoes and clods by their reflectance. Journal of Agricultural Engineering Research 6(1):104.

Petrov, G.D. and E.B. Karev. 1972. Separation potatoes from hard admixtures with use of radio-activated radiation. Trakt. i Selkhomash. 42(1). (In Russian)

Pflug, I.J., M.W. Brandt and D.R. Istler. 1955. Specific gravity potato separator. Quarterly Bulletin, Michigan Agricultural Experiment Station 31(1):29.

Rohrs, F. 1964. Trennung von Kartoffeln und Steinen auf einen Gummifingerband mi Burstenwaezen. Landtechnische Forschung 14(4):106-110, Munch.

Rosel, W. 1963. Trenneinrichtengen zu Machinensystemen fur den Kartoffenhanbau auf gut siebfahigen Boden mit mittlerem bis hohen Steinbesatz. Dtsch. Agrartech. 13(7):324-327, Berl.

Schafer, E. 1959. Tennung der Beimengunen von Kartoffeln in Sammelrodern. Landb. Forsch. 9(2):42, Volkenrode.

Schafer, E. 1960a. Tennung von Kartoffeln und Steinen mit geneigten Bandern. Landtechnische Forschung 10(5):131-137, Munch.

Schafer, E. 1960b. Separating systems according to the coefficient of rolling resistance and specific gravity. Paper, 1st Triennial Conference, European Association for Potato Research, Braunschweig-Volkenrode, 12-17 Sept.

Schafer, E. 1961. Untersuchungen uber die Trennung von Kartoffeln und Steinen mit umlaufenden Trennbursten. Landtechonische Forschung 11(6): 170-175, Munch.

Sides, S.E. and N. Smith. 1970. Analysis and design of potato-stone separation mechanisms. ASAE Paper No. 70-673, ASAE St. Joseph, MI 49085.

Sides, S.E., N. Smith and C.W. Kitteridge. 1974. A summary of potato harvesting developments in Maine. ASAE Paper NO. 74-1510, ASAE St. Joseph MI 49085.

Slight, D.L. 1961. Potato separation using electronic discrimination. Journal of Agricultural Engineering Research, 6:136.

Slight, D.L. 1966. Some x-ray absorption and scatter properties of potatoes and stones. Journal of Agricultural Engineering Research 11(3):148-151.

Srapenyants, R.A. and S.A. Said-Khodzhaev. 1963. Radiosotope method of separating potatoes from clods and stones. Trakt. i Selkhomash. 33(2): 36-39. (In Russian)

193

Srapenyants, R.A. and S.A. Said-Khodzhaev. 1964a.
On the radiometric separation of potato tubers
from admixtures. Trakt. i Selkhomash. 34(3):19-
21. (Translation 154, National Institute of
Agricultural Engineering, Silsoe, England).

Srapenyants, R.A. and S.A. Said-Khodzhaev. 1964b.
Fundamentals of the theory of a gamma-ray detec-
tor for a radiometric potato separator. Mekh.
Electrif. sel. Khoz. 22(1):37-40. (In Russian)

Sohst, J. 1959. Two-stage potato harvest. Tag Ber.
22, dtsch. Akad. LandwWiss.

Story, A.G. and G.S.V. Raghavan. 1973. Sorting
potatoes from stones and soil clods by infrared
reflectance. Transactions of ASAE 16(2):304-
309.

Zabeltitz, C. 1967. Uber die Trennung von Korpern
verschiedener Dichte in einem Fliessbett. VDI-
Zeitschrift. Reihe 14, Nr. 3.

Zaltzman, A., A. Mizrach and Z. Schmilovitch. 1982.
Fluidized bed separator. United States Patent
No. 4, 322, 287.

Zaltzman, A., R. Feller, A. Mizrach and Z.
Schmilovitch. 1983. Separating potatoes from
clods and stones in a fluidized bed medium.
Transactions of ASAE 26(4):987-990, 995.

Zaltzman, A., A. Mizrach and Z. Schmilovitch. 1985a.
Analytical model of a gravitational separation
process in fluidized bed medium. (Unpubl.)
Submitted to the Journal of Agricultural Engineering Research.

Zaltzman, A., Z. Schmilovitch and A. Mizrach. 1985b.
Separating flower bulbs from clods and stones
in a fluidized bed. (Unpubl.). Accepted for
publications in Canadian Agricultural
Engineering.

Zinnovev, E. 1959. Investigation of a fluidized
soil bed as a medium for the separation of
potato tubers from clods and stones. Trakt.
i Selkhomash. 29(12):25-28. (In Russian)

DISCLAIMER

Reference to commercial products, companies, or trade names is with the understanding that no discrimination is intended and no endorsement implied.

ACKNOWLEDGEMENTS

Thanks are due to Dr. Y. Alper for advice in designing the third experimental separator, and Mr. H. Agozi and Mr. A. Hoffman of the Institute of Agricultural Engineering, ARO, The Volcani Center, Bet-Dagan, Israel, for their assistance in experimental works, to Dr. S. Prussia of the University of Georgia (Experiment) for his assistance and advice during the paper preparation, and to Mrs. Kellie Meza and Mrs. Mary Story for typing.

This research was supported by a grant from the United States - Israel Binational Agricultural Research and Development Fund (BARD).

TABLE 1. RESULTS OF FIELD TESTS WITH THE SECOND POTATO PROTOTYPE.

TEST NO.	% Pota-toes in the mixture	Feed rate of the mixture t/h	Feed rate of pota-toes t/h	Percent distribution in the potato-clod-stone mixture								Variety
				clods and stones size, mm				Potato weight, g				
				6.3	6.3-12.5	12.5-25	12.5-50	50	60	60-120	120	
1-4	61.66	20.68	12.75	0.23	1.37	1.58	50.34	46.48	1.10	30.10	68.80	Desire
5-7	79.82	14.75	11.77	0.06	0.11	1.50	81.13	17.20	1.09	7.61	91.30	Dezansa
8-9	82.30	18.90	15.55	0.02	0.05	0.90	98.02	1.01	3.70	21.00	75.30	Care

TABLE 2. TYPICAL RESULTS OF THE FIELD TESTS WITH THE THIRD EXPERIMENTAL FBM SEPARATOR IN COMPARASION WITH X RAY SEPARATOR.
(Potatoes of Alfa variety)

Test No.	Type of Separator	Feed rate of the mixture t/h	% Potatoes in the mixture	% Potato recovery * (A)	% Clod and stone rejec- tion** (B)	Separation effectiveness (A X B, %)
1	FBM	1.17	50.2	100.0	100.0	100.0
2	FBM	2.29	47.7	100.0	98.00	98.0
3	FBM	2.82	52.7	100.0	97.00	97.0
4	FBM	2.95	50.2	100.0	98.0	98.0
5	FBM	4.56	50.2	100.0	98.0	98.0
6	FBM	6.90	50.2	98.0	98.0	96.0
7	X ray	4.60	50.2	64.8	90.0	58.3

* Ratio of potatoes that were discharged at the product exit, to potatoes in the mixture.

** Ratio of clods and stones that were discharged at the rejection exit, to clods and stones in the mixture.

197

TABLE 3. COMPARATIVE CHARACTERISTICS OF FBM EXPERIMENTAL SEPARATORS.

Separator No.	Dimensions of FBM, m			Coefficients of effective usage of FBM		Maximum theoretical capacity of FBM (for potatoes) t/h	Actual achieved capacity t/h	Power expense for air supply per 1 t/h of actual capacity hp	Amount of sand per 1 t/h of actual capacity m^3	Actual capacity per 1m^2 area of FBM, t/h
	Length/Width/Depth			Width k	Depth n					
1	2.5	1.80	0.60	0.4	0.28	11.6	5.0	1.40	0.54	1.11
2	2.5	2.2	0.60	0.9	0.83	26.0	22.0	0.74	0.15	4.00
3	2.5	0.64	0.30	1.0	0.66	20.9	8.0	0.30	0.06	5.00

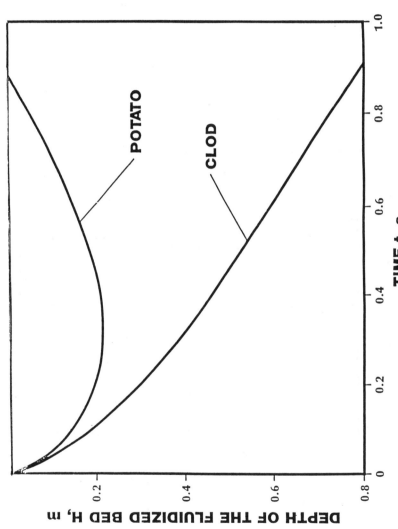

FIG. 1 Trajectories of potatoes and clods introduced in a sand FBM with initial velocity (sizes of potato and clod 0.1m; clod density 1700 kg/m³; potato density 1050 kg/m³; clod density 2300 kg/m³; diameter of sand particles 0.3mm; drop height of the mixture μ = 0.5m). ¯

199

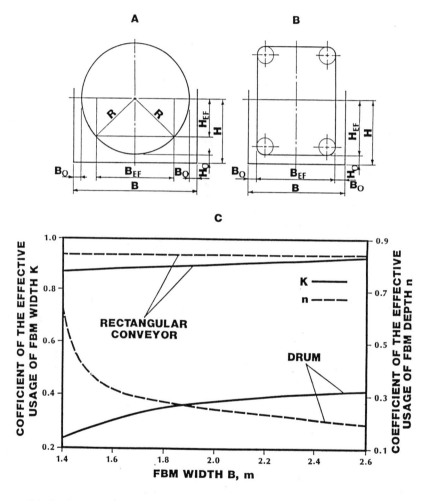

FIG. 2. Schemes and comparative characteristics of drum and rectangular conveyor.
a) drum; b) rectangular conveyor; and c) the characteristics.

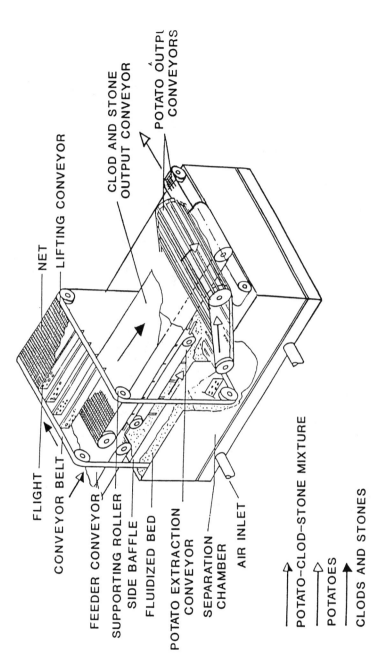

FLIGHT

CONVEYOR BELT

FEEDER CONVEYOR

SUPPORTING ROLLER

SIDE BAFFLE

FLUIDIZED BED

POTATO EXTRACTION
CONVEYOR

SEPARATION
CHAMBER

AIR INLET

NET

LIFTING CONVEYOR

CLOD AND STONE
OUTPUT CONVEYOR

POTATO OUTPU
CONVEYORS

POTATO-CLOD-STONE MIXTURE

POTATOES

CLODS AND STONES

FIG. 3. Schematic drawing of the second experimental potato FBM separator.

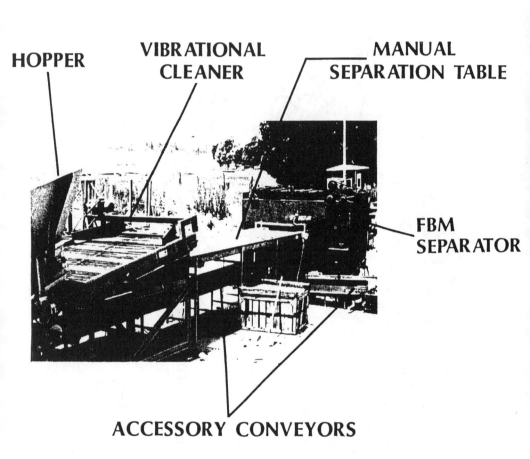

HOPPER **VIBRATIONAL CLEANER** **MANUAL SEPARATION TABLE**

FBM SEPARATOR

ACCESSORY CONVEYORS

FIG. 4. Line for preparing and supplying the mixture into second potato FBM separator.

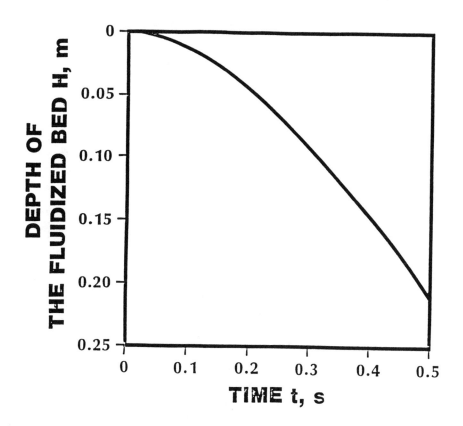

FIG. 5. A trajectory of clod introduced in a sand FBM with zero-order initial
velocity (size of clod 0.1m; clod density 1700 kg/m^3; density of sand
particles 2300 kg/m^3; diameter of sand particles 0.3 mm).

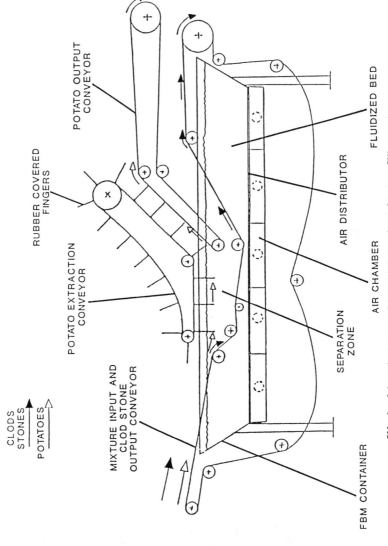

CLODS
STONES ▲
POTATOES ⇨

MIXTURE INPUT AND
CLOD STONE
OUTPUT CONVEYOR

POTATO EXTRACTION
CONVEYOR

RUBBER COVERED
FINGERS

POTATO OUTPUT
CONVEYOR

SEPARATION
ZONE

AIR CHAMBER

AIR DISTRIBUTOR

FLUIDIZED BED

FBM CONTAINER

FIG. 6.   Schematic drawing of the third experimental potato FBM separator.

POTATO EXTRACTION CONVEYOR

FEEDING AND CLOD-STONE OUTPUT CONVEYOR

FLUIDIZED BED MEDIUM CONTAINER

AIR CHAMBER

FIG. 7. The third experimental potato FBM separator.

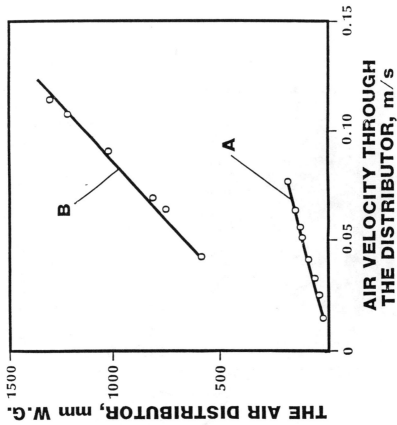

RESISTANCE OF THE AIR DISTRIBUTOR, mm W.G.

AIR VELOCITY THROUGH THE DISTRIBUTOR, m/s

FIG. 8. Comparative characteristics of air distributors: a) New air distributor, and b) Air distributor in 250 hours of operations.

THE SIZE AND SHAPE OF TYPICAL SWEET POTATOES

by

Malcolm E. Wright, Professor; John H. Tappen, Undergraduate; Fred E. Sistler, Associate Professor; Agricultural Engineering Department, Louisana Agricultural Experiment Station, Baton Rouge, Louisiana

ABSTRACT

A total of 457 U.S. grade number one sweet potatoes of four common commercial varieties, 199 from the 1983 crop and 258 from 1984, were measured using an image analysis system. Each potato was suspended in front of a light source and image edge data was taken for 18 views, 10 degrees of rotation apart, about its longitudinal axis. These data, plus measured weight and volume, were recorded on diskettes. The acquired data were used in an algorithm to calculate volume and surface areas. The mean difference for calculated minus measured volume was −1.92 percent. The range of differences was from −10.58 to +8.77 percent. Several possible sources of measurement error are discussed. Other programs were written to determine normalized averaged shapes for comparison of varieties and

ASAE Paper No. 85-6017

growing areas, to compare sweet potato shapes with
prolate spheroids, and to determine functional
relationships with which to predict surface area from
easily obtained measurements.

INTRODUCTION

The mensural characteristics of agricultural
products are very important in many engineering
design and research applications. Knowledge of
length, width, volume, surface area, and location of
center of mass may be applied in the design of
sorting machinery, in predicting amounts of surface
applied chemicals, in describing heat and mass
transfer during thermal processing, in quantification
of bruise, abrasion, and insect damage, and in
estimating yield in peeling operations. Minvielle,
et al. (1981) presented a brief history of
mensuration of agricultural products. Before the
advent of video image analysis techniques, the
acquisiton of size and shape data was very tedious
and time consuming, often of questionable accuracy.
For example, one method of finding surface area was
to carefully peel the fruit or vegetable, photograph
the flattened peeling and then use a planimeter on
the image. Because the amount of work involved, only
a limited number of samples could be measured. One
standard procedure was to attempt to fit this limited
data to a known geometric shape which could then be
substituted into the engineering design process as a
best estimate of the actual product. Apples,
oranges, and white potatoes might be represented by
spheres; bananas and ear corn by cylinders; and
carrots by cones.

Minvielle, et al. also reported on an algorithm
developed to acquire image edge data from solid
objects with convex surfaces and used it to calculate
volume, surface area and location of center of mass.
All points on the cross section peripheries were
connected by straight lines and the surface was
estimated from the polyhedron formed by a series of
contiguous triangular planes. This algorithm was
improved by fitting parabolic line segments to
adjacent points on the periphery of each cross
section (Sistler, Wright and Watson; and Wright,
Sistler, and Watson, 1984). It was tested on 12
sweet potatoes with acceptable results.

Few agricultural products are as irregular in shape as are sweet potatoes, although a "standard" shape is easily recognized. The size range for U.S. grade number 1 sweet potatoes includes diameters from 50.8 to 88.9 mm (2 to 3.5 in.) and lengths from 76.2 to 228.6 mm (3 to 9 in.). Many sizes and shapes lie within these specifications. Mechanical grading is used only to remove the smallest sizes (seed potatoes). Removing misshapen, damaged and oversized potatoes and selecting the number 1's is done subjectively by workers on packing lines when the potatoes are cleaned and packed for retail sale.

Tappan (1984) initiated the work reported in this paper by measuring 199 number 1 grade sweet potatoes using the video image analyzer. The objectives of this research were:

1. To acquire and store image data for a large number of number 1 grade sweet potatoes, and

2. To use the stored data to determine certain physical characteristics of the potatoes.

EXPERIMENTAL EQUIPMENT AND METHODS

The major components in the image analysis system are depicted in Figures 1 and 2. They included a vertically mounted light table with object holder, a video camera, a black and white video monitor, a color digitizer monitor, and a Datacube, Inc. model VG-120D digitizer board mounted in an Intel system 86/330A microcomputer. The first batch of 199 potatoes from the 1983 harvest was analyzed using a Cohu model 4410 vidicon camera with a 17.5 to 105 mm zoom lens. The second batch of 158 potatoes from the 1984 harvest was measured with Pulnix TM-34 KAB CCD camera using a 12.5 to 75 mm zoom lens.

Samples of approximately 20 to 40 potatoes were obtained from growers and from the Sweet Potato Research Station, Agricultural Experiment Station, LSU Agricultrual Center. The potatoes were selected at random from storage bins or packing lines and represented number 1 U.S. grade as normally selected by packing line workers for retail sale. The

209

varieties sampled were Centennial, Jewel, and Travis; the four most common commercial varieties in Louisana.

The dry weight of each potato was measured to 0.01 gram on a Mettler balance. Its volume was then obtained by measuring the buoyant force required to submerge it in water. Corrections were made in these measurements to account for the temperature of the water.

Prior to making any measurements with the image analyzer both the mounting stand and the camera were leveled. A calibration factor was obtained by measuring the length and height, in pixels, of a flat metal plate of known size placed in the potato holder in front of the light table.

For data collection each potato was held with a skewer in front of the light table. It was initially oriented so that the principal curve of its "backbone" was in a plane normal to the axis of the camera and lens with the concavity facing to the left when viewed from the camera.

The data collection program was interactive, requesting a descriptor code for each potato, weight, volume and pixel calibration factor. A cutoff grey level to separate the image from the lighted background could be set by the operator. To initiate data collection, a cursor was placed at the juncture of the skewer and the top of the potato on the first digitized image. From this point the program followed the outline of the potato, taking location data on the leftmost and rightmost pixel in each row of the image. When this process was completed, a tone sounded to signal the operator to turn the indexing wheel (see Figure 2) that held the skewer so that the next image could be captured. A four-second delay was built in to the program to allow for this operation. The indentations on the indexing wheel were 10 degrees apart, yielding 18 images per potato.

A second program used the acquired data to calculate the volume and surface area of each potato. A cross section was formed at each pixel row within the length of the potato by making calculations on the data. Because each cross section was one pixel high its area represented volume and its perimeter, area. Volume and surface area for the whole potato were then found by summation. These calculations, done in FORTRAN, required approximately one minute per potato.

A third program was written to normalize the individual potato data so that "typical" potato shapes could be generated. Using the data bank, each potato was "sliced" at ten equally spaced increments Thirty-six radii were generated from the center of each slice to the surface. All of the dimensions thus produced were then divided by the length of the potato. These dimensionless numbers could then be averaged for groups of potatoes to produce composite shapes.

RESULTS AND DISCUSSION

Figure 3 shows the composite outlines of the four varieties as generated from the measured data for all of the 457 potatoes. The shapes were similar with few distinctions, except overall length.

The slight curve to the central axis or "backbone" was as expected. The lengths and the width/length ratios, listed below, correspond with subjective evaluations of the relative characteristics of the varieties. They also confirm that size and shape are relatively consistent from year to year.

	1983	1984	Combined
Jasper	.377	.409	.392
Centennial	.392	.384	.386
Travis	.420	.437	.427
Jewel	.442	.466	.455

These composite volumes will be used in future studies to develop algorithms for sweet potato sorting routines. Because the shapes of individual potatoes vary so much within the number 1 grade it is possible that one or more standard deviations could

211

be added to the composite shape to provide an envelope volume with which to compare potatoes being sorted.

For the 199 potatoes from the 1983 harvest the overall results of calculated minus measured volume were:

Mean difference = -7.21%
Standard deviation of difference = 1.76%
Minimum difference = -10.58%
Maximum difference = -0.24%

For the 258 potatoes from the 1984 harvest the overall results of calculated minus measured volume were:

Mean difference = 2.63%
Standard deviation of difference = 2.27%
Minimum difference = -6.84%
Maximum difference = 8.77%

Several sources of error are being studied as possible explanations of the differences between measured and calculated values. Diffused light from the light table did not always produce silhouettes with clearly defined edges. Ambient light also may have had some effect.

The vidicon camera had an auto-black circuit which changed the image size as a function of the amount of darkness in the viewed scene. This feature was not discovered until the data for the 1983 potatoes had been taken.

Pixel shape tended to be rectangular rather than square, a fact discovered during calibration procedures. Moreover, the aspect ratio tended to vary slightly from test to test.

Image area also tended to vary with screen location. The effect of this source of error was probably negligible because all measurements in these tests were made in the same general area of the screen.

The color digitizer board did not use all of the available 64 grey levels because internal switches were not set to maximum scale. Instructions on the feature were not in the manual available at the time the data was taken. Histograms of the grey levels were compressed between levels 24 and 63. The distribution patterns of the grey levels were always bimodal, but selecting the best cutoff level between the light and dark peaks was made more sensitive by the diminished range.

The algorithm for calculating volume and surface area was also a source of error but earlier curve fitting tests using generated data (Sistler, Wright, and Watson, 1984) indicated that these errors could be assumed to be small in comparison to the measurement errors cited above. The volume of an irregularly-shaped object can be measured accurately and with a good degree of repeatability. The surface area, on the other hand, is extremely difficult to measure with either accuracy or repeatability. Because volume is a function of length cubed and surface area a function of length squared it may be assumed that the error in the surface area calculations will always be less than the volume error.

Table 1 displays the consolidated data on the physical properties of the sample potatoes arranged by variety. These data indicate that the Jasper variety was the largest in physical size but the lowest in density. The Jewels had the smallest ratio of surface area to volume (0.75) indicating that they were the most compact. They were also the most dense, although a high specific gravity does not imply a high dry matter content. One possible future use for data of this type would be the comparison of promising experimental varieties with those currently in commercial production.

Table 2 contains the same data as does Table 1 but rearranged according to source. This demonstrates that shape analysis has the potential of showing individual growers how the quality of their product compares with others. Image analysis may also prove useful in the future as a quality control on a regional or soil-type basis.

The prolate spheroid appears to be the most logical common geometric shape with which to compare the sweet potato. Several variations of prolate spheriods based on the measured volumes of the potatoes were fitted to the data. As a measure of goodness of fit in each case, the mean surface area as calculated directly from the acquired data was compared with that calculated by using the surface area equation for the spheriod. In the third case, the measured and calculated volumes were also compared.

The equations of the prolate spheroid are:

$$V = 4/3 \; \pi \; ab^2 \quad\text{--(1)}$$

$$A = 2\pi b \; + 2\pi ab \; \frac{\sin^{-1} e}{e} \quad\text{----------------------------(2)}$$

Where:
  V = volume
  A = surface area
  a = the semi-major axis
  b = the semi-minor axis

  $e = \dfrac{\sqrt{a^2 - b^2}}{a}$, the eccentricity

The three best cases and their results were:

1. Using equation (1), the measured volume, and the measured length, a semi-minor axis, b, was calculated for each potato. Then, using equation (2), the surface areas were calculated. The mean error for surface area was 7.73 percent with a standard deviation of 4.50 percent.

2. The ratio of the maximum width to the length was determined for each potato from the stored data. Using this ratio, the measured volume and equation (1) the dimensions a and b were calculated. These dimensions were then used to calculate surface areas. The mean error for surface area was 5.12 percent with a standard deviation of 4.95 percent.

3. An assumption was made that fixed ratio of the major and minor axes of the prolate spheroid to the length and maximum width of each potato could be used to generate comparable volumes. Using an iterative approach, a ratio of 0.918 was found to produce the best combination of

volumes and surface areas of the actual potatoes. For these conditions the mean error for volume was -2.784 percent with a standard deviation of 12.67 percent. The mean error for surface area was 2.80 percent with a standard deviation of 8.16 percent.

In all three of the above cases the range of error for individual potatoes was quite wide. In the future other shapes or combinations of shapes can be tested against the stored data with ease. The large quantity of data available for these tests, compared to previous techniques of measurement, will give greater credence to the results.

Four sets of calculations were made to develop means of predicting surface area. These results are depicted in Figures 4 through 8. The length times width parameter gave the best prediction with a correlation coefficient of r^2 = 0.901. This parameter is, unfortunately, not the most convenient to measure; nor is the volume, which also correlated well with surface area. Because most mechanical sorters sort on the basis of width, it is the parameter most easily measured under commercial conditions. However, its correlation with surface area was only r^2 = 0.467. These and similar relationships may prove useful in future studies of surface applied chemicals and peeling operations.

REFERENCES

Minvielle, D.P., F.E. Sistler, M.E. Wright, and T.R. Way. 1981. Digital analysis of the shape characteristics of agricultural products. ASAE paper no. 81-3536. St. Joseph, MI.

Sistler, F.E., M.E. Wright, and R.M. Watson. 1984. Measurement of physical properties of biological products with a video analyzer. Proceedings of the National Conference on Agricultural Electonics Applications. ASAE Publication 9-84, St. Joseph, MI.

Tappan, J.H. 1984. Image analysis of sweet potatoes --a report on volume calculations and sources of error. Unpublished undergraduate research report. Agricultural Engineering Department, Louisiana State University, Baton Rouge, La.

Wright, M.E., F.E. Sistler, and R.M. Watson. 1984. Measuring sweet potato size and shape with a computer. Louisiana Agriculture, 28(1):12-13.

TABLE 1. PHYSICAL PROPERTIES OF SWEET POTATOES
BY VARIETY

Variety		Minimum	Maximum	Mean	Std. Dev.
CENTENNIAL	Length (cm):	10.1	23.6	15.44	2.56
Sample Size: 131	Weight (g):	103.2	513.9	237.0	72.3
	Specific Gravity:	0.785	0.951	0.885	0.034
	Surface Area (cm2):	133.1	342.8	215.5	44.9
	Measured Volume (cm3):	118.1	569.0	268.3	82.6
	Calculated Volume (cm3):	119.6	585.6	263.8	83.0
	Volume Difference (%):	-10.53	6.03	-1.69	5.08
JASPER	Length (cm):	11.3	24.7	15.83	2.65
Sample Size: 124	Weight (g):	99.9	577.6	246.9	84.9
	Specific Gravity:	0.674	0.920	0.846	0.044
	Surface Area (cm2):	146.5	454.5	227.7	56.2
	Measured Volume (cm3):	136.3	634.3	291.1	97.1
	Calculated Volume (cm3):	126.7	673.3	291.0	106.0
	Volume Difference (%):	-8.81	8.77	-0.87	5.48
JEWEL	Length (cm):	8.5	19.8	13.68	2.12
Sample Size: 133	Weight (g):	117.5	507.5	268.6	85.8
	Specific Gravity:	0.800	1.004	0.956	0.037
	Surface Area (cm2):	122.8	341.1	205.5	45.9
	Measured Volume (cm3):	121.6	526.1	272.4	87.9
	Calculated Volume (cm3):	123.4	552.0	268.9	93.0
	Volume Difference (%):	-10.58	6.28	-1.74	5.46
TRAVIS	Length (cm):	9.5	20.6	14.08	2.48
Sample Size: 69	Weight (g):	106.9	529.9	231.5	101.1
	Specific Gravity:	0.862	0.986	0.932	0.034
	Surface Area (cm2):	122.2	337.4	192.6	50.0
	Measured Volume (cm3):	115.1	569.9	247.9	106.1
	Calculated Volume (cm3):	103.4	579.9	242.7	110.4
	Volume Difference (%):	-10.24	4.96	-2.85	4.91

TABLE 2.   PHYSICAL PROPERTIES OF SWEET POTATOES

BY SOURCE

Source		Minimum	Maximum	Mean	Std. Dev.
BRUCE	Length (cm):	10.5	17.5	13.71	2.00
Sample Size: 20	Weight (g):	130.4	507.5	346.1	100.5
	Specific Gravity:	0.954	1.004	0.977	0.011
	Surface Area (cm2):	136.8	336.8	242.2	53.6
	Measured Volume (cm3):	134.4	526.1	354.0	111.0
	Calculated Volume (cm3):	138.4	552.0	371.6	116.8
	Volume Difference (%):	2.96	6.17	4.92	0.86
CHASE	Length (cm):	9.5	21.7	14.40	2.24
Sample Size: 206	Weight (g):	106.9	529.9	239.6	70.8
	Specific Gravity:	0.744	1.003	0.915	0.051
	Surface Area (cm2):	122.2	337.4	203.7	41.9
	Measured Volume (cm3):	115.1	569.9	262.7	78.3
	Calculated Volume (cm3):	103.4	579.9	256.6	83.9
	Volume Difference (%):	-10.24	8.77	-2.95	5.08
DUCOTE	Length (cm):	10.1	24.7	15.66	2.67
Sample Size: 97	Weight (g):	99.9	460.6	221.2	78.1
	Specific Gravity:	0.674	0.928	0.855	0.044
	Surface Area (cm2):	134.7	327.6	211.3	48.2
	Measured Volume (cm3):	136.3	517.4	258.3	89.6
	Calculated Volume (cm3):	126.7	488.3	251.1	86.6
	Volume Difference (%):	-10.53	8.27	-2.71	5.09
FIELDS	Length (cm):	12.4	19.1	15.42	1.59
Sample Size: 14	Weight (g):	171.6	481.2	294.0	90.6
	Specific Gravity:	0.845	0.958	0.924	0.039
	Surface Area (cm2):	167.2	326.2	229.0	45.0
	Measured Volume (cm3):	181.8	507.4	318.9	98.8
	Calculated Volume (cm3):	162.6	471.8	293.5	93.5
	Volume Difference (%):	-10.58	-6.67	-8.22	1.17
E. FONTENOT	Length (cm):	11.0	23.3	15.25	2.78
Sample Size: 40	Weight (g):	103.2	477.4	243.5	86.3
	Specific Gravity:	0.852	1.002	0.942	0.041
	Surface Area (cm2):	133.1	341.1	212.4	49.8
	Measured Volume (cm3):	118.1	490.5	257.7	88.1
	Calculated Volume (cm3):	119.6	503.3	261.4	90.3
	Volume Difference (%):	-0.24	5.47	1.33	1.06
NEWTON	Length (cm):	8.5	24.7	14.90	3.26
Sample Size: 80	Weight (g):	114.8	577.6	258.9	96.6
	Specific Gravity:	0.726	0.997	0.884	0.055
	Surface Area (cm2):	122.8	454.5	226.1	66.8
	Measured Volume (cm3):	121.6	634.3	294.3	111.3
	Calculated Volume (cm3):	123.4	673.3	299.4	120.7
	Volume Difference (%):	-10.29	8.32	0.95	5.20

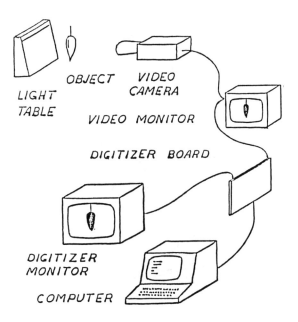

OBJECT VIDEO
CAMERA

LIGHT
TABLE

VIDEO MONITOR

DIGITIZER BOARD

DIGITIZER
MONITOR

COMPUTER

Figure 1. Image Analysis System.

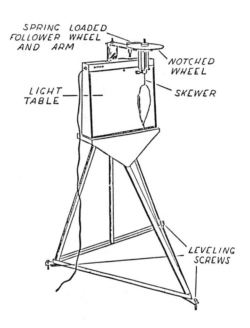

Figure 2. Potato Mounting Stand.

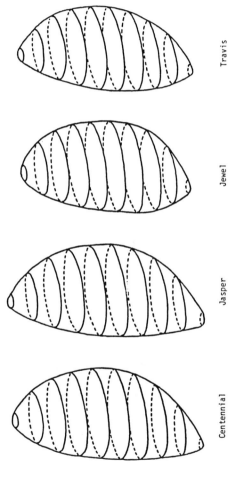

Centennial   Jasper   Jewel   Travis

Figure 3. Composite shapes for each variety of sweet potato measured.

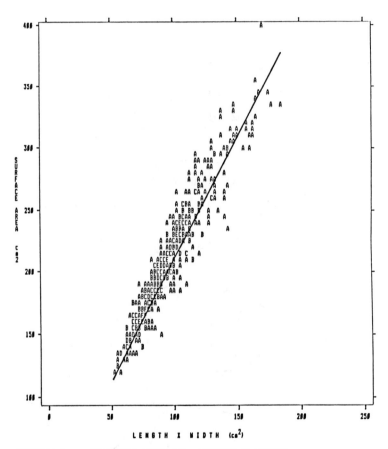

FIGURE 4.   SURFACE AREA VS. LENGTH X WIDTH

NOTE: A = 1 occurrence, B = 2, etc. 456 observations shown, 1 hidden.
Linear regression equation: Y = 1.918 I + 25.08. Correlation coefficient: r^2 = 0.901.

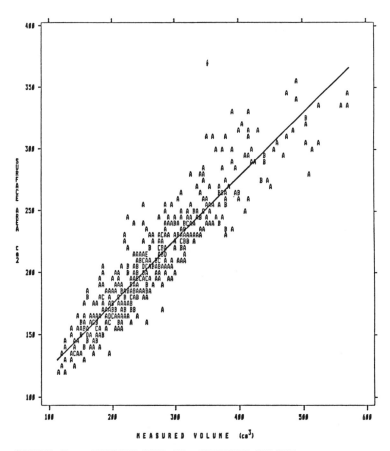

FIGURE 5.   SURFACE AREA VS. MEASURED VOLUME

NOTE: A = 1 occurrence, B = 2, etc. 455 observations shown,   2 hidden.
Linear regression equation: Y = 0.511 X + 73.15. Correlation coefficient: r^2 = 0.879.

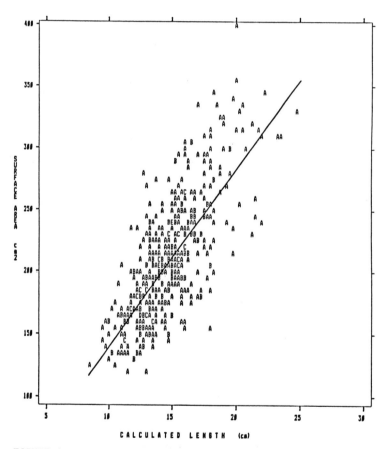

FIGURE 6.   SURFACE AREA VS. CALCULATED LENGTH

NOTE: A = 1 occurrence, B = 2, etc. 456 observations shown, 1 hidden.
Linear regression equation: Y = 14.57 X + 3.56. Correlation coefficient: r^2 = 0.568.

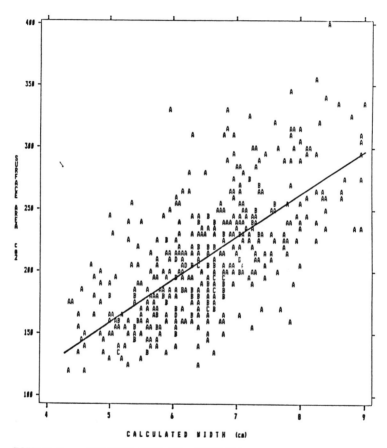

FIGURE 7.   SURFACE AREA VS. MAXIMUM WIDTH

NOTE: A = 1 occurrence, B = 2, etc.   451 observations shown,   6 hidden.
Linear regression equation: Y = 34.20 X - 11.96.   Correlation coefficient: r^2 = 0.467.

ALGORITHMS FOR DETERMINING TUBER SHAPE AND CUTTING POTATO SEED PIECES

by

Marvin J. Pitts, Assistant Professor and Gary M.
Hyde, Associate Profesor, Agricultural Engineering
Department; Robert E. Thornton, Extension
Horticulturist, Horticulture Department,
Washington State University

ABSTRACT

Conventional potato seed cutting produces a
variety of shapes and waste. Tubers were modeled as
an elliptical surface of revolution. Seven seed
piece shapes were defined. Criteria for seed piece
shape and tuber cutting patterns were given. Cutting
patterns were predicted by tuber length and width.

BACKGROUND

Lack of uniform stands in potato (Solanum
Tuberosum) fields may be costing Pacific Northwest
potato growers over $150 per hectare ($60.75 per

ASAE Paper No. 85-6018

acre) in lost production and inefficiency due to inappropriate seed sizing and irregular seed spacing (Schotzko et al., 1983). Commercial potatoes are grown in North America by planting pieces of potato tubers especially grown for that purpose. This planting procedure (really cloning) requires over a tonne (22cwt) of seed pieces per hectare (2.47 c) and is used because planting true seed would result in large variability in tuber type and quality from plant to plant.

The lack of uniformity in seed piece size and spacing is the accumulation of many minor problems related not only to the potato planter but to the potato seed cutting operation and even to the seed potato production.

The two most common types of potato planters currently used in the Pacific Northwest are cup-type and pick-type planters. In the former, cups attached to an endless chain move upward through a seed reservoir, pick up seed pieces, and convey them to the point where they drop into the planting shoe. In the pick planter, sharp picks are mounted on arms, which in turn are mounted on a wheel. As the wheel rotates the arm through the seed reservoir (or picking bowl), a seed piece is impaled on the picks and then is conveyed by the arm to a point where the picks are retracted and the seed piece drops into the planting shoe.

Difficulties arise when the cup or pick mechanism fails to convey a seed piece, or when it conveys two or more at a time. Irregular spacing of seed pieces in the field results in loss of efficiency and yield potential.

A large portion of the difficulty in selecting and conveying seed pieces one at a time arises from the lack of uniformity in size and shape of the cut seed pieces. Two basic systems of automatic cutters are currently used. One type used fixed blades to cut the tubers into four or six pieces. The other type uses a combination of a set of closely spaced rotating disk blades mounted on a common shaft to cut the tubers transversely into short lengths, and then a fixed knife makes one longitudinal cut for large tubers. For medium size tubers, the longitudinal cut is eliminated.

227

Both types of cutters generally use roll sizing systems to separate the seed tubers into three fractions: large tubers, medium tubers, and "single drop" tubers (those that need not be cut at all). The difficulty with the roll sizers is that they size by the smallest rather than the greatest dimension of the tuber. With the fixed-blade cutters, people are required to help direct the tubers through the appropriate blades. In the rotating disk-type cutters, there is no means of referencing tuber position with respect to one end, and many of the tubers end up with small slices (chips) cut off both ends with resultant waste or, if the chips are not sorted out, a worse situation where the chips are planted in the field in place of viable seed pieces.

From the standpoint of handling and singulation, ideal potato seed piece shapes would be spheres of uniform size. Whole tubers may approach this ideal, but since cut seed performance is as good as or superior to that of whole tubers (Cordner 1940; Iritani et al., 1972, and Thornton et al., 1985), and production of whole tubers of the desired size (45 to 60g) is much too low to meet seed requirements in North America, the best alternative is to cut the seed potatoes into blocky pieces of uniform shape and size (each with at least one eye, of course).

Likhyani (1981) found in planter experiments that planting precision improved if only end cut seed pieces were used. End cut seed pieces gave a higher percentage of correct spacings than center cut seed pieces for both Norland and Netted Gem (Russett Burbank) cultivars. He speculated that the end cut pieces have more rounded surface area, while the center cut pieces have more flat cut surface area and thus an increased chance of seed pieces sticking either together or to the planter hopper, in turn increasing the chances of both doubles and misses. The shape of the center cut pieces was not described by Likhyani, but relatively thin disk shaped pieces (large amount of cut surface area) would tend to adhere more than blockier shapes (those with minimized cut surface-to-volume ratio). Cut surface-to-volume ratio should probably be minimized also to maintain seed vigor by minimizing dehydration and exposure to seed piece decay (Nelson 1976).

OBJECTIVE

The overall goal of this research effort is to increase the uniformity of spacing between potato plants in production fields. As a first step toward this goal, we have attempted to improve potato planter performance by cutting seed pieces into more uniform shapes. To model the tuber and seed pieces, the following objectives were identified:

1. define a mathematical model of a potato seed tuber
2. select criteria (based on geometrical properties) to judge individual seed pieces
3. select criteria (based on geometrical properties) to judge the cutting of the seed tuber
4. choose a method to determine individual cutting pattern of a seed tuber in a production environment

Potato tubers are approximately ellipsoidal in shape; i.e., they are approximately elliptical in both longitudinal and transverse cross sections. The amount of eccentricity varies considerably within a given cultivar. Some cultivars, such as the Russett Burbank, are elongated while other cultivars, such as Norchip, are more blocky or spherical in shape.

There are two ellipse-based models which could be used to describe the tuber. In one model, each of the three diameters are distinct, and the potato is modeled as an ellipsoid, ie.

$$1 = \frac{x^2}{a^2} + \frac{y^2}{b^2} + \frac{z^2}{c^2}$$

where
$a = \frac{1}{2}$ the major axis of the ellipse
$b = \frac{1}{2}$ the second axis
$c = \frac{1}{2}$ the third axis   (1)

If the two smaller diameters are the same, the tuber can be defined by a surface of revolution of an ellipse.

$$1 = \frac{x^2}{a^2} + \frac{y^2 + z^2}{b^2}$$

where   a and b are defined as above   (2)

The first model (eq. 1) is a more complete description of the tuber shape, but requires three independent measurements of the tuber (length, width, and height). The second model (eq. 2) assumes that the width is equal to the height, and reduces the number of measurements to two, at the expense of a less complete description of the tuber.

In preliminary experiments the length, width, height, and mass were determined for over 50 seed tubers of each two cultivars (Russett Burbank, and Norchip). Linear regression analysis showed that the Russett Burbank tuber mass could be estimated with an R-square of .96 from the length and width or length and height of the tuber; or with an R-square of .97 using length, width and height. For the Norchip cultivar, the length, width R-square was .95 and the length-width-height R-square was .96. Simply stated, it is possible to estimate the mass of the tuber within 5 percent simply by measuring its length and width. The result is precise enough for cutting seed potatoes, and means that we need only use the silhouette maxima and minima dimensions to determine the size and shape of the tuber.

In this study, the surface of revolution of an ellipse was used to model seed tubers. The volume of a tuber defined by equation 2 is:

$$\text{tuber volume} = \frac{8 \pi ab^2}{3}$$

where   a = ½ major axis
        b = ½ minor axis   (3)

230

SEED PIECE DESCRIPTION

As stated earlier, a viable seed piece must contain at least one eye, enough mass (45 to 60g or 1.2 to 2 oz.) to support the plant during germination, be of blocky shape, and minimize the amount of cut surface. For this study, an assumption was made that a seed piece of at least the minimum mass and whose surface area is mostly skin-covered rather than cut, will contain at least one eye. This assumption is valid for Russett Burbank, and Norgold (two common varieties in Washington).

The potential variation in seed piece shape is quite large. In this study, four basic shapes were chosen. The first shape is that of a whole tuber (0-cut) whose mass is too low to require cutting (Figure 2a). The second shape is a disk (1-cut) formed by slicing the seed piece from the tuber in only one plane. The cross section of a 1-cut seed piece is a full circle (Figure 2b). The third shape (2-cut) is formed by cutting a 1-cut piece in half along a plane perpendicular to the plane of the first cut. The cross section of a 2-cut seed piece is a half circle (Figure 2c). The last seed piece shape (4-cut) is formed by cutting the 2-cut piece in half along a plane perpendicular to the planes of the two previous cuts. The cross section of a 4-cut is a quarter circle (Figure 2d).

Because the last three seed piece shapes can appear anywhere in the seed tuber, six distinct shapes are possible, three shapes in which the seed piece contains a tuber end (Figure 3a) and three shapes which do not include tuber end (Figure 3b). Addition of the 0-cut shape (whole tuber) brings the total number of seed piece shapes to seven.

The blockiness of a given seed piece shape depends on the shape of the seed tuber. For example, a 4-cut seed piece from a spherical shaped seed tuber would be very blocky, but a 4-cut from a tuber of similar mass but long and slender would be quite long and thin and not blocky.

In examining ways to measure the relative amount of cut surface area on a seed piece to the amount of

surface covered by potato skin, it became apparent
that in the four shapes defined above, a small cut
surface-to-skin covered surface ratio indicated not
only that the seed piece had a relatively small
amount of cut surface area but also that the seed
piece was blocky in shape.

The ratio is also a good indicator of the amount
of cut surface. A 0-cut seed piece has a ratio of
zero, a computationally valid value, and only a seed
piece with no skin covered surface (an impossible
situation) will have an infinite ratio value.

A second criteria to judge the amount of cut
surface area is the ratio of cut surface area to the
total surface area (cut surface area plus the skin
covered surface area) of the seed piece. The extreme
values for this ratio are zero (0-cut piece) and one
(no skin covered area).

Comparison of the ratios indicate that the
cut/skin surface ratio increases parabolically with
increasing cut surface area while the cut/total
surface area ratio increases linearly with increasing
cut surface area. Either ratio would serve as a
measurement for the criteria to minimize cut surface
area. Because the cut surface area-to-the-skin
covered area ratio has the potential to go to
infinity, this ratio was used in the study to
determine an actual range of ratio values that would
occur in production.

In order to predict the mass of a seed piece, an
equation computing the volume of the seed piece was
found by applying the starting and ending points
(Figure 1) to the seed piece (measured along the
major axis) to the integration which formed equation
3. The equation to compute seed piece volume is:

$$\text{Seed piece volume} = \text{Spovl} = \frac{2\pi b^2}{N}\left(X - \frac{X^3}{3a^2}\right)\Bigg|_{X_{low}}^{X=X_{high}}$$

where a and b = ½ major and ½ minor axis
       X_{high} = right end of seed piece
       X_{low} = left end of seed piece
       N = number of cuts
              (1 for 1-cut, 2 for 2-cut,
              4 for 4-cut)

(4)

232

In most applications, the desired mass of the seed piece and X_{low} , one boundary edge of the seed piece (the mathematics assume the left end as shown in Figure 1), are known, and X_{high} (the other boundary edge) must be found. Equation 4 can be solved for X_{high}, but will require solving a third order polynomial which contains one real and two imaginary roots. Equation 4 rearranged to find X_{high} is:

$$X_{high}^3 - 3a^2 X_{high} + 3a^2 (\frac{N*spvol}{2\pi b^2} + X_{low}$$

$$- \frac{X_{low}^3}{3a^2}) = 0 \qquad (5)$$

Substituting c for $-3a^2$, d for the last term and X for X_{high}: $\qquad X^3 + cX + d = 0 \qquad (6)$

This form of a cubic equation can be solved by algebraic form, by trigonometric substitution, or by an iterative process (Selby 1970). The computation of the roots directly will require complex math. Solving the roots using the trigonometric substitution may require the use of a hyperbolic cosine. Because computer implementations of complex math and hyperbolic functions are computationally intensive, the iterative process was chosen using an increment of 1/100 of the length of the major axis. The error in the determination of X_{high} is no more than 1 percent. and the error in the mass of the seed piece is less than 0.33 percent.

Once the volume is determined, mass can be computed by multiplying the volume by the density of potatoes (about 1.05 g/ml or .061 oz. per cubic inch).

The cut surface area of the seed piece was computed as:

cut surface area =

$$\frac{\pi}{N} b (2 - \frac{X_{high}^2 + X_{low}^2}{a^2}) \qquad (7)$$

and the skin covered surface as:

$$\frac{2\pi}{N} b \sqrt{\frac{a^2-b^2}{a^2}} \left(\frac{X}{2} \sqrt{\frac{a^4}{a^2-b^2} - X^2} + \frac{a^4}{a^2-b^2} \sin^{-1} \right.$$

$$\left. (\frac{X}{a^2} \sqrt{a^2-b^2}) \right) \Bigg|^{X=X_{high}}_{X_{low}} \tag{8}$$

CUTTING PATTERN CRITERIA

In the section above, criteria were established to judge cutting on an individual seed piece. Because of geometrical restrictions, the shape of a seed piece is directly related to how other seed pieces are cut. For example, a 140g (4.95 oz.) seed tuber should be divided into three seed pieces. Two patterns of cuts are possible: one consisting of three 1-cut pieces (111 pattern), and a second pattern consisting of one 1-cut piece and two 2-cut pieces (12 pattern). These two patterns result in different seed piece shapes (Figure 4). Which pattern is better for the overall tuber performance is not obvious.

The eccentricity of the ellipse also affects the way in which a seed tuber should be divided. Two tubers with an equal mass of 190g (6.71 oz.) should be divided into four seed pieces each. If one tuber is spherical in shape, the tuber would be cut into four 4-cut seed pieces. If the other tuber is cylindrical in shape, the cutting pattern would most likely be four 1-cut seed pieces (Figure 5). Interchanging the cutting patterns for these two tubers would be clearly inappropriate-the cylindrical tuber would yield four 4-cut seed pieces that resembled french fries, and the four 1-cut seed pieces from the spherical tuber would look like potato chips!

In attempting to find a cutting pattern criteria it is natural to extend the criteria used for individual seed pieces; every seed piece must contain at least one eye, every seed piece must have a mass between the minimum mass required for a viable plant

234

and twice the minimum mass, and each seed piece should have a blocky shape with a minimum amount of cut surface area.

The range of seed piece mass is a result of the limitations that no seed piece should have a mass less than the minimum. Because fractional seed pieces are not allowed, the number of seed pieces in a tuber were rounded down to an integral number and the mass redistributed among the seed pieces. As a result the distribution of seed piece mass is zero below the minimum mass value, is at a peak at the minimum value, decreases as the mass increases to twice the minimum value, and is zero for larger masses (Figure 6).

To extend the blocky shape (and cut surface) criteria to the tuber cutting pattern, the average blocky shape should increase (cut surface area decrease) across the tuber at the expense of an individual seed piece, but each seed piece in the tuber must remain viable (cut surface not too great) and plantable (not too slender).

To measure the overall blockiness of the seed pieces from a tuber, the cut surface area from each seed piece was summed and a ratio of summed cut surface area to the surface area of the seed tuber was defined. As the ratio decreases, the blockiness of the seed pieces increases. A 0-cut seed piece (whole tuber) has a ratio of zero, indicating that there are no cut surfaces.

The steps needed to determine the cutting pattern, given the length and width of the seed tuber, are to: determine the number of seed pieces, list the unique cutting patterns, determine the cut skin surface ratio for each pattern, and choose the pattern with the smallest ratio. The number of unique patterns increases quickly with the number of seed pieces in the tuber (Table 1).

Computing the cut/skin surface ratio for all the possible cutting patterns of a large seed tuber is time-consuming. In a product environment, the mass flow rate of seed tubers (10t/hr or 220 cwt/hr) does not allow enough time for an exhaustive search of the cutting patterns.

235

Attempts were made to correlate the cutting pattern with the length and width of the seed tuber (the two independent variables in the model). Two parametric variables, width to length ratio (w/l ratio) and the number of seed pieces in the tuber were used to select the cutting pattern which produced blocky seed pieces (Figure 8). The table was compiled by varying the length and width of the seed tuber (within the tuber sizes of 45 to 360g [1.59 to 12.69 oz.]), computing the cut/skin ratio for each pattern, and selecting the cutting pattern with the minimum ratio. For most tuber sizes, the optimum cutting pattern was identified by the number of seed pieces in the tuber. For the other tubers the cutting pattern selection was dependent on both the number of seed pieces in the tuber and the width/length ratio. The w/l ratio is an indication of the eccentricity of the ellipse used to generate the tuber shape. Intuitively, the shape of the seed tuber affects the way the tuber should be cut, as the 4 seed piece example above indicates.

The steps needed to determine the cutting pattern for a seed tuber in a production enviroment (given the length and width of the seed tuber) are: determine the number of seed pieces in the tuber and the w/l ratio; look up the cutting pattern from Table 1; and compute the edges of the seed pieces.

SUMMARY

In this paper the use of a revolved surface of an ellipse as a model of potato seed tuber was explored. The revolved surface model was less precise than an ellipsoidal model, but required one less measurement as an input. Statistical analysis of seed tubers indicated that the mass of the tuber can be predicted by the length and width of the tuber, indicating that the surface-of-revolution model was acceptable.

Criteria for a good seed piece was listed as: the seed piece must contain at least one eye, contain enough mass to support the shoot, be of a blocky shape, and have a minimum of cut surface area. Four types of seed piece cuts were defined (0-cut, 1-cut, 2-cut, and 4-cut), and seven seed piece shapes were identified. Blocky shape and cut surface area were measured using the ratio of cut surface area to skin covered surface area. Minimizing this ratio increased blockiness and decreased the cut surface area.

Criteria for choosing the cutting pattern of the seed piece were identified as: every seed piece must contain at least one eye, each seed piece must contain at least a minimum amount of mass, and the seed piece should be blocky with minimal cut surface area. The ratio of the sum of the cut surface area of all the seed pieces to the surface area of the seed tuber was used to measure the overall blocky shape and cut surface area of the seed piece.

The pattern which is used to cut the seed pieces from the seed tuber directly affects the viability of the seed pieces. Larger tubers have a large number of possible patterns. Exhaustive search of all the patterns was thought to be too time-consuming to use in a production seed cutting operation. A table of patterns based on the number of seed pieces and the ratio of tuber width to length was built to simplify the choice of the cutting pattern.

REFERENCES

Cordner, H.B. 1940. Seed preparation and cultural treatments in relation to stand of plants in full crop potatoes in Oklahoma. Proceedings of the American Society of Horticultural Sciences. 37:849-883.

Iritani, W.M., R.E. Thornton, L.D. Weller and G. O'Leary. 1972. Relationships of seed size, spacing, stem numbers to yield of Russett Burbank potatoes. Amer. Potato Journal, 49:463-469.

Likhyani, Surendar Kumar. 1981. Effect of seed piece variables on performance characteristics of potato planters. M.S. Thesis, Agricultural Engineering, University of Alberta, Edmonton, Alberta.

Nelson, D.C. 1976. Potato Production in North Dakota. Extension Bulletin 26, North Dakota State University of Agriculture and Applied Science, Fargo, ND 58102, March, pp. 15-20.

Thornton, R.E., R.Conlon, G.S. Lee and G.M. Hyde. 1985. Some new ideas about planting and cutting potato seed. Proceedings, 1985 Washington Potato Conference and Trade Fair. Washington State Potato Commission, 108 Interlake, Moses Lake, Washington 98837.

Schotzko, R. T., G.M. Hyde and R.E. Thornton. 1983. The dollars and cents of the 1982 potato seed size and spacing survey. Proceedings, 1983 Washington Potato Conference and Trade Fair. Washington State Potato Commission, 108 Interlake, Moses Lake, Washington 98837.

Selby, Samuel M. (editor). 1970. CRC standard math tables. The Chemical Rubber Co., Cleveland, Ohio. pp. 103-105.

Table 1. Number of unique cutting patterns for increasing number of
seed pieces in a tuber, and the tuber cutting pattern with
a minimum cut surface to tuber surface area ratio.

Number of pieces	w/l ratio	Number of unique patterns	Pattern with minimum cut surface
1	--	1	1
2	--	2	1 1
3	<0.9	3	1 1 1
	>0.9		2 1
4	--	5	1 2 1
5	<0.86	6	2 2 1
	>0.86		4 1
6	<1.0	13	1 4 1
	1.0		2 4
7	--	17	1 4 2

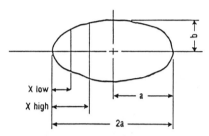

Fig. 1   Nomenclature used to describe seed tuber geometry.

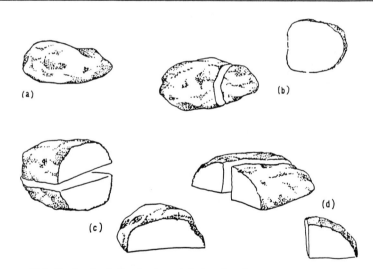

Fig. 2   Seed piece shapes: (a) 0-cut, (b) 1-cut, (c) 2-cut, (d) 4-cut.

Fig. 3   Seed piece shapes (a) at the end of a tuber and (b) in the center of the tuber.

 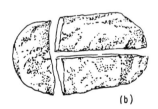

Fig. 4   Two possible cutting patterns for a 140g seed tuber (a) 111 pattern (b) 12 pattern.

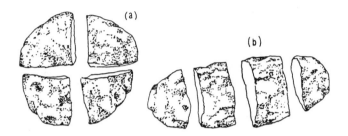

Fig. 5 Two possible cutting patterns for a (a) spherical tuber and a (b) tubular tuber.

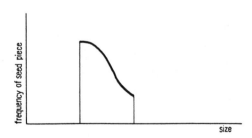

Fig. 6 Seed piece size distribution which contains no waste or over sized seed pieces.

POTATO PRODUCTION FROM TRUE SEED IN
WARM CLIMATE

by

Casimir A. Jaworski, Soil Scientist, USDA-ARS;
Sharad C. Phatak, Professor, Horticulture
Department; Suhas R. Ghate, Associate Professor,
Agricultural Engineering Department; Ronald D.
Gitaitis, Associate Professor, Plant Pathology
Department; University of Georgia, Coastal Plain
Experiment Station, Tifton, Georgia 31793

ABSTRACT

True seed of open-pollinated potato lines and of
tuber-forming Solanum species were evaluated for
transplant and/or tuber production under warm
climates. In a once over harvest 1.3 x 10^6
marketable potato transplants/ha (3.2 x 10^6 /A) were
produced from precision seeding at 164 mixed lite-
coat seeds/m row. Open pollinated line LA 31-124 in
a gel seeding at 98 seeds/m row produced 3.28 x 10^6
tubers weighing 31.9 t/ha (14.2 tons/A), thus, the
average weight of the tubers was less than 10 g (.35
oz.). Ninety-two tuber-forming Solanum species were
evaluated for tuber production under hot climate.

ASAE Paper No. 85-6019

<u>Solanum</u> species of <u>S. pinnatisectum, S. jamesii</u>, <u>S. kurtzianum</u>, <u>S. polytrichon</u>, <u>S. commersonii</u>, and <u>S. cardiophyllum</u> produced large number of tubers of 1 to 2 g with tuber rot resistance.

INTRODUCTION

Potato is the most important dicotyledonous food crop in the world and the tuber is used to plant the crop (Hooker, 1981). Potato production with true seed under warm and hot climates is of increasing interest even though the potato is a temperate climate crop (Accatino and Malagamba, 1982; Accatino et al., 1979; Malagamba, 1982; Van Der Zaag and Horton, 1983). The use of true potato seed (TPS) instead of seed tubers would reduce planting cost and virus diseases (Accatino and Malagamba, 1982; Accatino et al., 1979). Some of the variables affecting TPS germination are presented by Clarke and Stevenson (1943) and by Stier and Cordner (1936). Use of TPS in direct field seeding has been reported by several scientists (Ghate et al., 1983; Jaworski et al., 1983, 1985; Martin, 1983; Phatak et al., 1983, 1985). Ghate et al. (1981) developed a system and equipment for gel sowing germinated vegetable seeds. TPS germination under optimum laboratory temperature and gel sowing into warm solids resulted in improved emergence and plant stand (Ghate et al., 1983). Over a seven-year period involving many trials, Martin (1983) developed many cultural practices for direct seeding TPS under temperate climate conditions. Some of his TPS lines had tuber yields and quality equal to that of commercial cultivars. However, tubers produced from TPS were as a group inferior to commercial cultivars. Phatak, et al., (1983, 1985) demonstrated that several herbicides provided excellent weed control without phytotoxicity and that daminozide will protect potato seedlings from metribuzin injury. Jaworski et al. (1983, 1985) demonstrated that high seeding rates of open-pollinated TPS lines under a warm climate will produce large number of very small tubers while under a hot climate will produce very poor yields.

The objectives of this study were: (1) to determine if marketable potato transplants can be produced using present cultural practices for tomato transplants, (2) to determine tuber production from high seeding rates of TPS, and (3) to evaluate high seeding rates of tuber-forming Solanum species under a hot climate.

MATERIALS AND METHODS

Seeding Rate and Transplant Production

This test was conducted on Dothan loamy sand near Tifton, Georgia in the spring of 1982. Routine land preparation was used and 144 cm (57 in.) wide beds were formed. The soil was fumigated on January 20 with DD-MENCS (20% methyl isothiocyanate + 80% 1, 3-dichloropropene, 1,2-dichloropropane and related chlorinated hydrocarbons, Vorlex, 280 liters/ha [74 gal/h]) injected 18 cm (7 in.) deep with chisels 23 cm (9 in.) apart and water sealed with 1.3 cm (1/2 in.) of water via sprinkler irrigation. Seed bed received 44-39-112 kg/ha (39-35-100 lb/A) of N, P, and K, respectively, broadcast and rototilled to 15 cm (6 in.) immediately prior to seeding. TPS of mixed origin from Dr. S. Peloquin, University of Wisconsin, were coated with Asgrow lite-coat . All plots, which consisted of 11.7 m (38 ft.) bed, were precision seeded on March 19 with Stanhay planters in twin rows with row spacing of 35 cm (14 in.) and with 4 twin rows/bed. Seeding rates were 79, 131 and 164 seeds/m of twin row and all rates were replicated 4 times in a complete randomized block design. Diphenamid (N, N-dimethyl-2, 2-diphenylacetamide, 4.5 kg (10 lb.) a.i./ha) was applied for weed control immediately after seeding. Additional N was broadcast and watered in as needed.

Transplants were harvested, graded and counted for yield from a representative 0.9 m (3 ft.) of twin row in each plot on May 17, 57 days after seeding. Marketable potato transplant size was one + with a stem diameter greater than 2.0 mm (1/16 in.) and shoot length of 9 cm (3.5 in.) and larger.

Open-Pollinated TPS Lines and Tuber Yields

This test was conducted on Fuquay loamy sand near Tifton, Georgia in spring of 1982. Land preparation, soil fumigation, fertilization, and weed control were the same as in previous test. The eight open-pollinated TPS lines of LA 31-124, New

Haig, W 231, W 744, DP 63, W 639, Mixed, and Merrimack were germinated in the laboratory for three days prior to field gel seeding at 98 seeds/m row on March 12, 1982. Plots consisted of 12 m (39 ft.) bed with four single rows on 35 cm (14 in.) centers. All TPS lines were replicated four times in a completely randomized block design. Most of the TPS in the gel were placed on the soil surface. Plant stands were easily established by maintaining a moist soil surface with frequent irrigations.

Plant stands, tuber number, tuber weight and average tuber weight were collected on June 29, on 78 day old plants.

Tuber-Forming Solanum Species and Tuber Yields

Soil of Fuquay loamy sand was fumigated with DD-MENCS at 140 liters (15.4 gal/A) on February 10, 1984. Land preparation and weed control was as in the previous tests and the preplant fertilization rate was 55-47-44 kg/ha (49-42-39 lb./A) of N, P and K, respectively. Plot size was 30 cm (12 in.) of bed containing four rows for a total of 120 cm (48 in.) of row/plot. All entries were replicated two times. True seed of 1,504 entries representing 92 different tuber-forming Solanum species were hand seeded during April 14-20 (Table 1). Seeding rate was approximately 43 seeds/m row.

Tubers were harvested in late September and in October and only tuber yields in number/ha and t/ha are reported in this test.

RESULTS AND DISCUSSION

Seeding Rate and Transplant Yields

Marketable potato transplant yields increased with increasing seeding rates, with the highest seeding rate producing 1.3×10^6 plants/ha (3.2×10^6 plants/A) (Table 2). Marketable potato transplant yields averaged about 86 percent of the total transplants and was not affected by the range of seeding rates used. Potato transplants can be produced from true seed under field conditions provided TPS lines have hot climate adaptation.

246

Open Pollinated TPS Lines and Tuber Yields

The plant stand ranged from 33 plants/m (10 plants/ft.) for New Haig to 75 plants/m (23 plants/ft.) for LA 31-124 (Table 3). Large numbers of tubers were produced with LA 31-124 producing the largest number of 3.28×10^6 tubers/ha (1.33×10^6 tubers/A). The tubers were small and all entries averaged less than 10 g/tuber (0.35 oz/tuber) (Table 3). Even with the small tubers, tuber yields ranged from 13.6 to 31.9 t/ha (12.1 to 284.8 cwt/A) with LA 31-124 having the largest yield. Increasing tuber size through plant breeding could dramatically increase yield. Tuber rots were insignificant in this test since plants were alive at harvest.

Tuber-Forming Solanum Species and Tuber Yield

Average yields for the eight highest yielding Solanum species are presented in Tables 4 and 5. These are average yields for all entries of that species. Solanum pinnatisectum produced the largest yield, 4.7×10^6 tubers/ha (1.9×10^6 tubers/A) weighing 8.25 t/ha (73.5 cwt/A). Solanum pinnatisectum tubers averaged less than 2 g (0.07 oz.) each. Other Solanum species producing large number of tubers under hot climates were S. jamesii, S. kurtzianum, S. polytrichon, S. commersonii, and S. cardiophyllum. All of the higher yielding Solanum species not only have high tuberization at high temperatures, but also high tuber-rot resistance. Many entries produced no tubers because of lack of tuberization under hot climates and/or lack of tuber-rot resistance. This test was a good evaluation for tuber-rot resistance since plants were dead at harvest and tubers were in a hot-moist soil. Remnant potato skins from decayed tubers were observed in maybe poor or non-yielding plots.

CONCLUSIONS

These tests are preliminary evaluations in the use of true seed of tuber-forming Solanum species in potato production under hot climates. Only potato transplant production and tuber production from direct seeding at high rates were evaluated in this

study. Field production of marketable potato
transplants is possible using tomato transplant
production cultural practices from south Georgia in
early spring (Jaworski et al., 1983). Yields of
(averaging less than 10 g/tuber or 0.35 oz/tuber)
small tubers as high as 31.9 t/ha (284 cwt/A) were
obtained with open-pollinated line LA 31-124. None
of the advanced TPS lines produced high tuber yields
when plants were allowed to die prior to tuber
harvest. These advanced TPS lines do not have tuber-
rot resistance at high soil temperatures after plant
senescence. Tuber-forming Solanum species of S.
pinnatisectum, S. jamesii, S. kurtzianum, S.
polytrichon, S. ommersonii and S. cardiophyllum have
tuberization and tuber-rot resistance. The weight
yields per area of these species are small due to the
very small tubers. However, these Solanum species
may have more potential for adaptation to hot
climates than the S. uberosum by increasing tuber
size through screening and breeding.

Many engineering aids and mechanization will be
needed in the use of TPS. Precision seeding of TPS
and of the even smaller tuber-forming Solanum species
seeds, harvesting of small tubers as small as several
grams, and planting of small seedling tubers are some
of the areas needing engineering research.

REFERENCES

Accatino, P. and P. Malagamba. 1982. Potato
production from true seed. Bul. International
Potato Center, Lima, Peru, 20 pp.

Accatino, P., J.L. Rueda, and C. Berrios. 1979.
Agronomic technology to produce consumer
potatoes from botanical potato seed. Amer.
Potato J. 56:455 (Abst.)

Clarke, A.E. and F.J. Stevenson. 1943. Factors
influencing the germination of seeds of the
potato. Amer. Potato J. 20:247-258.

Ghate, S.R., C.A. Jaworski, and S.C. Phatak. 1983.
Emergenece and plant stand of pregerminated
true potato seed in warm climate. Amer.
Potato J. 60:557-562.

Ghate, S.R., S.C. Phatak, and C.A. Jaworski. 1981. Seeding pregerminated vegetable seeds in plots. Trans. ASAE 24:1099-1102, 1107.

Hooker, W.J. (Editor). 1981. Compendium of potato national Potato Center, Lima, Peru. 19 pp.

Martin, Mark W. 1983. Techniques for successful field seeding of true potato seed. Amer. Potato J. 60:245-259.

Phatak, S.C., C.A. Jaworski, and S.R. Ghate. 1983. Weed Control in transplant production from true potato seed. Proc. South. Weed Sci. Soc. 36:164 (Abst.).

Phatak, S.C., C.A. Jaworski, and S.R. Ghate. 1985. Daminozide protects potato seedlings from metribuzin injury. HortScience 20: (in press).

Stier, H.L. and H.B. Cordner. 1936. Germination of seeds of the potato as affected by temperature. Proc. Amer. Soc. Hort. Sci. 34:430-432.

Van Der Zaag, D.E., and D. Horton. 1983. Potato production and utilization in world perspective with special reference to the tropic and sub-tropic. Potato Research 26:323-362.

Table 1. Tuber-forming *Solanum* species and number of entries in each specie.

Solanum species	No. of entries	*Solanum* species	No. of entries
S. abancayense	3	S. laxissimum	1
S. acaule	35	S. leptophyes	6
S. acroglossum	1	S. lesteri	1
S. acroscopicum	2	S. lignicaule	4
S. agrimonifolium	6	S. limbaniense	2
S. alandiae	6	S. lycopersicoides	2
S. amabile	6	S. marinasense	11
S. ambosinum	4	S. medians	9
S. andreanum	1	S. megistacrolobum	38
S. berthaultii	30	S. microdontum	40
S. blanco-galdosii	1	S. mochicense	2
S. boliviense	10	S. morelliforme	1
S. brachistotrichum	2	S. multiinterruptum	7
S. brachycarpum	9	S. ochranthum	1
S. brevicaule	6	S. oplocense	32
S. brevidens	4	S. oxycarpum	5
S. bukasovii	32	S. pampasense	4
S. bulbocastanum	32	S. papita	8
S. canasense	36	S. pascoense	1
S. candolleanum	4	S. paucijugum	1
S. capsicibaccatum	2	S. paucissectum	3
S. cardiophyllum	14	S. pennellii	2
S. chacoense	36	S. phureja	122
S. chancayense	3	S. pinnatisectum	7
S. chomatophilum	11	S. piurae	3
S. circaeifolium	2	S. polyadenium	10
S. clarum	2	S. polytrichon	12
S. colombianum	6	S. raphanifolium	15
S. commersonii	16	S. sanctae-rosae	7
S. demissum	37	S. santolallae	2
S. doddsii	2	S. sogarandinum	2
S. etuberosum	4	S. sparsipilum	3
S. fendleri	26	S. spegazzinii	2
S. fernandezianum	2	S. stenophyllidium	2
S. gandarillasii	2	S. stenotomum	21
S. gourlayi	36	S. stoloniferum	2
S. guerreroense	2	S. sucrense	3
S. hjertingii	6	S. tarijense	3
S. hougasii	7	S. toralapanum	2
S. huancabambense	4	S. trifidum	2
S. immite	3	S. tuberosum	527
S. infundibuliforme	49	S. tuguerrense	1
S. iopetalum	3	S. venturii	1
S. jalcae	1	S. vernei	2
S. jamesii	14	S. verrucosum	4
S. kurtzianum	47	S. weberbaueri	1

Table 2. Potato transplant yields in relation to seeding rates.[z]

Seeding Rate (No./M Row)	TRANSPLANT YIELDS			
	Marketable (1000s/HA)	Culls (1000s/HA)	Total (1000s/HA)	% Marketable
79	650[a]	104[a]	754[a]	86[a]
131	1,080[b]	200[a]	1,280[b]	84[a]
164	1,315[c]	175[a]	1,490[c]	88[a]

[z]Mean separation within column by Duncan's multiple range test at 5% level.

Table 3. Plant stand, tuber yields, and weights from true potato seed of eight open pollinated lines gel seeded at high rates.[z]

Open Pollinated Lines	Plant Stand (No./m Row)	Tuber Yield		
		Number (1000s/ha)	Weight (t/ha)	Weight/Tuber (g)
LA 31-124	75^a	3,280^a	31.9^a	9.7^a
New Haig	33^e	3,010^{ab}	19.0^b	6.5^c
W 231	50^{cd}	2,500^{bc}	17.1^b	7.0^{bc}
W 744	58^{bc}	2,470^{bc}	18.8^b	7.7^{bc}
DP 63	66^{ab}	1,970^c	17.6^b	8.9^{ab}
W 639	40^{de}	1,950^c	13.8^b	7.2^{bc}
Mixed	61^{bc}	1,940^c	13.6^b	6.7^c
Merrimack	57^{bc}	1,880^c	18.1^b	9.5^a

[z]Mean separation within column by Duncan's multiple range test, 5% level.

Table 4. Tuber yield in numbers of tuber-
forming *Solanum* species under hot
climates.[z]

Solanum Species[y]	Number (1000s/ha)
S. *pinnatisectum*	4,696[a]
S. *jamesii*	1,046[b]
S. *kurtzianum*	1,040[b]
S. *polytrichon*	900[bc]
S. *commersonii*	859[b-d]
S. *cardiophyllum*	768[b-e]
S. *spegazzinii*	547[b-f]
S. *hjertingii*	431[b-f]

[z]Mean separation within column by Duncan's
multiple range test, 5% level.

[y]Only the highest producing species are
presented.

Table 5. Tuber yield in weight of true
potato seed (TPS) and tuber-
forming *Solanum* species under
hot climates.[z]

Solanum Species[y]	Weight (t/ha)
S. pinnatisectum	8.25[a]
S. cardiophyllum	2.30[b]
S. polytrichon	2.09[bc]
S. tarijense	1.99[b-d]
S. kurtzianum	1.87[b-e]
TPS (WIS, Peloquin)	1.50[b-f]
TPS (CIP, Bryan)	1.40[b-g]
TPS (IPRI)	1.29[b-h]

[z]Mean separation between columns by Duncan's
multiple range test, 5% level.

[y]Only the highest producing species or TPS
sources are presented.

ENGINEERING NEEDS FOR POTATO PRODUCTION
FROM TRUE SEED

by

Suhas, R. Ghate, Associate Professor, Agricultural
Engineering Department; Casimir A. Jaworski, Soil
Scientist, USDA-ARS; Sharad C. Phatak, Professor,
Horticulture Department; and Ronald D. Gitaitis,
Associate Professor, Plant Pathology Department,
University of Georgia, Coastal Plain Experiment
Station, Tifton, Georgia 31793-0748

ABSTRACT

Potatoes grown from the true potato seed (TPS)
are generally small and nonuniform in size and shape,
compared to the ones produced conventionally from
seed tubers. Potato production from TPS would be
considerably less expensive than from seed tubers
because of the negligible storage and handling cost
of the TPS. Potato production from the TPS would,
therefore, have the greatest potential in the
developing countries. In developed countries, this
production method would have some potential in

ASAE Paper No. 85-6020

commercial production as well as in home gardening. Research related to the TPS potato production has been mostly directed toward investigating suitable cultural practices, screening breeding lines for higher yield and warm climate adaptability, weed control in the field, and other similar production areas. Research concerning mechanization of TPS potato production has been limited. Engineering input to the TPS potato production, handling and storage needs considerable attention to develop practical and ecnomical practices. This paper highlights some research areas which the authors believe are worth investigating. Some engineering research that is conducted at the Coastal Plain Experiment Station related to the TPS potato production has been outlined along with some future plans.

INTRODUCTION

Potatoes are grown commercially from seed tubers. Good quality potato tubers are cut into several pieces each with an "eye" and then seeded into the soil for production. Generally, it takes about 1t to 2t of seed tubers to plant one ha (8.91 to 17.8 cwt/A) of potato field. Production, transportation, handling and storage of seed tubers are expensive operations because they are bulky. In addition, some seed tubers get infested with viral, fungal and bacterial diseases during production, in storage and transit. Cost of potato seed tubers range as high as 30 to 50 percent of the total production cost.

True potato seed (TPS) is obtained from potato berries and is very small. There are approximately 1.5 to 1.6 million seed per kg (70,000 seed/lb) of the seed weight. It takes about 200 to 300 g of TPS to sow one ha (2.85 to 4.28 oz/A) of potato field. Storage, handling and transporation of the TPS is easy and inexpensive. Moreover, TPS can be stored for many years and do not get readily infested as seed tubers do. Using TPS for potato production can considerably reduce the cost of production (Accatino and Malagamba, 1982; Martin, 1983).

However, the potato tubers produced from the TPS are nonuniform, varying from just a few g to several

256

hundred g each. This product is therefore no match for the large uniform potatoes produced from the seed tubers. Because of the small and nonuniform size and shape, potatoes from TPS have not been commercially produced in the U.S.A. and other potato producing countries. Nevertheless, due to the low cost of production, TPS is still a viable alternative for potato production in many countries of the world. In the USA and other industralized nations, TPS can be extensively used in commercial production of small tubers and in home gardening.

Researchers are working on the screening and selection techniques of TPS breeding lines which are suitable to various climatic conditions of the world including warm climate. Their research is leading to the selection of TPS lines which can produce large quantities of potato tubers. Even though nonuniform size is a problem, high yields of tubers would substantially decrease the production cost, hence TPS can be considered as an attractive choice for some potato producing farmers in the near future.

Although a good amount of research is currently being conducted related to TPS in the areas of its selection, production and cultural practices (Jaworski et al., 1985; Martin, 1983; Phatak et al., 1983, 1985), there is not much reseach being done in the engineering areas such as mechanization and handling. The purpose of this paper is to outline some of the engineering needs related to potato production from TPS.

SEEDING TECHNIQUES

TPS can be used in three different ways to produce potatoes: (1) TPS is sown equidistant in rows and potatoes are produced similar to other vegetable crops by direct seeding; (2) TPS is sown to obtain thick stands in rows for transplant production and the plants are harvested after several weeks of growth and then transplanted in another field. This technique is similar to the one used in the production of tomatoes, peppers, etc. but is currently under research for its feasibility and efficiency; (3) TPS is sown directly in a virus and insect free area in rows and small seedling tubers are produced. These small seedling tubers are then planted into the production area just like the seed tubers. Potatoes produced in this way are relatively more uniform and the final tubers are generally larger than the seedling tubers.

The seeding technique determines appropriate seeder to be used. For direct seeding and for transplant production, small seeders using cone, disk and vacuum principles can be used. It has been demonstrated that germination of TPS before sowing improves plant stand of some breeding lines in warm climates (Ghate et al., 1983). In this case, using a fluid drill is essential. In this method of seeding, germinated seed is thoroughly mixed with some carrier medium, typically a gel, and then the seed gel mixture is deposited into the soil furrow (Ghate et al., 1985). Gel seeders may be based on a compressed air principle (Figure 1) or a peristaltic pump principle for the seed gel extrusion (Figure 2).

Equipment is not available to seed small tubers if the potatoes are to be produced from the third seeding technique mentioned above. A planter which can place these small seedling tubers at equidistant locations is necessary in order to produce potatoes from TPS in this indirect fashion. This technique would still be less expensive than the production from seed tubers even though both approaches appear to be similar. These seedling tubers are much smaller than conventional seed tubers. Their storage and transportation would be less expensive than those for the conventional seed tubers. In addition, this type of vegetative propagation is limited to a two season cycle (production of seedling tubers from TPS in one season and production of potatoes from seedling tubers in the next season or year) unlike the conventional method in which vegetative propagation continues for unlimited time.

CLIPPING

The second technique of TPS potato production requires growing and shipping potato transplants. These transplants would require clipping before shipment similar to the other vegetable transplants. The mechanical clippers used in the production of

TPS potato transplant clipping would not be ideal in commercial use. These clippers could transmit viral, bacterial and other diseases in tomatoes and other vegetable transplants. Potato is highly susceptible to many viral diseases, hence these clippers, even though widely used on other transplants, would not be suitable for potato transplants. It is necessary to design and contruct a transplant clipper which would either eliminate or reduce the possibility of disease spread. Research related to potato production from TPS transplants would be greatly enhanced by the design construction and use of a new clipper.

HARVESTING

Because of the small size and nonuniformity of tubers, currently available potato diggers and harvesters are not suitable for harvesting potatoes grown for TPS. Two different types of equipment or one with two attachments might be necessary. The potato harvester should harvest the nonuniform marble like seedling tuber (less than 10 g [0.353 oz]) for replanting if the third approach of seeding techniques described in the previous section is used. The same harvester should be able to harvest larger tubers either grown from seedling tubers or from direct sowing of the TBS. These potatoes are small and nonuniform and the harvester should be able to pick all of them. This machine may be a semiautomatic harvester or may be just a harvesting aid. Its use is anticipated only in small fields at this time.

MATERIAL HANDLING AND SIZING

The potatoes produced from TPS are nonuniform and will require a considerable amount of sizing. A sizing station should be designed where potatoes as small as 2 cm (0.787 in.) in diameter can be easily sorted. These potatoes may have various ultimate uses. For example, the small potatoes can be used as salad potatoes or in canning while the large ones can be used as fresh market vegetables and the odd sizes can be used by industries for making reconstituted potato products. The equipment should similarly be manually operated, material handling aids because these will be used mostly on small farms.

STORAGE STUDIES

Storage studies related to potato transplants and final products are necessary if the potato production from TPS is to be commercialized. Some studies on transplant storage have been done (Risse et al., 1984). The results of these studies may be adopted to potato production from TPS if the TPS potato production follows the production patterns of several vegetables in the U.S.; e.g., growing transplants in warm areas and transporting them to cool areas for final production. Storage studies on the potatoes from TPS are necessary because of their small size and tender skin. The temperature, humidity and air circulation requirements for these tubers could be different from the conventionally grown potatoes.

PHYSICAL PROPERTIES STUDIES

Determination of physical properties of any fruit, vegetable, nut, root or tree is essential whenever mechanization of its production is planned. Many studies have been conducted on tomatoes, apples, potatoes and several other products which are (or could be) machine harvested and are handled several times before reaching the consumer (Garret et al., 1960; Huff, 1967; Nelson and Mohsenin, 1968; Somer, 1965). The seedling tubers or the potatoes produced seedlings can be used as a good quality product for consumption as a salad product or as a fresh market vegetable. Physical properties such as density, bioyield point, hardness, skin texture, time relaxation, etc. should be studied as they have been in the case of many fruits and vegetables. Most of these studies can be done using an Instron Universal testing machine. These studies will provide valuable information which can be used to design handling equipment, mechanical aids, sizer, harvester and transportation containers.

PROGRESS AT COASTAL PLAIN EXPERIMENT STATON

For the past several years, we have worked on techniques for producing potatoes from TPS. Considerable research has been conducted related to the screening and selection of TPS for warm climate, to general practices, and to weed control studies. Even though engineering research has been limited, we have done some preliminary work that is promising.

We evaluated the performance of germinated seeds using the fluid drill designed at CPES. We also studied the performance of TPS using pelleted seed with a precision Stanhay planter (Jaworski et al., 1983). We have also designed and constructed equipment (Figure 3) to mass innoculate potato plants in the field with Pseudomonas solanacearum (Ghate et al., 1982). Even though this innoculator is not meant for use in potato production, it is extensively used in our potato research program to screen potato breeding lines which are bacterial wilt resistant and heat tolerant. It could also have applications in studying clones of potato grown from TPS.

We have modified a sweet potato harvester to dig small nonuniform tubers produced from TPS (Figure 4). The digging mechanism was only partially successful since separation of soil clods and very small stones from potatoes still remains a problem. We have designed a mechanical aid (Figure 5) which can be used to hand seed very small research plots. The same equipment can also be used to pick potatoes from the ground once they are dug and thrown back on the soil by the modified sweet potato harvester. Our future research plans include physical properties studies (Figure 6) and development of a sizer for potatoes produced from TPS.

SUMMARY

Production of potatoes from TPS would be considerably less expensive than from seed tubers. However, because of the small and nonuniform sizes of the TPS tubers, this production practice is not widely accepted. Engineering research concerning the TPS potato production is necessary to develop practical and economical production practices. Some of the engineering needs which the authors believe worth investigating are (1) to develop a seeder to sow TPS and to seed seedling tubers grown from TPS, (2) to develop clippers to clip TPS grown potato transplants without transmitting any viral or bacterial diseases, (3) to design and construct a harvester or a mechanical aid to harvest all of the

small and uniform TPS tubers, (4) to construct
equipment for sizing and handling of small tubers,
(5) to do storage studies on small tubers, and (6) to
investigate physical properties such as bioyield
point, density, skin texture of the small tubers
grown from TPS.

REFERENCES

Accatino, P. and P. Malagamba. 1982. Potato produc-
    tion from true seed. Bul. International Potato
    Center, Lima, Peru, 20 pp.

Garrett, A.W., N.W. Desrosier, G.D. Kuhn and M.C.
    Field. 1960. Evaluation of instruments to
    measure firmness of tomatoes. Food Technology
    14:562.

Ghate, S.R., R.D. Gitaitis, S.C. Phatak and C.A.
    Jaworski. 1982. A field inoculator for
    potatoes. Trans. of ASAE 25(4):919-920.

Ghate, S.R., S.C. Phatak and C.A. Jaworski. 1985.
    A new seeder for fluid sowing germinated seed.
    Acta Horticulturae. (In press)

Huff, E.R. 1967. Measuring time-dependent
    mechanical properties of potato tubers, equir-
    ment, procedure, results. Transactions of As.
    10(3):414-419.

Jaworski, C.A., S.C. Phatak, S.R. Ghate, and R.D.
    Gitaitis. 1983. Potato transplant and tuber
    production at high seeding rates of true potato
    seed. American Potato Journl 60:811 (Abstract).

Jaworski, C.A., S.C. Phatak, and S.R. Ghate. 1985.
    Potato performance from high seeding rates of
    true potato seed under hot climates. HortScience
    20:(Abstract).

Martin, Mark W. 1983. Techniques for successful
    field seeding of true potato seed. American
    Potato Journal 50:245-259.

Nelson, C.W. and N.N. Mohsenin. 1968. Maximum
    allowable static and dynamic loads and effect of
    temperature for mechanical injury in apples.
    Journal of Agricultural Engineering Research
    13(4):317-329.

Phatak, S.C., C.A. Jaworski, and S.R. Ghate. 1983. Weed control in transplant production from true potato seed. Southern Weed Society Proceedings: 164.

Phatak, S.C., C.A. Jaworski, and S.R. Ghate. 1985. Daminozide protects potato seedlings from metribuzin injury. HortScience 20:(In press).

Risse, L.A., C.A. Jaworski, S.C. Phatak and S.R. Ghate. 1984. Effect of storage temperature and duration on quality and survival of potato transplants. American Potato Journal 61:261-265.

Somers, G.F. 1965. Visoelastic properties of storage tissue from potato, apple and pear. Journal of Food Science 30(6):922-929.

Figure 1. A compresed air fluid drill.

Figure 2. A fluid drill using peristaltic pumps.

Figure 3. A mass inoculator for inoculating potato plants.

Figure 4. A modified sweet potato harvester for digging potatoes from TPS.

Figure 5. A mechanical aid for handling farm products.

Figure 6. Instron Universal testing machine.

III. QUALITY AND UTILIZATION

Sugar Changes and Chipping Responses of Norchip
    Tubers After Handling From Storage -
    Paul H. Orr

The Economic Importance of Bruising to Idaho
    Potatoes in Transit - N.L. Meyer

Potato Bruising During Transport - S.W. Grant

Research Needs in Handling and Transporting
    Potatoes for the Chip Market - Paul H.
    Orr

Tuber Quality Control in Potatoes for Chip
    Production From Vine Kill to Storage -
    Maurice Eddows

An Approach Towards Potato Utilization and
    Third World Countries - Robert H. Booth

Postharvest Handling Systems Analysis of Fresh
    Produce - D.T. Campbell

SUGAR CHANGES AND CHIPPING RESPONSES OF
NORCHIP TUBERS AFTER HANDLING FROM STORAGE*

by

Paul H. Orr, Agricultural Engineer, USDA-ARS-NSA,
RRV Potato Research Lab; Joseph R. Sowokinos,
Research Biochemist, University of Minnesota, RRV
Potato Research Lab; Jerry L. Varns, Research
Chemist, USDA-ARS-NSA, RRV Potato Research Lab,
East Grand Forks, Minnesota

ABSTRACT

A handling treatment providing potato-on-potato
tumbling in a rubber-lined rotating drum concentrated
and magnified the effects of handling on internal
quality. Chip color and sugar concentrations were
measured 0, 5, 10, and 20 days after handling
treatments on Norchip tubers stored 1 to 10 months @
9°C (48°F), 90 RH. Month-by-month, the handled
samples produced higher sugar concentrations and
darker chips than controls. Results identified the
potential for internal quality losses via industrial
storage, handling and shipping systems when marketing
chipping potatoes.

ASAE Paper No. 85-6021

269

INTRODUCTION

Producing, storing and transporting potatoes (Solanum tuberosum L.) for processing into chips is an important part of the nation's potato industry. Approximately 13 percent of the potatoes utilized in the United States each year are consumed as potato chips (USDA, 1984). Potato chips contributed to over 46 percent of the salted snack sales volume of 6.7 billion dollars in the U.S. in 1984 (Potato Chip/Snack Food Association, 1985).

The potato chip industry maintains product freshness via minimal finished product inventories. Therefore, a steady, year-round supply of high quality raw potatoes is required to, in turn, provide consumers with a steady, year-round supply of fresh, high quality potato chips.

Most potatoes for chipping are harvested and stored in their raw form in storages located in the U.S. fall crop production areas. Then, over a period of about 9 months, the stored crop is continuously removed from storage and transported to processing plants located near large metropolitan market areas throughout the U.S. Potatoes grown in the U.S. spring and summer crop production areas, which provide the raw material for chipping during the remaining three months, are generally moved directly from field or short term storage to the processing plant.

In recent years, as the industry lengthened total storage time from 6 months to 9 months, Norchip, a major chipping cultivar, began yielding off-color chips when stored beyond the 6 month requirement. Off-colored product is often seen after potatoes arrive at the processing plant even though chips made at the storage site just prior to handling and shipping exhibit good chip color. This specific

----

*This paper was prepared on official Government time and reports research paid for by U.S. taxpayers. The article and the reseach information, therefore, are in the public domain and cannot be copyrights.

problem may not be unique to Norchip because other cultivars, such as Monona, exhibit similar color problems during transit.

Norchip is the most important cultivar for chipping in the U.S. because of its high solids and generally acceptable finished product color. Although Lulai and Orr (1979) and Orr and Graham (1983) demonstrated the importance of high dry matter content of raw potatoes for chipping, acceptably light color after frying is absolutely essential to the chipping industry. Entire lots of otherwise high quality raw potatoes are rejected when chip color fails to meet a processor's minimum standard.

Dry handling of raw potatoes is normally practiced in the chip processing industry. Powered bulk scooping, as described by Orr (1971), continues today as a major method of dry handling chipping potatoes from storage. It is generally recognized that handling methods for potatoes destined for the chipping market are rather harsh, e.g., use of bulk scoops, hoppers and multi-tiered conveyors.

The purpose of our handling treatment was to mimic and/or magnify the commercial handling effect in order to concentrate visually quality changes with measureable sugar differences. A modified rotating drum appeared to be effective in providing a vigorous handling situation. This handling technique utilizing potato-on-potato tumbling in a rubber-lined rotating drum was shown earlier to provide repeatable, linearly increasing rates of CO_2 generation with time of tuber treatment (number of revolutions) (Varns, 1985).

METHODS AND EQUIPMENT

Norchip potatoes were grown in Grand Forks County, North Dakota under cultural practices common to the Red River Valley production area. The potatoes were harvested commercially and placed into a commercial storage bin. The harvested potatoes were preconditioned for 24 days at ambient conditions (approx. 20°C [68° F] and 90 percent (RH) to suberize surface scuffs. Potatoes used in our tests were then selected (approx. 250 g size [8.75 oz.]) from the commercial storage bin, placed in wire-bound crates

(25 kg or 55 lb. capacity) and transferred to a controlled temperature storage room equipped with forced ventilation. The storage conditions were then altered over a period of 3 days from 20° C (68 °F), 90 percent RH to 9 °C (48 °F), 90 percent RH for long-term storage. Sprout inhibition of the stored samples was accomplished with a gaseous application of CIPC (isopropyl N-(3-chlorophenyl) carbamate) during the third month of storage.

A "control sample" and a "handled sample", each consisting of 80 tubers, were taken from the total lot of stored potatoes each month for 10 months for handling treatment and subsequent evaluation of chip color and internal sugars. The 80 tubers removed each month and designated as the control sample were returned untreated to storage, whereas the 80 tubers designated each month as the handled sample were given a handling treatment before being returned to storage. After each monthly handling treatment, chipping tests and sugar evaluations were subsequently performed at intervals of 0, 5, 10 and 20 days on 10 tubers taken from both the control and handled lots.

All data were given a statistical analysis of variance using a general linear model procedure with a Student-Newman-Keul test for significance.

Handling Treatment

The handling treatment was accomplished in a specially adapted clothes dryer (Hotpoint[1] , Model #3LL775) having a cylindrical metal drum rotating about a horizontal axis. The dryer's rotating drum, which was originally 62 cm (25 in.) in diameter and 43 cm (17.2 in.) deep, had 3 smooth, prism-shaped baffles, integrally indented centripetally parallel to the axis of rotation and 120 apart on its interior circumference. Each indented baffle was 18 cm (7.2 in.) wide at its base, 43 cm (17.2 in.) in length and had an 8 cm (3.2 in.) centripetal projection. The dryer's original metal drum was modified by lining

----

[1]Mention of a trade name or a company name does not constitute a guarantee or warranty of a product by the U.S. Department of Agriculture and does not imply its approval to the exclusion of other products that may also be suitable.

272

its interior circumferencial surface with a 1-cm (.4 in.) thickness of soft neoprene rubber (Durometer reading from 5 to 6 on the "A" scale[2]). The drum's rotational speed was slowed to 0.31 r/s and a revolution counter was added.

To perform the handling treatment, 20 tubers[3] from the appropriate 80-tuber sample were placed in the drum of the dryer, the door was closed and the drum was rotated for 40 revolutions. The potatoes were then removed from the drum and returned to storage.

Analytical Procedures

At 0, 5, 10, and 20 days following handling treatments, 20-tuber replicates were taken from the appropriate 80-tuber sample for evaluation of sugar concentrations and finished chip color. Ten tubers were randomly selected for sugar analysis from the 20-tuber replicate.

Twenty slices consisting of 2 slices from each of the 10 raw tubers destined for sugar analysis, were obtained and chipped using the procedure of Lulai and Orr (1980). Each individual chip from the 20-chip sample was assigned a PC/SFA chip color value (scale 1 to 5) and an "equivalent" Agtron number according to the following scale:

------

[2]Durometer reading according to ASTM:D2240-81.

[3]Approximately 20-25 tubers were used to obtain reproducible tuber-on-tuber tumbling during a handling treatment (Varns, et al., 1985). Four repetitions of this procedure were used to complete the treatment on the 80-tubers making up the handled sample.

PC/SFA chip color value	PC/SFA equivalent Agtron value
1.0	70
1.5	65
2.0	60
2.5	55
3.0	50
3.5	45
4.0	40
4.5	35
5.0	30

(Potato Chip/Snack Food Association, 1978)

Mean equivalent Agtron values of the chipping samples from the handling replicates (0, 5, 10 and 20 days following handling) were plotted by computer (Hewlett Packard, Model 9830A) utilizing a spline curve-fitting program and x-y plotter (Hewlett Packard, Model 9872) for all treated and control samples for the 10 months of storage (data not available for month 3).

An industrial analyzer (Yellow Springs Instrument Co., Model #27) measured glucose and sucrose concentrations (Sowokinos, et al. 1985) at each 0-, 5-, 10- and 20-day interval following handling treatment. The mean of five readings was used for the reported sugar value.

Electron microscopy was used to examine the sub-cellular components, particularly the integrity of amyloplast membranes, in control and handled samples. These tests and results will be reported elsewhere.

RESULTS AND DISCUSSION

Commercial practices of production, harvesting, and storage were used for the preparation of the raw potatoes in these tests. An extended holding period, following the suberization process, is commonly referred to as "preconditioning" to metabolize excess reducing sugars prior to cooling the tubers for long-term storage. The latter half of the 24-day period at

20 ° C (68°F) was sufficient to stabilize chip color prior to reducing tuber pulp temperature to 9°C (48 °F).

Chipping Tests

Figure 1 illustrates the results of the chipping tests at 0, 5, 10 and 20 days following handling treatment of Norchip potatoes stored at 9° C (48 ° F), 90 percent RH for periods of 1 to 10 months (no data for month 3). Chip tests at 0-, 5-, 10- and 20-day intervals represent the approximate chronology involved for potatoes that are handled and transported commercially from storage to processing. The controls at 0-time also represent the handling samples at 0-time and were plotted accordingly.

Month-by-month the handled samples produced darker chips than the control samples at 5, 10, and 20 days following handling treatment (Figure 1). Mean differences, in PC/SFA equivalent Agtron values, between the handled and the control samples were significant (P<0.01) at 5, 10, and 20 days for each duration of storage (1-10 months). The largest difference at each interval was 16 at 5 days following 10 months of storage, 18 at 10 days following 1 month of storage and 23 at 20 days following 5 months of storage.

As shown in Figure 2, the difference in mean chip color was 13 PC/SFA equivalent Agtron values at 5 days, 12 at 10 days and 16 at 20 days when data were combined across the entire 10-month storage period. Differences at each interval were significant (P<0.01). A 12- to 16-point loss in PC/SFA equivalent Agtron value in finished potato chip color, as shown by our handling treatments, represents a serious decrease in quality. In many cases, entire bins of potatoes are rejected as unsuitble raw product for processing because of similar losses in final product quality.

Examination of the raw data used to determine means and ranges of the figures showed most chips in the figures in the control samples were spread more evenly across the range from light to dark. In industry, the few dark chips from potatoes similar to our control samples could possibly be removed during final product inspection at the processing plant. However, when darker chips are broadly distributed, as indicated in the handled samples, little corrective action can be anticipated during final product inspection at the plant.

Figure 3 presents the overall mean differences when 5-, 10-, and 20-day intervals were combined and shown at storage periods 1 through 10 months. Differences between the control and the handled samples are signifiant (P<0.01) at each storage period compared.

By utilizing the spline curve-fitting plot of the data in Figure 3, we illustrate the presence of an underlying effect (interaction) of storage duration on chip color. Note the similar "tracking" of the control and handled curves from month 5 through month 10 of storage time. Since chip color is primarily related to the presence of reducing sugars, this tracking is likely associated with changes in glucose content at those storage periods. This glucose effect, in part, would be a result of the stress of physiological aging in storage. The large difference in chip color occurring after one month of storage indicates that potatoes may be very sensitive to handling at this time. The "overshooting" of the curves at inflection points is inherent in the spline curve-fitting program/plot.

Comparing the two curves in Figure 3 shows that the handling treatment caused a severe color difference when performed very early (1st month) in the storage period, this lessened somewhat, mainly due to changes in control tubers (2-4 months), then intensified later (> 4 months), again, mainly due to changes in control tubers.

Potato Sugars

Table 1 provides an example of the mean concentration of glucose and sucrose found in our Norchip tubers at the 10-day interval following handling treatment of potatoes previously stored for the periods shown in the table. Glucose and fructose are the reducing sugars of concern in the Maillard (nonenzymic) browning reaction that results in dark colored potato chips during frying. Glucose is the

276

accepted sugar to monitor in raw potatoes, immediately prior to frying, as an indicator of expected finished chip color. If glucose is maintained at less than 0.04 percent in raw potatoes, acceptable color will generally be found in the finished chips. Sowokinos (1978) has identified sucrose in raw tubers as the major sugar that changes as tubers mature.

Figure 4 shows sucrose and glucose patterns obtained in control and handled samples 0, 5, 10, and 20 days following handling treatment after 7 months storage at 9 °C (48°F), 90 percent RH. Note that sucrose increased at a rapid rate to a high concentration, relative to the control sample, following handling treatments; whereas, glucose varied only slightly from the concentrations found in the control sample. This pattern was typical in every monthly interval tested. It was our observation that the higher concentrations of sugars (especially sucrose) were present in the handled samples having undergone the longer storage durations (5-10 months).

Given the extremely high sucrose concentrations developed in samples receiving 5 to 10 months of storage, subsequent handling treatment and up to 20 days response time and the relatively low concentrations of glucose under those same conditions (Table 1 and Figure 4), a major portion of this increased sucrose due to handling is not automatically cleaved to glucose and fructose, but is somehow sequestered away from further enzymatic action.

Schallenberger, et al. (1959), indicated hydrolysis of sucrose into glucose and fructose might occur in the presence of hot cooking oil and amino acids typical of chip frying environments. This would result in dark chip color if the sucrose concentration is high enough (>0.5% fresh wt.). We believe that the slight changes in glucose found in our samples are the primary cause of chip color changes. The sequestering phenomenon of sucrose and effects of various sugar concentrations will be discussed more fully in a separate publication.

Relevance to Potato Industry

The rapid buildup of sucrose in the handled
samples indicates that the handling treatments caused
some type of biochemical stress in the tubers. One
visual result of this stress is generally poorer chip
color, as shown in our tests. These chipping data
illustrate the need for handling potatoes from
storage as gently as possible in order to avoid loss
of quality (color) in the final processed chips.
This precaution applies even if the time between
handling and chipping is as short as 5 days (Figure
2). Simliarly, in industry Norchip potatoes destined
for the chip market may, potentially, lose internal
quality because of rough handling methods. Note in
Figure 4, that a period of 5 days was sufficient time
for potatoes to develop high concentrations of sugars
when previously stored 7 months. As reflected by the
sugar concentrations seen in Table 1, total sugar
concentration appears to increase with tuber age,
indicating senescense is approaching. Stored
potatoes may senesce slowly, but this process may
still cause tubers to be more sensitive to handling
stress. This aspect of our tests also will be
published elsewhere.

The increasing sucrose concentration appeared
reversible, to some extent, late in the 20-day
testing period following handling treatment if the
potato sample had been stored less than 8 months
(Figure 4). For longer storage periods, the trend
was a continual increase in sucrose during the entire
20-day testing period following handling treatment.
This reversibility/irreversibility of sucrose is part
of a dilemma that now exists for the potato industry,
where loads of raw potatoes are sometimes held at the
processing plant at a relatively high temperature (13
°C to 21 °C [55.4 to 70 °F]) for up to 4 weeks with the
expectation that excess sugars found upon arrival
will revert to starch or be respired. Sometimes the
reversal is accomplished; sometimes it is not.
Reversals are usually accomplished with potatoes
previously stored less than 6 months; whereas,
irreversiblity will occur more often with potatoes
stored longer than 6 months.

The industry also struggles with varying color
analyses for chipping samples from seemingly

278

identical (but actually changed) lots of potatoes. The storage operator usually samples the potatoes in the bulk storage bin for chip color analysis prior to handling and shipping to market. The processor samples the load of potatoes for chip color analysis upon arrival at the processing plant. Although both parties probably feel they are looking at a chip sample from the same lot of potatoes, they are not. The storage operator is essentially looking at a sample similar to the "control" sample in our tests; the processor is essentially looking at a sample similar to our "handled" sample at a specific time following the handling treatment. As shown by our data, "control" and "handled" samples may be quite different in sugar development and chip color.

Handling Methods and Equipment

Better methods and equipment to handle bulk potatoes out of storage are needed. The bulk scooping method is quite rough on raw potatoes even if extreme care is used in its operation. Bulk bin unloaders of the type used by the Western U.S. potato industry appear to handle bulk potatoes more gently, but these operations still offer many damage opportunities for potato-on-potato tumbling at conveyor drops and damage at the surface of the bulk pile.

In theory, the storer and handler should attempt to equate all storage/handling operations to the "control" samples of our tests by eliminating all handling out of storage if possible. For example, a pallet box method of handling raw potatoes into and out of storage would eliminate the rough out-of-storage handling operation. The loaded boxes could be shipped to the processing plant where final dumping (handling) of the potatoes could take place only minutes prior to processing. The practicality and economics of such a method would have to be considered.

Fluming potatoes (Schaper, et al. 1985) might be possible when unloading bins for the chipping market. The method is gentle when done properly, but industry has some concern about possible temperature changes in the potatoes whenever water used for fluming is colder than the raw potatoes being moved. There is also concern about water removing protective surface films from the potatoes, plugging lenticels and spreading bacterial diseases. Cargill (1981) and Orr (1985) found that bacterial diseases can be controlled when an appropriate concentration of chlorine is maintained in the water used to wash potatoes.

Our data suggest it would be helpful if stops and starts could be avoided when unloading the potatoes from bulk bins. For example, those potatoes at the lower face of a partially removed pile receive excessive handling by being bumped by the scoop, whereas those at the upper face roll down the slope of the remaining pile. Therefore, with chipping delays, sugars could accumulate and cause these potatoes to be in a category of poorer quality for chips.

It is also important that the transport vehicle be ventilated when carrying potatoes to the chip processing plant to avoid accelerating sugar accumulation via a respiratory buildup of CO_2. The choice of transportation should insure the shortest possible transport time to limit the time available for sugars to increase, especially in the first 5 days following handling. In this respect, scheduling of the load for processing immediately upon arrival at the plant is important. Any delays at the processing plant simply allow more time for increases in sugars which result in dark chips.

Long-Term Needs

Our results emphasize the continued need for alternative storage, handling, and shipping systems to provide more gentle handling of potatoes destined for chip processing plants. System criteria also include high capacity and relatively low cost to function in the potato storage/processing industry.

The optimal location of storage facilties with respect to the processing plant should be examined in terms of delivery time. The requirement that huge volumes of raw potatoes be moved into storage in a very short time (2-4 weeks) at harvest does not allow lengthy transportation times from field to storage. Thus, storage facilities are generally located near the production area. Processing plant locations are influenced by various concerns, such as distance to final product distribution areas, but it may be possible to optimize plant location in a way that also minimizes raw potato delivery time.

Our results also emphasize the need to increase the internal durability of potatoes grown for the chipping market. This would necessitate changes in long-term breeding programs to develop a potato that responds better to handling as measured by internal quality. Speculation also includes the possible treatment of the potato with a metabolic "regulator" that would stabilize the raw potato against an undesirable response to handling.

It is postulated that the data reported herein may be varietal, and thus limited to Norchip; however, the possibility exists that the responses shown may be representative for other chipping cultivars. Future research is recommended to determine the response of additional chipping cultivars to handling following long-term storage.

Additional research is also recommended to determine the sugar changes and chipping responses of Norchip and other chipping cultivars during the 5-day period immediately following handling. Note that in our tests, essentially all quality loss pertaining to finished chip color occurred in the first 5 days. Evaluations at 1-day increments during that period would seem appropriate.

ACKNOWLEDGEMENTS

We thank: K.G. Janardan, Statistician, North Dakota State University for the statistical analyses and Marilyn E. Nelson, Engineering Technician, USDA-ARS-NSA for the computer plotting of the data.

REFERENCES

Cargill, B.F., H.S. Potter, R.L. Ledebuhr and M.W. Glover. 1981. Prestorage chemical application techniques to minimize potato losses in storage. Unpublished presentation, Pot. Assoc. Amer. Annual Meeting.

Lulai, E.C. and P.H. Orr. 1979. The influence of specific gravity on yield and oil content of chips. Amer. Potato J. 56:379–390.

Lulai, E.C. and P.H. Orr. 1980. Quality-testing facilities for grower use at the Potato Research Laboratory. Amer. Potato J. 57:622–628.

Orr, P.H. 1971. Powered bulk scooping in potato storages. Marketing Res. Rept. No. 916. U.S. Dept. Agr.

Orr, P.H. and C.K. Graham. 1983. Determining least-cost sources of chipping potatoes by use of mathematical models. Trans. of ASAE. 261:297–300 & 304.

Orr, P.H. Unpublished data.

Potato Chip/Snack Food Association. 1978. Fry color standards for potatoes for chipping.

Potato Chip/Snack Food Association. 1978. PC/SFA announces brand new chip color chart. Chipper Snacker 35 (6):19–20.

Potato Chip/Snack Food Association. 1985. PC/SFA 1985 snack food management report. Chipper Snacker 42(7):CS1–CS20.

Schaper, L.A., P.H. Orr, N. Smith and J.H. Hunter. 1985. Hydraulic transport of potatoes. Technical Bulletin 84-24. Agr. Res. Service. U.S. Dept. Agr.

Schallenberger, R.S., O. Smith, and R.H. Treadway. 1959. Role of sugars in the browning reaction in potato chips. Agr. and Food Chem. 7(4):274–277.

Sowokinos, J.R. 1978. Relationship of harvest sucrose content to processing maturity and storage life of potatoes. Amer. Potato J. 50:333–334.

Sowokinos, J.R., E.C. Lulai, and J.A. Knoper. 1985. Translucent tissue defects in Solanum Tuberosum L. I. Alterations in amyloplast membrane integrity, enzyme activities, sugars and starch content. Plant Physiol. 78:489-494.

United States Department of Agriculture. 1984. Agricultural Statistics. U.S. Gov't. Printing Office. Washington, D.C.

Varns, J.L., J.R. Sowokinos and E.C. Yaeger. 1985. Heterogeneity in bulk storage of potatoes; Changes in respiration, sugar content, and chipping at different pile levels. Amer. Potato J. 62:446-447 (Abstract).

Table 1. Percentage of sucrose and glucose in control and handled potatoes subjected to increasing periods of storage (sugars were measured at constant 10-day period following handling treatment).

Sugar	Sample Handling Treatment	Means of 5 measured values at each storage period (months at 9C)			
		1	4	7	10
		----------Percent(fw)----------			
Sucrose	Handled	0.450	0.475	0.597	0.958
	Control	0.177	0.156	0.123	0.304
Glucose	Handled	0.048	0.059	0.048	0.046
	Control	0.016	0.023	0.025	0.036

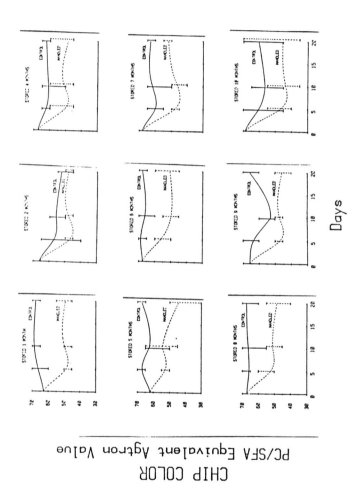

CHIP COLOR
PC/SFA Equivalent Agtron Value

TIME FOLLOWING HANDLING TREATMENT

Days

Fig. 1. The influence of storage duration and handling on chip color (cv. Norchip). Color measurements (means, ranges) were made 0, 5, 10 and 20 days after handling treatments on potatoes stored 1 to 10 months (Significant differences between handled and control means, $P < 0.01$).

285

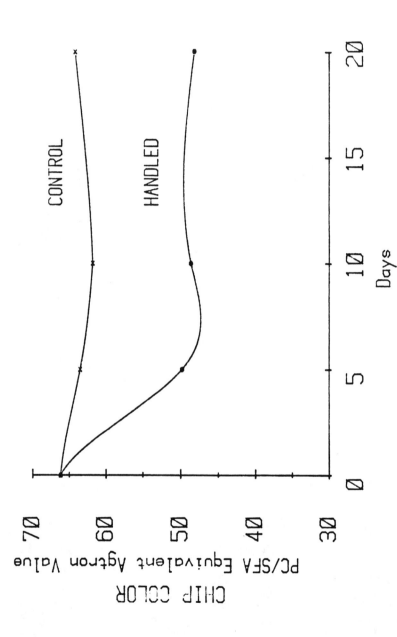

CHIP COLOR

PC/SFA Equivalent Agtron Value

TIME FOLLOWING HANDLING TREATMENT

Fig. 2. The influence of increasing time between handling and processing upon chip color &cv. Norchip), regardless of storage duration. Data represents all the color means for the 0-, 5-, 10- and 20-day intervals following handling treatment. (Significant differences between handling and control composite means, P < 0.01).

286

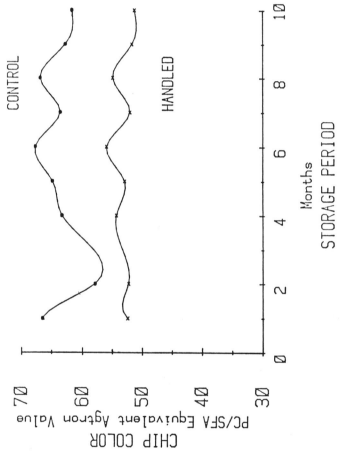

Fig. 3. The influence of storage duration (1 - 10 Months) upon chip color (cv. Norchip), regardless of time interval between handling and processing. Data points represent the handling sample and control composite means (0, 5, 10, and 20 days) for each storage duration.

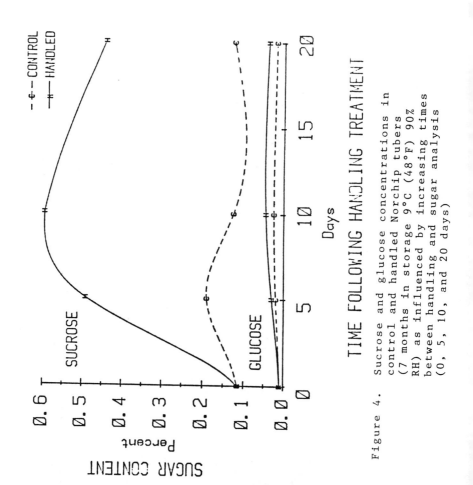

Figure 4. Sucrose and glucose concentrations in control and handled Norchip tubers (7 months in storage 9°C (48°F) 90% RH) as influenced by increasing times between handling and sugar analysis (0, 5, 10, and 20 days)

THE ECONOMIC IMPORTANCE OF BRUISING
TO IDAHO POTATOES IN TRANSIT

by

N.L. Meyer, Associate Professor; R.L. Phelps,
Research Assistant; G. Kleinschmidt, Extension
Potato Specialist; R.G. Beaver, Extension Potato
Specialist; M.L. Devoy, Research Associate;
College of Agriculture, University of Idaho,
Moscow, Idaho

ABSTRACT

This study classifies fresh potato shatter
bruise occurring in transit after grading and
inspection. Then the economic cost to the Idaho
fresh pack industry is established.

INTRODUCTION

The potato industry is important to Idaho.
Idaho farmers received $287,983 million of cash
receipts from potatoes in 1983, making potatoes 14.3
percent of producers' cash receipts in terms of value

ASAE Paper No. 85-6022

for production. This figure does not include the value added to the potato crop beyond the farm gate. Additional state and regional income comes from processing and marketing activities carried out in the state. Much of this value added income takes the form of wages and salaries paid to employees working in the processing and packing plants. The economy of Idaho also benefits from the plant construction, the purchase of equipment and its installation, purchases of packaging materials and supplies, the hiring of transport services, the payment of state and local taxes, and all the other expenditures made by the potato industry.

When it comes to shipping potatoes, nearly two-thirds of the U.S. population lives east of the Mississippi River. This means Idaho producers must transport potatoes greater distances to the major markets than producers from areas such as New York, Maine, the Red River Valley of North Dakota and Minnesota, Colorado and Wisconsin. For example, while Idaho paid around $3/cwt to ship to Chicago, Wisconsin potato producers pay about 60 cents (Nelson, 1984). This suggests consumers must pay more for Idaho potatoes.

Idaho's potato industry has a reputation for marketing a high quality product. To maintain this reputation potatoes shipped out of Idaho are required by law to pass federal-state inspections. Even so, there are occasional complaints from consumers and retailers about bruising found in Idaho potatoes. To protect Idaho's reputation for marketing quality potatoes, it is necessary to discover why and how these bruises are occurring after the potatoes have passed inspection. Since bruised potatoes bring a lower sales price, if they are marketable at all, and since they already have the production, packing and transport costs invested in them, there is an economic cost associated with bruising. The Idaho potato industry and producers and packers in particular will benefit if the economic cost of bruising Idaho potatoes in transit can be reduced.

OBJECTIVES

This study examines the economic cost of bruising to Idaho potatoes while in transit from the fresh pack shipping point to the retail distributor. Specifically, the objectives are as follows:

1. Examine the potato marketing chain from the fresh pack shipping point to the terminal market or wholesale distributor to determine:

    a. where bruising occurs
    b. how the bruising occurs
    c. what is the degree and cost of the bruising to the Idaho potato industry

2. To provide the above information to interested parties permitting them to identify cost effective means for reducing bruising in transit from the fresh pack shipping point to the retailer distributor.

CONSTRAINTS

This study focuses on one variety of potatoes, the Russett Burbank. It is primarily concerned with shatter bruise occurring to Idaho potatoes between the fresh pack shipping point in Idaho and the terminal market or wholesale distributor in Maryland. It is done in conjunction with Steve Grant and Mark Turzcin's work at the University of Maryland and USDA Beltsville.

Only one common handling and packaging system, 50 pound boxes, used for shipping fresh Idaho potatoes is examined. Though it would have been ideal to examine all the various handling systems and packaging materials actually used for shipping Idaho potatoes, the time and resource requirements were beyond the means of this study. Nevertheless, by choosing one of the two common modes for shipping Idaho potatoes, rail, this study should be of value to future researchers and those presently concerned with reducing the cost of bruising to Idaho potatoes while in transit (Table 1).

BRUISE DEFINED

Throughout the literature concerning potato bruising several terms are used. A bruise may be described as a pressure bruise, blackspot, shatter bruise, or a mechanical injury. A pressure bruise is a flattened or sunken area resulting from the pressure of adjacent tubers in a pile. Blackspot refers to a discoloration of the potato tissue just beneath the skin. Shatter bruise appears as a break in the tuber surface which may penetrate deeply into the tuber (Thornton 1979). Mechanical injury refers to cutting, breaking, or any other damage mechanically inflicted on the tuber. In much of the bruise literature, the mention of mechanical injury primarily refers to the bruising which develops after impact. Shatter bruise is the form of bruising emphasized in this study.

BRUISING THROUGH THE MARKET CHAIN

Shatter bruises occur more frequently as tuber turgidity increases. In general, shatter bruise decreases with maturity. Tuber temperature at the time of impact has a considerable effect on the amount of shatter bruise but the temperature effects have not been consistent (Ophuis, et al. 1958; Johnston and Wilson, 1966, 1969; Shippers, 1971a, 1971b). Johnston and Wilson found that damage severity was less during late harvest than during early harvest at the same temperature. Other researchers have reported an increase in damage at lower temperatures. Thornton has found that "shatter bruise is the primary bruise problem with cold potatoes." (Thornton, 1979).

SHIPPING POINT TO CONSUMER STUDIES

Bruising and other injuries to potatoes occur after the potatoes leave the shipping point. Many of these bruises actually occur before the potatoes are shipped but do not develop until in route to the consumer (Sparks, 1957; DeLoach and Moore, 1948). Still, additional bruising does occur as a result of rough handling and improper loading (DeLoach, 1942; DeLoach and Moore, 1948; Heson and Kroesbergen, 1960; Rion, 1945; Rose, 1946; Sparks, 1957). "Rough handling between the sackers, the carriers, and the reefer by the loaders is the source of much of the damage" (DeLoach and Moore, 1948). Heson and Kroesbergen recommend that the potatoes should be carefully handled during transit:

292

Sacks should not be dropped on the floor of
trucks, railway wagons, etc.; one should
not walk on the sacks, and it is advisable
to line the floor surfaces as it is
particularly the potatoes in the lowermost
sacks that suffer extensively during
transport. Nor should very heavy
(packaging) units be employed (sacks,
crates) as these are difficult to handle
and are often roughly deposited on the
floor. When potatoes are packed in
cardboard boxes (25 or 12.5 kilos [55 or
27.5 lbs.]) tubers are not damaged to the
same extent as in wooden crates (Heson and
Kroesbergen, 1960). (The samples in this
study were packed in cardboard boxes.)

Sparks noted that the process of loading the car
at the shipping point increased hard and serious
bruises by 2.5 percent and that the method of loading
will to some extent determine the amount of injury
caused in transit. He found that hand loading
results in less injury than dump-loading. The actual
transporting of the potatoes increased bruising by 5
percent but the unloading of sacks from the railroad
car caused less injury than any other operation from
the time of harvest onward. However, just the
opposite was true with distributing the potatoes as
more bruising was caused in distribution than in any
other operation (Sparks, 1957).

Rose discusses bruising as an avenue for
diseases and decay to occur which will damage the
appearance and the shipment and thus lower its market
value and also lead to waste when the potatoes are
prepared by the consumer. Rose concedes that the
prices potatoes bring do not warrant the same care
and handling as given to apples or pears but
nevertheless there is room for serious reduction in
mechanical injury. Finally, Rose talks about the
economic loss associated when only part of a shipment
is damaged:

A type of injury frequently occurring on
potatoes is that caused in carlot shipments
by the pressure of the load on the lower

layers, particularly the lower side of the bags in the bottom layer... [On heavier than normal loads] shippers and receiver were inclined to blame all of the so-called floor bruising on the use of the heavier load, although more or less damage of this kind always prevailed even in the lighter loads. In considering the damage sustained in this connection it should be noted that in the wholesale trade the bag is the unit; therefore, damage done to the potatoes on only one side of a bag affects the market value of the whole bag and the number of bags that are thus affected similarly influences the return on the whole carload when it is sold as a unit. This effect is often out of all proportion to the number of potatoes that show injury and is especially important if the crushing or bruising releases juice that causes dirty or wet spots on the bags or if holes are worn in the bags by rubbing against the walls or floor rack of the car while in transit.

Bruising from whatever cause is sometimes so serious a problem to receivers and distributors of potatoes in large terminal markets that they find it necessary to recondition the shipments which they handle. In doing this the receiver discards badly bruised tubers and resacks them in clean bags. Bruised potatoes which are still fit for food are graded out of a No. 1 pack and are either trimmed or sold at a discount (Rose, 1946).

A similar action occurs today when loads are rejected. The actual discount depends on the degree of divergence from grade standard. An average discount of $2 per box would result in $4,000 less for a load of 2,000 50-pound boxes. For the higher value count boxes the discount needed to move the grade rejected potaotes could be even larger. In cases where the potatoes must be repacked the price discount is often as high as 50 percent.

294

DATA COLLECTION AND SAMPLING PROCEDURES

Fifty-six percent of Idaho potatoes were shipped by railcar in 1983-84 (Table 1). Three rail car shipments of potatoes to the Washington, D.C. area in 50-pound corrugated boxes were monitored for this study. This research was a cooperative effort of USDA-OT, University of Maryland, National Potato Councils Anti-Bruise Committee and the University of Idaho Extension Service. For this project, assessment of shatter bruise involved visually locating cuts or shatter bruise, measuring the length of the cut with a caliper rule and using a kitchen rule to measure the depth of cut (Grant, p. 6).

RAILCAR EXPERIMENTAL DESIGN

The location of the 13-22.7 kg (30-50 lb.) boxes of sample potatoes which at origin in Idaho are shown in Table 2, and Figure 1. The boxes were marked with an alpha-numeric code for easy detection and recovery at destination. During the trip, which lasted ten days, the inside temperature of the railcar was monitored. Chart temperature recorders were placed inside three test sample boxes. The first recorder at the front of the car in the center box, A-3; the second recorder at the middle of the car in the top test box, B-6; and the third recorder at the rear of the car in the center box, C-3.

DESTINATION SAMPLING

Railcar shipments from Idaho were received at the Jessup, Maryland produce center. The 22.7 kg (50 lb.) test boxes were identified and removed from the cars during the unloading procedure. All test sample containers were taken to the University of Maryland, College Park for bruise analysis.

DESTINATION STORAGE

Test sample potatoes once removed from the vehicle were then taken to Holzapfel Hall on the University of Maryland campus. The refrigeration unit was set at 10°C (50 °F) to keep the deterioration of the external and internal quality of sample potatoes to a minimum (The Potato Association of

America, 1980). Sample potatoes needed to be tempered for at least 24 hours in storage before bruise analysis could be performed, because following injury, a potato sometimes requires 24 hours to reach maximum bruise color development (The Potato Association of America, 1980).

TEST 1 - SHATTER BRUISE MEASUREMENT

The 4.54 kg (10 lb.) sample bags from the trucks were opened and every other potato was set aside on a tray which was marked with the bag location (i.e., A-1, A-2, ...) for use in the shatter bruise test. The other potatoes were placed in a similar tray and were used for the blackspot test described elsewhere by Grant. The procedure of choosing every other potato minimized systematic error and observer bias. Each potato was individually weighed in grams on a calibrated electronic scale and any cuts or cracks were visually located and measured for length and depth in millimeters using a stainless steel hand-held caliper.

A five-pound sample was selected from each 22.7 kg (50 lb.) sample railcar box. Each box was emptied on a flat surface and one tenth of the potatoes were separated from the total 50 lbs.

GRADING STANDARDS

If there are questions about the quality of a load when it arrives, a re-inspection can be called for. (All potatoes are required by the Idaho Marketing Order to be ingrade when they are shipped. See USDA Standards for Grades of Potatoes.) Shatter bruise is classified as an external effect because it is visible through examination of the exterior surface of the potato. It is one of several types of bruises. For U.S. No. 1 grade a tolerance of eight percent by weight is acceptable subject to the fact that not more than five percent of the tolerance can be of external defects. In the three test carloads, all were accepted as U.S. No. 1 grade.

For the experimental samples shipped, all were hand picked to be free of external injury. Thus all shatter bruise occurred during transit or unloading.

The proxy used for degree of shatter bruise is
depth of split in mm. There is strong correlation
between the length and depth, the longer the split
the greater the depth. To rate bruise severity,
three categories were developed based on depth of
split. Slightly split were no splits or splits less
than 3 mm (.12 in.). Moderate bruises were those
with split depth of 3.1 mm to 6 mm (.12 to .24 in.).
Severe bruises were splits greater than 6 mm in
depth. The specific number and percentage in each
category is shown in Table 3. Eighty-three percent
of the sampled potatoes were shatter bruise free,
that is, had no splits or they were less than 3 mm in
depth. Eleven percent had splits of 3.1 to 6 mm.
Six percent had splits of more than 6 mm which we
classified as severe shatter bruise. This
classification is an arbitrary decision by the
authors.

ECONOMIC EFFECT OF LOAD REJECTION

Idaho's market order which permits enforcement
of grade standards for exports from the state,
enhances Idaho's ability to control the movement of
nonquality product from Idaho. The result has been a
reputation for quality product from the state. This
has enabled a premium to be charged for "Idaho
Bakers." To evaluate the importance of shatter
bruise for the individual shippers and the industry I
spoke with members of the Federal Inspection Service
concerning the frequency of reinspection. [1] It has
ranged from 4.7 to 8.0 percent in recent years. For
this example we will use a 6.5 percent reinspection
rate. He stated that the number of calls for
reinspections was closely related to changes in
market price. Further, upon reinspection, the
failure rate has been 5.5 percent for Idaho
inspection for the 1984/85 crop year. Based on these
two assumptions, there would be an estimated 118
inspection failures at destination for Idaho
potatoes. Thirty-six would be for rail cars and 82
for trucks (Table 3). The economic importance of
these failures to the fresh pack industry are noted
in the following section.

----

[1]Conversations with Pat Brubaker of Federal
Inspection Service office in Boise, Idaho, June 11-
12, 1975.

It is assumed the volume of potatoes involved is so small that it does not affect national potato prices. Therefore losses are only shown as decreases in revenue and extra costs to the packer.

The scenarios possible when a load fails to pass inspection are: 1) sell the load at a discounted price, 2) repack the load taking out the below grade product thus permitting the remaining product to make grade, and 3) dispose of the total load by dumping.

For the following analysis a situation of 60-70 count cardboard boxes will be used and a base revenue is calculated at $25 per 50-pound box. Annual estimated losses to the Idaho fresh pack industry because product does not make grade are based on 36 cars, and 82 trucks being rejected (Table 4).

Assuming that all reinspection failures can be discounted and marketed for ten percent less than anticipated and that the receiver will cover freight, the revenue loss to the industry is $131,200 (82 loads x $1,600 per load) for truck shipments and $165,600 (36 cars x $4,600 per car) for a total of $296,800 annually. That's $.0154 per cwt for all fresh pack per year.

In cases where the loads failing reinspection must be replaced and assuming shipper must accept a 50 percent price discount and pay transport, the revenue losses to the Idaho fresh pack industry are considerably greater. They are estimated at $1,025,000 (82 loads x $12,500 per load) for truck shipments and $1,229,400 (36 cars x $34,150 per car) resulting in an etimated revenue loss to the industry of $2,254,400. This would be $.11 for each hundred weight of potatoes exported from Idaho in 1983/84.

The worst case scenario is where the product must be dumped resulting in the loss of all revenue plus paying the transport charges. In this case, the revenue loss to the industry would be $1,845,000 ($22,500 per load x 82 loads) from truck shipments and $2,264,400 ($62,900 per load x 36 rail car loads) for a total revenue loss to the industry of $4,109,400. That is estimated to be $.20 per hundred weight for all potatoes exported from the state.

In actuality each case of carload inspection failure is decided on its own merits. Factors such as price rot[2] strongly influence the number of reinspections and the discount needed to move product. On the other side, strong demand can decrease the discounts necessary to move a product which fails reinspection. In the scenarios discussed, Case 1 is a situation of strong demand and very little discount which will not affect fresh pack price a great deal. Case 3 will affect the overall Idaho price by $.20 per cwt.

All Idaho producers lose from bruise and spoilage in potatoes. Therefore, it is to producers', transporters', packers' and distributors' advantage to reduce bruise whenever possible, thereby permitting Idaho producers to continue to receive the premium which permits them to compete in Eastern markets.

IMPLICATIONS FOR FURTHER RESEARCH

This work is just a beginning step in defining steps to reduce the losses resulting from transport of potatoes. First the real losses to the shipper/packer occur when the load fails reinspection. Therefore his main goal is to pack a product which will pass reinspection and meet the buyers' needs at destination. Research needs to be key to what factors are most prevalent in reinspection failures.

Second, it would be good to compare modes (ie., railcar, truck, piggyback) and containers as well as packing materials (ie. 50-pound cardboard boxes, mesh bags, and poly balers) to quantify differences. There are advantages to certain packing or shipping methods that potentially reduce risk of reinspection failure and therefore economic loss.

Economic analysis must also look at the macro level as well as the micro level. A major assumption

----

[2] Price declining between the date of purchase and the date of delivery.

in this analysis was that increases in quantities marketed because of less bruising, waste and spoilage would not affect price. At the macro level the increase in supply would have a depressing effect on price. This would cause the estimated benefits to bruise reduction to be over stated. Price and demand elasticity must be included in the analysis.

REFERENCES

DeLoach, D.B. and James C. Moore. Trial shipment of Oregon late-crop potatoes. Oregon Agr. Exp. Sta. Bulletin No. 460. 1948.

Grant, Steven W. 1985. Potato bruising during transportation. Masters Thesis. Univ. of Maryland. Ag. Engineering Dept.

Johnston, Edward F. and J.B. Wilson. Effect of soil temperatures at harvest on the bruise resistance of potatoes. American Potato Journal, Vol. 46, 1969, p. 75-82.

Johnston, Edward F. and J.B. Wilson. Soil, air and tuber temperature and bruise resistance. Maine Agr. Exp. Sta. Misc. Report No. 119, 1966.

Nelson, James H. World of potato fresh shippers: gamble begins upon purchase. Potato Grower of Idaho, Sept. 1984, p. 18-27.

Ophuis, B.G., J.C. Hesen and E. Kroesbergen. The infuence of the temperature during handling on the occurrence of blue discolorations inside potato tubers. European Potato Journal. Vol. 1, 1958, p. 48-65.

Rose, D.H. Handling and shipping early potatoes. USDA Cir. No. 744. 1946.

Sparks, Walter C. Mechanical injury to potaotes from harvester to consumer. Idaho Agr. Exp. Sta. Bulletin No. 280. 1957.

Thornton, Robert. Potato tuber condition and the harvester operation. Chipper Snacker, Nov. 1979, p. 41-42.

Table 1   Idaho Fresh Potato Movements in Pounds by Month for 1983-84 Crop Year

Month	Carlot Summary (lbs)	(#)	Truck Summary (lbs)	Piggyback Summary (lbs)	Total Rail Truck, Pig. (lbs)	Total Fresh Movement (cwt)
August	4,725,150	45	16,185,738	84,050	20,994,930	209,949
September	34,541,946	310	45,721,131	169,000	80,432,077	804,320
October	107,204,899	943	87,270,060	536,750	195,011,709	1,950,117
November	139,138,036	1,211	96,936,812	857,000	236,931,848	2,369,318
December	120,614,985	1,054	75,837,440	1,322,550	197,774,975	1,977,750
January	143,056,876	1,238	83,385,046	1,033,300	227,475,222	2,274,752
February	109,806,105	957	81,869,316	728,450	192,403,871	1,924,039
March	129,183,879	1,114	82,098,211	722,800	212,045,890	2,120,549
April	123,078,349	1,051	92,027,209	798,750	215,904,308	2,159,043
May	123,337,358	1,062	109,732,572	639,750	233,709,680	2,337,097
June	101,708,450	876	115,735,012	426,500	217,869,962	2,178,700
July	2,473,450	23	11,569,346	88,000	14,130,796	141,308
TOTALS	1,138,869,483	9,884	898,368,246	7,456,900	2,044,699,276	20,446,992

Average Carlot Wt. = 115,223.54   Rail Movement = 55.7%   Truck = 43.94%   Piggyback = .36%

Source: USDA Market News Report

301

Table 2. Identification code for 22.7 kg (50 lb.) boxes

Rear of Car	Center of Car	Front of Car
C-1		A-1
C-2	B-6	A-2
C-3	B-7	A-3
C-4		A-4
C-5		A-5

Grading Standards

If there are questions about the quality of a load when it arrives, a re-inspection can be called for. (All potatoes are required by the Idaho Marketing Order to be ingrade when they are shipped. See USDA Standards for Grades of Potatoes.) Shatter bruise is classified as an external effect because it is visible through examination of the exterior surface of the potato. It is one of several types of bruises. For U.S. No. 1 grade a tolerance of 8 percent by weight is acceptable subject to the fact that not more than 5 percent of the tolerance can be of external defects. In the three test carloads, all were accepted as U.S. No. 1 grade.

302

Table 3. Shatter Bruise Classifications in Sample Potatoes
          from Idaho Test Shipments

Degree Bruise	Number	Percent
Slight (0 to 3 mm)	284	83
Moderate (3.1 to 6 mm)	36	11
Severe (over 6 mm)	22	6
TOTAL	342	100

Table 4 Potential Loss Summarys Under Three Scenarios[1]

	Carlots[2] (lbs)	Trucks[3] (lbs)	Piggyback[2] (lbs)	Total cwt
Total 1983-84	1,138,869,483	898,368,246	7,456,900	20,446,992
Number Cars/ Trucks	9,903	22,459	186	-
Inspection at Destination[4]	644	1,460	12	-
Inspection failures at destination[5]	36	81	1	

[1] All fresh table stock potatoes exported from Idaho must be graded.

[2] Carlot average load of 115,000 pounds.

[3] Truck loads average 40,000 pounds.

[4] Based on conversations with Pat Brubaker, 6/12/85, Federal Inspection Service, Boise, Idaho, the reinspection rate for Idaho inspected shipments has varied from 4.7 to 8 percent. For purposes of this example a 6.5 percent reinspection rate is used.

[5] Based on conversations with Pat Brubaker, 6/12/85, Federal Inspection Service, Boise, Idaho, recent experience has been a 5.5 percent inspection failure rate.

Table 5 Revenue Losses From Failure to Make Grade Under 3 Scenarios

Scenarios	Truck 800 boxes[1]	Railcar 2300 boxes
(1) Base Revenue to Idaho Shipper per load ($25/box)	$20,000	$57,500
(2) Discount ($2 per box) Revenue to Shipper Lost from base revenue/load	$18,400 ($1,600)	$52,900 ($4,600)
(3) Discount to repacker ($12.50 per box) Transport cost to Maryland ($6.25 per cwt Net revenue Loss from Base per load	 $ 2,500 ($12,500)	 $ 5,400 (34,150)
(4) Spoiled Load must dump Transport cost Total revenue lost	 $20,000 $ 2,500 ($22,500)	 $57,500 $ 5,400 ($62,900)

[1] Assume 50 pound cardboard boxes of #60-70 Idaho U.S. 1 potatoes
    valued at $25 per box

305

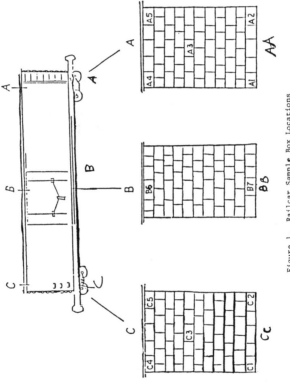

Figure 1. Railcar Sample Box Locations

306

POTATO BRUISING DURING TRANSPORT

by

S.W. Grant, Graduate Research Assistant,
Horticulture Department, University of Maryland;
M.T. Turczyn, General Engineer and B.H. Ashby,
Marketing Specialist, U.S. Department of Agriculture;
N.D. Hallee, Extension Agricultural Engineer,
University of Maine; G.D. Kleinschmidt, Extension
Potato Specialist, Idaho Research and Extension
Center, Twin Falls, Idaho; and F.W. Wheaton,
Professor, Agricultural Engineering Department,
University of Maryland

ABSTRACT

Test shipments of potatoes were conducted to
determine the amount of shatter bruise and blackspot
incurred by table stock potatoes during truck and
rail transportation. Shatter bruising averaged 45
percent at destination to potatoes shipped from
storage and 20 percent to new potatoes shipped

ASAE Paper No. 85-6023

shortly after harvest. However, shatter bruises severe enough to cause reduction in grade averaged only three percent. Rough handling at the loading docks rather than transport stresses appear to cause considerable shatter bruising. Blackspot trim loss was found to be less than one percent for stored potatoes after transport and zero percent for new potatoes.

INTRODUCTION

The National Potato Council estimates that their industry losses are over 125 million dollars annually due to bruising which occurs while harvesting, storing, handling, packing and shipping table stock potatoes. Although bruising occurs at every phase of the distribution cycle, the bulk of the current research has only reported on the amount of bruising that occurs during harvesting and storage. Therefore, he Council requested help in determining the amount and the severity of bruising that occurs due to handling and transporting table stock potatoes from the packing shed to terminal wholesale warehouses. This paper reports on a series of test shipments conducted to provide baseline data on bruises incurred by table stock potatoes during transportation.

A few past studies have presented bruise data associated with handling and transport. While informative, new developments in packaging, new handling practices such as palletized loading, and increasing load density for potatoes shipped in railcars have been introduced. These new practices may influence the amount of bruising that occurs. Bakken (1934), Sparks (1950, 1957), and Weber (1964) reported that the percentages of bruising to table stock potatoes caused by handling and transport were 10, 20, and 9 percent, respectively. Their grading methods were not the same so comparison of data is not possible. They agreed that handling of the potatoes was the primary cause of the bruising rather than vehicle shock and vibration.

METHODOLOGY

Test loads of table stock potatoes from Maine, Florida, and Idaho, representing three major production areas, were monitored for intransit bruising during shipment to the Washington, D.C. area. The potatoes from Maine and Florida were shipped in refrigerated tractor trailer trucks, and those from Idaho were transported by railcar. Shatter bruise-free potato samples were inserted in each commercial shipment at origin to assure that only transport bruises were measured. A test plan that specified the procedure for sampling, bruise measurement, packaging and test sample bag location within the vehicle at origin was used.

Sample preparation at origin was performed by State personnel and retrieval of samples and bruise measurement at destination was performed by USDA personnel. Sample potatoes from Florida were prepared by the same USDA personnel at both origin and destination.

Origin

The potatoes transported and tested were U.S. graded No. 1 table stock. Test sample potatoes were randomly selected and visually free of shatter bruises. Samples of stored potatoes were taken from the same lot that had been designated for the commercial load. Samples of new or freshly harvested potatoes were taken from the sorting line during the bagging operation from the same lot being packed for the commercial shipment. The use of bruise free potatoes at origin, as applied in this study, was patterned after Harding and Chace (1961) to insure that injury found at destination occurred in transit. At origin initial bruise analyses for blackspot, which is not visible until the potato is peeled, were performed on the lot of potatoes from which the shipment samples were taken and those potatoes were discarded. All potatoes shipped were commercially graded before packing.

Pulp temperatures were obtained during the vehicle loading operation. In addition, temperature chart recorders were placed throughout the load of potatoes to monitor the potato's environmental temperature during the trip.

Truck Shipments

For the truck shipments, the bruise-free sample potatoes were packed into 4.54 kg (10 lb.) paper/mesh window bags similar to those used for the other potatoes in the commercial load. Twenty-five sample bags were used in each test load. Each sample 4.54 kg (10 lb.) bag was packed by shipper personnel with four other commercial 4.54 kg (10 lb.) bags in a paper or nylon mesh master baler bag. These five baler bags in turn were loaded by shipper at a designated position on one of five pallets (Figure 1). Each test pallet was placed at the designed position within the commercial load on alternating sides of the trailer to give a representation of the entire load (Figure 1).

Railcar Shipments

For the railcar shipments, the potatoes were not palletized and shipped in 22.7 kg (50.0 lb.) corrugated fiberboard boxes. The sample potatoes were bulk packed in 12 boxes. These samples boxes were marked and inserted at locations within the commercial load as shown in Figure 2.

Destination

Upon arrival at the wholesale chain store or terminal wholesale warehouse in the Washington, D.C. area, each vehicle was unloaded and the sample potatoes and temperature recorders were retrieved. Pulp temperatures were obtained. Sample potatoes were stored under refrigeration at 10° C (50° F) and 70 percent relative humidity. The sample potatoes were stored at least 24 hours before bruise determinations were made. Bruise determinations for each sample bag were made by using 2.27 kg (5.0 lb.) of each sample for shatter bruise measurements and the remaining 2.27 kg for blackspot measurement.

Measurement of Shatter Bruise

Shatter bruises break the potato skin and are recognizable as a crack or fissure. Shatter bruise was determined through visual examination. The length of each bruise in the skin was measured using a hand-held caliper. The bruise depth was located by slicing into the potato meat perpendicular and along the length of the cut. Removing the meat of the potato revealed the bruise depth. The depth was then measured using a hand-held caliper.

Measurement of Blackspot

Blackspot is defined as uniformly discolored areas beneath the skin, not visible until a potato is peeled (The Potato Association of America, 1980). The blackspot seldom penetrates deeper than 0.32 cm (0.126 in.) to 0.64 cm (0.252 in.) and is rarely accompanied by a rupture of the potato skin. Blackspot was determined by first peeling each 2.27 kg (5.0 lb.) sample of potatoes in a ten percent lye bath solution. Each potato was then weighed and visually examined for bruising. Blackspot was removed with a kitchen knife and weighed. The length, width, and depth of each blackspot removed was measured using a hand-held caliper.

Data Analysis

Differences in the frequency and severity of shatter bruise and blackspot by shipper and location within the vehicle were analyzed statistically using Analysis of Variance (ANOVA) and Duncan's Multiple Range Techiques.

Due to the general nature of this study and the necessity of using commercial shipments from diversified geographic regions and limited duration of time, some vairables could not be controlled. Examples are distance shipped, mode of transportation, shipper, and variety. Therefore, no attempt is made in this study to make any comparison between growing area, variety, or mode of transport.

RESULTS

Shatter Bruise

Frequency and Severity

Table 1 shows that approximately 45 percent of the potatoes shipped from storage and 21 percent of new potatoes incurred some shatter bruise. This reflects the overall amount of abuse the potatoes incur during loading and transport, it is not indicative of the marketability of the potatoes at destination.

Table 2 defines the severity of damage by bruise depth. This was accomplished by dividing the sample potato bruise measurements into four bruise severity categories: (1) There is no bruise damage, (2) Slight bruise severity where depth is less than 3 mm (0.12 in.), (3) Medium bruise severity where bruise depth is greater than 3 mm (0.12 in.) but less than 6 mm (.24 in.) and (4) Severe damage where bruise depth is greater than 6 mm. (0.24 in.).

Based on observations of subjective commercial grading techniques, it was assumed that only potatoes showing severe damage (category 4) were bruised enough to possibly affect their marketability.

Effect of Pallet or Stack Location Within Vehicle

No significant differences (P<0.05) were found for the amount of shatter bruise by location of the pallet within truck or stack locations within the railcars.

Effect of Position Within Pallet or Stack

No significant differences (P<0.05) in the amount or severity of shatter bruise were found by bag position within pallet for new potaotes shipped by truck. In addition, no significant differences were found for shatter bruise damage at different box locations within the stack for stored potatoes shipped by railcar. Significant differences were found for bruise area (length x depth) by bag position for stored potatoes shipped by truck (Table 3). This table indicates that a considerable amount of the bruising damage was concentrated on the bottom layers of the pallets. Further analysis on a shipper basis revealed that the bruising at the lower layers may have been caused by one shipper's poor loading method rather than by transport stresses.

Effect of Shipper

Railcar shippers showed no significant differences (P<0.05) in shatter bruise damage.

Table 4 shows significant (P<0.05) differences in both the frequency and cumulative depth of shatter bruise for both new and stored truck transported potatoes originating at different packing sheds. Each group of these potatoes was of the same variety and transported by the same mode.

Further analyses comparing truck shippers found significant (P<0.05) differences in the frequency of bruises by bag position within the pallet for only shipper A of stored potatoes (Table 5). For this shipper the highest amount of bruising incurred on potatoes on the bottom layers of the pallets. Loaders were observed dropping the baler bags directly on the wooden pallets at this packing shed, thus possibly accounting for the increased brusing.

Effect of Pulp Temperatures and Handling

Table 6 illustrates that shatter bruise damage is related both to the type of handling and pulp temperature. For stored potatoes, both test loads were loaded at non-recommended temperatures. Shipment A received rough handling and shipment B received careful handling while loading at an incorrect temperature. The rough handling resulted in a 44 percent increase in the total percentage of shatter bruise damage.

For new potatoes, Shipper C loaded potatoes at a non-recommended temperature and roughly handled the potatoes while stacking on pallets. Shipper D handled the potatoes carefuly and at a recommended temperature, thus total percentage bruising was reduced by about 16 percent.

These findings agree with the Potato Association of America (1980) who found that increased brusing in stored potatoes loaded at temperatures below 10 °C, and the findings by Stiles and Hallee (1981) who showed that newly harvested potatoes handled at pulp temperatures between 2 to 4 °C (35.6 to 39.2 °F) or 16

313

to 18 °C (60.8 to 64.4°F) were more susceptible to
bruising than at other temperatures. Table 6 also
confirms that new potatoes are more susceptible to
severe damage from rough handling than stored
potatoes. Much research has shown that early or new
potatoes are more sensitive to damage from bruising
than mature or stored potatoes because the skins have
not had time to mature or set (Rose, 1946; Sparks,
1977).

Blackspot

After transport, blackspot trim loss in stored
potatoes was one percent and none for new potatoes.
There were no significant differences (P<0.05) in
blackspot development at different locations within
the railcar or truckloads, nor by different locations
within pallets or stacks.

CONCLUSIONS

From this study it may be concluded that a
relatively high frequency of shatter bruise is
incurred by potatoes during transport, but the amount
of severe damage due to transport shock and
vibrations is relatively low. A considerable amount
of bruising damage results from rough handling during
loading. Bruising due to rough handling is further
compounded when the potatoes are loaded at non-
recommended loading temperature.

Practically no blackspot bruising was found as a
consequence of transport conditions.

REFERENCES

Bakken, H.H. 1934. The market for midwestern
    potatoes. Wisc. Univ. Ext. Circular 272, Univ.
    of Wisc., Madison, Wisc.

Hann, P.H. 1981. Damage to potatoes (transport and
    handling). Center for Agricultural Publications
    and Documentation, the Netherlands. Wageningen,
    the Netherlands.

Harding, P.L. and W.G. Chace. 1961. Effect of heavy
    loading on quality of Sebago potatoes shipped
    from Florida by rail. USDA, MRR-441.

Idaho Growers Shippers Association Newsletter.
   December 18, 1983.

Commercial potato production in North America.   1980.
   The Potato Assoc. of Amer., Univ. of Maine
   at Orono, Orono, Maine.

Rose, D.H.   1946.   Handling and shipping early
   potatoes.   USDA Circular 744.

Smith, Ora.   1968.   Potatoes: production, storing,
   processing.   The Avi Publishing Co., Westport,
   Conn.

Sparks, W. August 1950. Injury studies on Idaho grown
   Russett Burbank potatoes, Part I, shipping and
   handling.   Amer.   Potato J. 27(8):   287-303.
   August.

Sparks, W. June 1957. Mechanical injury to potatoes
   from harvester to consummer.   Bulletin 280.
   Idaho Agric. Experiment Station, Univ. of Idaho,
   Aberdeen, Idaho.   June.

Sparks, W. January 1977.   Potato brusing can cost
   you $$.   Amer. Veg. Grower 25(1):1416.

Stiles, D. and N. Hallee.   1981.   Anti-bruise cam-
   paign: harvest phase.   Univ. of Maine Exten-
   sion Service Publication.   Orono, Maine.

Weber, J., W.M. Iritani, and J.E. Dixon.   1964.
   Shipping damage to potatoes shipped in sacks
   and bulk.   Idaho Agric. Res. Progress Report
   No. 86, University of Idaho College of Agri.
   Idaho Falls, Idaho.

TABLE 1.   NUMBER AND PERCENT OCCURRENCES OF SHATTER BRUISES FOUND ON
POTATOES BY INDICATED TRANSPORT AND PHYSIOLOGICAL CONDITIONS

| Shatter Bruise Per Potato | TRUCK | | RAILCAR |
	New Potatoes 1/	Stored Potatoes 2/	Stored Potatoes 3/
0	79.14	57.97	52.30
1	15.71	21.98	27.75
2	3.38	10.75	10.40
3	1.48	4.70	5.78
4	0.14	2.30	2.02
5	0.14	1.15	0.86
6	--	1.40	0.86
7	--	0.28	--

1/   Mean of three truck shipments approximately 1,600 km (1000 mi.).

2/   Mean of three truck shipments approximately 1,120 km (700 mi.).

3/   Mean of three railcar shipments approximately 3,860 km (2412 mi.).

316

TABLE 2. SHATTER BRUISE SEVERITY AND PERCENTAGE OF OCCURRENCE

| Bruise Severity Category | TRUCK | | RAIL |
	New Potatoes	Stored Potatoes	Stored Potatoes
No damage	79.44	57.91	51.90
Slight bruise 1/	9.84	36.05	27.99
Medium bruise 2/	8.81	4.22	10.79
Severe bruise 3/	1.91	1.82	9.33

1/ Bruise depth less than 3 mm (0.12 in.).

2/ Bruise depth less than 6 mm (0.24 in.).

3/ Bruise depth greater than 6 mm (0.24 in.).

TABLE 3. SHATTER BRUISE AREA PER 2.27 kg (5 lb.) BAG BY
POSITION WITHIN PALLET ON STORED
POTATOES SHIPPED BY TRUCK 1/

Bag Position Within Pallet 2/	Cumulative Bruise Area (Mean)
	(mm^2)
5	460abc*
4	226c
3	410bc
2	480ab
1	653a

1/ Based on three shipments trucked 1,120 km (700 mi.).

2/ See Figure 1 for bag position.

* Means with the same letter are not
significantly different (P<0.05) by Duncan's
Multiple Range Test.

TABLE 4. SHATTER BRUISE PER 2.27 kg SAMPLE BAG DEVELOPED DURING TRUCK
TRANSPORTATION

Stored Potatoes 1/		
Shipper	Bruise Per Bag (mean)	Cumulative Bruise Depth Per Bag (mean)
	No.	mm (m)
A	14.6a*	36.6a (1.44)
B	3.4b	7.8b (0.307)

New Potatoes 2/		
Shipper	Bruise Per Bag (mean)	Cumulative Bruise Depth Per Bag (mean)
C	3.0a	12.1a (0.476 in.)
D	0.8b	3.7b (0.146 in.)

1/ Stored potatoes of one variety shipped by truck approximately 1,120 (700 mi.) km

2/ New potatoes of one variety shipped by truck approximately 1,600 km (1000 mi.)

* Means in the same column with the same letter are not significantly different (P<0.05) by Duncan's Multiple Range Test

319

TABLE 5. SHATTER BRUISE FREQUENCY BY BAG
POSITION WITHIN PALLET BY SHIPPER

Bag Position 2/ Within Pallet	Stored Potatoes 1/	
	Shipper A 3/ (Mean)	Shipper B 4/ (Mean)
	No.	No.
5	9.6b*	4.0a
4	13.6b	1.6a
3	10.8b	?.4a
2	20.0a	4.4a
1	24.0a	4.4a

1/ Potatoes of same variety shipped approximately
1,120 km (700 mi.).

2/ See Figure 1 for bag position.

3/ Rough handling observed.

4/ Careful handling observed.

* Means in the same column with the same letter
are not significantly different (P<0.05) by
Duncan's Multiple Range Test.

TABLE 6. EFFECT OF LOADING TEMPERATURE AND HANDLING ON THE AMOUNT OF SHATTER BRUISE

Potato Physiological Condition	Shipper	Type of Handling Observed	Average Pulp Temperature °C	Bruise Category by Percent			Total Percent
				Slight 1/	Medium 2/	Severe 3/	
Stored	A	Rough	5.5 4/	66.29	0.75	0.38	67.42
	B	Careful	3.9 4/	16.82	4.20	1.20	22.22
New	C	Rough	16.2 4/	11.69	12.36	2.25	26.30
	D	Careful	23.8 5/	6.36	2.12	1.27	9.75

1/ Bruise depth less than 3 mm (0.12 in.).

2/ Bruise depth less than 6 mm and greater than 3 mm (0.12 in.).

3/ Bruise depth greater than 6 mm (0.24 in.).

4/ Non-recommended loading temperature (below 10° C or 16° to 18° C) (50°F or 60.8 to 64.4°F).

5/ Recommended loading temperature.

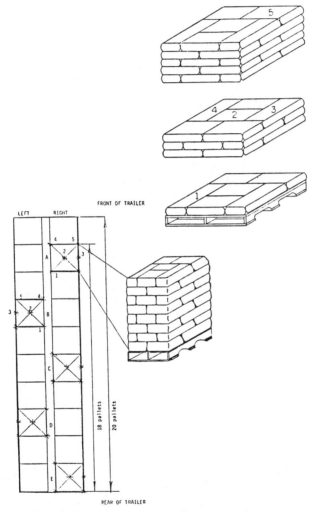

FIG 1 Top view of truck trailer showing sample pallets within trailer and
bag positions within pallets.

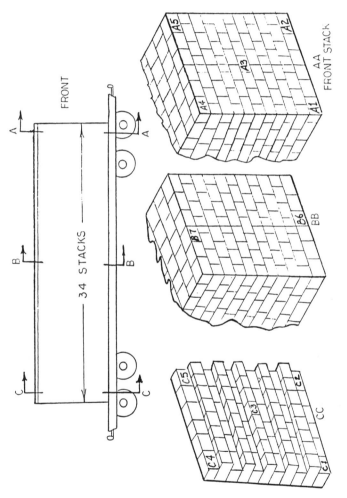

FIG 2 Railcar sample box locations.

323

RESEARCH NEEDS IN HANDLING AND TRANSPORTING
POTATOES FOR THE CHIP MARKET

by

Paul H. Orr,   Agricultural Engineer, USDA-ARS-NSA,
RRV Potato Research Laboratory, East Grand Forks,
Minnesota

ABSTRACT

Raw potatoes of stable high quality (internal
and external) are necessary on a year-round basis in
the   chipping   industry.   Handling potatoes from
storage   has   recently   demonstrated   a   quality
destabilizing effect.   Multi-discipline research is
suggested on   1) location   models   for   production/
storage/processing/consuming   areas,   2)   handling
methods and equipment, 3) cultivar improvement,   and
4) sorting via internal quality parameters.

ASAE Paper No. 85-6024

INTRODUCTION

In the U.S., the consumer trend continues to shift from fresh consumption of potatoes toward various processed forms. About 70 percent of the U.S. fall-crop potato production is ultimately processed for use. Long-term storage of potatoes to supply raw material having stable quality for conversion into various types of processed products is becoming one of the more important apsects of the potato industry. Handling large volumes of raw potatoes into and from storage and transporting them to the various market locations has also developed into an important part of the processed potato industry, particulary in relation to maintaining quality during the sometimes lengthy shipping process. In this report, we will concentrate on requirements of the U.S. potato industry for research to aid in handling and transporting to market the approximately 1.8 million metric tons (40,000,000 cwt) of potatoes utilized annually for chipping (PC/SFA, 1985).

Ideally, raw potatoes having relatively stable quality for processing into potato chips must be available in relatively large volumes year-round to meet the industry's chip production strategy calling for small inventories of finished products in order to maintain freshness.

STORAGE/PLANT LOCATION

Potatoes for chipping are produced in quantity in the U.S. fall-crop production areas where tubers having high total solids can be grown and a cool climate presents opportunities for long-term storage without costly refrigeration. Then, over several months time, the stored raw potatoes are removed from

----

*A Laboratory cooperatively operated by the Agricultural Research Service, U.S. Department of Agriculture; the Minnesota Agricultural Experiment Station; the North Dakota Agriculture Experiment Station; and the Red River Valley Potato Growers Association. This paper was prepared on official Government time and reports research paid for by U.S. taxpayers. The article and the research information, therefore, are in the public domain an cannot be copyrighted.

storage and shipped to chipping plants located in or near large metropolitan consumption areas around the country. The storage/shipping season from the fall production areas generally ranges from September through May/June. Two to three months of direct use of newly harvested potatoes from the field of the summer-crop production areas of the U.S. completes the 12-month production-processing-utilization year.

Location Models

There is need for research utilizing a total systems approach to thoroughly evaluate production/ storage/process-plant/market locations (Figure 1). Processing schedules would, of course, be paramount, but handling and transporting effects on quality stability during storage unloading and shipping need to be included. Orr and Graham (1983) formulated a model that included a linear programming approach to determine least-cost sources of chipping potatoes as a means of minimizing finished product costs when potatoes having different specific gravities are available at different prices from several different sources and a series of constraints are affecting the choices. Orr and Ebeling (1976) developed a computer model that simulated potato packinghouse operations. The model is concerned with the response of packinghouse workers and machines to certain physical and biological characteristics of the potatoes during packinghouse operations. Micro-processor capabilities currently allow consideration of models to assist in automatic grading of fruits and vegetables (Miller, 1985). Such models could become part of a larger more comprehensive model that evaluates the total system, optimizing size and location of storages and processing plants in relation to producing and consuming areas. The biological nature of raw potatoes required for the chipping industry introduces relatively uncontrolled variability into such systems analyses and must be included if a model is to be effective. Good databases are required to ultimately exploit the concept, but research to develop the structural interrelationships within a systems model is needed at this time.

HANDLING FROM STORAGE

Effects on Potatoes

Orr, et al. (1985) addressed the problem of off-color product frequently seen after potatoes arrive at the processing plant even though chips obtained via samples at the storage site prior to shipping exhibited good color. They postulated that dry handling methods such as powered bulk scooping, (Orr, 1971) are rather harsh to the potatoes and could cause development of sugars in the raw potatoes given adequate time following handling. Figure 2, from their work, illustrates that, month-by-month, the samples given handling treatments produced darker chips than did the controls. Additional research to trace the progress of the de-stabilizing effects during the period immediately following handling is needed since, essentially, all color change occurred in the five-day period immediatley following handling (Orr, et al.). Research of this nature is also needed to determine if other primary chipping cultivars respond similarly, or whether some cultivars are better or worse in resisting the effects of post storage handling. Only Norchip was examined by Orr, et al. Research underway at Cornell University may identify some of these responses using other cultivars (Siecka). Sowokinos, et al. (1985) examined the sugar concentrations found during their handling tests and attempted to determine if membrane deterioration was involved. In general, they found that slight changes in glucose concentration following handling treatments causes chip color deterioration, and significant membrane degradation occurred only with senescense. The capability of predicting internal quality for processing would be of practical benefit to the industry.

Better Handling Methods Needed

The work of Orr and Sowokinos identified a need for better methods for handling bulk potatoes from chip potato storages. The bulk scooping method is quite rough on potatoes, even if extreme care is used in its operation. Bulk bin unloaders utilizing conveyors are less harsh, but still offer many potato-on-potato damage opportunities. Orr, et al. (1985) showed that, though externally unharmed, the chipping potato is extremely sensitive to potato-on potato contact in a tumbling situation and expresses that sensitivity in the form of increased sugar concentrations which ultimately result in off-colored potato chips.

In theory, all handling from storage should be eliminated if possible. For example, pallet boxes might serve as the storage and shipping container without removing the potatoes until final dumping at the plant. However, such a system is not always practical and realistically economical. Some system to minimize handling while removing potatoes from chip storages is needed.

Established concepts such as fluming potatoes (Schaper, et al., 1985) may be possible. Research is needed to determine if open channel fluming and pipelining can be used specifically to handle chipping potatoes from storage without adversely affecting quality. The method is gentle when systems are properly designed and operated but industry has some concern about possible temperature changes of the potatoes and the related internal quality effects whenever water used for fluming is colder than the raw potatoes. There is also concern about water removing protective surface films from potatoes, plugging lenticels and spreading bacterial diseases. Cargill (1981) and Orr (1985) found that bacterial diseases can be controlled by maintaining appropriate concentrations of chlorine in the fluming water.

Research to develop better methods and equipment to gently handle potatoes from storage would benefit the entire potato industry. Agricultural engineers interested in equipment design and development could find a challenge in providing new concepts for gently handling large volumes of potatoes at a rapid rate within the cost constraints of a low-priced commodity.

Altered Bin Environments

Research is needed to determine if altered bin environments that occur during bin unloading activities are detrimental to final chip color. The industry itself tends to provoke this situation by the practice of partially unloading a bulk storage bin then stopping activity for several days, only to begin again later. The practical question of whether or not these practices affect final chip color needs to be answered. If there is an effect, how rapidly should a bin be emptied? Round-the-clock? In 3 or 4 days? Ten days? Knowledge about the sequence of events that takes place in those potatoes remaining in the altered storage environment would be helpful in determining appropriate bin sizes based on unloading system capabilities.

BETTER CULTIVARS

Research is needed to genetically increase external and internal durability of potatoes grown for the chipping market. A method of testing for this durability is also needed in order to know whether a breeding selection will be a good handling cultivar, or a poor handler, when released to the industry. Those selections determined to be good handlers can be used as crossing materials in the breeding programs. Handling characteristics could then become a known entity when a cultivar is released, rather than the current costly practice of trial and error on a large scale by the industry.

Research is needed to determine if some metabolic "regulator" can be identified that will toughen internal cellular components and assist in maintaining compartmentalization and stabilization of metabolic processes during and immediately following the handling period. The longer-term research effort should include routine selection for externally and internally tougher potatoes. Some means of identifying and quantifying the appropriate handling characteristics of potatoes would be of help to the breeders. Varns (1985) has developed an experimental potato-on-potato bruising concept that appears to give valid, repeatable results in initial tests. Work by Orr and Varns (1985) at the Potato Research Laboratory may provide a method for testing differences in handling characteristics of cultivars.

SORTING FOR QUALITY

It is postulated that changes in carbohydrate content and metabolism are the primary influences affecting the final product quality of processed

329

potatoes. Undesirable changes, which can occur in healthy potatoes, result in losses of approximately 11 million dollars annually to the processing industry alone. Research is needed to develop a method of sorting potatoes that includes the effects of bruising, disease and stress on the quality of potatoes for processing via analyses of sugar-starch transformations, physical and chemical changes of membranes, and gas exchanges. If a means of sorting potatoes based on internal quality could be achieved, one could avoid the current practice of moving all externally acceptable tubers to market and having entire lots rejected when a portion of the tubers have excessive reducing sugar concentrations. Potatoes with unacceptable internal quality need never leave the production area to become a further liability in the marketing channels. The industry might then avoid increased costs due to handling and transporting to market ultimately unacceptable raw materials and subsequent production of excessive waste materials requiring disposal in overloaded systems of most metropolitan areas.

LONG-TERM RESEARCH

Because of the biological variability inherent in potatoes, all research that examines production, storage, handling, transporting, and processing becomes a long-term effort. Year-to-year differences between crops must be identified and evaluated in any such research. Variability within years and cultivars, and a host of other factors requires careful analysis and interpretation to be meaningful. A multi-discipline effort appears to be a proper approach to address the potato industry's research needs in handling and transporting potatoes for the chip market.

REFERENCES

Cargill, B.F., H.S. Potter, R.L. Ledebuhr and M.W. Glover. 1981. Prestorage chemical application techniques to minimize potato losses in storage. Unpublished presentation, Pot. Assoc. Amer. Annual Meeting.

Miller, W.M. 1985. Decision model for computer-based grade separation of fresh produce. Trans. of Amer. Soc. Agr. Eng. 28(4):1341-1345.

Orr, P.H. 1971. Powered bulk scooping in potato storage. Marketing Res. Rpt. No. 916, U.S. Dept. Agr.

Orr, P.H., and C.K. Graham. 1983. Determining least-cost sources of chipping potatoes by use of mathematical models. Trans of Amer. Soc. Agr. Engr. 26(1):297-300 & 304.

Orr, P.H., J.R. Sowokinos and J.L. Varns. 1985. Sugar changes and chipping responses of Norchip tubers after handling from storage. Amer. Soc. Agr. Engr. Paper No. 85-6021.

Orr, P.H. and K. A. Ebeling. 1976. Computer simulation of potato packinghouse operations. Trans. of Amer. Soc. Agr. Engr. 19(5):978-983 & 988.

Orr, P.H. Unpublished data.

Orr, P.H. and J.L. Varns. Unpublished data.

Potato Chip/Snack Food Association. 1985. PC/SFA 1985 snack food management report. Chipper Snacker. 42(7):CS1-CS20.

Schaper, L.A., P.H. Orr, N. Smith and J. H. Hunter. 1986. Hydraulic transport of potatoes. Tech. Bul. 84-24. Agr. Res. Service. U.S. Dept. Agr.

Sowokinos, J.R., P.H. Orr, J.A. Knoper and J.L. Varns. 1985. Influence of aging and handling stress on sugars, chip quality and integrity of the starch (amyloplast)membrane. Amer. Potato J. 62:(Abstract).

Sieczka, J.B. Unpublished data.

Varns, J.L. Unpublished data.

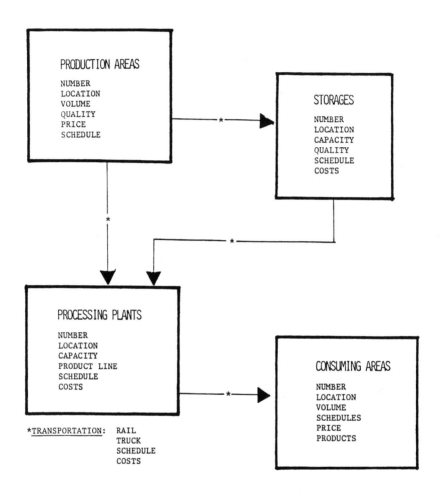

Fig 1. Any total systems approach to evaluating and optimizing production/storage
/process-plant/market locations should contain a raw product <u>quality</u> component.

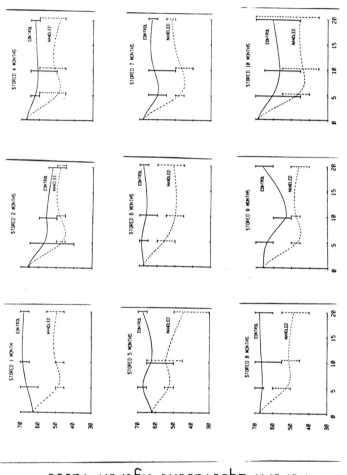

CHIP COLOR
PC/SFA Equivalent Agtron Value

TIME FOLLOWING HANDLING TREATMENT

Days

Fig. 2. The influence of storage duration and handling on chip color (cv. Norchip). Color measurements (means, ranges) were made 0, 5, 10 and 20 days after handling treatments on potatoes stored 1 to 10 months (Significant differences between handled and control means, P < 0.01).

TUBER QUALITY CONTROL IN POTATOES FOR CHIP
PRODUCTION FROM VINE KILL TO STORAGE

by

Maurice Eddowes, Newport, Shropshire, England

ABSTRACT

About 40 percent of the processed potato crop in
the United Kingdom is processed for chips (french
fries). Large tubers over 50 mm (1.97 in.) in size
are required with high dry matter and low reducing
sugar contents. Tuber quality is most important.
The most frequent cause of rejection is through
mechanical damage and bruising. Greening of tubers
must be avoided, skins must be well set, harvesting
and handling damage minimized, and controlled
temperature and air conditions maintained in storage.

INTRODUCTION

The potato processing indutry in the UK has not
achieved the preeminent position that it has held for

ASAE Paper No. 85-6026

sometime in the United States. Nevertheless it has increased significantly over the last 20 years and now uses about 25 percent of the total UK crop.

Processors need a reliable supply of UK or imported potatoes of a predetermined quality, throughout the year. This requirement is met, usually, in UK by producers growing suitable varieties to specification under contact, but a variable proportion of the processor's requirement will be purchased as opportunity arises in the open market.

Size and appearance of the potatoes are most important in the chip (fry) sector to qualify for useful quality premiums. Tuber size should be over 50 mm (1.97 in.) with not more than 60 tubers in a 10 kg (22 lb.) sample. The specific gravity should be over 1.080 (dry matter over 20%) and the reducing sugar content should be below 0.25 percent. Varieties with white skins and shallow eyes are preferred. Long oval tubers produce the best quality chip (fry) grade.

PRODUCTION TECHNOLOGY

Graded seed, preferably 45-55 mm (1.77-2.17 in.) should be used to ensure accurage spacing of seed, according to tuber seed count, and even depth of planting.

The object is to achieve the appropriate plant population for variety and seed size. Adequate supply of balanced nutrients for a 20-tonne (440 cwt) plus yield per acre, effective crop protection against weeds, diseases and pests, and systematic irrigation as needed to maintain soil moisture close to field capacity, are basic to high output of potentially marketable processing potatoes.

Whether or not the potential marketable yield is feasible will depend upon the tuber quality factors considered below.

TUBER QUALITY CONTROL

The final ridge must have been constructed to provide complete soil coverage to protect a large bulk of tubers from exposure to light and subsequent greening. A rounded, well shouldered ridge usually provides maximum stability against soil movement and tuber exposure in the ridge. Green potatoes are a waste and counter-productive.

Vine Killing

This should be carried out about mid-September to destroy green foliage as the crop nears maturity and to hasten skin setting of tubers. An interval of three weeks should be left from the time of chemical destruction of the vine until harvesting to ensure that the vitally important protective skin is properly set. Harvesting in UK should be completed by mid-October to avoid the onset of cold weather and frost.

Harvesting and Handling of Crop

Mechanical damage is the most frequent reason for rejection of potatoes by processors. Every effort must be made to avoid tuber damage, especially external cuts and bruises and internal bruising. Most of the mechanical damage occurs during harvesting and it is most important to ensure that harvesting and handling equipment is correctly set and maintained, and operated according to soil and weather conditions. For example, under very dry conditions bruising is a major problem, and under wet conditions tubers are more susceptible to rotting diseases. All places in the harvesting system where damage is likely to occur should be carefully checked throughout the harvesting operation. Make sure that hard metallic surfaces are cushioned and that the potatoes do not drop onto hard surfaces by using rubber or plastic padding as protection against tuber damage. To monitor possible sources of damage during harvesting, take random samples of 5-10 kg (11 - 22 lb.) of potatoes from different points, wash them and examine them carefully for mechanical damage. If damage is found check the following potential sources: stones and clods, pressure on ridges; disc/share setting; primary web; sharp cutting surfaces on machinery; and height of drops in the flow system.

Storage

Whichever method of storage is used (bulk or boxes) attention must be paid to the following standards:

1. Potatoes for storage should be mature with skins properly set.

2. Wet potatoes should not be put into long-term storages because of the risk of bacterial rots.

3. Excess soil, stones and debris should be removed before storing.

For chipping potatoes the holding temperature in the storage should be 8°C (46.4 ° F) to maintain quality and to prevent the build-up of reducing sugars. The storage environment and temperature above and within the potatoes should be checked regularly.

AN APPROACH TOWARDS POTATO UTILIZATION
AND THIRD WORLD COUNTRIES

by

Robert H. Booth and P. Keane, Postharvest
Scientists, International Potato Center
Apartado 5969, Lima, Peru

ABSTRACT

An increasing number of potato producing
countries are becoming interested in processing.
This is commonly manifested in a desire to copy
present industrialized nations products and
processes. Such approaches are commonly not
appropriate. This paper describes an attempt to
apply underlying food processing principles to
consumer needs in developing countries.

INTRODUCTION

An increasing number of potato producing
countries throughout the world are showing interest

ASAE Paper No. 85-6027

in processing. Frequently, in third-world countries, this interest is based on ill-conceived ideals of helping to smooth-out the gluts and deficiencies, and accompanying high price fluctuations, of prevailing supply patterns. Similarly, this interest is commonly manifested in desires to copy products and processes presently being used in industrialized nations. Such thinking, which fails to consider food processing as part of an overall food plan of the country or region concerned, rarely leads to the establishment of successful research and development projects and even less frequently to the establishment of new food products and industries.

However, in defense of this unfortunate but prevailing approach, it must be mentioned that: a) almost all food manufacturing processes of today cater exclusively for the middle/high income consumers, who constitute a minority of the population in many developing countries, and b) most of the training which has been provided in food processing has been based in the industrialized nations with focus on individual components e.g. nutrition, new products, processing or marketing of the food system with relatively little attention being placed on the underlying principles of these components and their application to and integration into a total food program.

In the industrialized nations, sophisticated processes and techniques are available to exploit the consumers requirements and can offer a wide choice of products to satisfy even the most demanding market criteria. Consumer analysis and market study is continuous by most food processing companies and there is a consistent effort to improve and streamline their product development programs. This is based on the understanding that all successful products go through four main phases in the market place: introduction, penetration, maturation, and decline. The duration of each phase depends on many factors but one thing is certain, all products have a beginning and an end.

In contrast, nothing by way of a parallel is directed towards the abundant low-income consumers in third-world countries. Typically, these consumer types are financially unable to benefit from the wide array of food products on the supermarket shelves. This linked with seasonably, perishability and accompanying high price fluctuations means that nutritious fruit, vegetables and root crops, like the potato, are excluded from their diets during certain periods of the year. The effect of seasonal production on continuity of supply and associated price fluctuations are greatest where, for any reason, only one crop is produced each year. This is the case in numerous tropical potato producing countries where, for example, potato production is limited to the cooler winter months. In such situations potatoes need to be stored for long periods, commonly in hot humid environments, if a constant supply of fresh potatoes is demanded by the consumer. Such storage frequently requires refrigeration which, if at all feasible, is expensive and results in a high cost product to the consumer. In such situations, the processing of potatoes into a more stable and acceptable food product could greatly assist in maintaining the required supply of this nutritious vegetable to low-income consumers.

However, most food manufacturers are not concerned with these low-income groups and so the available advanced technologies and research inputs remain largely for the benefit of the upper classes. Where attempts have been made to apply existing food science and processing technologies for the benefit of these consumers, these have largely been approached from either a nutritional or technological stand-point and have met with limited success. The food value of highly nutritious products remain unrealized unless they are organoleptically acceptable to and liked by target consumer groups.

Potato Processing at the International Potato Center (CIP)

The objective of the small potato processing project at CIP is to attempt to remedy some of the above mentioned deficiencies. The project aims, through illustrating how underlying industrial food processing principles can be applied to simple potato processing, to develop a relevant approach for initiating food processing enterprises in developing countries. Simultaneously, the project aims to illustrate how consumer use of potatoes could be expanded in third-world countries. Specifically, the project can be considered as having four basic phases: consumer study, product development, process development and transfer of technology.

The Consumer

Any successful food processing project must be based on an identified consumer need or opportunity. This requires a knowledge and understanding of the target consumer group. This in turn requires an organized research input aimed at developing a product feasibility brief. Such a methodical approach should reduce risk and hopefully eliminate irrelevant data and allow a potential project to emerge. Due to shifting patterns in target consumer groups such studies must be a continuing process in any food processing project.

In Peru, which has an estimated population of 18 million, a continually growing and significant proportion of the population live in city slum settlements. Lima, the capital city, has close to 300 such settlements with a population in excess of 1.2 million. Other cities and towns have similar settlements.

The average income for a family living in such settlements has been calculated to be certainly no more than U.S.$130 per month. The present minimum wage is much lower than this in dollar terms. In Peru, as a whole, an average family spends 60 percent of their income on food, 24 percent on clothing and medicine and the remainder on fuel, travel and electricity. Rice and potato account for one third of the money spent on food and approximately 30 kgs (66 lbs.) of each are consumed per family each month. As high rates of inflation continue to push food prices upward an ever increasing percentage of income is being spent on food, particularly in the lower income settlements.

The severe economic pressure under which these consumer types live force all family members to seek employment thus leaving little time for domestic work and food preparation. This, contrary to much common thinking, is creating a greater demand for convenience foods in the lower income groups than in upper income groups. Upper income groups commonly employ domestic help and so the time spend on food preparation is less critical to them. In spite of this, however, the small existing food processing sector caters primarily for these upper classes. For example, of the 250,000 ha (617,000 acres) of land dedicated to potato production in Peru, only two percent of the total production is processed. The conventional processed products, (chips and French fries) are destined for the higher income groups.

In target areas information was collected on existing food habits as a means of helping to define market opportunities. It was found that, although along with rice, potatoes share first place in consumer buying preference for agricultural produce. It was also found that price fluctuations cause potatoes to become too expensive for many families within the low-income areas during certain periods of the year. A specific objective of the project involved finding a way of utilizing the nutritional and organoleptically acceptable potato in processed foods that are within the economic constraints of low-income target consumers.

Product Development

If a potato based food is to have a long shelf life it must be processed. Of the conventional processes: freezing, canning and dehydration, the latter is the least expensive when one takes into account the overall costs and is the most relevant to the majority of developing countries. In must developing countries an extensive frozen marketing chain is not in place and the cost of canned produce places them financially out of reach to the majority of consumers.

If one produced a pure potato dried product, its cost based on the dry matter content of potatoes and not considering any processing costs must be approximately six times the cost of the fresh potatoes. Applying this to the cost of potatoes in Peru would make the price of a dried potato product too expensive compared with other dehydrated food products available in the market place. However, if one dilutes the potato with other lower cost national products such as cereals and legumes, it becomes theoretically possible to produce a product with a competitive price. Having been forced for economic reasons to consider the idea of potato extension or potato based food mixes, it becomes possible to consider enhancing the nutritional value of the potato by selecting other ingredients to strengthen the nutritional weaknesses of the potato.

Based on this, a number of dehydrated blends of predominantly cereals, legumes and potatoes were prepared in proportions which acknowledged the economic necessity for low priced foods. Based on flavour and cost some of the products were selected for consumer testing. One such mixture appears to have a wide acceptance with Peruvian consumers. This mixture in its dried form contains 30 percent potato with the balance composed of flours of rice, beans, oats, barley and maize, all of which are produced within Peru.

The approximate nutritional value of this mixed product, calculated from food data tables, is 10.6 percent protein and 333 kcal of energy per 100 grams (3.53 oz.) of product. The accuracy of this estimate has been confirmed through chemical analysis. Based on a method used by FAO/WHO, the calculated probable efficiency value of the products protein is 86 percent as compared to 82, 70 and 41 percent respectively for the proteins of potato, rice and beans alone. The dried product is reconstituted and prepared by the addition of approximately one litre (0.264 gal.) of water to 80 grams (2.82 oz.) of the mix and boiling for about 25 minutes. The cooked product, which has the consistency of a thick soup or porridge, has a neutral or bland taste which can be used as a base for breakfast, savory or dessert foods. For example, in some tests, consumers have added a little cocoa, sugar and cinnamon at the final stages of cooking and have made an appetizing breakfast food.

In initial consumer acceptability tests, more than 1,000 individuals in two cities of Peru sampled the product. In some tests families were given half a kilogram(1.1 lb.) of product for "in-home" evaluation after a brief demonstration and tasting of the mixture. The results in all these tests were encouraging indicating a broad acceptance of the product. At this stage a product brief was developed. Confirmations of these initial consumer acceptability tests have been obtained from the continued daily use over an 18 month period in a common kitchen providing lunch for approximately 100 children and in an extensive school feeding test involving 6000 kg (13,200 lbs.) of product.

Process Development

The process used for producing the test mixture was simple. Potatoes are cooked and mashed. Flours produced from the selected cereals and legumes are then mixed with the mashed wet potato. The mixing spreads the moisture content of the potato over the whole mix thereby facilitating easier drying. Drying has been accomplished by means of solar energy through, of course, artificial means can also be applied at a higher cost.

The sequence and process details may vary with different production scales, conditions and needs, and thus should not be regarded as fixed. In response to national interest in different levels of production, two demonstrative lines have been developed in the small experimental pilot plant CIP Huancayo research station. Huancayo, at an altitude of 3,200 m (10,500 ft.) above sea level is situated in a major potato producing region in the central highlands of Peru and where the other mix ingredients are also readily available.

One line has the capability of producing 100 kg (220 lbs.) of dried product per week. One hundred kilograms (220 lbs.) of product would produce 5,000 food portions of 20 grams (0.70 oz.) of mix in 250 ml (8.33 fl. oz.) of water. This would be enough for a family of six to eat the product three times a day for nine months. This small line is aimed at the individual farm or urban family. For the farm family the advantages of simply converting a portion of the harvested potatoes into a processed product to give year-round food stability is being stressed. Also, by processing the poorer quality tubers, storage and marketing of the fresh tubers could be improved.

The approximate raw material requirements and prepared raw material inputs are shown in Table 1.

344

The process steps used in the CIP line are illustrated in Figure 1. The processing implements used for this scale of operation are commonly available in most family kitchens or can readily be purchased locally.

The second line is directed to the community or small factory scale of operation and has the capacity of 1000-2500 kg (2200-5500 lbs.) per week. One ton of product will provide 50 thousand 20 gram/250 ml (.70 oz./8.33 fl oz.) food portions, which would be sufficient for 396 families of six to eat the product three times a day for a week. The approximate ingredient requirements to produce one ton (2200 lbs.) of product are ten times those illustrated in Table 1. All the small scale processing equipment used in this line (Figure 2) has been manufactured locally in Peru. Experience with this line has given a recovery rate of 54 percent on the prepared raw materials, the wet mix having a moisture content of around 50 percent and the final product 8 to 10 percent. The product is sun dried in a walk-in solar drying chamber. The central Andes region of Peru commonly has an eight month dry season and a four month rainy season. The potato harvest coincides with the beginning of the dry season during which period radiation levels are approximately 3000 kcal/ m^2/day (279.0 kcal/ft^2/day). The drying chamber has a mean temperature of 21 °C (69.8 °F). This rises to 50-65 ° C (122-149 ° F) on sunny cloudless days but remains below 35 °C (95°F) on rainy days. This means that even on the poorest drying days, from every 500 kg (1100 lbs.) of wet mix placed in the chamber on 100 one meter square (10.7 ft^2) trays 270 kg (594 lbs.) of dried mix is produced every 48 hours. The capacity of the line is largely determined by the size and efficiency of the drying facilities.

When producing and preparing foods for human consumption great care should always be exercised. During processing good manufacturing practices should be adhered to including personal hygiene, control of incoming ingredients, and quality control of process and finished product. It is always an advantage, from a microbiological point of view, to have a processed product which requires cooking prior to consumption, as is the case with the above described

potato based food mix. Notwithstanding the safeness
of this approach, it should always be the intention
to produce the best and most hygienienic product
possible, consistent with the available resources.
Although the CIP pilot lines are not operated
commercially, product samples have been analyzed in
both the USA and Europe. In both cases all
bacteriological counts were below the limits set for
this product type in those countries. This simply
serves to illustrate that products of acceptable
bacteriological quality can be produced on simple
lines relaying on solar drying. Similarly, shelf
life studies have illustrated that the product can be
stored simply for periods of at least 12 months with
no loss in consumer acceptability.

Transfer of Technology

As stated earlier, the overall objective and aim
of this CIP potato processing project is to develop
an approach to incorporate simple processing, of
local produce into stable foods, acceptable to low
income consumers, within local food systems. Thus,
although important, primary attention in transfer
efforts, outside of Peru, should not be placed on the
specific product or production processes. Potato, or
other commodity based dry food mixes can be modified
according to consumer taste preferences, costs and
availability of ingredients. Local crops with
specifically desirable attributes can readily be
incorporated into such processed foods. As already
mentioned, the sequence and process details will vary
according to many location specific factors.

In Peru, itself, and with assistance from
various national institutions, transfer efforts are
being concentrated at three levels of operation.
Commercial enterpreneurial interest is beginning to
be shown in the product and small factory scale
operations. The CIP pilot plant line has been
demonstrated to interested parties. In both urban
and rural communities that have been exposed to
the product, interest is being expressed in the
possibility of producing such a produce within and
for the community. Here again, emphasis must be
placed on local availability and cost of ingredients,
and specific local crops to satisfy consumer
preferences. In the central Andes region efforts

346

have commenced on transferring this approach of potato utilization to individual families and one or two families in three selected areas have started to experiment with the product and process. All these efforts will be strengthened and continually evaluated in the coming months.

Outside of Peru, interest in this approach of potato utilization has already been shown by a number of countries including Bolivia, Colombia, Guatemala, Mexico, Bangladesh, Bhutan, Sri Lanka, Thailand and the Philippines. Food scientists from Guatemala and Bangladesh have received training at CIP and are being assisted in establishing similar projects in their own countries. Additional training will be given to scientists from Bolivia, Colombia and Bhutan in 1985. Also, and as a means of illustrating the flexibility of the approach examples of different potato and sweet potato based dried food mixes have been sent to interested scientists in several countries.

All these transfer efforts require additional strengthening through more training and back up visits and research. However, preliminary indications are that an industrialized approach can be applied to the development of simple processed potato products for low-income consumers in third world countries provided that emphasis, from the beginning and throughout product and process development and transfer phases, is placed on the specific needs of the target consumer group.

Table 1. Ingredient requirements to produce 100 kg of product

	Fresh Potato	Whole Rice	Broad Beans	Oats	Barley	Maise Corn	Salt
Raw Ingredient and Quantity (kg)	170	17	21	21	23	12.5	4
	Boiled Mashed Potatoes	Rice Flour	Broad Bean Flour	Oat Flour	Barley Flour	Maise Corn Flour	Salt
Prepared Ingredient and Quantity (kg)	120	16	16	16	16	12	4

348

Figure 1

Flow diagram for 100 kg (220 lb.) per week production line

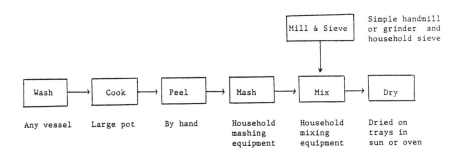

Figure 2

Flow diagram for 1-2.5 tons (2200-5500 lb.) tons per week production line

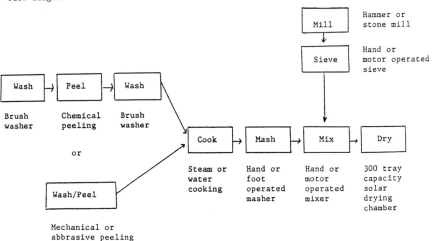

349

POSTHARVEST HANDLING SYSTEMS ANALYSIS OF
FRESH PRODUCE

by

D.T. Campbell, Research Assistant and S.E. Prussia,
Assistant Professor, Agricultural Engineering
Department; R.L. Shewfelt, Assistant Professor,
Food Science Department; W.C. Hurst, Associate
Professor, Food Science Extension, University of
Georgia, Athens, Georgia; J.L. Jordan, Assistant
Professor, Agricultural Economics Department,
The Georgia Experiment Station, Experiment,
Georgia

ABSTRACT

A method of evaluating losses and damages of
fresh produce from specific postharvest handling
systems was developed and is demonstrated by
analyzing an example system. Various systems
analysis techniques were evaluated, and computer
simulation was chosen as the most appropriate to
incorporate into the proposed method. The method was

ASAE Paper No. 85-6028

found to be an excellent tool for formulating and evaluating potential solutions to loss or damage problems that exist within a typical system.

INTRODUCTION

The typical postharvest handling system of a fresh fruit or vegetable is a complex system comprised of many diverse, yet interrelated components. Any or all components may lead to the damage or loss of the product as it travels through the system. A number of researchers working in the field of postharvest handling have recognized a need for a research method that is capable of evaluating an _entire_ postharvest handling system, instead of one or more components of the system that may be suspected of causing damage (Schoorl and Holt, 1982; Schaper and Varns, 1982; Shewfelt et al., 1985). Damage that appears at one component of a system can be caused by the exposure of the product to some damaging agent at a previous component. This delayed evidence of damage in fresh produce is fairly common (Halsey, 1963; MacLeod et al., 1976), and in some cases damage may not be detected until the fruit or vegetable is used by the consumer (Deponis and Butterfield, 1979). For these reasons, some researchers have concluded that latering one specific component of a system (i.e., minimizing damage at that component), without evaluating other components, may have no effect, or even a detrimental effect, on the performance of the overall system (Schoorl and Holt, 1982). A research method that incorporates systems analysis (SA) techniques would allow the evaluation of the overall system, as well as the individual components.

In order to utilize SA techniques in developing a method of evaluating produce damage and losses within a postharvest handling system, the most appropriate SA technique must first be chosen. Before the technique that is chosen can be used, however, two initial phases of the method will have to be completed. Phase one must be the formulation of a black-box model of the handling system that will show the physical structure of the system and the flow of produce through the system, both in terms of damaged and undamaged produce. Phase two should be collection of data that is needed for the systems

351

analysis, such as the time it takes for products to complete processes, or the magnitude of product loss or damage found at each component experimentally. Using the model and the collection of data as inputs into the systems analysis technique that is chosen, the postharvest handling system can be analyzed in terms of the sources and magnitudes of lost and damaged produce, the relationship between components in causing damage, the performance of the overall system, and potential solutions to any damage or loss problems that are found.

OBJECTIVES

The objectives of this paper are to:

1. Evaluate various SA techniques to determine which is the most appropriate to use as part of a method for analyzing losses and damages in postharvest handling systems.

2. Develop and demonstrate a research method, that utilizes the SA technique chosen in Objective One, for evaluating damage and losses in a hypothetical postharvest handling system.

REVIEW OF LITERATURE

It is important to distinguish a specific postharvest handling system from an overall marketing or distribution system. A postharvest handling system may be defined as the processes that a particular fruit or vegetable undergoes from the time it is harvested until the time it reaches the consumer (Campbell, 1985). Usually, the term "postharvest handling system" refers to the specific handling system of a particular fruit or vegetable at a specific location. Although no two postharvest handling systems are exactly alike, the components that make up handling systems are basically the same for all fruits and vegetables. Generally, these components include cleaning, sorting, grading, packaging, storing, wholesaling, retailing, and the transportation necessary to take the product from one point to the next.

A few researchers have evaluated specific postharvest handling systems by determining the quality loss or damage present at each component of the system. An approach such as this enables a better understanding of the structure and performance of the overall system, and to some degree, the effect that each component has on damage as the product flows through the system. Shewfelt et al., (1985), for example, evaluated quality changes that take place in Southern peas at each component as they travelled through an operational postharvest handling system. Jordan et al. (1984) used quality characteristic data from a similar study to determine the stages in a postharvest handling system that most affected the price of tomatoes. Research methods such as these enable the damage that occurs within a specific handling system to be evaluated both in terms of the performance of individual components of the system, and in terms of the performance of the system as a whole.

An overall marketing or distribution system of a fresh fruit or vegetable is usually thought of as an overview of the processes that the product typically undergoes from production to consumption, with no regard to specific handling systems at specific locations. Thus, research into marketing or distribution systems of produce are of little value in evaluating and correcting damage problems within specific handling systems. Mongelli (1984), for example, provides an overview of the total fresh tomato marketing system from harvest to retail market in terms of product flow and associated costs. While such an overview is useful in understanding the general flow of produce, it is of little value to a researcher interested in minimizing produce damage within a specific system.

Halloran, et al. (1982) evaluated losses of many food products (including fresh produce) during marketing and distribution by compiling data from many sources, but again, the information is of little value in evaluating specific handling systems. Schaper and Varns (1982) did a similar study specifically for potatoes that evaluated both mass and energy losses in the potato marketing chain. Data from such a study could be used to estimate the losses that occur in a specific handling system, but without an evaluation of the system in question, there is no guarantee that such estimates are correct.

It is clear that there is a need for a research method that is capable of evaluating specific handling systems at specific locations, yet general enough to be used for evaluating damage within any handling system. A systems approach, such as that taken by Jordan et al. (1985) and Shewfelt et al. (1985), is a good start in evaluating the structure and performance of a specific system. The methods used by these researchers, however, could be expanded to include evaluation of the system via systems analysis techniques. Systems analysis techniques would not only allow the identification of the true magnitudes and sources of damage in the system, but would also be useful in developing and evaluating potential solutions to damage problems once they have been identified.

EVALUATING SYSTEMS ANALYSIS TECHNIQUES

Many system-oriented industries utilize the advantages of SA techniques to identify the true origins and magnitudes of problems, and even to identify potential solutions to problems. Since postharvest handling systems are similar to other industrial systems, in that they are often complex systems composed of many functional components, the same SA techniques can be used to form the basis of a method for evaluating damage that occurs within them. By using such a method, researchers can evaluate both a postharvest handling system, and the components that make up the system. Further, SA techniques will enable the researcher to formulate and evaluate potential solutions to the damage problem with little or no disturbance to the actual system. These, in fact, are the major advantages of using SA techniques.

At this point, a decision must be made as to which SA technique is the most appropriate for evaluating damage within postharvest handling systems. The typical postharvest handling system is complex and, as such, there are many variables that have to be taken into account when evaluating damage problems. Further, postharvest handling systems are dynamic, and parameters that affect damage may change from day to day, or even minute to minute. These facts complicate the choice of the most suitable SA technique to use in evaluating postharvest damage. In order to make this decision, however, it is necessary to briefly review and compare the various SA techniques that are available.

Linear Programming

Probably the most widely used SA technique today, linear programming (LP) has been used to analyze problems in such diverse areas as agriculture, communication systems, and petroleum distribution. In analyzing a problem with LP, however, the analyst must usually make simplifying assumptions about the problem. In order to use LP for example, the objective of the analysis must be to maximize or minimize some parameter such as profits or costs, respectively. Further, there must be only one objective, and it is subject to constraints or restrictions, based on the availability of resources that are needed for production. Naturally, the analyst must assume linearity, or the proportionality between the objective function and constraints to the production level of each product, in order to use LP to analyze a system (Davis and McKeown, 1984).

After expressing the objective function, constraints, and other assumptions in a linear, mathematical form, the result is a set of equations that must be solved simultaneously. This may be accomplished mathematically or graphically, but is more typically done via computer algorithms.

Goal Progamming

It is not uncommon in any industry to encounter problems in which there are numerous objectives. In the postharvest handling industry, for example, a few of the objectives may be to minimize damage, minimize the time of handling, and maximize the profits. The tools that are generally utilized to analyze problems with multiple objectives are called multicriteria models and methods. Of the muticriteria methods used, goal programming (GP) is perhaps the most common.

An off-shoot of linear programming, GP treats the objectives of a problem as constraints and utilizes an assigned priority system for satisfying the objectives. Solutions to a multicriteria problem via GP are obtained by minimizing deviations from the objectives while satisfying each objective as closely as possible considering its priority ranking. The key advantages of GP over linear programming are that it can provide more information about a problem and is capable of evaluating situations in which there are multiple goals. The solution techniques used in GP are similar to those used in LP.

Integer Progamming

Basically, integer programming (IP) is analogous to LP with the exception that fractional solutions to problems are not allowed. This technique was devised to account for situations in which the assumption of divisibility does not hold, but all other LP assumptions are applicable.

Obviously, one solution technique that can be used to solve an IP problem is to use LP and simply round off the results. Additionally, there are both graphical and mathematical methods that yield approximate solutions to an IP problem, but no one computer algoritm has been developed and tested.

Dynamic Programming

All of the SA techniques discussed thus far have relied on the use of static models (models in which the parameters remain the same regardless of the time period being considered) for their analysis. Obviously, there are cases where some parameters change over time, and an optimal solution to a problem for one time period may not be optimal for the next. For this class of problem, the most commonly used SA technique is known as dynamic programming (DP).

Rather than finding an optimal solution for a single problem with constant parameters, DP solves larger problems that may span many time periods and handles changes in parameters by breaking problems down into sets of small problems. DP then solves each problem of this set sequentially, where the parameters of each small problem depend on the time period being considered.

Two basic assumptions must be made in order to use DP. First, it must be assumed that the problem can be decomposed into smaller, solvable problems; second, the problem must adhere to the theory that, if a given decision is optimal, then all subsequent decisions based on the given decision are also optimal (Bellman's Principle of Optimality). One can reason that, if these assumptions hold true, then the best approach would be to work backwards to solve each problem. This, in fact, is the essence of the DP solution technique. DP begins at the end of the process and works backwards, always using the optimal solution from an earlier decision (Davis and McKeown, 1984). DP uses no single algorithm to solve the overall problem, but rather uses different solution techniques to individually solve the set of smaller problems it is made of.

Queing System Analysis

There are many businesses and industries in which the entities that flow through them (i.e. people, machines, etc.) require some service, and that service is not immediately forthcoming. As a result of having to await the service, the entities form "queues" or waiting lines. The collection of components that make up a queuing arrangement (entities, waiting area, service facilities, etc.) is known as a queuing system. The field of study involving queuing systems is commonly referred to as queuing theory.

Typically, the objective of a queuing system analysis is to reduce the amount of time that an entity spends in the system (and thus the number of entities in the system). The models used in queuing system analysis, however, do not "solve" the problems, but rather describe the queuing system in terms of average waiting times, average queue lengths, etc. The analyst must vary the parameters of the system (such as the number of servers or the service times) in order to arrive at optimal solutions for a particular problem.

Queuing models, like LP, IP, and GP models, are static, but differ from those models in that they are generally nonlinear. Additionally, queuing models are stochastic in that queuing system parameters are seldom known with certainty and are usually described by probability distributions.

Solution algorithms do exist for a few special queuing models, however, assumptions need be made for most real world problems in order for them to be analyzed via queuing systems analysis.

Markovian Processes

With the exception of queuing system analysis, all of the SA techniques and models discussed thus far have been deterministic. Likewise, with the exception of dynamic programming, the methods and models described previously were static--the parameters remained the same over the time period under investigation. Utilizing the advantages of both Queuing theory and DP, Markovian Processes are a family of models that are both stochastic as well as time dependent. Further, like Queuing theory, Markovian processes are descriptive of a situation, and optimization can only be achieved by varying the parameters of the process to determine the best course of action. The objectives of Markovian analyses, however, are always to determine sequentially the probabilities that certain events will or will not occur (Davis and McKeown, 1984).

As powerful as Markovian processes are as an SA technique, however, there still exists the need for making simplifying assumptions pertaining to the situation being studied. For example, it is assumed that the uncertainty about the path than an entity takes from one point to the next may be measured with probabilities. Further, it must be assumed that there will be repeated occurrences (trials) of events under identical conditions, and each identical event occurs in equal time periods. Assumptions such as these somewhat limit the capability of Markovian Processes in analyzing real-world situations.

The solution technique behind most Markovian processes involves matrix operations in which there exists a transition matrix and a probability vector.

The transition matrix contains the probabiities of events occurring in several possible ways. The probability vector defines the starting conditions of each event before it occurs. Using matrix multiplication, a new probability vector is obtained that defines the end conditions after an event occurs over a certain time period. This vector becomes the starting probability vector for the next time period to be considered. In this manner, Markovian processes describe the probabilities of events in a sequential fashion.

Since well defined algorithms exist for solving most Markovian process problems, most situations can be analyzed mathematially or via computer algorithms that incorporate matrix operations.

Computer Simulation

Perhaps the most powerful of the SA techniques used today, simulation allows a situation to be analyzed without making many of the simplifying assumptions that are necessary to use other techniques. A simulation model need not be linear, in fact a correct model will be only as linear as the system it represents. A simulation may be stochastic, deterministic, static, dynamic, or combinations of all four, again depending on the system that it represents. Because such assumptions are not necessary, and because analytical solutions are not required in simulation, larger, more complex systems may be studied under real world conditions. Although computer simulation is descriptive (like Queuing theory and Markovian Processes), perhaps its biggest advantage is that it allows experimentation on the system without disturbing the system if it exists. Again, optimization is achieved only by varying the parameters of the system and by choosing the parameters that yield the most optimal results. It must be kept in mind, however, that each simulation is merely an experiment, and a number of runs may be necessary in order to obtain valid results.

A computer simulation is performed by moving entities through a process via a computer algorithm that models the process and defines the flow of entities through it. Many special purpose simulation languages have been developed that vary according to the timing system of events that occur in the system. Additionally, simulations may be written in the fundamental programming languages such as FORTRAN, BASIC, or PASCAL.

Because the cost of computing is continually decreasing, and because simulation allows processes to be examined under more realistic conditions than other SA techniques, the attractiveness of using simulation to evaluate and solve problems is great.

The Best Technique

Since postharvest handling systems are usually fairly complex, and because they may be static, dynamic, deterministric, stochastic, or combinations of all four, computer simulation is clearly the most suitable SA technique for evaluating them in terms of losses or damage. Many of the simplying assumptions that are necessary in order to use other SA techniques are simply not needed when using simulation. Thus, the simulation model may mimic the existing system as closely as the modeler wishes. Although simulations are descriptive, many problems and parameters can be evaluated using only one simulation model. Further, with the exception of some data collection, the system need not be disturbed in order to evaluate changes in the model. These facts indicate that computer simulation is the best SA technique for evaluating postharvest handling systems.

DEVELOPMENT AND DEMONSTRATION OF A RESEARCH METHOD

After the most appropriate SA technique for evaluating postharvest handling systems has been chosen, a research method capable of evaluating damage and losses within specific systems can be developed and demonstrated. The proposed research method will be discussed and demonstrated, mostly by way of an example of a typical, hypothetical postharvest handling system analysis. The research method is composed of four distinct phases:

1. The model development process,

2. Data collection,

3. Development of the simulation model, and

4. System analysis via computer simulation.

The Model Development Process

The first step in evaluating any system is to clearly define the system of concern. In order to correctly evaluate the damage that occurs within any postharvest handling system, it is essential that the researcher has an understanding of:

    a. the structure and operation of the specific system in question,

    b. the relationship between components of that system, and

    c. the interactions between components of the system as produce flows through it.

In order to accomplish such an understanding, it is necessary for the researcher to spend as much time as is needed observing the system in operation. As the system is being observed, a black-box model or flow diagram may be formulated to show the static structure of the system, as well as the flow of the produce through it. Only when the model is complete should attempts be made to formulate a computer simulation model to analyze the system.

As an example of the model development process, let us consider a postharvest handling system of some typical, ficticious fresh market product that will be called a "Fruitable." Because we are interested only in evaluating one specific Fruitable postharvest handling system, we must travel to the location of the system in question in order to begin to observe and define the system, and to collect information for the black-box model.

We begin our observation of the system in a field at one of the farms where the Fruitables are being grown, and we follow the Fruitables through every process or component of the system until they reach the hands of the consumer. We note every process or component in the system, as well as the

361

order in which the Fruitables encounter them. We then repeat the process of following Fruitables through this system until we are comfortable that we have accurately recorded both the static and dynamic structure of the system. We may then begin to formulate a black-box model of the system that will accurately portray this structure.

For the purpose of this example, let us assume that this ficticious system is composed of the following components or processes.

a. Harvesting of the Fruitables at the farm.

b. Transportation of the Fruitables to a specific packinghouse.

c. Receiving of the Fruitables at the packinghouse where they are graded, size-sorted, color-sorted, boxed or packaged, and then stored to await transportation to a wholesale distribution center.

d. Transportation of the Fruitables from the packinghouse to the wholesale distribution center.

e. Grading and storage of the Fruitables at the wholesale distribution center.

f. Transportation of the Fruitables from the wholesale distribution center to the retail markets or other institutions.

g. Grading of the Fruitables at the retail market or institution and storage or display of them to await purchase by a consumer.

Since we are interested in evaluating the damage and loss of the Fruitables as they travel through the system, we make some observations and notes in addition to those above. These include the following:

a. Grading of the Fruitables occurs only at four distinct components, those being the farm during harvesting, the packinghouse, the wholesale distribution center, and the retail market or institution. These are the only places that Fruitables may be lost from the system.

b. At least to some extent, every process in the system causes some amount of damage in the Fruitables. Thus, at any given point in time there may be damaged Fruitables flowing through the system as well as undamaged Fruitables.

c. Although grading is done at the four components noted earlier, not all the damaged produce is discarded by the graders. This may be because the damage is not apparent, the damage was not caught by the grader, or the damage was of such little significance that, at that point in the system, the Fruitable was allowed to continue through the system.

d. The graders, occasionally discard undamaged Fruitables due to carelessness, haste, or other reasons.

Using these observations and notes, we are now ready to formulate our complete black-box model of the Fruitables postharvest handling system. As we do so, care should be taken to assure that the black-box model correctly represents the actual system under investigation. It may be desirable, once the model is complete, to follow the Fruitables through the system a final time with the model in-hand to assure that it is correct.

Figure 1 indicates a black-box model of the Fruitable postharvest handling system that was observed and discussed above. Note that every component or process encountered by the Fruitables is adequately represented in this model. Further, the notes pertaining to the locations of grading stations, the flow of damaged and undamaged Fruitables through the system, and the losses of both damaged and undamaged Fruitables have been incorporated into the model. At this point, the black-box model development phase of the research method is complete. This model, along with data that may be collected from the system, will be used to formulate a computer simulation model that can be used to evaluate the origins and magnitudes of losses of Fruitables from this specific postharvest handling system.

<u>Data</u> <u>Collection</u>

Once we are satisfied that our black-box model
is complete, and that our knowledge of the operating
characteristics of the system is adequate, some
further data must be collected in order to develop
the simulation model.

First, data must be obtained pertaining to the
amount (percent) of produce that is found to be
damaged at each component of the system. Second, of
the damaged produce reaching a grading station, the
amount that is discarded (lost from the system), as
well as the amount that is allowed to continue
through the system must be investigated. Similar
data need to be collected for the undamaged produce
reaching a grading station. Finally, the times
associated with each process or component need to be
investigated and recorded. This is due to the fact
that every fresh market product has an expected
shelf-life, and should the product not make it out of
the system within that amount of time, it too will be
lost from the system.

At first glance, it may seem that the data
collection phase of the research method would be time
consuming and expensive: Two things should be noted
here:

1. The data collection phase need only be as
long as the researcher feels necessary to provide
good estimates for his simulation model.

2. The amount and cost of the data collection
phase is proportional to the complexity of the system
and the accuracy desired by the researcher.

It should be kept in mind that the formulation
and evaluation of potential solutions to damage and
loss problems within the system may well cover the
cost of the research project.

For our Fruitable example, let us assume that
the following data was collected from the actual
operating system:

*Of the Fruitables hanging on the vines in the field, 25 percent are damaged and 75 percent undamaged.

*Of the damaged Fruitables, 80 percent are not harvested and left on the vine to decay. The remaining 20 percent are harvested and continue through the system.

*The time that it takes to harvest a Fruitable and deliver it to a position in the field to await transportation to the packinghouse is normally distributed with a mean of .5 hours and a standard deviation (SD) of .1 hours.

*The harvesting operation damages 10 percent of all the Fruitables harvested.

*The time that Fruitable sits in the field waiting to be taken to the packinghouse is normally distributed with a mean of 6 hours and an SD of 2 hours.

*While the Fruitables sit in the field waiting, 3 percent are damaged.

*Loading the Fruitables and trucking them to the packinghouse requires a time that is normally distributed with a mean of 1 hour and an SD of .25 hours.

*This trucking process damages 3 percent of all the Fruitables.

*The time that passes in between the arrival of the Fruitables to the packinghouse and the beginning of their processing is normally distributed with a mean of 1 hour and an SD of 0.30 hours.

*Of all the damaged Fruitables reaching the graders in the packinghouse, 90 percent are discarded and lost from the system. Ten percent continue through the system.

*Of all the undamaged Fruitables reaching the graders, 3 percent are discarded and 97 percent continue through the system.

*Size-sorting the Fruitables takes a time that is normally distributed with a mean of .025 hours and an SD of .005 hours.

*The size-sorting process damages 1 percent of all the Fruitables passing through it.

*Color-sorting the Fruitables takes a time that is normally distributed with a mean of .03 hours and an SD of .005 hours.

*The color-sorting process damages 1 percent of all the Fruitables passing through it.

*The time that it takes to box the Fruitables is normally distributed within a mean of .05 hours and an SD of .01 hours.

*Boxing the Fruitables damages 2 percent of all that are boxed at the packinghouse.

*After boxing, the Fruitables sit in storage at the packinghouse for a time that is normally distributed with a mean of 10 hours and an SD of 4 hours.

*Two percent of the Fruitables are damaged during this storage.

*Loading the Fruitables onto a truck and shipping them to the wholesale distribution center requires a time that is normally distributed with a mean of 14 hours and an SD of 3 hours.

*Ten percent of the Fruitables are damaged during this shipping.

*The Fruitables stay at the wholesale distribution center for a time that is normally distributed with a mean of 18 hours and an SD of 6 hours.

*Of all the damaged Fruitables that reach the grader at the wholesale ditribution center, 95 percent are discarded and 5 percent are allowed to continue through the system.

*Of all the undamaged Fruitables reaching the graders, 2 percent are discarded and 98 percent are allowed to continue.

*Loading and shipping the Fruitables from the wholesale distribution center to the retail market requires a time that is normally distributed with a mean of 3 hours and an SD of 1 hour.

*This shipping damages 4 percent of the Frutiables in the system at this point.

*Upon arrival at the retail market, the Fruitables sit in storage for a time that is normally distributed with a mean of 4 hours and an SD of 1 hour.

*Of all the damaged Fruitables reaching the grader at the retail market, 50 percent are discarded and 50 percent are allowed to stay in the system.

*Of all the undamaged Fruitables reaching the grader, 1 percent is discarded and 99 percent stay in the system.

*At the retail market, after grading, Fruitables sit either in storage or display for a time that is normally distributed with a mean of 14 hours and an SD of 4 hours awaiting purchase by a consumer.

This data, along with information from the black-box model of the system, is all that is required to formulate a simulation model of the system that is capable of evaluating losses and damages of Fruitables while within the system.

Note from the above data that damage probabilities were deterministic, while process times were stochastic. In fact, damage probabilities and process times may have been stochastic or deterministic and could have been modeled as either. Further, note that while this system is hypothetical, it is realistic of many fresh market products. In fact, Campbell (1985) and Shewfelt (1985) studied postharvest handling systems of tomatoes that were completely analogous to the hypothetical Fruitable system.

Since we have defined and observed the postharvest handling system in question, developed a black-box model of the system, and collected the necessary data, we can now develop the computer simulation model.

Development of the Simulation Model

Drawing information from our black-box model, our notes, and the data we collected, we can now begin to formulate a computer simulation model that can be used to study the system. As noted earlier, many special purpose simulation languages have been developed to accommodate simulationists, although some simulationists still use the common programming languages such as FORTRAN, BASIC or COBOL. Since the purpose of this paper is to present a research method, and not to study simulation languages, the special purpose language SLAM - Simulation Language for Alternative Modeling (Pritsker and Pegden, 1978) - was chosen to use in developing and analyzing the simulation model. SLAM was chosen because of availability and because it is one of the simplist, yet most powerful simulation languages used today. Further, the software for the Network portion of SLAM, which we will use in developing our simulation model, is available for use on some personal computers. It should be noted, however, that any simulation language with Network features could have been used to develop the simulation model.

Figure 2 indicates the SLAM network diagram of the hypothetical Fruitable postharvest handling system. This example simulation model was created to study damage with emphasis on losses of Fruitables from the system, and where the losses occur. With the information provided by the black-box model, the data that was collected as discussed in the previous section, and the SLAM variable descriptions provided in Table 1, the reader should easily be able to understand the Network diagram. However, a brief discussion of the diagram is presented below to aid in this understanding.

The purpose of the very first mode in the diagram is to create 500 entities (Fruitables) and enter them into the system. At this point, the model represents the state of the system where the

Fruitables are on the vine in the field before harvesting. This is indicated by the node labeled "Vine." Now, using only probabilistic branching, activity arrows to indicate process durations, and ASSIGN nodes to alter the values of the variables indicated in Table 1, a simulation model is created that mimics the behavior of the actual operating system.

Two main concepts were utilized in developing the simulation program and diagram. The first concept, illustrated in Figure 3, is the logic used to model a process such as harvesting or trucking. When all the Fruitables flowing through the system (both damaged and undamaged) arrive at the node labeled "HARV" (for harvesting), they pass through an activity (arrow) that represents the time that it takes to complete the process. The statement "RNORM(.5,.1)" indicates that the time it takes to harvest a Fruitable and sit it in the field when the harvester is full requires a time that is normally distributed with a mean of .5 hours and a standard deviation of .1 hours. Upon the arrival of the Fruitables to the second node, 90 percent of them are routed directly to the node labeled "FLD" for field, which is the beginning of another process. The remaining 10 percent are routed through an "ASSIGN" node before being routed to the node "FLD." The "ASSIGN" node changes the value of the variable "ATRIB(2)" to 1 for each Fruitable passing through it to indicate that it was damaged by the harvesting process. If a Fruitable passes through this node whose ATRIB(2) value is already 1, it's ATRIB(2) value remains 1. As indicated in Table 1, the ATRIB(2) variable is used as a flag to indicate whether an entity is damaged [ATRIB(2)=1] or undamaged [ATRIB(2)=0]. Every process that the Fruitables undergo, with the exception of grading, are modeled in the exact same manner. For convenience, node label definitions are provided in Table 2.

The concept behind simulation of the grading process is illustrated in Figure 4. When Fruitables reach the nodel labled "GRD", they are routed to the node labeled "BD2" if they have been damaged by any of the previous processes. Undamaged Fruitables that reach the "GRD" node are routed to the node labeled

"OK2." The nodes "BD2" and "OK2" both model the single grader or set of graders that grade the produce. Ninety percent of the Fruitables reaching the "BD2" node are discarded from the system, and the number of Fruitables that are discarded are counted via an ASSIGN node and the variable XX(2). These Fruitables are then routed to the node labeled "LOSS," which will be discussed later. The remaining 10 percent of the Fruitables that reach the node "BD2" are routed to the next process (node SST) and allowed to continue through the system. The Fruitables that reach the node "OK2" are undamaged and, as such, 97 percent of them are routed to the next process to continue through the system. The remaining 3 percent are discarded by the grader, counted by the variable XX(3), and routed to the node labeled "LOSS." Every grading process is modeled in this way.

Figure 5 indicates the logic used at the end of the simulation diagram. At the node labeled "CON," every Fruitable that is still in the system at this point is checked to see if it has been in the system for more than 144 hours, the expected shelf life of the Fruitables. If so, it is routed to the node labeled "TIM", counted by the variable XX(8), and routed to the node labeled "LOSS." The Fruitables that pass through the system in less than 144 hours are routed to the node labeled "END," where they are again sorted into damaged Fruitables (and sent to the node labeled "BD5") or undamaged Fruitables (and sent to node "OK5). The number of Fruitables that make it through the entire system undamaged are counted by the variable XX(10) at node "OK5" and are then terminated by the simulation. The number of damaged Fruitables that make it through the entire system are counted by the variable XX(9) and are then routed to the node labeled "LOSS." The node "LOSS" and the variable XX(11) counts these Fruitables, as well as every other Fruitable that has been lost from the system. These entities are then terminated by the simulation. When all 500 Fruitables that were entered into the system have been terminated, the simulation run is ended.

Note that every process, duration, and probability indicated by the black-box model and the collection of data is incorporated into the simulation model. The flow of both damaged and undamaged Fruitables is modeled, as well as the performance of the graders. It is of utmost importance that no process that damages produce or requires a significant amount of time be left out of this model. The simulation model, after all, can be only as correct as the simulationist makes it.

The SLAM computer code for this simulation is given in Appendix A. With the exception of some initial SLAM control statements, the code corresponds to the network diagram precisely. For more information concerning the use of the SLAM computer code, consult Pritsker and Pegden (1978).

It should be noted once again that, although SLAM was used for the purposes of illustrating the research method, any simulation language that provides the user with networking capabilities could have been used. Most simulation languages that incorporate network features utilize their own set of node symbols for network diagrams, and thus, the diagram for this model may appear slightly different if another language is used. The logic, however, should be the same.

Now that our simulation model is complete and the simulation program is running, we must verify the program to assure that it is performing correctly. Most simulation languages provide the user with a "TRACE" statement that can be used to accomplish this. Further, output of the simulation can be compared to data used to build the simulation to assure that it is functioning properly. Once these things have been accomplished, we may proceed to the fourth and final phase of the research method--the postharvest handling systems analysis via the computer simulation model.

Analysis via Computer Simulation

Once the computer simulation model is completed, running properly, and is checked for accuracy, the postharvest handling system of concern may be evaluated in terms of damages and losses. Most simulation languages provide the user with the results of simulation runs in the form of a report once the simulation being performed is completed.

371

From this report, the researcher may assess the performance of the system under the conditions that were specified in the simulation model. It should be noted, however, that the output of only one simulation run is merely an observation. A number of runs are necessary in order to obtain a statistically correct estimate of the parameter(s) that are of concern. Once these estimates have been obtained, the researcher will have data from which he may evaluate the existing system.

The analysis of the postharvest handling system actually begins after the existing system has been simulated and evaluated. By merely changing one or more of the parameters specified in the original model, depending on the process(es) that the researcher wishes to investigate, the researcher may evaluate the effect of changing these parameters in the real system on the performance of the system. This can be done without further data collection or any disturbance what-so-ever to the existing system. To evaluate changes in the existing system by actually changing the operating parameters of the system would be difficult and costly, if not impossible to do. Further, all the data that was required in order to evaluate the system under the normal operating conditions would have to be recollected every time a change in an operating condition is investigated. It is clear that computer simulation could save the researcher much time and money when evaluating postharvest handling systems. It should be noted again, however, that when changes are made in the simulation, a number of runs are required to correctly re-evaluate the parameters in question. Changes in the simulation model may continue to be made until the researcher has evaluated all the changes in all the processes that he deems necessary in order to find feasible solutions to any damage or loss problems that were present in the existing system under normal operating conditions.

For our Fruitable postharvest handling system example, the output report provided by SLAM for the simulation of the system under normal operating conditions is shown in Figure 6. The variables of interest in this output report are the XX(N) variables indicated in Table 1 and underlined in

Figure 6. The "current values" of these variables
are of interest in this case, as they provide the
final count of Fruitables that leave the system in
the various places. For example, one can see from
Figure 6 that, out of 500 Fruitables hanging on the
vine, 100 of them were never harvested, and therefore
lost, due to damage. Out of the 400 Fruitables that
were harvested, 82 were lost at the packinghouse.
Seventy-eight of these were thrown out because they
were damaged, while 4 undamaged Fruitables were
inadvertantly discarded by the grader at the
packinghouse. The three variables at the end of this
list indicate the number of damaged Fruitables that
made it through the system, the number of undamaged
Fruitables that made it through the system, and the
total number of Fruitables lost from the system,
respectively. From Figure 6, it can be seen that 8
damaged Fruitables reached the end of the system, 259
reached the end of the system undamaged, and a total
of 241 Fruitables were damaged or considered lost
from the system. Again, Tables 1 and 2 will aid the
reader in identifying the variables presented in the
section of the report marked "Regular Activity
Statistics" give the user a count of the number of
Fruitables that pass through activities numbered in
the square boxes in the diagram of Figure 2. This
data is found in the column marked "Entity Count."
The "Activity Index" corresponds to the number of the
activity in the small square boxes in Figure 2. For
example, it can be seen that only 267 of the possible
500 Fruitables ever made it to the grocer (node
labeled "GRO"). Of these Fruitables, 8 were damaged
and 259 undamaged.

From the data presented in the SLAM simulation
output report for this model, under the normal
operating conditions of the existing system, we can
assess the performance of the system. For example,
we can see the following:

*Of 500 Fruitables hanging on the vines, 48.2
percent (241/500) were lost due to damage or being
unnecessarily discarded.

*20 percent (100/500) of the Fruitables,
however, were never harvested due to being damaged,
so the actual amount lost in the operating system was
28.2 percent ([241-100]/500).

373

*Since only 400 Fruitables were actually harvested, 19.5 percent (78/400) were damaged prior to reaching the packinghouse and were discarded at the packinghouse.

Estimates such as these provide us with measure of the operating performance of the existing Fruitable postharvest handling system.

Now, let us begin to analyze the system via our computer simulation model. For the purpose of this illustration, let us assume that we would like to investigate the effect of reducing the amount of damage in the Fruitables hanging on the vine on the performance of the entire system. To do so, all we need do is change the parameter that specifies the amount of Fruitables that are damaged on the vine. This is done merely by altering the simulation program in line number 00240 of the code in Appendix A to the line number 00240 of the code in Appendix B. This will allow us to investigate the effect on system performance of reducing the amount of damage present in the field before harvesting from 25 percent to 5 percent. The SLAM report in Figure 7 shows us that the effect that this one change had on the system performance was to reduce the total loss from 48.2 percent to 38.4 percent (192/500). Thus, we may conclude that the farmers need to better care for the crops by better irrigating, applying pesticides or herbicides, or by reducing decay by harvesting sooner or more often. Note that in order to evaluate this change, no further data was collected from the existing system, and no changes in the operating conditions of the system were necessary. In fact, this analysis could have been accomplished in the cold of winter when the physical system was not even operational!

By continuing to change parameters in our simulation model of the Fruitable postharvest handing system, we can identify the greatest sources of loss and damage, and continually improve the performance of the system until feasible solutions to the loss an damage problems have been formulated. The solutions (changes), however, must be implemented into the existing system by farmers, packinghouse managers, wholesalers, etc. for them to affect the operation of

the real, existing postharvest handling system.
Normally, however, this is not the job of the
researcher.

SUMMARY AND CONCLUSIONS

In this paper it was sought to develop and
demonstrate the use of a research method for
evaluating losses and damages within specific
postharvest handling systems of specific fresh market
products. It was desired that the method be general
enough for use in nearly any postharvest handling
system of any product, yet complete enough to be able
to evaluate components of the system of concern as
well as the performance of the overall system. By
evaluating various systems analysis techniques,
computer simulation was chosen as the most suitable
for use in this application.

The research method developed consisted of four
distinct phases: 1) The Model Development Process,
2) Data Collection, 3) Development of the Simulation
Model, and 4) Analysis via Computer Simualtion. Each
phase of the research method was discussed in detail
and demonstrated with an example of a typical,
hypothetical postharvest handling system.

Results of simulations showed the method
presented in this paper is a feasible, extremely
useful tool in evaluating specific postharvest
handling systems in terms of damages and losses of
produce within them. Solutions to damage and loss
problems found to exist in a system can be easily
evaluated, and potential solutions to the problems
may be formulated and assessed to determine the most
suitable solutions for the system in question.
Finally, the method is general enough so that nearly
any postharvest handling system of any fresh market
product may be examined by using the techniques
presented here.

REFERENCES

Campbell, D.T. 1985. A systems analysis of post-
harvest damages to fresh fruits and vegetables.
Unpublished Research Proposal. Dept. of
Agric. Engr., University of Georgia.

Campbell, D.T., S.E. Prussia, and R.L. Shewfelt. 1985. Evaluating postharvest damage to fresh market tomatoes. ASAE Paper No. 85-3031.

Ceponis, M.J. and J.E. Butterfield. 1979. Losses in fresh tomatoes at the retail and consumer levels in the Greater New York Area. J. Amer. Soc. Hort. Sci. 104(6):751-754.

Davis, K.R. and P.G. Mceown. 1984. Quantitative Models for Management. Kent Publishing Company. Boston, MA.

Halloran, J.M., T.R. Pierson, and J.W. Allen. 1982. Losses of food commodities during marketing and distribution. ASAE Paper NO. 82-6502.

Halsey, L.H. 1963. Studies of tomato bruising. Proc. of Am. Soc. for Hort. Sci., 83:710-715.

Joran, J.L., R.L. Shewfelt, S.E. Prussia, and W.C. Hurst. 1984. Hedonic price estimation for tomatoes using a flexible functional form: evaluating the postharvest system. Paper presented at the 18th Atlantic Economic Conference, Montreal, Canada, October 13, 1984.

MacLeod, R.F., A.A. Koder, and L.L. Morris. 1976. Damage to fresh tomatoes can be reduced. California Agriculture, Dec. 10-12.

Mongelli, R.C. 1984. Marketing fresh tomatoes. USDA Marketing Research Research Report MRR-1137.

Pritsker, A.A.B. an C.D. Pegden. 1978 Introduction to Simulation and SLAM. John Wiley and Sons. New York, NY.

Pritsker, A.A.B. 1984. Introduction to Simulation and SLAM II. Jonn Wiley and Sons. New York, NY.

Schaper, L.A. and J.L. Varns. 1982. Mass and energy losses in the potato marketing chain. ASAE Paper No. 82-4025.

Schoorl, D. and J.E. Holt. 1982. Fresh fruit and vegetables distribution-management of quality. Scientia Hertic., 17:1-8.

Shewfelt, R.L., S.E. Prussia, J.L. Jordan, and W.C. Hurst. 1985. A systems approach to the evaluation of changes in quality during postharvest handling of Southern Peas. J. Food Sci. In press.

Shewfelt, R.L. 1985. Personal communication.

TABLE 1. Descriptions of the functions of SLAM variables used in the simulation diagram and program of the example Fruitable postharvest handling system.

SLAM VARIABLE	VARIABLE FUNCTION
ATRIB(1)	Marks the time that each Fruitable is harvested.
ATRIB(2)	Indicates whether a Fruitable is damaged or undamaged. The value of ATRIB(2) for an undamaged Fruitable is 0, while the value for a damaged Fruitable is 1. In this sense, the ATRIB(2) variable is used as a flag in the simulation program.
XX(1)	Counts the number of Fruitables damaged in the field and not harvested.
XX(2)	Counts the number of Fruitables discarded at the packinghouse due to damage.
XX(3)	Counts the number of Fruitables discarded at the packinghouse that were undamaged.
XX(4)	Counts the number of Fruitables discarded by the wholesale grader due to damage.
XX(5)	Counts the number of Fruitables discarded by the wholesale grader that were undamaged.
XX(6)	Counts the number of Fruitables discarded at the retailer due damage.
XX(7)	Counts the number of Fruitables discarded at the retailer that were undamaged.
XX(8)	Counts the number of Fruitables lost from the system due to their shelf life being exceeded.
XX(9)	Counts the number of damaged Fruitables that reach the end of the system without being discarded.
XX(10)	Counts the number of undamaged Fruitables that reach the end of system.
XX(11)	Counts the total number of Fruitables lost or damaged in the system.
TNOW	The time that passes in between the harvesting of a Fruitable and the time it reaches the end of the system.

Table 2. Node Labels used in the simulation network diagram and the function they model when they occur (See Figure 2).

Node Label	Function
Vine	Fruitables hanging on the vine
BD1	Damaged Fruitables in the Field
OK1	Undamaged Fruitables in the Field
HARV	Harvesting process
FLD	Fruitables sitting in the field after harvest
TRK	Fruitables being trucked from field to packinghouse
PH	Arrival of Fruitables at packinghouse
GRD	Grading Fruitables at Packinghouse
BD2	Damaged Fruitables reaching grader at packinghouse
OK2	Undamaged Fruitables reaching grader at packinghouse
SST	Size-sorting at packinghouse
CST	Color-sorting at packinghouse
BOX	Boxing operation at packinghouse
STG	Storage at packinghouse
TR1	Trucking Fruitables from packinghouse to wholesaler
WLS	Fruitables at wholesaler
GRW	Grading Fruitables at Wholesaler
BD3	Damaged Fruitables reaching grader at wholesaler
OK3	Undamaged Fruitables reaching grader at wholesaler
TR2	Trucking Fruitables from wholesaler to retailer
RTL	Fruitables at retailer
GRR	Grading Fruitables at retailer
BD4	Damaged Fruitables reaching grader at retailer
OK4	Undamaged Fruitables reaching grader at retailer
GRO	Fruitables reaching grocery display at storage.
CON	Fruitables reaching consumer
TIM	Fruitables whose shelf life is exceeded are counted
END	Fruitables reaching the end of the system are counted
BD5	Damaged Fruitables at the end of the system are counted
OK5	Undamaged Fruitables reaching the end of the system are counted
LOSS	All Fruitables lost or damaged in the system are counted
AD1-AD3	Nodes labeled simply to show connections on the diagram

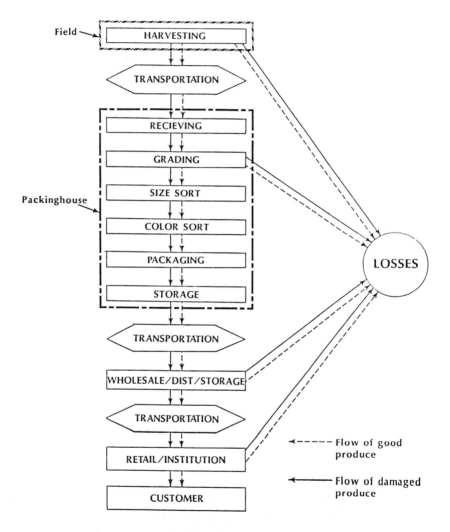

Figure 1: Black-box model of the example, hypothetical postharvest handling system of "Fruitables".

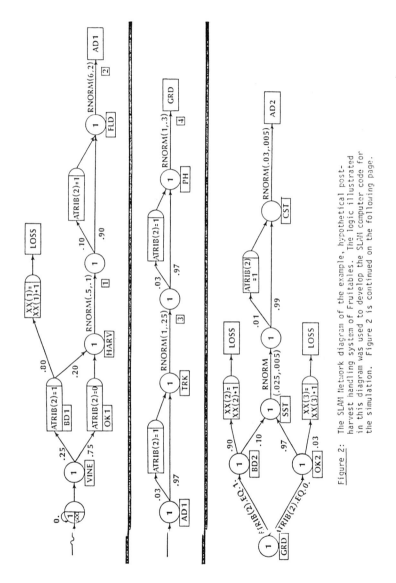

Figure 2: The SLAM Network diagram of the example, hypothetical post-harvest handling system of Fruitables. The logic illustrated in this diagram was used to develop the SLAM computer code for the simulation. Figure 2 is continued on the following page.

381

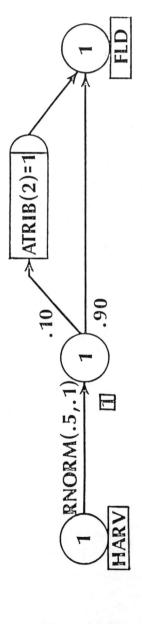

Figure 3: A portion of the SLAM Network diagram of Figure 2 that illustrates the logic used to model a process such as harvesting
or trucking.

382

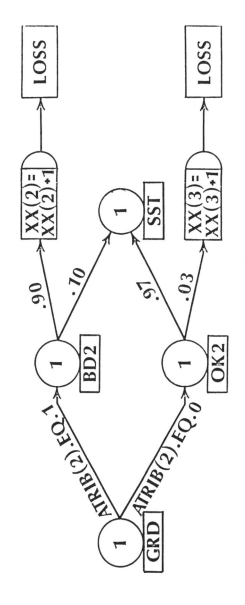

Figure 4: A portion of the SLAM Network diagram of Figure 2 that illustrates the logic used to model the grading processes.

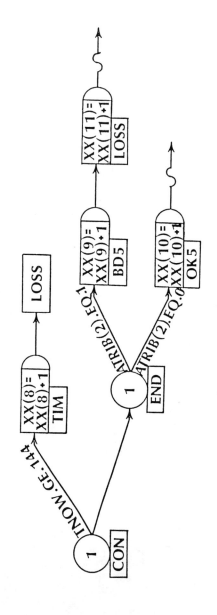

Figure 5: The portion of the SLAM Network diagram of Figure 2 that is used to collect data at the end of the simulation.

S L A M   S U M M A R Y   R E P O R T

SIMULATION PROJECT POSTHARVEST   BY TIM C.

DATE 6/ 1/1985   RUN NUMBER   1 OF   1

CURRENT TIME   0.1008E 03
STATISTICAL ARRAYS CLEARED AT TIME 0.0

STATISTICS FOR TIME-PERSISTENT VARIABLES

	MEAN VALUE	STANDARD DEVIATION	MINIMUM VALUE	MAXIMUM VALUE	TIME INTERVAL	CURRENT VALUE
NO.BAD..NOT HARV	0.1000E 03	0.6250E-01	0.0	0.1000E 03	0.1008E 03	0.1000E 03
NO.BAD LOSS @ PH	0.7119E 02	0.2040E 02	0.0	0.7900E 02	0.1008E 03	0.7900E 02
NO.GOOD LOSS PH	0.3637E 01	0.1068E 01	0.0	0.4000E 01	0.1008E 03	0.4000E 01
NO.BAD LOSS GRW	0.1692E 02	0.1625E 02	0.0	0.3500E 02	0.1008E 03	0.3500E 02
NO.GOOD LOSS GRW	0.2992E 01	0.2709E 01	0.0	0.6000E 01	0.1008E 03	0.6000E 01
NO.BAD LOSS GRR	0.3388E 01	0.3685E 01	0.0	0.8000E 01	0.1008E 03	0.8000E 01
NO.GOOD LOSS GRR	0.7571E 00	0.8948E 00	0.0	0.2000E 01	0.1008E 03	0.2000E 01
NO. TIME LOSS	0.0	0.0	0.0	0.0	0.1008E 03	0.0
NO.BAD AT END	0.2232E 01	0.3189E 01	0.0	0.8000E 01	0.1008E 03	0.8000E 01
NO.GOOD AT END	0.7580E 02	0.1025E 03	0.0	0.2590E 03	0.1008E 03	0.2590E 03
TOTAL LOSS	0.2011E 03	0.3887E 02	0.0	0.2410E 03	0.1008E 03	0.2410E 03

REGULAR ACTIVITY STATISTICS

ACTIVITY INDEX	AVERAGE UTILIZATION	STANDARD DEVIATION	MAXIMUM UTILIZATION	CURRENT UTILIZATION	ENTITY COUNT
1	1.9872	26.4439	400	0	400
2	24.6292	86.1349	399	0	400
3	4.0257	15.0031	100	0	400
4	3.9644	14.8322	95	0	400
5	0.1589	0.7351	11	0	318
6	31.1549	73.8611	286	0	318
7	44.5422	82.1217	276	0	318
8	56.0969	86.6499	262	0	318
9	37.4966	53.3646	162	0	267

Figure 6:   The SLAM output report that indicates the results of the simulation of the example system under normal operating conditions.

385

****SIMULATION LANGUAGE FOR ALTERNATIVE MODELING (SLAM)****
****VERSION 1.0 * RELEASE 1.4****
****COPYRIGHT 1979 BY PRITSKER AND ASSOCIATES, INC. AND C. DENNIS PEGDEN****
****WEST LAFAYETTE, INDIANA 47906****
****THIS JOB PROCESSED AT****
****UNIVERSITY OF GEORGIA****
****JUN. 09, 1985****

S L A M   S U M M A R Y   R E P O R T

SIMULATION PROJECT POSTHARVEST   BY TIM C.

DATE 6/ 4/1985   RUN NUMBER   1 OF   1

CURRENT TIME   0.1015E 03
STATISTICAL ARRAYS CLEARED AT TIME 0.0

STATISTICS FOR TIME-PERSISTENT VARIABLES

	MEAN VALUE	STANDARD DEVIATION	MINIMUM VALUE	MAXIMUM VALUE	TIME INTERVAL	CURRENT VALUE
NO.BAD..NOT HARV	0.1800E 02	0.2210E-01	0.0	0.1800E 02	0.1015E 03	0.1800E 02
NO.BAD LOSS @ PH	0.7753E 02	0.2213E 02	0.0	0.8500E 02	0.1015E 03	0.8500E 02
NO.GOOD LOSS PH	0.1878E 01	0.4583E 00	0.0	0.2000E 01	0.1015E 03	0.2000E 01
NO.BAD LOSS GRW	0.2335E 02	0.2194E 02	0.0	0.4300E 02	0.1015E 03	0.4300E 02
NO.GOOD LOSS GRW	0.5611E 01	0.4954E 01	0.0	0.1100E 02	0.1015E 03	0.1100E 02
NO.BAD LOSS GRR	0.4460E 01	0.4417E 01	0.0	0.1000E 02	0.1015E 03	0.1000E 02
NO.GOOD LOSS GRR	0.1511E 01	0.1412E 01	0.0	0.3000E 01	0.1015E 03	0.3000E 01
NO. TIME LOSS	0.0	0.0	0.0	0.0	0.1015E 03	0.0
NO.BAD AT END	0.3552E 01	0.5054E 01	0.0	0.1500E 02	0.1015E 03	0.1500E 02
NO.GOOD AT END	0.9178E 02	0.1222E 03	0.0	0.3080E 03	0.1015E 03	0.3080E 03
TOTAL LOSS	0.1359E 03	0.4939E 02	0.0	0.1920E 03	0.1015E 03	0.1920E 03

REGULAR ACTIVITY STATISTICS

ACTIVITY INDEX	AVERAGE UTILIZATION	STANDARD DEVIATION	MAXIMUM UTILIZATION	CURRENT UTILIZATION	ENTITY COUNT
1	2.3812	31.8195	482	0	482
2	29.4383	103.3607	481	0	482
3	4.8154	18.0249	108	0	482
4	4.8249	17.9548	105	0	482
5	0.1961	0.8737	10	0	395
6	37.5038	91.0341	349	0	395
7	53.6433	101.3891	346	0	395
8	70.8844	108.2382	333	0	395
9	45.2391	62.0239	183	0	323

Figure 7: The SLAM output report that indicates the results of the simulation of the example system after the model was modified to examine the effect of reducing in-field damage.

SLAM computer code for the simulation program of the hypothetical postharvest handling system under normal operating conditions.

```
00050 GEN,TIM C.,POSTHARVEST,6/4/85,1,,NO;
00060 LIMITS,2,3,500;
00070 INTLC,XX(1)=0,XX(2)=0,XX(3)=0,XX(4)=0,XX(5)=0;
00080 INTLC,XX(6)=0,XX(7)=0,XX(8)=0,XX(9)=0,XX(10)=0;
00090 INTLC,XX(11)=0;
00100 TIMST,XX(1),NO.BAD,.NOT HARV;
00110 TIMST,XX(2),NO.BAD LOSS @ FH;
00120 TIMST,XX(3),NO.GOOD LOSS FH;
00130 TIMST,XX(4),NO.BAD LOSS GRW;
00140 TIMST,XX(5),NO.GOOD LOSS GRW;
00150 TIMST,XX(6),NO.BAD LOSS GRK;
00160 TIMST,XX(7),NO.GOOD LOSS GRK;
00170 TIMST,XX(8),NO. TIME LOSS;
00180 TIMST,XX(9),NO.BAD AT END;
00190 TIMST,XX(10),NO.GOOD AT END;
00200 TIMST,XX(11), TOTAL LOSS;
00210 NETWORK;
00220      CREATE,0,,,1,500;
00230 VINE GOON,1;
00240      ACT,,,25,RD1;
00250      ACT,,,75;
00260      ASSIGN,ATRIB(2)=0;
00270      ACT,,,HARV;
00280 RD1  ASSIGN,ATRIB(2)=1,1;
00290      ACT,,,20,HARV;
00300      ACT,,,80;
00310      ASSIGN,XX(1)=XX(1)+1;
00320      ACT,,,LOSS;
00330 HARV GOON,1;
00340      ACT/1,RNORM(.5,.1);
00350      GOON,1;
00360      ACT,,,90,FLD;
00370      ACT,,,10;
00380      ASSIGN,ATRIB(2)=1;
00390      ACT,,,FLD;
00400 FLD  GOON,1;
00410      ACT/2,RNORM(6,2);
00420      GOON,1;
00430      ACT,,,97,TRK;
00440      ACT,,,03;
00450      ASSIGN,ATRIB(2)=1;
00460      ACT,,,TRK;
00470 TRK  GOON,1;
00480      ACT/3,RNORM(1,.25);
00490      GOON,1;

00500      ACT,,,97,FH;
00510      ACT,,,03;
00520      ASSIGN,ATRIB(2)=1;
00530      ACT,,,FH;
00540 FH   GOON,1;
00550      ACT/4,RNORM(1,.3),,GRD;
00560 GRD  GOON,1;
00570      ACT,,ATRIB(2).EQ.1.0,RD2;
00580      ACT,,ATRIB(2).EQ.0.0;
00590      GOON,1;
00600      ACT,,,97,SST;
00610      ACT,,,03;
00620      ASSIGN,XX(3)=XX(3)+1;
00630      ACT,,,LOSS;
00640 RD2  GOON,1;
00650      ACT,,,10,SST;
00660      ACT,,,90;
00670      ASSIGN,XX(2)=XX(2)+1;
00680      ACT,,,LOSS;
00690 SST  GOON,1;
00700      ACT,RNORM(.025,.005);
00710      GOON,1;
00720      ACT,,,99,CST;
00730      ACT,,,01;
00740      ASSIGN,ATRIB(2)=1;
00750      ACT,,,CST;
00760 CST  GOON,1;
00770      ACT,RNORM(.03,.005);
00780      GOON,1;
00790      ACT,,,99,BOX;
00800      ACT,,,01;
00810      ASSIGN,ATRIB(2)=1;
00820      ACT,,,BOX;
00830 BOX  GOON,1;
00840      ACT/5,RNORM(.05,.01);
00850      GOON,1;
00860      ACT,,,98,STG;
00870      ACT,,,02;
00880      ASSIGN,ATRIB(2)=1;
00890      ACT,,,STG;
00900 STG  GOON,1;
00910      ACT/6,RNORM(10,4);
00920      GOON,1;
00930      ACT,,,98,TR1;
00940      ACT,,,02;
00950      ASSIGN,ATRIB(2)=1;
00960      ACT,,,TR1;
00970 TR1  GOON,1;
00980      ACT/7,RNORM(14,3);
00990      GOON,1;
01000      ACT,,,90,WLS;
01010      ACT,,,10;
```

```
00500        ACT,,.97,PH;
00510        ACT,,.03;
00520        ASSIGN,ATRIB(2)=1;
00530        ACT,,,PH;
00540   PH   GOON,1;
00550        ACT/4,RNORM(1,.3),,,GRD;
00560   GRD  GOON,1;
00570        ACT,,ATRIB(2).EQ.1.0,BD2;
00580        ACT,,ATRIB(2).EQ.0.0;
00590        GOON,1;
00600        ACT,,.97,SST;
00610        ACT,,.03;
00620        ASSIGN,XX(3)=XX(3)+1;
00630        ACT,,,LOSS;
00640   BD2  GOON,1;
00650        ACT,,.10,SST;
00660        ACT,,.90;
00670        ASSIGN,XX(2)=XX(2)+1;
00680        ACT,,,LOSS;
00690   SST  GOON,1;
00700        ACT,RNORM(.025,.005);
00710        GOON,1;
00720        ACT,,.99,CST;
00730        ACT,,.01;
00740        ASSIGN,ATRIB(2)=1;
00750        ACT,,,CST;
00760   CST  GOON,1;
00770        ACT,RNORM(.03,.005);
00780        GOON,1;
00790        ACT,,.99,BOX;
00800        ACT,,.01;
00810        ASSIGN,ATRIB(2)=1;
00820        ACT,,,BOX;
00830   BOX  GOON,1;
00840        ACT/5,RNORM(.05,.01);
00850        GOON,1;
00860        ACT,,.98,STG;
00870        ACT,,.02;
00880        ASSIGN,ATRIB(2)=1;
00890        ACT,,,STG;
00900   STG  GOON,1;
00910        ACT/6,RNORM(10,4);
00920        GOON,1;
00930        ACT,,.98,TR1;
00940        ACT,,.02;
00950        ASSIGN,ATRIB(2)=1;
00960        ACT,,,TR1;
00970   TR1  GOON,1;
00980        ACT/7,RNORM(14,3);
00990        GOON,1;
01000        ACT,,.90,WLS;
01010        ACT,,.10;
```

```
01020        ASSIGN,ATRIB(2)=1;
01030        ACT,,,WLS;
01040   WLS  GOON,1;
01050        ACT/8,RNORM(18,6),,GRW;
01060   GRW  GOON,1;
01070        ACT,,ATRIB(2).EQ.1.0,BD3;
01080        ACT,,ATRIB(2).EQ.0.0;
01090        GOON,1;
01100        ACT,,.98,TR2;
01110        ACT,,.02;
01120        ASSIGN,XX(5)=XX(5)+1;
01130        ACT,,,LOSS;
01140   BD3  GOON,1;
01150        ACT,,.05,TR2;
01160        ACT,,.95;
01170        ASSIGN,XX(4)=XX(4)+1;
01180        ACT,,,LOSS;
01190   TR2  GOON,1;
01200        ACT,RNORM(3,1);
01210        GOON,1;
01220        ACT,,.96,RTL;
01230        ACT,,.04;
01240        ASSIGN,ATRIB(2)=1;
01250        ACT,,,RTL;
01260   RTL  GOON,1;
01270        ACT,RNORM(4,1),,,GRR;
01280   GRR  GOON,1;
01290        ACT,,ATRIB(2).EQ.1.0,BD4;
01300        ACT,,ATRIB(2).EQ.0.0;
01310        GOON,1;
01320        ACT,,.99,GRO;
01330        ACT,,.01;
01340        ASSIGN,XX(7)=XX(7)+1;
01350        ACT,,,LOSS;
01360   BD4  GOON,1;
01370        ACT,,.50,GRO;
01380        ACT,,.50;
01390        ASSIGN,XX(6)=XX(6)+1;
01400        ACT,,,LOSS;
01410   GRO  GOON,1;
01420        ACT/9,RNORM(14,4),,,CON;
01430   CON  GOON,1;
01440        ACT,,TNOW.GE.144.0,TIM;
01450        ACT,,,STP;
01460   TIM  ASSIGN,XX(8)=XX(8)+1;
01470        ACT,,,LOSS;
01480   STP  GOON,1;
01490        ACT,,ATRIB(2).EQ.1.0,BD5;
01500        ACT,,ATRIB(2).EQ.0.0;
01510        ASSIGN,XX(10)=XX(10)+1;
01520        TERM;
01530   BD5  ASSIGN,XX(9)=XX(9)+1;
01540        ACT,,,LOSS;
01550   LOSS ASSIGN,XX(11)=XX(11)+1;
01560        TERM;
01570        END;
01580 FIN;
```

The simulation program of the hypothetical postharvest handling
system after alteration to examine the effect of reducing in-
field damage. Note that the only alteration was made in line
number 00240.

```
00050 GEN,TIM C.,POSTHARVEST,6/4/95,1,NO,NO,,NO;        00500      ACT,,,97,PH;
00060 LIMITS,2,3,500;                                   00510      ACT,,,03;
00070 INTLC,XX(1)=0,XX(2)=0,XX(3)=0,XX(4)=0,XX(5)=0;    00520      ASSIGN,ATRIB(2)=1;
00080 INTLC,XX(6)=0,XX(7)=0,XX(8)=0,XX(9)=0,XX(10)=0;   00530      ACT,,,,PH;
00090 INTLC,XX(11)=0;                                   00540  PH  GOON,1;
00100 TIMST,XX(1),NO.PAD..NOT HARV;                     00550      ACT/4,RNORM(1,.3),,GRD;
00110 TIMST,XX(2),NO.PAD LOSS @ PH;                     00560  GRD GOON,1;
00120 TIMST,XX(3),NO.GOOD LOSS PH;                      00570      ACT,,ATRIB(2),EQ,1.0,BD2;
00130 TIMST,XX(4),NO.PAD LOSS GRN;                      00580      ACT,,ATRIB(2),EQ,0,0;
00140 TIMST,XX(5),NO.GOOD LOSS GRN;                     00590      GOON,1;
00150 TIMST,XX(6),NO.PAD LOSS GRR;                      00600      ACT,,,97,SST;
00160 TIMST,XX(7),NO.GOOD LOSS GRR;                     00610      ACT,,,03;
00170 TIMST,XX(8),NO. TIME LOSS;                        00620      ASSIGN,XX(3)=XX(3)+1;
00180 TIMST,XX(9),NO.PAD AT END;                        00630      ACT,,,LOSS;
00190 TIMST,XX(10),NO.GOOD AT END;                      00640  BD2 GOON,1;
00200 TIMST,XX(11), TOTAL LOSS;                         00650      ACT,,,10,SST;
00210 NETWORK;                                          00660      ACT,,,90;
00220     CREATE,0,,,1,500;                             00670      ASSIGN,XX(2)=XX(2)+1;
00230 VINE GOON,1;                                      00680      ACT,,,LOSS;
00240     ACT,,,05,BD1;                                 00690  SST GOON,1;
00250     ACT,,,95;                                     00700      ACT,RNORM(.025,.005);
00260     ASSIGN,ATRIB(2)=0;                            00710      GOON,1;
00270     ACT,,,HARV;                                   00720      ACT,,,99,CST;
00280 BD1 ASSIGN,ATRIB(2)=1,,1;                         00730      ACT,,.01;
00290     ACT,,,20,HARV;                                00740      ASSIGN,ATRIB(2)=1;
00300     ACT,,,80;                                     00750      ACT,,,CST;
00310     ASSIGN,XX(1)=XX(1)+1;                         00760  CST GOON,1;
00320     ACT,,,LOSS;                                   00770      ACT,RNORM(.03,.005);
00330 HARV GOON,1;                                      00780      GOON,1;
00340     ACT/1,RNORM(.5,.1);                           00790      ACT,,,99,BOX;
00350     GOON,1;                                       00800      ACT,,.01;
00360     ACT,,,90,FLD;                                 00810      ASSIGN,ATRIB(2)=1;
00370     ACT,,,10;                                     00820      ACT,,,BOX;
00380     ASSIGN,ATRIB(2)=1;                            00830  BOX GOON,1;
00390     ACT,,,FLD;                                    00840      ACT/5,RNORM(.05,.01);
00400 FLD GOON,1;                                       00850      GOON,1;
00410     ACT/2,RNORM(6,2);                             00860      ACT,,,98,STG;
00420     GOON,1;                                       00870      ACT,,.02;
00430     ACT,,,97,TRK;                                 00880      ASSIGN,ATRIB(2)=1;
00440     ACT,,,03;                                     00890      ACT,,,STG;
00450     ASSIGN,ATRIB(2)=1;                            00900  STG GOON,1;
00460     ACT,,,TRK;                                    00910      ACT/6,RNORM(10,4);
00470 TRK GOON,1;                                       00920      GOON,1;
00480     ACT/3,RNORM(1,.25));                          00930      ACT,,,98,TR1;
00490     GOON,1;                                       00940      ACT,,.02;
                                                        00950      ASSIGN,ATRIB(2)=1;
                                                        00960      ACT,,,TR1;
                                                        00970  TR1 GOON,1;
                                                        00980      ACT/7,RNORM(14,3);
                                                        00990      GOON,1;
                                                        01000      ACT,,,90,WLS;
                                                        01010      ACT,,,10;
```

```
00500        ACT,,.97,PH;
00510        ACT,,.03;
00520        ASSIGN,ATRIB(2)=1;
00530        ACT,,,PH;
00540   PH   GOON,1;
00550        ACT/4,RNORM(1,.3),,GRD;
00560   GRD  GOON,1;
00570        ACT,,ATRIB(2).EQ.1.0,BD2;
00580        ACT,,ATRIB(2).EQ.0.0;
00590        GOON,1;
00600        ACT,,.97,SST;
00610        ACT,,.03;
00620        ASSIGN,XX(3)=XX(3)+1;
00630        ACT,,,LOSS;
00640   BD2  GOON,1;
00650        ACT,,.10,SST;
00660        ACT,,.90;
00670        ASSIGN,XX(2)=XX(2)+1;
00680        ACT,,,LOSS;
00690   SST  GOON,1;
00700        ACT,RNORM(.025,,.005);
00710        GOON,1;
00720        ACT,,.99,CST;
00730        ACT,,.01;
00740        ASSIGN,ATRIB(2)=1;
00750        ACT,,,CST;
00760   CST  GOON,1;
00770        ACT,RNORM(.03,.005);
00780        GOON,1;
00790        ACT,,.99,BOX;
00800        ACT,,.01;
00810        ASSIGN,ATRIB(2)=1;
00820        ACT,,,BOX;
00830   BOX  GOON,1;
00840        ACT/5,RNORM(.05,.01);
00850        GOON,1;
00860        ACT,,.98,STG;
00870        ACT,,.02;
00880        ASSIGN,ATRIB(2)=1;
00890        ACT,,,STG;
00900   STG  GOON,1;
00910        ACT/6,RNORM(10,4);
00920        GOON,1;
00930        ACT,,.98,TR1;
00940        ACT,,.02;
00950        ASSIGN,ATRIB(2)=1;
00960        ACT,,,TR1;
00970   TR1  GOON,1;
00980        ACT/7,RNORM(14,3);
00990        GOON,1;
01000        ACT,,.90,WLS;
01010        ACT,,.10;
```

391

```
01020        ASSIGN,ATRIB(2)=1;
01030        ACT,,,WLS;
01040   WLS  GOON,1;
01050        ACT/8,RNORM(18,6),,,GRW;
01060   GRW  GOON,1;
01070        ACT,,ATRIB(2).EQ.1.0,BD3;
01080        ACT,,ATRIB(2).EQ.0.0;
01090        GOON,1;
01100        ACT,,.98,TR2;
01110        ACT,,.02;
01120        ASSIGN,XX(5)=XX(5)+1;
01130        ACT,,,LOSS;
01140   BD3  GOON,1;
01150        ACT,,.05,TR2;
01160        ACT,,.95;
01170        ASSIGN,XX(4)=XX(4)+1;
01180        ACT,,,LOSS;
01190   TR2  GOON,1;
01200        ACT,RNORM(3,1);
01210        GOON,1;
01220        ACT,,.96,RTL;
01230        ACT,,.04;
01240        ASSIGN,ATRIB(2)=1;
01250        ACT,,,RTL;
01260   RTL  GOON,1;
01270        ACT,RNORM(4,1),,,GRR;
01280   GRR  GOON,1;
01290        ACT,,ATRIB(2).EQ.1.0,BD4;
01300        ACT,,ATRIB(2).EQ.0.0;
01310        GOON,1;
01320        ACT,,.99,GRO;
01330        ACT,,.01;
01340        ASSIGN,XX(7)=XX(7)+1;
01350        ACT,,,LOSS;
01360   BD4  GOON,1;
01370        ACT,,.50,GRO;
01380        ACT,,.50;
01390        ASSIGN,XX(6)=XX(6)+1;
01400        ACT,,,LOSS;
01410   GRO  GOON,1;
01420        ACT/9,RNORM(14,4),,,CON;
01430   CON  GOON,1;
01440        ACT,,TNOW.GE.144.0,TIM;
01450        ACT,,,STP;
01460   TIM  ASSIGN,XX(8)=XX(8)+1;
01470        ACT,,,LOSS;
01480   STP  GOON,1;
01490        ACT,,ATRIB(2).EQ.1.0,BD5;
01500        ACT,,ATRIB(2).EQ.0.0;
01510        ASSIGN,XX(10)=XX(10)+1;
01520        TERM;
01530   BD5  ASSIGN,XX(9)=XX(9)+1;
01540        ACT,,,LOSS;
01550   LOSS ASSIGN,XX(11)=XX(11)+1;
01560        TERM;
01570        END;
01580 FIN;
```

IV   STORAGE ENVIRONMENT

INFLUENCE OF PRESTORAGE CHEMICAL TREATMENTS
ON OUT-OF-STORAGE MARKET QUALITY OF POTATOES

by

B.F. Cargill, Professor; R.L. Ledebuhr, Engineering
Specialist; K.C. Price, Engineering Specialist; and
T.D. Forbush, Research Assistant, Department of
Agricultural Engineering, Michigan State University,
East Lansing, Michigan

ABSTRACT

This paper is part of a continuing report on the
influence of prestorage mechanical handling and
chemical treatments on the market quality of potatoes
out of storage. Treatments using low volume solutions
of fungicides and bactericides are compared to check
treatments. New chemical application technology is
used and two controlled droplet application systems
are discussed.

ASAE Paper No. 85-4028

INTRODUCTION

Mechanical systems for harvesting and handling result in tuber damage and the degree of this damage influences the storability and market quality of the potatoes coming out of storage.

Various prestorage chemical treatments have been shown to influence losses and market quality out of storage. The present practice is to treat mechanically handled potatoes going into storage with a fungicide suspension containing 0.42 fl oz (12.4 ml) of a thiabendaxole formulation containing 42.28 percent active [2-(4-Thiazolyl) benzimidazole]. The recommendation has been to apply the thiabendazole at the rate of 0.42 fl oz (12.4 ml) in 1 gal (3.79 liters) of water per short ton (909 kg) of potatoes. Commercially in the USA this chemical is referred to as Mertect 340F (a product of the Merck Chemical Co., Rahway, New Jersey).

A one-gallon (3.79 liters) solution per ton (909 kg) of potatoes is considered excessive. It results in free surface water on the potatoes and presents a serious overload to the storage ventilation system. To more clearly comprehend the problem, consider a typical potato storage bin containing 16,500 cwt (6825 short tons) in which 15 barrels (over 2800 liters) of a water chemical solution are dumped. If this free surface water is allowed to cover the potato lenticles for 24 hours, oxygen starvation will occur and create a storage disorder.

Since 1983, prestorage chemical application research at Michigan State University has been shifting emphasis toward the development of a commercial, low-volume, controlled droplet application system. The purpose of the research was to develop a commercially acceptable application system, while maintaining or enhancing the market quality of potatoes being removed from storage.

OBJECTIVES

The objective of the research was to develop a commercially acceptable, low-volume, controlled droplet, prestorage application system. More specific objectives were: 1) enhance the out-of-storage market quality of the commercially harvested potatoes, 2) improve chemical deposition on the potatoes going into storage, and 3) reduce the water solution required to apply these chemicals.

PROCEDURE

Potato Samples

The 1983 and 1984 Atlantic and 1984 Monona potatoes were grown at the Michigan State University Potato Research Farm at Entrican, Michigan. These potatoes were harvested using the MSU one row plot harvester. The Monona potatoes used in the commercial phase of this project were grown and harvested by Sackett Ranch, Inc., Stanton, Michigan.

Equipment

The Lockwood bin piler (with prestorage chemical application equipment) at Sandyland Farm's Inc., Howard City, Michigan, was used to treat all of the MSU grown Atlantic and Monona potatoes in 1983 and 1984. The potato flow rate was controlled at 30 tons/hr (approximately 27.3 metric tons/hr).

The Lockwood bin piler (with prestorage chemical application equipment) at Sackett Ranch Inc., Stanton, Michigan, was used to treat the potatoes during the commercial phase of the project. The potato flow rate over this bin piler was approximately 80 tons/hr (72.7 metric tons/hr).

In 1983 all the chemical application was performed with the Microtec spray system provided by Micron Corp., Houston, Texas. This unit consisted of a chemical solution reservoir with mechanical agitation, a water flush system for cleaning, plastic plumbing, liquid filled gauges, diaphram pump, a Spraying Systems, Inc. orifice disk for chemical metering, and a Micromax nozzle fitted with a model airplane propeller. The entire system was powered by a 12v battery.

In 1984 two different chemical application systems were used. The first system was a Micronair AU7000 CDA (controlled droplet application) nozzle without propeller blades mounted in a cross-flow fan

(prototype II), see Figures 1-4. This system was
mounted at the boot where the cleaning bed empties
onto the piling boom. The second system used a heavy
duty shroud/mounting (prototype III), mounted with a
Micronair AU7000 with propellers. This system was
mounted at the junction between the stationary and
telescoping boom conveyors on Sandyland Farms
Lockwood bin piler. Both systems used stacked
peristaltic pumps for metering the chemicals. All
of the components used in the 1984 chemical
application systems were powered by a 120v source.

Chemical Solution

The chemical solution used in 1983 and 1984
consisted of a fungicide, bactericide, and a chemical
carrier.

In 1983 the chemical solution was applied at a 3
oz/ton (97.7 ml/metric ton) rate. This 3 oz solution
consisted of 0.42 oz (12.4 ml) of Mertect 340-F
(42.28%) active ingredient [2-(4-thiazolyl)
benzimidazole]; 0.64 oz (18.9 ml) chlorine (6% active
ingredients), with a 1.94 oz (57.4 ml) of water or
food grade soybean oil used as a carrier.

In 1984 the chemical solution was applied at
approximately 2.6 oz/ton (85.3 ml/metric ton). This
2.6 oz solution consisted of 0.42 oz of Mertect 340-F
(12.4 ml) and 2.1 oz (61.9 ml) of water or food grade
soybean oil with 5 percent Rohm Hass food grade
emulsifier. Chlorine dioxide was mixed into the water
at the rate of 200 ppm to control bacterial soft rot.

Chemical Treatment

All chemical treatments for 1983 and 1984 were
low volume treatments and contained 0.42 oz/ton (12.4
ml/short ton) of Mertect-340F. Tables 1 and 2 give a
detailed description of the chemical treatments for
the 1983 MSU Atlantic and commercially produced
Monona potatoes respectively. Tables 3, 4 and 5 give
a detailed description of the chemical treatments
used for the 1984 MSU Atlantic, Monona and the
commercialy produced Monona potatoes respectively.

Storage Environment

Immediately after treatment, bagging, tagging, etc. samples[1] of the 1983 and 1984 Atlantic potatoes were placed in controlled environment cubicle storage on the MSU campus and in the center of a commercial potato storage at Sandyland Farm's Inc., Howard City, Michigan. The potatoes in the cubicles were suberized for two weeks; one week at 60°F (15.6 ° C) and 95 percent r.h. and one week at 55 °F (12.8°C) and 95 percent r.h. After suberization these potatoes were lowered 5 F/week (2.7 °C) until the desired storage temperatures of 45°F (7.2 °C) and 50 °F (10 ° C) were reached.

Samples of the MSU grown Atlantic (1983 and 1984) and Monona (1984) potatoes were stored in a commercial bulk storage at Sandyland Farms, Inc., Howard City, Michigan. These potatoes had 24 hour ventilation (continuous circulation) and were lowered in storage temperature approximately 1 F every 2 days until the desired storage temperature of 45 F (7.2 C) was reached. The potatoes at Sandyland Farms were stored in a 15,320 cwt (690 metric tons) uniformly ventilated storage.

Samples of the 1983 and 1984 commercially produced and treated potatoes were stored in the MSU cubicles and in 1984 in the commercial bulk storage at Sackett Ranch, Inc., Stanton, Michigan. Samples in the MSU cubicle storage were suberized in the same manner as the Atlantic potatoes in the cubicle storage as described above. The samples in the commercial storage were suberized at 55-60 F with continuous recirculation ventilation for approximately 30 days. After suberization the potatoes stored at Sackett Ranch were gradually lowered to their storage temperature 45°F (7.2 ° C) over a 30-day period. The potatoes at Sackett Ranch, Inc. were stored in a 14,000 cwt (640 metric tons) uniformly ventilated storage.

----

[1] Sample bags weighted approximately 25 lbs (11.4 kg) and are bagged in flat mesh plastic bags.

Residue Analysis

Ten pounds (4.5 kg) of randomly selected tubers were removed from selected treatments for evaluation of TBZ residue. The potato assay for thiabendazole was performed from opposite quarters of each tuber by the Ag Chem Division of the Merck Chem. Co., Rahway, New Jersey.

Evaluation

Bruise Analysis: A bruise analysis (combined shatter/blackspot) of the 1984 MSU grown Atlantic and Monona potatoes was performed. Various lots of 80 lb (36 kg) samples of potatoes were taken: 1) after harvesting with the MSU plot harvester and 2) at the end of the bin piler just prior to placement in the storage bin. These samples were delivered to Ore-Ida Foods, Greenville, Michigan where they were held at room temperature for 48 hours before the bruise evaluation. The bruise-free percent for the 1984 MSU grown Atlantic and Monona potatoes is presented in Table 6.

Weight Loss: All bagged potato samples were weighed after treatment. The samples stored in the MSU cubicals were weighed after two weeks of suberization and at the market quality evaluation dates. Samples stored commercialy were weighed upon removal from storage. Weight loss is represented by a percentage and is determined by.

$$\text{Weight loss \%} = \frac{Wi-We}{Wi} \times 100$$

Wi = initial weight

We = evaluation weight

Market Quality: Market quality evaluations of the potatoes in the cubicals were made at various times during storage. Market quality evaluation of the commercially stored potatoes were made upon the removal of the samples from storage. These evaluations involved removal of the respective bag from storage, emptying the bag, and, cutting and examining each individual tuber.

Tubers were classified as follows:

A. Marketable

This includes potatoes that have 0-5 %, by weight of dry rot

B. Non-marketable

Dry rot   Soft rot

1.   5.1-10.0%   4.   0-5.0%
2.   10.1-25.0%   5.   5.1-10.0%
3.   25.1% and over   6. 10.1-25.0%
                                 7. 25.1% and over

C. Non-storage related problems and defects (scab, nematodes, insects, sunburn, etc.)

After the potatoes were classified, the various categories of non-marketable potatoes were counted and weighed.

Market quality is represented by a percent and is determined by tuber weight and numbers. Market quality evaluation by weight and number are compared for potential variations due to potato size variations within the sample bags. These two methods are as follows:

1. By number of tubers:

Marketable quality ($\%$) = $\frac{Mn}{Tn}$ x 100

Mn = number of marketable potatoes in each sample

Tn = total number of potatoes in each sample

2. By weight of tubers:

Marketable quality ($\%$) = $\frac{Mw}{Tw}$ x 100

Mw = weight of marketable potatoes in each sample

Tw = total weight of potatoes in each sample

RESULTS AND DISCUSSION

Equipment

The Microtec application system used in 1983 had several mechanical problems. The majority of these problems were results of the corrosive, low-volume chemical solutions used. These mechanical problems can be divided into three areas: 1) the pumping (metering system), 2) the application system, and 3) the power source.

The pumping (metering) system, which consisted of the chemical solution reservoir, diaphragm pump, plumbing system, liquid filled pressure gauges, and a Spraying Systems, Inc. orifice for chemical metering, had three basic problems: 1) excessive pressure differentials across the diaphragm pump which resulted in reduced diaphragm head life (less than 24 hours of operation in some instances) and difficult control of solution metering at desired flow rates; 2) the diaphragm was not well suited for pumping these materials. Even with adequate size plumbing the diaphragm head life was less than 48 hours of operation and 3) the orifice metering system was difficult to calibrate and control with the low volume solutions desired.

The application system consisted of a direct drive Micromax nozzle with a model airplane propeller mounted on the nozzle. At the low flow rates used, 3 oz./ ton (88.6 ml/909 kg) which translates to approximately 3 oz/min (88.6 ml/min) at commercial rates, there was excessive chemical build-up in the rotor-cup styrations. This chemical build-up caused a "slinging" of the chemical solution and neutralized the controlled-droplet producing ability of the nozzle. This build-up also caused excessive bearing wear on the nozzle drive motor and bearing failure. The nozzle spray pattern was difficult to control and fit to different size conveyors. The application area also had to be extensively shrouded in order to prevent drifting.

The 12v power system presented problems. A battery charger had to be continously recharging the

403

12v battery in order to supply enough power to the
Microtec system. The 12v system was very susceptible
to power fluctuations on the bin loading system.
This made chemical flow control difficult due to the
pressure changes in the system caused by power
fluctuations to the pump.

The Microtec unit used in 1983 was the first low-
volume application system used on a trial commercial
basis in this project. While there were some
promising results from this equipment, these results
could not overcome the inconsistencies and frequent
mechanical failures of the machine. For this reason
a different application system had to be developed
for 1984.

Two CDA[1] spray systems were used in 1984: a boom
mounted Micronair 7000 and a Micronair AU7000 fitted
in a cross-flow fan and mounted at the boot between
the boom and the cleaning table. Both systems used a
120v power source and stacked peristaltic pumps for
metering each individual chemical.

The Micronair AU7000 unit (Prototype III)
displayed good results. The Micronair nozzle handled
the low-volume, viscous, materials with no clogging.
Clean-up was fast and simple compared to the
Microtec. However, the prototype III was noisy,
experienced a problem with chemical drift, and is
subject to damage by operator error, due to its
location on the boom.

The Micronair AU7000 nozzle mounted in the cross
flow fan (Prototype II) had several advantages over
Prototype III and the Microtec. First, due to its
location, it is easily accessible for repairs and
cleaning. The circular pattern of the CDA nozzle
system is charged to a rectangular pattern, (see
Figure 4) which is more adaptable to the geometry of
a conveyor. The straight stream air flow increased
chemical impingement, nearly eliminated chemical
drifting, and gave more consistent chemical
deposition on the potatoes.

----

[1]Controlled Droplet Applicator

The stacked peristaltic pumps, driven by a DC motor with a 120 v infinite voltage regulator, gave excellent control of the chemical application rate. The stacked pumps allowed the chemicals to be pumped separately and directly from the commercial container. This eliminates the need for mixing and mechanical agitation of the chemical solution. Maintenance and clean-up to the pumping system was minimal. The 120v power source was not susceptible to the power fluctuations as the 12v source. All components of the power system are OEM parts and readily available.

Weight Loss

The weight loss for the 1983 Atlantic potatoes stored at 45°F (7.2°C) and 50°F (10°C) at the MSU cubicles and at Sandyland Farms is shown in Table 7.

A statistical analysis shows that there is a 0-1.8 percent difference (at the 25% level of significance) in weight loss for treatment 4 for the 45°F storage temperature at the 125 and 184 day storage duration. This suggests the possibility that the potatoes treated with the 3 oz/ton solution with soybean carrier may have a slightly lower weight loss at longer storage durations.

The statistical analysis also showed a 1.1 percent difference (at the 25% level of significance) between treatment 1 and treatments 2-4 at the 83 day storage duration.

Treatment 1 is a check from the MSU plot harvester and it would be expected to have a slightly lower weight loss than treatments 2-4 which due to more mechanical handling had a lower bruise-free percentage than treatment 1.

Weight loss for the 1984 Atlantic potatoes stored at 45°F (7.2°C) and 50°F (10.0°C) at the MSU cubicles is presented in Table 8. The statistical analysis showed the following:

1. A difference of 2.3 percent (at the 10% level of significance) between treatments 2 and 4 stored at 45°F (7.2°C) for 180 days.

405

2.   A difference of 1.1 percent (at the 10% level
of significance) between treatments 2 and 3 stored at
50°F (10.0°C) for 110 days.

3.   A difference of 0.8 percent (at the 1% level
of significance) between treatments 2 and 3 stored at
45°F (7.2°C) for 110 days.

The lower weight loss for treatment 4 suggests
that potatoes treated with the oil carrier will have
a lower weight loss at the longer storage duration.

Market Quality

The market quality of the treated 1983 Atlantic
potatoes stored at 45°F (7.2°C) and 50°F (10°C) at
the MSU cubicles and at Sandyland Farms is presented
in Table 9.

A statistical analysis of treatment 1   vs
treatment 2 stored at 45°F and 50°F for 83 days shows
a difference of 10.0 and 5.5 percent respectively (at
the 20% and 25% level of significance respectively)
in market quality for these treatments.

Treatment 1 is a check from the MSU plot
harvester and treatment 2 is a check taken after
equivalent potatoes had run over the bin piler at
Sandyland Farms. Treatment 2 has a lower bruise-free
percentage so it is expected that it would have a
decrease in market quality due to the increased
bruising from mechanical handling.

The analysis showed a difference of 7.4 and 4.5
percent   (25%   and   15% level   of   significance
respectively) between treatments 2 and 3 at the 45 F
and 50 F storage temperatures (respectively) for the
83 day storage duration.   The analysis also showed a
difference of 6.3 and 5.4 percent (at the 25% and 10%
level   of   significance   respectively)   between
treatments 2 and 4 at the 45°F and 50°F temperatures
(respectively) for the 83 day storage duration.
There is also a difference of 4.6 percent (10% level
of significance) between treatment 2 and 4 stored at
45 F for 184 days.

Bacterial soft rot was not a significant factor
in either the check or treated samples.

Table 10 presents the data for the low volume commercial prestorage chemical treatment at Sackett Ranch, Inc., Stanton, Michigan.

A statistical analysis shows that there is a very significant difference (11.4%), (at the one percent level of significance) between the treated and non-treated potatoes. The market quality percentage of the check samples is influenced less than 2 percent by bacterial soft rot. Treated samples had no bacterial soft rot.

Table 11 presents the data for the 1984 low volume commercial prestorage treatment at Sackett Ranch, Inc., Stanton, Michigan. No significant difference was found for the potatoes stored at Sackett Ranch due to the large variability in the samples. However, the averages suggest an improvement in market quality with chemical treating.

The market quality of the treated 1984 Atlantic potatoes stored at 45° F (7.2 °C) and 50 °F (10° C) at the MSU cubicles is presented in Table 12.

A statistical analysis of the 1984 Atlantic potatoes stored at 45° F and 50° F at the MSU cubicles showed the following results:

For Atlantic potatoes stored at 45° F for 112 days there was a difference of 6.3 percent (2.5% level of significance) between treatments 2 (check) and 3 (treated, water carrier). There was also a difference of 6.8 percent (2.5% level of significance) between treatments 2 (check) and 4 (treated, soybean oil carrier).

For Atlantic potatoes stored at 45° F for 187 days there was a difference of 10.9 percent (0.5% level of significance) between treatments 2 and 4. There was also a difference of 7 percent (20% level of significance) between treatments 3 and 4.

For Atlantic potatoes stored at 50° F for 187 days there was a significant difference of 4.7 percent (15% level of significance between treatments 2 and 3. There was also a difference of 6.6 percent (10% level of significance) between treatments 2 and 4.

407

The market quality data from the 1984 Atlantics suggest that a very significant increase in market quality will be obtained by treating the potatoes. The data also suggests an additional increase in market quality when an emulsified soybean oil is used as a chemical carrier.

The market quality and residue analysis of the 1984 Monona potatoes stored at 45 ° F at Sandyland Farm is presented in Table 13.

A statistical analysis on the 1984 Monona potatoes showed a difference of 2.9 percent (10% level of significance) between treatments 2 (check, bruised) and 3 (treated, prototype II, water carrier). The analysis also showed a difference of 3 percent (20% level of significance) between treatemtns 1 and 2.

CONCLUSIONS

The following conclusions can be drawn from this study:

1. The Micronair "basket" type nozzle is better suited to handle the solution used in this study.

2. For metering the chemical, peristaltic or "squeeze" pumps are superior to the diaphragm pump-orifice combination.

3. Weight loss is not influenced by the fungicides and bactericides used in this study. However, the results suggested that using soybean oil as a chemical carrier may reduce weight loss.

4. Market quality of the potatoes can be improved from 0-11.4 percent using the low volume solutions. Since the cost of the chemicals used is less than $0.02/cwt ($0.20/metric ton), only a small increase in market quality is necessary to cover application costs and provide a return for the producer.

ACKNOWLEDGEMENTS

The researchers involved in this project wish to acknowledge and thank the following organizations for their support:

1. Michigan Potato Industry Commission, E. Lansing, Michigan.

2. Merck & Co. Chemical Corp., Ag Chemical Division, Rahway, New Jersey.

3. Soybean Promotion Committee of Michigan, E. Lansing, Michigan.

4. Sackett Ranch, Edmore, Michigan.

5. Sandyland Farms, Howard City, Michigan.

6. Ore-Ida Foods, Greenville, Michigan.

Table 1. Chemical and Mechanical Treatments of the 1983 MSU Grown Atlantic Potatoes.

Treatment	Mechanical Handling	Chemical applied[1] per short ton (909 kg)
1	Plot harvester	None (check)
2	Plot harvester and bin piler	None (check)
3	Plot harvester and bin piler	0.42 oz (12.4 ml) Mertect 340-F 0.64 oz (18.9 ml) chlorine[2] 1.94 oz (57.4 ml) water
4	Plot harvester and bin piler	0.42 oz (12.4 ml) Mertect 340-F 0.64 oz (18.9 ml) chlorine[2] 1.94 oz (57.4 ml) soybean oil

[1]All chemical treatments were applied with the Microtec spray system, supplied by Micron, Inc.

[2]Household chlorine bleach with 5.25% active ingredients.

Table 2. Prestorage Chemical Treatment used on 1983 Commercially[1] Produced and Handled Monona Potatoes.

Treatment	Chemical Applied[2] per short ton (909 kg)
1	None (check)
2	0.42 oz (12.4 ml) Mertect 340-F 0.64 oz (18.9 ml) chlorine[3] 1.94 oz (57.4 ml) water

[1]Potatoes were grown and stored by Sackett Ranch, Inc., Stanton, Michigan
[2]The chemicals were applied with the Microtec spray system, supplied by Micron, Inc.
[3]Household chlorine bleach with 5.25% active ingredients.

Table 3. Prestorage Chemical and Mechanical Treatments of 1984 MSU Grown
Atlantic Potatoes.

Treatment	Mechanical Handling	Chemical applied[1] per 2000 lbs. (909 kg)
1	Plot harvester	None (check)
2	Plot harvester and bin piler	None (check)
3	Plot harvester and bin piler	0.42 oz (12.4 ml) Mertect 340-F 2.1 oz (65.1 ml) water[2]
4	Plot harvester and bin piler	0.42 oz (12.4 ml) Mertect 340-F 2.1 oz (65.1 ml) emulsified soybean oil[3]

[1]The chemicals were all applied with the MSU Prototype II, see Equipment under PROCEDURE
[2]Also contains 200 ppm of chlorine dioxide
[3]Contains 5 % Rohm Haas food grade emulsifier and 200 ppm of chlorine dioxide

Table 4. Chemical and Mechanical treatments of the 1984 MSU grown Monona
Potatoes.

Treatment	Mechanical Handling	Chemical Application System[1]	Chemical Applied per 2000 lbs. (909kg)
1	Plot harvester	None	None
2	Plot harvester and bin piler	None	None
3	Plot harvester and bin piler	Prototype II	0.42 oz (12.4 ml) Mertect 340-F 2.1 oz (65.1 ml) water[2]
4	Plot harvester and bin piler	Prototype III	Same as Treatment 3.
5	Plot harvester and bin piler	Prototype II	0.42 oz (12.4 ml) Mertect 340-F 2.1 oz (65.1 ml) emulsified soybean oil[3]
6	Plot harvester and bin piler	Prototype III	Same as Treatment 5.

[1]See Equipment under PROCEDURE
[2]Also contains 200 ppm of chlorine dioxide
[3]Contains 5% Rhom Haas food grade emulsifier and 50 ppm of chlorine dioxide

Table 5. Prestorage Chemical Treatment used on 1984 Commercially Produced[3]
and Handled Monona Potatoes.
==
Treatment   Chemical Applied[1] per 2000 lbs. (909 kg)

| 1 | None (check) |
| 2 | 0.42 oz (12.4 ml) Mertect 340-F
2.1 oz (62.0 ml) water[2] |

==

[1]Chemical applied with Prototype II application system. See Equipment
under PROCEDURES
[2]Also contains 200 ppm of chlorine dioxide.
[3]Sackett Ranch Inc., Stanton, Michigan

Table 6. Bruise-Free Percentage of the 1984 MSU Grown Atlantic and Monona
Potatoes at Various Stages in the Mechanical Handling System[1]

==

Variety	Samples location	Bruise-free percentage
Atlantic	Plot harvester	86.5%
Atlantic	After bin piler	82.6%
Monona	Plot harvester	92.4%
Monona	After bin piler	87.7%

==

[1]Bruise evaluations were performed by Ore-Ida Inc., Greenville, Mich.

Table 7. Weight Loss (%) for the 1984 Treated Atlantic Potatoes Stored at 45 and 50F and 95% r.h. at the MSU cubicles and Sandyland Farms.

	Storage duration[1] and storage temperature				
Treatment[2]	83 days		125 days	184 days	
	45F 7.2C	50F 10C	45F 7.2C	45F 7.2C	50F 10C
1	3.9	4.8	-	-	-
2	5.0	5.6	5.7	9.5	12.7
3	4.9	6.3	5.9	10.6	12.3
4	4.5	5.4	5.7	8.8	11.0

[1]Potatoes were stored in the MSU cubicles for the 83 and 184 day storage duration. Potatoes at the 125 day storage duration were stored at Sandyland Farms.
[2]See Table 1 for a detailed description of the treatments

Table 8. Weight Loss (%) for the 1984 Atlantic Potatoes Stored at 45F (7.72C) and 50F (10.0C) and 95% r.h. at the MSU Cubicles.

Treatment[1]	Storage Duration and Temperature			
	110 days		180 days	
	45F (7.2C)	50F (10.0C)	45F (7.2C)	50F (10.0)
2	5.38	4.16	9.10	9.87
3	4.56	3.27	11.52	7.82
4	4.94	3.82	6.78	9.32

[1]See Table 1 for a detailed description of the treatment

Table 9. Market Quality (% Marketable Weight) and Deposition for the 1983 Treated Atlantic Potatoes Stored at 45F and 50F and 95% r.h. at the MSU Cubicles and Sandyland Farms (Commercial Storage).

Treatment[2]	Storage duration[1]					Chemical deposition[3] (ppm)
	83 days		125 days	184 days		
	45F 7.2C	50F 10C	45F 7.2C	45F 7.2C	50F 10C	
1	96.8	95.1	-	-	-	-
2	86.8	89.6	92.6	89.6	94.3	-
3	94.2	94.1	91.0	86.8	91.9	.42 - .45
4	93.1	95.0	89.2	94.2	88.7	2.46 - 2.50

[1]Potatoes for the 83 and 184 day storage duration were stored at the MSU cubicles. Potatoes for the 125 day storage duration were stored at Sandyland Farms
[2]See Table 1 for a detailed description of treatments
[3]Mertect

Table 10. Market Quality (% by Weight) for Non-treated vs Low Volume Prestorage chemically treated Monona potatoes (1983) stored at Sackett Ranch.

Treatment[1]	Market quality (% by weight)
Check	81.3
Treated	92.7

[1]See table 2 for a detailed description of treatments

Table 11. Market Quality (% by Weight) and Deposition for Non-treated vs Low Volume Prestorage Chemically Treated Monona Potatoes (1984) stored at Sackett Ranch.

Treatment[1]	Market quality (% by weight)	Deposition ppm[2]
1	81.8	-
2	88.5	2.14-2.78

[1]See table 5 for a detailed description of the treatments
[2]Mertect

Table 12. Market Quality (% Marketable by Weight) for the 1984 Atlantic
Potatoes Stored at 45F (7.2C) and 50F (10C) and 95% r.h. at the
MSU Cubicals.

Treatment[1]	Storage duration			
	112 days		187 days	
	45F 7.2C	50F 10C	45F 7.2C	50F 10C
2	86.7	91.5	79.7	73.6
3	93.0	92.4	83.7	78.3
4	93.5	93.2	90.6	80.2

[1]See Table 4   for a detailed description of the treatments.

Table 13. Market Quality (% Marketable by Weight) and Chemical Residue for
1984 Monona Potatoes stored at 45F for 175 days at Sandyland Farms
commercial Bulk Storages.

Treatment1	Market Quality	Chemical residue (ppm)[2]
1	97.2	-
2	94.2	-
3	97.1	2.74 - 3.27
4	96.2	2.78 - 4.17
5	96.7	1.38 - 5.51
6	96.8	1.52 - 3.15

[1]See table 4 for a detailed description of the treatment

[2]Mertect

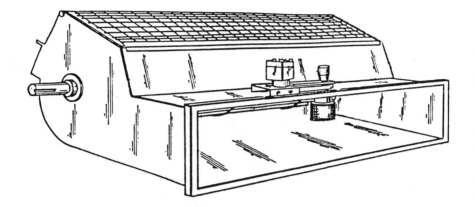

Figure 1. Overall schematic of prototype II used in the 1984
chemical application research.

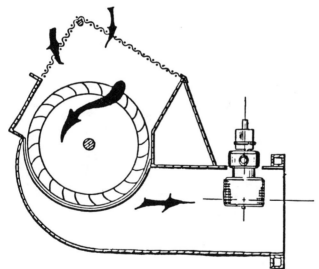

Figure 2. Side view of the prototype II used in the 1984
chemical application research.

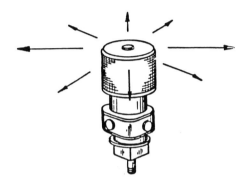

Figure 3. Schematic of the Micronair AU 7000 applicator used
in prototype II and III in the 1984 chemical application research.

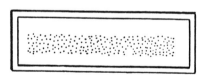

Figure 4. Schematic (plan view) of the spray pattern of
the prototype II.

NATURAL DIFFUSED LIGHT, A PRACTIAL ALTERNATIVE TO CONTROLLED ATMOSPHERE STORAGE OF POTATO SEED TUBERS

by

Robert H. Booth, Coordinator Postharvest
Technology, International Potato Center, Apartado
5969, Lima, Peru

ABSTRACT

This paper reports the more important technical features of the diffused light technology for storing seed potato tubers. It also discusses how interdisciplinary research, in the farmer-back-to-farmer approach was involved in its generation and transfer to many small potato farmers in developing countries.

INTRODUCTION

Potato production in many developing countries is characterized by large numbers of small growers. Much of the research at the International Potato

ASAE Paper No. 85-4029

Center (CIP) with headquarters in Lima, Peru, is geared to help national potato programs assist these small farmers. CIP's source research is organized in ten multidisciplinary "thrusts" with objectives ranging from collection and maintenance of a world germplasm bank, control of pests and diseases, agronomy for diverse climates, "seed" production and distribution, to postharvest technology and food systems.

Scientists in the postharvest thrust maintain that extensive knowledge on basic postharvest technologies and principles exist for potatoes. Thus, emphasis in developing countries should be on researching the low cost application of these principles to specific problems and together with national scientists transferring potential solutions to farmers or other clients (Booth and Burton, 1983). In attempting to use known principles and technologies to solve postharvest problems, lessons should be learned from many past failures. These have commonly occurred where attempts concentrated on the direct transfer of packaged technologies which were successfully developed for one location to another supposedly similar problem in another location. It must be understood that while basic technologies and principles are universal, their application is location specific and requires a good understanding of supply-demand patterns and the socio-economic as well as technical needs of each location. This suggests that the best use of limited resources in the application and transfer of known technologies could be achieved through the use of interdisciplinary teams (Booth and Burton, 1983).

Farmer-Back-To-Farmer

Based on the increasingly accepted view that agriculture is not merely a technical endeavour but a socio-economic one as well, social scientists are becoming more accepted into agricultural development teams. However, a review of the agricultural development literture shows that fully integrated interdisciplinary teams involving both biological and social scientists have rarely been constituted. Based on their truly interdisciplinary experiences, the CIP postharvest team developed the farmer-back-to-farmer model for generating and transferring acceptable agricultural technology (Rhoades and Booth, 1982).

The model stresses that applied research must both begin and end with the final client-farmer, merchant or consumer. It provides an alternative approach to strictly disciplinary research and extension. Starting with the philosophy that the clients circumstance is the spring board of research, the model then logically consists of a series of task-oriented goals aimed towards acceptable technological solutions to specific problems. These goals are linked in a circular form, by a number of activities (Table 1) (Rhoades and Booth, 1982).

This paper not only tries to illustrate the more important technical features of the diffused light technology for storing seed potato tubers, but also illustrates how interdisciplinary research in the farmer-back-to-farmer approach was involved in its generation and transfer to many small potato farmers in developing countries.

Diagnosis of the Problem

Farmers frequently perceive and define their problems differently from research scientists and change agents. While postharvest scientists may be content to research the reduction of specific storage losses, there is little hope of their findings being applied unless farmers also perceive the particular loss as being important. It is important that from the very beginning farmer and scientists arrive at a common agreement concerning the problem to be solved.

In this particular case the commonly defined problem was the excessive sprouting and associated losses during the traditional storage of seed tubers. In many countries small farmers traditionally store their seed tubers in heaps in poorly ventilated dark rooms. This frequently results in excessive sprouting requiring expensive desprouting and resulting in loss of seed quality.

Adequate storage practices are a requirement of any seed production system. It is possible that present traditional storage practices may have been

adequate for old traditional varieties, but as
varieties and seed production systems have changed
there is a clear need, understood by both farmers and
scientists, to improve upon these practices.

Interdisciplinary Team Research

The environmental conditions in which seed
tubers have to be stored in developing countries are,
of course, extremely varied. In general, sufficient
natural cool air does not exist to permit the
extensive use of naturally ventilated or forced draft
ventilated dark stores to maintain storage
temperatures low enough to prevent excessive
sprouting when seed tubers need to be stored for
periods longer than their natural dormancy.
Similarly, the use of electrically powered
refrigeration is not compatible with the needs of
small farmers in developing countries. The need is
for simple, low-cost, small scale storage units.

Although the effect of lights on reducing sprout
elongation has been known for a long time (Dinkel,
1963) it has not until recently been used as a seed
storage technique. However, natural diffused light
has been widely utilized as a preplanting green
sprouting technique (van der Zeeg, 1982). Only in
isolated examples has this diffused light technique
been used. Recently this technique has been well
researched, described, and widely advocated as an
appropriate seed storage technique suitable for the
needs of many potato farmers in developing countries.

To fully evaluate a seed storage technique, its
effects on both the storage behaviour and subsequent
field performance of stored tubers must be evaluated.
From 1978 to 1980, storage and field trials comparing
the effects of storing seed tubers in diffused light
and dark storages were undertaken at the CIP research
station at Huancayo. This experiment station is
located at 3,200 m (10,499 ft.) above sea level in
one of the major potato growing areas of Peru.

The results of these experiment station trials
(Table 2) demonstrate the effectiveness of natural
diffused light in restricting sprout elongation,
increasing sprout number per tuber, reducing total
storage losses, promoting rapid uniform emergence and

increasing total yields. In these experiment station trials, storage in natural diffused light resulted in an average yield increase of 17 percent.

In an additional series of trials, seed tubers stored in a cold store at 4 °C (39.2°F) were compared with seed tubers stored in natural diffused light stores in two different environments: 3200 m.a.s.l.* (10,499 ft.) with an average storage temperature of 12 ° C (53.6°F) and 800 m.a.s.l. , (2,625 ft.) with an average storage temperature of 24°C (75.2 °F). Only in 1 out of 10 compariosons at 3,200 m.a.s.l. result in 3 out 18 comparisons at 800 m.a.s.l. did cold storage result in significantly higher yields than storage in diffused light.

The first diffused light experimental storage constructed at CIP, Huancayo, had a capacity of about 5 tons (110 cwt) of seed tubers stored in seed trays and is now regarded as an "over engineered" structure. Throughout the research processes, the social science member of the postharvest team kept constant pressure on the technologists to make the physical structure compatible with the needs of small Andean potato farmers. Thus, following the initial successes at Huancayo, the structures which have since been built on research stations for research, training and demonstration purposes have become simpler and less costly. Also, storages were developed specifically for research station use where direct access to large number of cultivars is required. (Figure 1)

Interdisciplinary Team Testing and Adaptation

Where research is designed to find practical solutions to farmer's or other client's problems, the potential solution should clearly be tested under their conditions and evaluated against prevailing practices. This is necessary before the adoption of a given technology can be advocated. (Figure 2 and 3).

Following the successful application of natural diffused light to the storage of seed tubers on the

----
*
M.A.S.L. - Meters above sea level.

422

research station, on-farm trials were commenced with farmer cooperators (Figure 4). Prior inspection of farm buildings had revealed that the inner courtyard of many Andean farm houses has a veranda with a roof that allows for indirect light. Experiments were thus set-up under these verandas and using conventional seed trays taken from the research station storages. In other words, no new storages were built but advantage was taken of existing architecture. These on-farm trials yielded positive technical results similar to those obtained on the research station (Table 3).

However, while farmers expressed interest in the "new" technology, they also expressed concern over unavailability and cost of seed trays. As a result of this initial experience with farmers the second and third series of on-farm trials were conducted using simple collapsible shelves rather than unfamiliar seed trays. (Figure 5). The shelves were constructed of rough-hewn lumber common in the region. Again, results in terms of improved seed tuber quality and increased yields similar to those experienced on the research station were obtained. Due to lower costs, familiarity with materials and rustic design, farmers were now able to relate more closely to the diffused light storage concept. The technology now appeared ready for transfer and thus entered the final phase of the farmer-back-to-farmer cycle.

Farmer Evaluation

The validity of these research findings and the farmer-back-to-farmer approach rested on whether farmers were willing to test and use the technology at their own expense and time.

The actual patterns of farmer adoption and adaptation observed have been strikingly similar in most countries where the diffused light storage technology has been introduced and studied. Following the necessary training of national extensionists and the construction of simple demonstration storages, adoption begins by either a few individuals or the community as a unit taking the initial risks of experimenting with the "new" technology on their own (Figure 6). Farmers rarely accepted blindly technicians judgments and were not in a hurry to copy demonstration storages no matter how simple and low-cost these were. Instead, farmers commenced their own experimentation, initially on a small scale involving only small proportion of their seed tubers. If the farmers own experimentation proved positive, they commonly continued to make increased use of the technology and simultaneously other community members began the adoption process in their own cautious way.

Instead of copying prototype demonstration storages, most accepted the basic principle of using diffused light and adapted it to meet their particular circumstances – technical, economic and social (Figure 7). This has meant that the majority of adopters have not built new independent storages but instead have modified existing farm buildings. Even where new structures were built, farmers altered the design to meet their own needs and preferences. The variarion in these adaptations ranged from simply spreading potatoes in thin layers on the floor in front of windows or in open-sided stables, to the construction by cooperatives of new 100 ton capacity purpose built natural diffused light stores. Thus, while all diffused light storage are based on the same principles and have a similarity, each nationality and individual farmer have developed their own particular designs depending on local arcitecture, construction materials, and other particular local needs and considerations (Figure 8).

This great variability in farmer initiatives in adapting the basic technology to suit his particular needs and circumstances alerted the CIP scientists to the dangers of producing stereotyped engineering deisngs and plans for diffused light potato storages. Instead, CIP has produced several documents explaining and illustrating the principles of using natural diffused light (CIP undated; Booth and Shaw, 1981) and numerous collaborating national programs have produced their own extension materials including posters, slide sets and simple handouts. This approach has resulted in a continuous training program to ensure that extensionists and farmers alike understand enough about the principles they are applying. While this approach has resulted in numerous poor adapations, usually involving inadequate light penetration and overloading, it is considered more desirable and likely to have a longer lasting impact than the production of detailed plans which could be copied without understanding the underlying principles.

The adoption of the diffused light principle by small farmers is not only beginning to have the anticipated impact on reducing storage losses and improving seed tuber quality resulting in yield increases, but it is also affecting other aspects of potato production in some countries (Figure 9). In Sri Lanka, for example, where from 1980 to 1983 farmers built more than 500 diffused light storages and an estimated additional 1,000 farmers modified their existing storage systems, numerous additional effects on the farming system have been noted (Rhoades et al., 1984). The introduction of the diffused light storage technology has permitted Sri Lankan potato farmers to plant their potatoes when climatic and/or market conditions are optimal and not simply when imported seed tubers were available. This more optimal planting has resulted in as high as 133 percent yield increases and has altered the flow of seed tubers which in certain areas has allowed an extra crop of potatoes or an alternative crop to be grown in the rotation system. This capability for low-cost storage of locally produced seed tubers has also contributed to a reduction in the importation of seed tubers and has boosted the moral and prestige of those local researchers and extensionists involved.

The continued studies of farmer adoption, adaptation and use of this technology has not only revealed some of these wider implications of this simple storage technology but are necessary to continue to define new problems related to its use. For example, research is presently underway on trying to define the optimum light requirements, the effects of exposure to light on physiological aging of seed tubers and on the control of important pests and diseases which are being encountered in these storages. This continuing research process helps illustrate why technologies should not simply be designed, introduced and abandoned by applied scientists. A change in one part of a food production system frequently necessitates changes to other parts of the system. Thus, information must be collected on the technologies acceptance or rejection by clients, the final judges as to the appropriateness of a proposed solution.

We believe that this farmer-back-to-farmer approach is a useful way to harness the limited applied agricultural research resources to solving problems of food production systems. In this case we have illustrated how it was applied to the generation and transfer of the natural diffused light technology for storing seed potato tubers and which is proving to be a practical low-cost alternative to controlled low-temperature storage for many small potato farmers in developing countries (Figures 10 and 11).

REFERENCES

Booth, R.H. and R.L. Shaw. 1981. Principles of potato storage. The International Potato Center, P.O. Box 5969, Lima, Peru. 105 pp.

Booth, R.H. an W.G. Burton. 1983. Future needs in potato post-harvest technology in developing countries. Agriculture, Ecosystems and Environment 9:269-280.

Dinkel, D.H. 1963. Light-induced inhibition of potato tuber sprouting. Science, 141:1407-1408.

International Potato Center (undated) Low cost stores for seed potatoes. Pamphlet, CIP, Lima, Peru.

Rhoades, R.E. and R.H. Booth. 1982. Farmer-back-to farmer: a model for generating acceptable agricultural technology. Agricultural Adminis-tration, 11: 127-137.

Rhoades, R.E., W.V.D. Albert and R.H. Booth. 1984. Improving a farming system through post-harvest technology: Diffused light potato stores in Sri Lanka. Farming Systems Support Project Newsletter, 2:4-8.

van der Zaag, D.E. 1982. Seed potatoes, sources of supply and treatment. Netherlands Potato Consultative Institute, P.O. Box 17337, 2502 CH The Hague, The Netherlands. 39 pp.

Table 1. *

Farmer-back-to-farmer: Activities and Goals

Activities	Goals
1. Diagnosis	Common definition of problem
2. Interdisciplinary team research	Identify and develop a potential solution
3. Interdisciplinary team testing and adaptation	Better fit the proposed solution to clients needs
4. Evaluation by client	Understanding of clients acceptance or rejection

* from Rhoades and Booth, 1982.

Table 2. Effect of natural diffused light on storage behaviour and field performance of seed tubers stored at CIP, Huancayc , Peru.[1]

	Diffused light storage	Dark Storage
Sprout length cm (in.)	1.8 (0.71)	21.7 (8.54)
Sprout number/tuber	3.4	1.4
Total storage losses (%)	9.9	20.3
Days to full emergence	30.6	38.1
Total yield , t/ha (cwt/ac)	28.8 (256.4)	24.6 (219.0

[1]Mean results of three years trials with 8 cultivars stored for 180 days.

Table 3. Comparison of the effects of on farm storing of farmers seed tubers in diffused light and traditional dark storage.[1]

	Tubers stored in diffused light		Tubers stored in traditional dark storage	
Sprout length cm (in.)	1.0	(0.39)	13.1	(5.16)
Sprout number/tuber	3.4		1.6	
Total storage losses (%)	10.6		22.2	
Total yield., t/ha (cwt/ac)	18.2	(162.0)	15.2	(135.3)

[1]Mean results of three years trials with five farmers using a total of seven cultivars.

Figure 1. A 12 ton (254 cwt) diffused light potato storage used for CIP Research materials at the CIP Huancayo Research Station, Huancayo, Peru.

Figure 2. A 12 ton (264 cwt) diffused light potato storage under construction for Research materials at Huancayo, Peru.

Figure 3. An experimental demonstration type diffused light potato sotrage on the Coast of Peru.

431

Figure 4. A large 100 ton (22,000 cwt) Farmer Cooperative diffused light seed potato storage on the Coast of Peru.

Figure 5. An experimental diffused light seed potato storage showing small naturally ventilated bins in MSAC Philippines.

433

Figure 6.   An experimental diffused light seed potato storage, MSAC, Philippines.

Figure 7.   An on-farm diffused light storage for seed potatoes in Columbia.

435

Figure 8. A large 100 ton (22,000 cwt) farmer-owned diffused light storage for seed potatoes in the Philippines.

Figure 9. A small experimental diffused light potato storage, Fang, Thailand.

Figure 10. An experimental diffused light potato storage
designed by CIP for the hot conditions of
San Ramon, Peru.

438

Figure 11.   A diffused light storage   used for the hot areas
of San Ramon, Peru.

439

ASSESSMENT OF BACTERIAL SOFT ROT
POTENTIAL IN POTATOES

by

F.H. Buelow, Professor, Agricultural Engineering
Department;   Eileen Maher, Specialist and Arthur
Kelman, Professor, Plant Pathology Department;
University of Wisconsin-Madison, Madison,
Wisconsin 53706

ABSTRACT

Soft   rot potential in potatoes is determined by
incubating the tubers in a mist chamber.   A bruising
device   that delivers consistent impacts is used   for
some   tests.   Test   results show the   importance   of
maturity,   bruise damage, wound healing, temperature,
and dry tuber surfaces in the control of soft rot.

INTRODUCTION

One of the major causes of economic loss to   the
potato   industry   is the bruising that occurs   during
harvesting,   storing and grading of   potatoes.   Many

ASAE Paper No. 85-4030

research and extension publications document the
various ways in which tubers can be damaged and
possible approaches to minimize this damage (Smittle
et al., 1974). Notwithstanding this information, the
problem continues to plague growers. Current
estimation of the cost to the entire industry of
bruise-related losses range from 100 to 150 million
dollars annually (Stiles, 1983).

Bruising has a critical role in predisposing
potatoes to infection by soft rot bacteria and fungi.
Both visible and hidden bruises (blackspot) may
provide pathways for infection of the tubers not only
in storage, but also during the highly vulnerable
period after planting. Bacterial soft rot is caused
mainly by two closely related bacteria: the blackleg
and the common soft rot bacterium, Erwinia carotovora
pv atroseptic (Eca), and the common soft rot
bacterium, Erwinia cartovora pv cartovora (Ecc)."
These bacteria may be present mainly in the lenticels
or to a lesser extent at the stolon end of the tuber.
Many bacteria may be present in breaks or wounds in
the periderm that have occurred during harvesting and
handling procedures (Perombelon and Kelman, 1980).

Although a variety of internal factors determine
whether or not bacteria will be able to invade and
develop extensively in a potato tuber, perhaps the
single most important factor is the presence of a
direct opening into the tissue of the tuber. The
soft rotting bacteria do not have the mechanisms to
penetrate directly through the protective barrier
provided by the thick-walled cells of the peel of a
mature tuber; rather they invade through lenticels,
cuts and bruises.

In addition to the blackleg and soft rot
bacteria, other groups of bacteria may be present
that can contribute to the decay process. Among
these are certain spore forming bacteria that only
thrive when oxygen levels are very low. These
anaerobic bacteria belong to a group of widely
prevalent soil-inhabiting organisms called clostridia
(Campos et al., 1982). Under low oxygen conditions
that develop when tubers are covered with a film of
water, these clostridia are as destructive as the
soft rotting Erwinia strains. Certain strains of
Clostridium can convert a healthy tuber into a soft,

mushy, foul-smelling mass in a relatively short period of time, particularly when the temperatures rise above 20 ° C (68 °F).

The severity of bacterial soft rot may be reduced in a variety of ways. These are:

a. Eliminating the bacteria from the seed and environment of the tuber during growth, harvest and storage.

b. Reducing the bruising to the extent that direct openings into the tissues of the tuber do not occur.

c. Increasing the toughness of the peel sufficiently to resist bruising damage during harvesting and handling.

Given the widespread prevalence of the soft rot Erwinia in soil, on roots of some weeds, and in rivers and lakes, it is difficult to avoid contamination of tubers. Therefore, a major approach to reduce bacterial soft rot may be the reduction of bruise damage.

In order to conduct a research program aimed at reduction of bruise damage of potatoes, it is essential to have:

a. a means of assessing the potential for bacterial soft rot in a sample of potatoes, with results available in less than a week.

b. a means of inflicting a constant impact force to tubers, so that susceptibility to bruising can be evaluated.

This paper describes the equipment and techniques that were developed to assess the soft rot potential and provide uniform impacts on tubers. Results of various tests are presented that illustrate the use of the equipment and techniques.

EQUIPMENT AND TECHNIQUES

The Mist Chamber

The potential for soft rot development in potato tubers can be evaluated by a mist chamber procedure that maintains water films on the tubers for periods of four days at 20°C (68°F) (Lund and Kelman, 1977). Tubers covered with water become anaerobic after 2-1/2 hours at 21°C (69.8°F) (Burton and Wigginton, 1970). Under anaerobic conditions, susceptibility of tubers to bacterial soft rot caused by strains of pectolytic Erwinia is greatly enhanced (Perombelon and Lowe, 1975; DeBoer and Kelman, 1978; Kelman and Maher, 1979). At the temperature of 20°C (68°F) both Eca and Ecc can develop, and clostridia are usually not favored.

In general, the mist chamber must maintain continuously a film of water on the tubers at a temperature of 20°C (68°F). The tubers should not touch each other and should be supported by a wire or plastic rack so that water can drain away readily. Racks with one square meter area are adequate to handle 120 tubers at a time. At the time tubers are placed into the mist chamber, they should be thoroughly sprayed with water to be certain that a film of water covers the entire surface. It is also essential that the tubers not be permitted to become dry during the incubation period.

A one-square meter (10.7 ft.^{2}) chamber should have a generator that releases between 50 and 200 ml/min. (1.67 to 6.67 oz/min) of water. The droplet size must be such that all surfaces of all tubers are kept wet. A very satisfactory generator is a spray mist cooler for metal working that delivers a mixture of air and water with a very fine droplet size. Such a unit may be obtained from W.W. Grainger, Inc. (Item No. 4X663). This unit may be mounted outside the chamber with the nozzle inserted into the chamber. Another type of mist generator is a "sonic" nozzle manufactured by Sonic Development Corporation, 305 Island Road, Mahwah, New Jersey 07430. These units deliver droplets less than 10 microns (10 μm) in diameter. Temperature control is accomplished most easily by locating the mist chamber in a room that is maintained at 20°C (68°F). It is essential for reproducible results to maintain a constant temperature in successive experiments.

Construction of the chamber may be as simple as a one-square meter (10.7 ft) area box with 150 mm (5.9 in.) sidewalls and a bottom sloping toward a

443

drain opening. The cover may be constructed of a frame covered with 4 or 6 mil polyethylene. For another model, one-half inch plastic conduit was used for arches between the diagonally opposite corners. The arches were clamped together at the top and then covered with plastic. If several racks are installed one above the other, it is necessary to hang plastic sheets under each to prevent dripping of water and bacterial ooze from tubers on one shelf to those beneath.

Potato Bruising Device

The purpose of a potato bruising device is to inflict a constant impact force to tubers. Since large numbers of bruises are often required for a test program, it is desirable that the device be able to deliver constant blows quickly.

The level of bruising force delivered depends on the size and shape of the surface contacting the tuber, the mass of the body meeting the tuber, the mass of the tuber, and the velocity at which the tuber and surface meet. Kunkel and Gardner (1959) reported that "Energy expended during the impact is not a good measure of deformation, since energy could be expended in the entire potato (and possibly its support) or could be expended in an extremely small volume immediately adjacent to the point of contact."

Therefore, the design of a bruising device should be such that a constant mass impacts the tubers at a constant velocity. The mass of the bruising device should be much less than the mass of the tuber and its support so that all of the momentum of the impacter is converted to an impulsive force on the surface of the tuber. Potatoes are almost completely inelastic and so impact deformations result in tissue damage rather than elastic restitution.

No standard exists for tuber impacters. Kunkel and Gardner (1959) used a 100 gram (3.53 oz.) plug, dropping it 15.2, 30.5, 45.7 and 60.9 cm (6, 12, 18, and 24 in.). Similar plugs of various masses have been used by other researchers since then (Maas, 1966; Schippers, 1971; Peterson and Hall, 1974). Based on these previous researchers' procedures, a

444

100 gram (3.53 oz.) mass dropping 305 mm (12 in.) was selected as the bruising device design. The contacting surface was hemispherical with a 20 mm (0.787 in.) radius.

An apparatus with these specifications is shown in Figure 1. Many of the features of the device are intended to speed the bruising, since many replications on many lots are often necessary to assess the effects of temperature, humidity, maturity and other factors on soft rot potential.

Bruised potatoes are inoculated by immersion in a suspension of 10 - 10 Ecc per ml. Alternatively, a 20 drop of ten-fold dilutions of Ecc is applied at the bruise site. Potatoes are incubated in a mist chamber at 20°C (68° F) for 48-96 hours. The macerated tissue is removed and weighed at the end of the incubation period.

It has been noted that tubers with a pulp temperature at 8°C (46.4 °F) at the time of impacting are more prone to bruise injury than those impacted at 18 C (64.4 F) (Bartz and Kelman, 1984).

WOUNDS AND WOUND HEALING

The type of wound that is made in the surface of the potato affects the wound-healing process. Recent histological studies by Norman Thomson and Dr. Ray Evert (Unpublished data, University of Wisconsin Botany Department) confirm earlier observations that the rate and type of wound healing reflects whether the tissue is damaged by a clean cut (shatter bruise), or an impact bruise that may not be visible externally (blackspot).

In the case of a clean cut, suberin, a wax-like substance that is relatively impermeable to water, is deposited gradually in cell walls directly under the cut area (Kolattukudy, 1981). This process of suberization is followed by the development of a cork cambium of dividing cells that form a barrier of new cork-like cells called wound periderm under the suberized cells. A sharp contrast to this is when the tissue is bruised mechanically with a convex faced impact type bruising device, the outer periderm is only slightly cracked and injury is often not apparent externally. However, in this case, typical

445

suberized cells are evident only at the edges of the bruise and the wound periderm formation is greatly delayed. Formation of the wound-healed tissue is very irregular and deep fissures or cracks are evident in the tissue in the bruised area. Vital staining of the bruised tissue with neutral red shortly after the damage occurred indicates that normal cell functions are destroyed and deep layers of cells are killed along the cracks.

Studies by Drs. William Bland and Champ Tanner, (Unpublished data, University of Wisconsin Soil Science Department) on tubers from the same samples and similarly bruised indicate that the rate of water loss from cuts versus bruises is significantly lower over an extended time period. A very rapid decline in the rate of water loss occurred from a clean cut over a seven-day period when cut potato tubers were placed under optimal conditions for curing. However, the rate of water loss from mechanically bruised sites declined relatively slowly and continued to decline over seven days. These studies as well as those of other investigators provide strong evidence that the mechanical damage that results when tubers are subjected to pressure and impact forces creates injuries that heal slowly even under optimal conditions for healing.

Oxygen is a key factor in suberization and wound periderm formation. During the initial days in storage there is a race in progress between the formation of suberized cells and wound cork and the growth and spread of the soft rot bacteria into wounded tissue prior to the formation of effective barriers. Under normal conditions, its very unlikely that the level of oxygen passing through potatoes in a storage bin will be reduced to such low levels that adverse effects on the curing process will occur. However, if moisture condenses on tuber surfaces or condendation from the walls or roof areas in a storage bin drips on the tubers, the resulting water film can cause the tubers to become deficient in oxygen in a relatively short period of time because of internal respiration requirements (Burton and Wigginton, 1970). As potato tuber oxygen levels decrease below normal concentrations, the rate of wound healing declines; if oxygen concentrations remain very low, little or no wound healing will

446

occur (Wigginton, 1974). In addition, the bacterial infection process is markedly impeded in a well-aerated tuber; this occurs well before the oxygen-dependent wound healing processes have had an opportunity to limit the spread of the infection. Furthermore, the pectic enzymes produced by the bacteria that are involved in degrading the pectic materials between plant cell walls are less effective at ambient oxygen levels. The increased resistance of potato tissue to enzymatic degradation may be a response of the tuber which operates more effectively when adequate oxygen is present (Maher and Kelman, 1983).

The rate of suberization and wound cork formation also decline as temperatures drop below 20° C (68 ° F); the process will stop at 4 ° C (39.2 ° F) (Wigginton, 1974). Thus, it is necessary to balance the decrease in growth of the bacteria that also occurs with decrease in temperature with the concomitant decrease in the healing of wounds.

RESULTS AND DISCUSSION

In a typical experiment, tubers were placed at three different temperatures: 4 ℃, 16 ℃, 24 °C (39.2, 60.8 and 75.2 ℉) for a period of 48 hours; then each tuber was bruised at two points with the bruiser (Table 1). One group of tubers was incubated in the mist chamber; a second lot was placed at 27°C (80.6° F) and observed after 48 hours for the presence of shatter bruise and blackspot. The most severe soft rot and injury occurred in those tubers bruised at 5° C (41°F). In tubers incubated in the mist chamber, the percentage of bruised areas that decayed declined from 85 percent in tubers bruised at 4 ℃ (39.2°F) to 50 percent in the tubers bruised at 24 ℃ (75.2 ° F). However, when tubers that had been incubated dry were peeled, the percent blackspot or shatter bruise evident declined more rapidly as the temperature increased; thus, at 24 ℃ (75.2°F) the percentage of bruised areas that showed visible damage was only 25 percent. This indicates that the soft rot bacteria may be able to develop in bruise sites that cannot be seen by the naked eye and thus, the mist chamber assay provides a highly sensitive means for assessing bruising injury (Kelman and Maher, 1983).

At the time of harvest, the mist chamber assay has been used to detect bruise severity during the harvesting process. When samples were taken from a fresh pack operation after the tubers had passed from a digger, onto a truck, through a washer and grader, and placed in the plastic bags for shipment, over 80 percent decayed after mist chamber exposure; in contrast, less than 10 percent of the hand-dug potatoes were decayed (Table 2). Similar results were obtained in mist chamber assays when hand dug tubers were compared with tubers taken from the digger and bin piler (Table 3). At each major step in harvesting and storing potatoes the percent of tubers with soft rot and the number of soft rot bacteria/g of periderm increased (Kelman and Maher, 1983).

During the curing process, the ability of the potato to recover is conditioned to some extent by the type and amount of damage that occurred during the harvesting and bin piling procedure. In one series of experiments, tubers from one field were sampled from various points in the harvesting operation; samples were placed in the storage bin where the potatoes from that field were placed (Table 4). Samples were examined by the mist chamber procedure at the time of harvest and again after two months when the curing was presumably completed. The potatoes originally taken from the digger boom showed a remarkedable degree of recovery; initially, over 55 percent of the tubers had decayed, but after the curing procedure only one percent of the tubers in that particular lot decayed. However, a sample from the bin piler boom still showed a relatively high percentage of decayed tubers (55%), indicating the recovery of these potatoes had not been equal to that of the tubers from the digger boom. Tubers with moderately high soft rot potentials at the time they enter the storage bin can, under proper conditions, recover to the point where none will decay even when placed under the high stress conditions of the mist chamber. However, if the bruising is very extensive, curing procedures may not be as effective (Kelman and Maher, 1983).

When mechanically bruised potatoes were held under optimal conditions for wound healing for three

448

days (90% relative humidity and 20°C [68 ° F]), then inoculated and placed in the mist chamber, severity and number of infections decreased significantly indicating that invasion pathways had been partially closed during this relatively short curing period (Kelman and Maher, 1983).

Tubers that are badly bruised and damaged may not fully recover and, thus, provide a potential hazard if conditions in the storage are not maintained at a highly favorable level. It is necessary to emphasize that high soft rot readings under mist chamber conditions do not indicate necessarily that a problem will develop in storage, but merely that the potential for decay exists (Kelman and Maher, 1983).

Although tubers may have stored well during the period prior to grading, their soft rot potential may increase after grading and shipping has caused new bruises. This was illustrated in an experiment in which potato seed samples were taken from the bins of three different growers shortly before the seed potatoes were shipped to commercial growers in central Wisconsin (Table 5). At the time the seed lots arrived and were placed in temporary storage prior to planting, a second set of samples were taken from each of these seed lots. Both sets of samples were assayed by the mist chamber procedure. The percentage of seed tubers that decayed increased markedly after they had been subjected to the normal grading, shipping, and bin loading procedure. It is important to note that initially the seed had very low soft rot readings. The other interesting aspect of this particular test was the fact that these seed lots had the same relative ranking in the initial decay readings, and in the readings taken after shipment (Kelman and Maher, 1983).

SUMMARY AND CONCLUSIONS

It appears that the mist chamber incubation procedure has the potential for application in the following ways:

1. It may provide a means of evaluating seed quality and the potential for seed piece decay. A high soft rot potential index in the seed has, in general, indicated that a particular seed lot would

449

have also a high potential for seed piece decay or the development of blackleg. This may be greatly influenced by environmental conditions after planting.

2. The method can be used to detect those steps in the harvesting procedure that may be contributing to bruise damage. It appears that the bacteria can detect very slight damage to tuber tissue which is not visible to the naked eye.

3. The steps in packing procedures that increase soft rot potential can also be monitored, as well as the grading and movement of seed potatoes to the commercial grower.

A device that was found effective in inflicting a uniform impact to potatoes is one that has a 100 gram (3.53 oz.) plug dropping 305 mm (12 in.). The contacting end of the plug has a spherical radius of 20 mm (0.787 in.). The application of uniform impacts, with subsequent inoculation of the wounds and incubation in the mist chamber, appears to have potential applications for:

1. Monitoring the suberization of wounds on tubers placed into storage. It therefore may be used to determine optimum temperatures, humidities, and air flows for curing and storage and to determine whether a given lot of potatoes can be held for an extended storage period. As has been demonstrated, soft rot potential drops rapidly as the curing process continues; this decline can be used as a means of monitoring the effectiveness of the curing and holding procedures.

2. Determining which samples of potatoes are more prone to bruise injury. The procedure showed, for example, that tubers impacted at 8 °C (46.4 ° F) were more prone to bruise injury than those impacted at 18°C (64.4 °F).

REFERENCES

Bartz, J.A. and A. Kelman. 1984. Bacterial soft rot potential in washed potato tubers in relation to temperatures of tubers and water during simulated commercial handling procedures. Amer. Pot. J. 61:485-493.

Burton, W. and M.J. Wigginton. 1970. The effect of a film of water upon the oxygen status of a potato tuber. Potato Res. 13:180-186.

Campos, E., E.A. Maher, and A. Kelman. 1982. Relationship of pectolytic clostridia and Erwinia carotovora strains to decay of potato tubers in storage. Plant Disease 66: 543-546.

Cupples, D. and A. Kelman. 1974. Evaluation of selective media for isolation of soft rot bacteria from soil and plant tissue. Phyto-pathology 64:468-475.

DeBoer, S.H. and A. Kelman. 1978. Influence of oxygen concentration and storage factors on susceptibility of potato tubers to bacterial soft rot. Potato Res. 21:65-80.

Kelman, A. and E.A. Maher. 1979. Bacterial soft rot potential: A means of assessing potato tuber quality. Proc. 18th Annual Washington State Potato Conf. 35-40.

Kelman, A. and E.A. Maher. 1983. Potato bruises – pathways for bacterial infections. 2nd Ann. North Amer. Seed Pot. Seminar Proc. Dec. 1983.

Kolattukudy, P.E. 1981. Structure, biosynthesis, and biodegradation of cutin and suberin. Annu. Rev. Pl. Physiol. 32:539-567.

Kunkel, R. and W.H. Gardner. 1959. Blackspot of Russett Burbank potatoes. Proc. of the Amer. Soc. for Hort. Sci. 73:436-444.

Lund, B.M., and A. Kelman. 1977. Determination of the potential for development of bacterial soft rot of potatoes. Amer. Pot. J. 54:211-225.

Maas, E.F. 1966. A simplified potato bruising device. Amer. Pot. J. 43:424-426.

Maher, E.A. and A. Kelman. 1983. Oxygen status of potato tuber tissue in relation to maceration by pectic enzymes of Erwinia Carotovera. Phytopathology. 73:536-539.

Perombelon, M.C.M. and A. Kelman. 1980. Ecology of
    soft rot erwinias. Ann. Rev. Phytopathol.
    18:361-387.

Peterson, C.L. and C.W. Hall. 1974. Thermorhec-
    ological simple theory applied to the Russet
    Burbank potato. Trans of ASAE 17(3):546-552,
    556.

Schippers, P.A. 1971. Measurement of blackspot
    susceptibility of potatoes. Amer. Pot. J.
    48(3):71-81.

Smittle, D.A., R.E. Thornton, C.L. Peterson, and
    B.B. Dean. 1974. Harvesting potatoes with
    minimum damage. Amer. Pot. J. 51:152-164.

Stiles, D.G. 1983. The national potato antibruise
    committee. Amer. Pot. J. 60:821. (Abstract)

Wigginton, M.J. 1974. Effects of temperature,
    oxygen tension and relative humidity on the
    wound-healing process in the potato tuber.
    Potato Res. 17:200-214.

Table 1. Bacterial soft rot[1] and mechanical damage in relation to temperatures

Tuber temperature at time of bruising	Ave. wt. of decayed tissue	Injured area decayed	Shatter bruises	Visible damage
4°C	1.4 g	85%	50%	83%
16°C	1.0 g	76%	15%	48%
24°C	0.4 g	50%	8%	25%

[1] Tubers were incubated in a mist chamber for 96 hrs.

Table 2. Percent of tubers with bacterial soft rot and numbers of soft rot bacteria on potato tubers sampled at different steps in harvesting and packing

Sample point	Percent tubers with bacterial soft rot[1]	Number of soft rot bacteria/g of peel
Hand dug	8	55,000
On truck	16	380,000
Packed for shipment	83	10,000,000

[1] Based on 30-tuber samples incubated for 96 hrs.

Table 3. Percent of tubers with bacterial soft rot and numbers of
soft rot bacteria on tubers taken at different points in
harvesting and storing procedures

Sample point	Percent tubers with bacterial soft rot[1]	Number of soft rot bacteria/g of periderm[2]
Hand dug	20	100
Digger	30	1,500
Bin piler	100	700,000

[1] Based on 30-tuber samples incubated for 96 hrs.

[2] Based on periderm sample from 10 tubers; dilution platings on a
crystal violet pectate medium (Cuppels and Kelman, 1974).

Table 4. Percent soft rot in potatoes from the digger boom and the
bin piler at harvest and after curing

Sampling point	Percent tubers with bacterial soft rot at harvest[1]	Percent tubers with bacterial soft rot after curing[2]
Digger boom	55	1
Bin piler	100	55

[1] Tubers incubated in the mist chamber for 96 hrs.
[2] Digger boom tuber samples in open mesh bags were placed in area
of storage bin from which bin piler samples were taken after
two months of storage.

Table 5. Bacterial soft rot in seed potatoes sampled from bins of
certified growers prior to grading and shipment and after
arrival and placement in temporary storage prior to planting

Seed grower lot	% tubers with soft rot[1] From seed bins[2]	After shipment[3]
A	3	48
B	17[3]	89
C	5	78

[1] Tubers were incubated in a mist chamber for 96 hr.
[2] Based on two 30-tuber samples.
[3] Based on four 30-tuber samples.

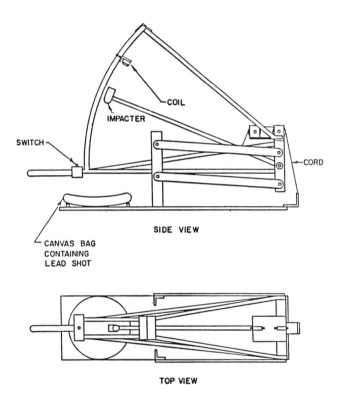

COIL

IMPACTER

SWITCH

CORD

SIDE VIEW

CANVAS BAG
CONTAINING
LEAD SHOT

TOP VIEW

Figure I.   Potato Bruising Device

EFFECT OF STORAGE TEMPERATURE ON COLOR CHANGES
AND CONTENT OF CAROTINOIDS OF DEHYDRATED DICED
POTATOES

by

W. Bergthaller, G. Tegge and W. Hoffmann, Federal
Research Center for Cereal and Potato Processing,
Detmold, Federal Republic of Germany

ABSTRACT

Yellowness of tuber flesh and of dehydrated
dices from German potato cultivars is related to
concentration of carotinoids. While storing of
potatoes results only in slight changes of carotinoid
concentration a drastic reduction occurs in
dehydration processes. Further losses in the dried
product accompanied by reduction of yellowness are
consequence of storing at elevated temperature (+35
°C resp. 95 °F).

ASAE Paper No. 85-4031

INTRODUCTION

General Considerations

Throughout central European countries, the yellow color of the tissue of potato tubers is certainly an important property, especially of culinary quality, (market-value of commercial potatoes) where dehydrated potato products are concerned. Tuber flesh color is closely connected with the variety. Therefore, in breeding and propagation, varieties are differentiated according to their flesh color which may vary from white to intensive yellow (Siebeneck, 1959; Anonymous, 1984). In potato processing or the dehydration branch of the German potato processing industry, varieties with intensive yellowness are preferred progressively. Priority of yellow colored potatoes is also confirmed by a list of registered varieties in the Federal Republic of Germany, and 95 percent belong to the light yellow or yellow type. The majority of them (56%) includes the yellow or intensely yellow ones (Anonymous, 1984).

Flesh color, in particular its yellowness, is strongly related to the concentration of total carotinoids. The relevant carotinoid pigments (xanthophylls) are shown in Figure 1. Single carotinoids contribute to formation of potato flesh color in a similar manner without having an outstanding importance to one of these components (Iwanzik et al., 1983). The composition of carotinoids of some German potato varieties (n=13), the flesh color of which ranged from white to intensely yellow regarding their concentration on fresh weight basis, is shown in Table 1. Violaxanthin is the most important pigment, especially in yellow-flesh tubers. Lutein (+zeaxanthin) and lutein-5,6-eposide (+antheraxanthin) follow according to their decreasing importance. Further carotinoid pigments are neoxanthin A and neoxanthin which were found in minor quantities.

Recently published studies (Tevini et al., 1985) prove the existence of mono-and diesters (15-30%) with palmitic, stearic and linolic acid as main fatty acid components. The fraction of carotinoid-diesters exceeds considerably the lutein-fraction, especially in the case of yellow-flesh varieties. White-flesh varieties contain only traces of these carotinoid esters.

For measuring the color of potato flesh in raw or cooked state as well as that of dehydrated potato products, several attempts were carried out on visual or instrumental basis (Siebeneck, 1959; Grunewald, 1974; Francis and Clydesdale, 1975; Erdelyi and Koncz, 1976; Bergthaller et al., 1978; Schaller et al., 1980; Berthaller et al., 1983). Dehydrated potato cube studies, in connection between sensory evaluation of color quality of dehydrated potato cubes and corresponding instrumental measurements, illustrate the significance of the a- and L-values using the color space of R.S. Hunter (Schaller et al., 1980). Nevertheless, further studies on the influence of blanching time during short-time storage (up to 29 days) showed also the importance of the b-value (according to R.S. Hunter) being highly comparable to yellowness of dehydrated diced potatoes. This above behavior is in good agreement with the angle of dominant wavelengths corresponding to the chromaticity of several samples which is rather small (575-578 mn) (Bergthaller et al., 1978; Schaller et al., 1980; Schaller et al., 1981/82). While stored at comparatively low temperatures +15 to 18 C (59 to 64 F), yellowness of dehydrated potato cubes decreased slightly showing also different behavior of the investigated cultivars (Schaller et al., 1971/82).

Color and Carotinoid Content in Stored Potato Tubers

As a result of storage, slight changes of tuber flesh color are a well known phenomena. However, some varieties react in a different manner. Color may change in both directions to increasing and decreasing intensity of yellowness. The direction probably depends on ambient storing conditions and year of harvest (Siebeneck, 1959).

Similar results have been reported by Tevini et al., (1985) with respect to total carotinoid concentration. Between November (after harvest) and April (after a six-month storage period) concentration of total carotinoids increased to about 15 percent in three of seven investigated cultivars, while somewhat lower losses (5 to 10%) could be found with three other cultivars (Figure 2). An increase of total carotinoid concentration in connection with effects of variety and temperature has also been described by Janave and Thomas (1979). However, irradiation reduced carotinoid concentration. The reported losses were very high (up to 50%).

The individual carotinoid pigments, especially violaxanthin and to a lower extent lutein, were reduced. On the other hand the fraction of carotinoid diesters was extended considerably in some cultivars (Figure 3). With respect to those changes, other varieties showed a partly different behavior, e.g. only slightly extended or unchanged values.

Carotinoid Concentration as Affected by Processing

In manufacture of dehydrated diced potatoes, tubers are prepared according to a production diagram as shown in Figure 4. The results of Tevini et al., (1985) as well as earlier published studies on vegetables and herbs (Cole and Kapur, 1957; Nutting et al., 1970; Sweeny and Marsh, 1971; Philip, 1975; Holmes et al., 1979; Baruffaldi et al., 1983) show a reduction of carotinoid concentration can be expected in consequence to blanching and drying.

By cooking potato tuber pieces, considerable amounts of the main component violaxanthin are converted (cis-trans isomerization). In this connection, cooking time had an important effect. Compared with violaxanthin, carotinoid esters remained relatively stable (Tevini et al., 1985).

Drying leads to further losses by epoxidation which may reach a detrimental extent. Structure of carotinoids, pre-treatment of drying products, drying conditions, oxygen concentration in drying atmosphere, and increase of product surface are responsible for various effects (Nutting et al., 1970; Spiess et al., 1968).

Considering carotinoid pigments characteristic to potatoes, Tevini and Bergthaller (in preparation) finally reported about the influence of treatment prior to dehydration and the drying step itself. Losses of total carotinoid concentration recently reported for dehydration in general (Tevini et al., 1985) are mostly due to poor stability of violaxanthin, while unidentified reaction products and lutein isomers are formed mainly in the blanching step (Figure 5). In addition to blanching and drying operations, peeling also proved to be responsible for demonstrated losses. The somewhat higher concentration of carotinoids in the cortex (Tevini et al., 1985) in connection with substance losses from peeling may explain the observed effect.

Deterioration of Carotinoids of Dried Products During Storage

Dehydrated potato products pretreated by blanching or cooking are very sensitive to oxidation deterioration. Highly unsaturated fatty acids are also sensitive to this property, but in oxidative decomposition, carotinoids are particularly involved. Later lipids deteriorated, too. Both reactions are manifested in sensory changes of bleaching of product yellowness and at least in occurrence of defective flavor (Stute, 1981). Oxidative deterioration of carotinoids during storage of dried vegetable products is accelerated by high temperatures and low moisture contents as well as high oxygen concentrations (Land, 1962; Spiess et al., 1969). Bleaching and formation of defective flavor are generally known reactions, particularly for potato flakes and granules (Talburt and Smith, 1975) and to a much lower, but not well known, extent for dehydrated potato cubes or slices (Schaller et al., 1981/82; Tevini et al., 1985; and Tevini and Bergthaller, in preparation).

MATERIALS AND METHODS

Source Material

For manufacture of dehydrated diced potatoes, 50 kg (110 lbs) of tubers of cultivars Bintje and Saturan grown in 1981 and stored for nearly eight months under controlled storage conditions of 8° C 0.5° C (46.4 °F ± 0.9°F) and relative humidity 94 percent 3 percent were used. Sprouts were suppressed three times during the eight month storage period, using IPC and CIPC.

460

Production of Dehydrated Diced Potatoes

Dehydrated diced potatoes were produced according to a discontinuous semi-technical process as described by Schaller et al., (1980). Five kg (11.0 lbs) of tubers were peeled discontinuously for 2.5 min using an abrasive peeler, followed by manual trimming. The peeled tubers were cut into dices of 10 mm (0.4 in.) These dices were washed for three minutes in tap water, blanched in boiling tap water for 165 seconds and washed for an additional two minutes. These prepared potato cubes were dried using a discontinuous, moving-tray heated air drier for 405 minutes [first cycle 180 minutes at 78 °C (172.4 °F) and second drying cycle at 225 minutes at 55° C (2131 F)]. At the end of the drying process (10 cycles per variety), samples of dehydrated diced potatoes were mixed to form homogeneous material for the storage experiment. The mixed material was divided into 48 representative subsamples of 200 g (0.44 lb.) product, each using a conical sample divider.

Storage procedure

Subsamples were packed in paper bags and one half of them stored in a refrigerated chamber at about +5 ° C (41° F) and about 75 percent relative humidity. The second half was stored in a storage unit with recirculating air of about +35°C (95 ° F). The relative humidity reached 25 percent. Storage times were fixed for: 1, 8, 165, 22, 29, 36, 43, and 50 days.

At the end of each storage time, three subsamples from each variable (variety and storage temperature) were taken for determination of color and concentration of total carotinoids.

Color

Color of dehydrated diced potatoes was measured instrumentally in five repetitions as described by Schaller et al., (1978) using a tristimulus colorimeter of Momcolor D-type (Magyar Optikai Muvek, Budapest). With respect to previously published results, (Schaller et al., 1981/82) the +b-value of the a,b,L-color space (after R.S. Hunter) was chosen to characterize yellowness.

461

Sample Preparation

To determine moisture content as well as concentration of total carotinoids aliquot (equal) parts of the subsamples were ground in a laboratory impact mill with screen perforation diameter of 0.8 mm (0.027 in.)

Moisture

Moisture content was determined by drying one part of ground sample at 105°C (221 ° F) for three hours in a drying oven (Adler, 1971).

Total Carotinoids

Carotinoids were extracted from a 20 g sample of ground dehydrated potatoes by shaking with 100 ml of methanol/aceton mixture (2:1, v/v) for one hour. This extraction procedure was repeated three times, the combined extracts mixed with 300 ml for a 19 percent sodium chloride solution, and finally shaken out several times for one minute with 100 ml petroleum benzine (b.p. 40-60°) in a 1 1-separating funnel until further added petroleum benzine remained colorless. The acetone-methanol layer was drawn off and discarded. Since carotinoids could not be extracted completely from ground dehydrated potatoes, the percolated residue was extracted once more with 100 ml portions of petroleum benzine until the residue remained colorless.

Both petroleum benzine extracts were combined and purified with 300 ml of a saturated solution of sodium chloride by shaking in a 2 1-separating funnel. The petroleum benzine layer, which had been dried overnight with 30 g anhydrous sodium sulfate, was finally concentrated in a rotary evaporator. The residual extract was once more percolated over anhydrous sodium sulfate to remove remaining moisture in a volumetric flask, filled up to 50 ml with petroleum benzine for measurement in a Zeiss DM 4 spectromphotometer (Carl Zeiss, Oberkochen). Extinction values were determined at 438 nm using petroleum benzine as zero. Concentration of total carotinoids in dry substance was calculated on the basis of measured extinction values and a mean

specific extinction coefficient ($E^{1\%}_{cm}$) of 2500. As a
precaution against oxidation, all sample
manipulations were carried out in nitrogen atmosphere
and in the dark.

Statistical Procedure

Mean values and values of standard deviation
of yellowness and total carotinoid concentration were
estimated on basis of subsamples (n=3) investigated
per variable. Following tests of homogeneity, one-way
analyses of variance were carried out concerning the
effect of storage time as influenced by temperature
and variety. Differences between successive mean
values of treatments were judged using the least
significant differences (LSD) for P = 0.05 or 0.01
respectively (Sachs, 1984).

RESULTS AND DISCUSSIONS

The results of analyses of yellowness (+b-value)
and concentration of total carotinoids in dehydrated
diced potatoes stored at +5°C (41°F) and +35°C (95° F)
are presented in Tables 2 and 3 for cv. Bintje and in
Tables 4 and 5 for cv. Saturan. It is clearly shown
that over a 50-day storage period similar, but
differently pronounced behavior of both varieties and
of temperatures studied could be observed.

It was observed that at +5°C (41 ° F), changes
in yellowness proved to be of little importance,
however at +35°C (95 °F), a decrease of about three units
of yellowness was observed within the first month (29
days). This was similar to previously reported data
concerning a considerable lower storage temperature
of 15 to 18 °C (59 to 65° F) (Schaller et al.,
1981/82). Apart from somewhat lower +b-values from
starting storage, the observed decrease at a higher
temperature level was unexpectedly small. With
continued storage further decrease of yellowness was
observed. This effect, which could be called a
bleaching effect, was of lower intensity, as may be
seen from Figure 6 and 7.

Regarding changes in carotinoids at +5°C (41°F),
concentration of total carotinoids decreased
according to negative, significant (P<0.001) and
linear (P.>0.10) connections within a period of about

29 days for cv. Bintje and 43 days for cv. Saturna. Following losses of about 200 μg/100μg dry substance, corresponding to a remainder of 65 to 72 percent within the test periods decomposition of carotinoids was stopped. Further significant changes (P = 0.05) did not occur.

Initial concentration of carotinoids, which could not be determined because of incomplete extraction, can be estimated at 586μg/100μg dry substance for cv. Bintje and at 726 g/100 g dry substance for cv. Saturna.

Although considerable losses (25 to 30%) in total carotinoid concentration have to be taken into consideration with storage time at storage temperatures of about +5 ℃ (41°F), comparable changes in yellowness were not observed. The phenomenon cannot yet be explained, as detailed information on decomposition of individual carotinoids at lower temperatures has not as yet been reported.

A completely different situation, however, is typical of higher storage temperatures, e.g. +35°C (or 95°F). Within the tested storage period (1 to 5 days) concentration of carotinoids decreased markedly with accelerated rate in initial storage time. At the end of designated storage time concentration of total carotinoids got to 138 or 173 μg/100 μg dry substance. In general, the remainder could be estimated at 26 percent which is rather high in comparison with data of Spiess et al. (1968) from freeze-dried paprika and carrots packed in oxygen containing atmosphere (0.5 mg/g). In our experiments, oxygen concentration was not controlled in accordance with practice requirements.

Nevertheless, decomposition of potato carotinoids proceeded very intensively under such conditions, as confirmed in a recent report (Tevini and Bergthaller, in preparation). Formation of isomers and numerous unknown reaction products takes place to a considerable extent. Though losses in carotinoid concentration were comparably high, changes in color, i.e. yellowness, remained relatively small, as mentioned above. This observation does not sufficiently agree with changes in carotinoid concentration and therefore reactions

of the Maillard-type should also be taken into
consideration for explaining color changes. This
should be the objective of further studies.

REFERENCES

Adler, G. 1971. Kartoffeln und Kartoffelerzeugnisse
(Potatoes and Potato Products). Verlag Paul
Parey, Berlin and Hambeug: 167-168.

Anonymus. 1984. Beschreibende Sortenliste 1984.
Kartoffeln. (Descriptive List of Registered
Varieties 1984. Potatoes) Verlag die Kartoffel-
wirtschaft (Deutscher Fachverlag GmbH),
Frankfurt/Main.

Baruffaldi, R., T.C. Vessoni Penna, G.F. Leonhardt
and L.e. Abe. 1983. Blanching of carrots.
Effects of processing on texture and carotenes.
Ciencia e Tecnologia Aliment. 3:144-154.

Bergthaller, W., K.H. Fehn and A. Schaller. 1978.
Ergebnisse instrumentller Farbmnessungen bei
Trockenkartoffel-Wurfeln (Results of instrumen-
tal colour measurements with dehydrated potato
cubes). (Confructa, Int. J. Technol. Fruit
Vegetable Process. 23:110-118.

Bergthaller, W., W. Kempf and A. Schaller. 1983.
Instrumentelle Farbmessung und sensorische
Farbbewertung von Trockenkartoffel-Wurfeln
(Instrumental measurement and sensory evaluation
of the colour of dried potato cubes). ZFL, Int.
Z. Lebensmittel-Technol. - Verfahrenstech. 34:
174, 177-178, 180, 182-183.

Cole, E.R., and N.S. Kapur. 1957. The stability of
lycopene. II. Oxidation during heating of
tomato pulp. J. Sci. Food Agric. 8:366-368.

Erdelyi, L., and L. Konzc. 1976. Burgonya es
burgonyapure szinenck objectiv merese (Objek-
tive colour measurement of potatoes and potato
puree). Hutoipar. 23:82-86.

Francis, F.J., and F.M. Clydesdale. 1975. Food
Colorimetry. Theory and Applications. The AVI
Publishing Co., Westport, Connecticut: 259-266.

Grunewald, T. 1974. Instrumentelle Farbmessung von Kartoffeln und Verarbeitungsprodukten (Instrumental colour measurement of potatoes and processing products). Confucta, Int. J. Technol. Fruit Vegetable Process. 19: 109-119.

Holmes, Z.A., L. Miller, M. Edwards and E. Benson. 1979. Vitamin retention during home drying of vegetables and fruits. Home Econ. Res. J. 7: 258-264.

Iwansik, W., M. Tevini, R. Stute and R. Hilbert. 1983. Carotinoidgehalt und -zusammensetzung verschiedener deutscher Kartoffelsorten und deren Bedeutung fur ide Fleischfarbe der Knolle (Carotinoid content and composition of various German potato varieties and its relationship to tuber flesh colour). Potato Res. 26: 149-162.

Janave, M.T., and P. Thomas. 1979. Influence of post-harvest storage temperature and gamma irradiation on potato carotinoids. Potato Res. 22: 365-369.

Land, D.G. 1063. Stability of plant pigments. In: Hawthorne, J., and J.M. Leitch (ed.): Recent Advances in Food Research. Vol. 2, Butterworth and Co., London: 50.

Nutting, M.D., H.J. Neumann and J.R. Wagner. 1970. Effect of processing variables on the stability of -carotenes and xanthophylls of dehydrated parsley. J. Sci. Food Agric. 21: 197-202.

Philip, T. 1975. Utilization of plant pigments as food colorants. Food Prod. Dev. 9: 50, 52, 54, 56.

Purcell, A.E. and W.M. Walter, Jr. 1968. Autoxidation of carotenes in dehydrated sweet potato flakes using C- -carotene, J. Agri. Food Chem. 16: 650-653.

Schaller, A., W. Bergthaller and W. Kempf. 1980.
Ergebnise von Studien uber den Zusammenhang
zwischen sensorischer Bewertung and instru-
menteller Messung der Farbe bei Trockenkartoffel-Wurfeln (Results of studies on the
connection of sensory evaluation and instrumental measurement of colour with dehydrated
potato cubes). Confructa, Int. J. Technol.
Fruit Vegetable Process. 25: 9-15.

Schaller, A., W. Bergthaller and E. Gabriel-Blanke.
198/82. Ergebnisse von Untersuchungen bezuglich
des Einflusses des Wasserblanchierens auf die
Farbe von Trockenkartoffel-Wurfeln wahrend einer
Kurzzeit-Lagerung unter besonderer Berucksichti-
gung des Gelbwertes (Results of investigations
relating to the influence of water-blanching on
the colour of dehydrated potato cubes during a
short-time storage under special consideration
of yellowness). Confructa, Int. J. Technol.
Fruit Vegetable Process 26: 8-17.

Siebeneck, H. 1959. Beobachtungen an der Fleischfarbe der rohen Kartoffel (Observations on
the flesh colour of raw potatoes). Potato
Res. (Eur. Potato J.). 2: 229-237.

Spiess, W.E.L., P. Sole, C. Askar and A.A. Askar.
1968. Die Haltbarmachung von Lebensmitteln
durch Gefriertrocknung (Conservation of food
by freeze-drying). Therapiewoche. 18: 1165-1186.

Stute, R. 1981. Die Bedeutung der Carotinoide fur
die Stabilitat und zur Stabilisierung von
Kartoffelpureeprodukten (Importance of carotinoids for stability and stabilization of
dehydrated mashed potatoes). Bericht 2. Karto-
ffel-Tagung 1980. Arbeitsgeme inschaft
Kartoffelforschung e. V., Detmold: 36-46.

Sweeny, J.P., and A.C. March. 1971. Effect of
processing on provitamin A in vegetables. J. Am.
Dietec. Ass. 59: 233-243.

Tevini, M., W. Iwanzik and G. Schoneker. 1984.
    Analyse, Vorkommen und Verhalten von Carotin-
    oiden in Kartoffeln und Kartoffelprodukten
    (Analysis, occurrence and behavior of cartotin-
    oids in potatoes and potato products). Jahrbuch
    1984, Forschungskreis der Ernahrungsindustrie
    e.V., Hannover: 36-53.

Tevini, M., and W. Bergthaller. 1985. Das Verhalten
    der Carotinoide der Kartoffel im Verlauf der
    Trocknung und Lagerung bei Trockenkartoffel-
    wurfeln (Behaviour of potato carotinoids during
    drying   and   storing   with   dehydrated   potato
    cubes). (In preparation).

Sachs, L. 1978. Angewandte Statistic (Applied
    statistics). Springer-Verlag. Berlin,
    Heidelberg, New York and Tokyo.

Table 1: Composition of carotinoids of German potato varieties (n=13) tested in 1980

	Concentration (µg/100 g fresh weight) Range		
Violaxanthin	7.9	-	244.5
Lutein (+Zeaxanthin)	15.7	-	88.0
Lutein-5,6-epoxide (+Antheraxanthin)	2.7	-	51.0
Neoxanthin A	1.1	-	15.5
Neoxanthin	0	-	8.7
β-Carotin		traces	
Total Carotinoids	24.4	-	342,7

(Iwanzik et al.: Potato Res. 26 (2) 149-162, 1983)

Table 2: Yellowness (+b-value) and concentration of total caro-
         tinoids in dehydrated diced potatoes from cv. Bintje
         after 1 to 50 days storage time at +5 °C (41 °F)

Storage time days	+b-value		Total carotinoids (µg/100 g dry substance)	
	mean[1]	s.d.[2]	mean[1]	s.d.[2]
1	22.45	0.136	-	-
8	21.80	0.127	534	22.1
15	22.20	0.155	484	18.8
22	22.60	0.278	436	12.4
29	22.53	0.343	405	8.3
36	22.44	0.201	397	9.5
43	21.60	(0.230)[3]	392	14.2
50	21.79	0.274	393	7.6
LSD (P = 0.05)	0.397		24.9	
LSD (P = 0.01)	0.548		34.5	

[1]Mean of 3 subsamples
[2]Standard deviation
[3]Estimated value

Table 3: Yellowness (+b-value) and concentration of total caro-
         tinoids in dehydrated diced potatoes from cv. Bintje
         after 1 to 50 days storage time at +35 °C (95 °F)

Storage time days	+b-value		Total carotinoids (µg/100 g dry substance)	
	mean[1]	s.d.[2]	mean[1]	s.d.[2]
1	22.28	0.113	-	-
8	21.59	0.479	4	23.2
15	2 .68	0.o66	291	25.6
22	2 .19	0.458	2 4	18.0
29	19.14	0.291	192	16.7
36	19.27	0.112	158	4.4
43	18.85	0.038	160	8.2
50	18.41	0.118	138	5.5
LSD (P = 0.05)	0.476		29.0	
LSD (P = 0.01)	0.656		40.2	

[1]Mean of 3 subsamples
[2]Standard deviation

Table 4: Yellowness (+b-value) and concentration of total
        carotinoids in dehydrated diced potatoes from cv.
        Saturna after 1 to 50 days storage time at +5 ^{o}C (41 ^{o}F)

| Storage time | +b-value | | Total carotinoids (μg/100 g dry substance) | |
days	mean[1]	s.d.[2]	mean[1]	s.d.[2]
1	21.05	.311	-	-
8	21.07	.326	683	20.8
15	21.39	.478	669	25.0
22	21.11	.326	618	7.7
29	21.42	.060	593	27.2
36	20.97	.274	537	11.4
43	20.79	.247	522	9.1
50	20.97	.265	522	8.8
LSD (P = 0.05)	0.529		30.7	
LSD (P = 0.01)	0.729		42.6	

[1]Mean of 3 subsamples
[2]Standard deviation

Table 5: Yellowness (+b-value) and concentration of total
        carotinoids in dehydrated diced potatoes from cv.
        Saturna after 1 to 50 days storage time at +35 ^{o}C (95 ^{o}F)

| Storage time | +b-value | | Total carotinoids (μg/100 g dry substance) | |
days	mean[1]	s.d.[2]	mean[1]	s.d.[2]
1	2 .93	0.197	-	-
8	2 .28	0.486	549	16.5
15	18.98	0.482	330	11.6
22	18.60	0.589	283	9.3
29	17.85	0.315	242	13.6
36	17.45	0.098	182	6.4
43	17.12	0.257	178	10.1
50	17. 4	0.251	173	7.1
LSD (P = 0.05)	0.638		17.6	
LSD (P = 0.01)	0.880		24.4	

[1]Mean of 3 subsamples
[2]Standard deviation

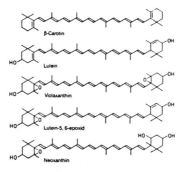

Figure 1: Structure of some carotinoid pigments (Xanthophylls) relevant for potatoes

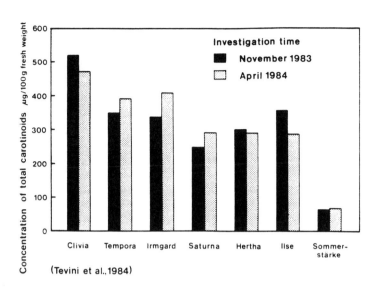

(Tevini et al., 1984)

Figure 2: Changes in carotinoid concentration of several German
potato varieties as influenced during storage

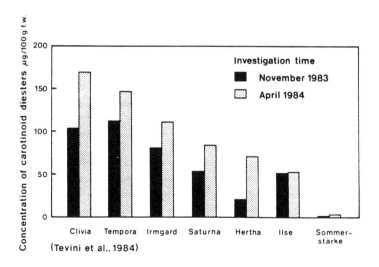

(Tevini et al., 1984)

Figure 3: Changes in concentration of carotinoid diesters of
several German potato varieties as influenced during
storage

```
Potato Store
     |
   Washer
     |
   Peeler
     |
   Washer
     |
Inspection and Trimming
     |
   Dicer
     |
  Blancher
     |
   Washer
     |
   Drier
```

Figure 4: Production diagram for manufacture of dehydrated
          diced potatoes

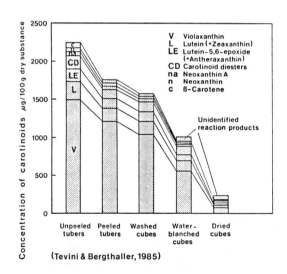

Figure 5: Reduction of carotinoid concentration during manufacture
          of dehydrated diced potatoes

474

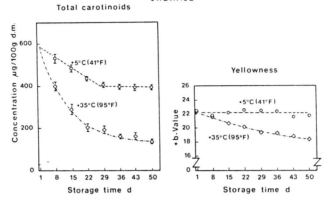

Figure 6: Effects of storage time (1 to 50 days) and storage temperature [+5 °C and +35°C (41°F and 95°F)] on yellowness and concentration of carotinoids in dehydrated diced potatoes (cv. Bintje)

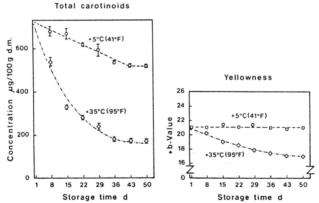

Figure 7: Effects of storage time (1 to 50 days) and storage temperature [+5°C and +35°C (41°F and 95°F)] on yellowness and concentration of carotinoids in dehydrated diced potatoes (cv. Saturna)

A MODEL FOR OPTIMIZING VENTILATION RATES
FOR POTATO STORAGE

by

Robert Y. Ofoli, Assistant Professor, and George
E. Merva, Professor, Department of Agricultural
Engineering, Michigan State University, East
Lansing, Michigan

ABSTRACT

A scheme is developed for the optimization o:
the ventilation rate for potato storages based on th(
principle of minimum entropy production. The schem(
involves calculating a parameter defined as th(
energy dissipation index (EDI). When the EDI i:
plotted against the ventilation rate, the grapl
provides a zone of minimum system entropy production
The procedure may be used to optimize the ventilatioı
rate.

INTRODUCTION

The subject of entropy has fascinated engineer:
and scientists for ages in spite of its abstrac·

ASAE Paper No. 85-4033

nature. Engineering applications of entropy usually involve the determination of the efficiencies or the degree of irreversibility of a process, especially in cases where the processes involve steam and other idealized gases for which standard thermodynamic tables or charts are available.

Given the abstractness of the concept, the analysis of entropy production in the potato storage environment would appear to be simply an academic exercise. However, entropy production is very intimately linked not only to energy transport, but to all mass transport and to any chemical reactions taking place in a given system. Thus, an examination of entropy generation can be used to gain further insight into these processes. It also provides a convenient vehicle for optimization.

The local production of entropy in any biological storage system is the result of heat transport, mass transport and chemical reactions in that system. Since it is nearly impossible to measure entropy production experimentally in a biological storage, the approach taken in this study was to use a model for heat and mass transport that predicts convective air temperatures and produce mass losses in the storage environment. The heat and mass transport relations were then used, in addition to appropriate chemical reaction equations, to examine the production of entropy and the dissipation of energy in the system.

The analysis of entropy production in a biological system has had very limited application. Briedis (1981) studied the link between engineering thermodynamics and experimental and theoretical biology. The work included the derivation of material and energy balance relations for open, growing systems far from equilibrium, and the use of these relations to study growth and development in the avian egg and microbial systems.

Fortes and Okos (1981a, 1981b) used the principles of irreversible thermodynamics to study heat and mass transport in corn kernels. The study postulated that the gradient of the moisture content provides the driving force for both liquid and vapor movement in the porous medium.

477

Several researchers have devised optimization techniques for the ventilation rates of agricultural storage medium. Misener (1973) studied the drying characteristics of potatoes immediately following suberization and developed a model for stimulating deep bed cooling of potatoes from known ambient conditions. The study included an optimization procedure for the ventilation rate as measured against potato shrinkage and ventilation costs.

Hunter (1976) developed a steady-state simulation model to predict air temperatures, relative humidity and weight loss for the white potato in storage. The model reported the critical range of velocities to be 0 to 3.05 meters per minute (10 ft./min.).

Lerew and Bakker-Arkema (1977) gave a finite difference solution of the simultaneous heat and mass transfer equations in bulk stored potatoes.

Temperature and weight loss were simulated for various types of instrumentation and ventilation system management schemes commonly applied to commercial storages. The effects on system efficiency of fan control by temperature sensors and time clock to that of continuous fan operation were examined.

Brugger (1979) developed a mathematical model for the two-dimensional air flow and heat and mass transfer within a potato pile. The objective of the study was to examine the effect of various parameters on the performance of the storage media. Temperature and humidity of the storage air were found to be the most important factors influencing the quality, weight loss, respiration rates and biochemical reactions.

Objectives

This study is motivated by the obvious relationship between entropy generation and the efficiency of engineering systems (Bejan, 1982) and the accompanying effects on system optimization. The study has as its objectives the application of the principles of non-equilibrium thermodynamics to an open biological system subjected to forced air convection in order to:

478

1. derive a model for the quantitative analysis of entropy production resulting from heat transport, mass transport and chemical reaction in the storage environment; and to

2. examine the feasibility of using the model as a tool for the optimization of the ventilation of agricultural storage media.

MATHEMATICAL ANALYSIS

The model presented here is for entropy production and energy dissipation resulting from non-isothermal heat transport, mass transport and chemical reactions in agricultural porous media. It accounts for:

    a. heat generation within the product;
    b. transport of water from the product to the void space;
    c. heat transport from the product to the void space;
    d. evaporation of water from solid surfaces; and;
    e. the respiration chemical reaction.

Assumptions

1. The medium is isotropic.
2. The only significant chemical reaction taking place in the storage environment is that of respiration.
3. The walls of the storage volume are impermeable and behave as perfect insulators.
4. The only transported quantity of significance in the storage volume is water vapor.

System Entropy Production

Entropy production is treated as a global quantity in this study. The control volume must therefore enclose the entire storage volume. Being an open system, it exchanges both heat and mass with its environment. By assumption #3, the points of these exchanges are restricted to the entry and exit points of the ventilation air (Figure 1).

The total rate of entropy production can be represented as

479

$$\frac{\delta S_v}{\delta t} = -\bar{\nabla} \cdot \bar{J}_s + \sigma \tag{1}$$

where $\bar{J}_s$ is the vector representing the flux of entropy and σ represents the local production of entropy due to the occurrence of irreversible processes in the system. The production of entropy (rather than entropy flows into and out of the control volume) is the quantity of interest in this paper since it relates directly to the dissipation of energy.

This local production of entropy, derived from the basic relationship of irreversible thermodynamics (Ofoli, 1984) is

$$\sigma = \frac{L_{QQ}}{TL} - \frac{2L_{KQ}}{TL^2} \left(\frac{\tau_{rz}}{\rho} - RT \right) + \frac{L_{KK}}{TL} \left(\frac{\tau_{rz}}{\rho} - RT \right)^2 + \frac{J_{ch}A}{T}$$

$$\tag{2}$$

where T is the absolute temperature, L is a characteristic dimension, ρ is the density, A is the chemical affinity.

$$L_{KK} = \frac{h_D \rho}{gD} \tag{3}$$

$$L_{KQ} = \frac{D^T T_p}{D} \tag{4}$$

$$L_{QQ} = hT \tag{5}$$

and

$$J_{ch} = L_{ch}A \tag{6}$$

with h_D the mass transfer coefficient, ρ the air density, g the gravitational constant used here to provide dimensional homogeneity, D a characteristic dimension of the storage volume, D^T a modified thermal diffusion coefficient and h the heat transfer coefficient.

The shear stress, developed from the relations of Ergun (1962) and Bennett and Myers (1974) is

$$\tau_{rz} = \frac{f_p u_s^2 \, \rho}{6\epsilon^2} \tag{7}$$

where f_p is the friction coefficient, u_s is the superficial velocity, and ϵ is the porosity of the medium. The superficial velocity is defined as the velocity that would exist in the storage volume if it were empty.

With the above relationships, Eqn. 2 can be written as

$$\sigma = \frac{h}{L} - \frac{D_{AB}\rho R f_p u_s^2}{3DL\epsilon^2 T} + \frac{2D_{AB}R\rho}{DL} + \frac{h_D \rho f_p u_s^4}{36gDL\epsilon T}$$

$$- \frac{h_D\rho R f_p u_s^2}{gDL\epsilon^2} + \frac{h_D\rho R^2 T}{gDL} + \frac{h A}{T} \tag{8}$$

It is clear from Eqn 8 that σ is a function of both the velocity and the temperature, with the velocity being the dominant parameter. Under normal modes of cooling, most agricultural storages operate in a narrow range of temperatures, therefore, the variation of σ with temperature is limited. It is apparent, then, that the minimization of the rate of entropy production can be done most effectively through control of the air velocity which, for a given structure, implies the ventilation rate.

OPTIMIZATION BY MINIMIZING ENTROPY PRODUCTION

The rate of system entropy production provides a key parameter for system optimization. It is a measure of the rate at which system energy is made unavailable for useful work. If a process is designed in such a manner that it operates in a zone of a minimum entropy production, the system energy utilization would be most efficient.

The energy dissipation is defined as

$$\Gamma = \sigma T \tag{9}$$

One approach to optimization might be for one to equate the partial derivative of Eqn. 8 (with respect to the velocity) to zero and determine the velocity at which σ is a minimum. While this approach is mathematically appealing, it would be physically meaningless because it ignores the dependence of the temperature on the velocity, implying that the temperatures in the storage volume would remain constant over a range of ventilation rates. This is quite unlikely.

The optimization approach used here is based on the total dissipation of energy, given by

$$\phi = A_{ac} \int_t \int_V \Gamma \, dV \, dt \tag{10}$$

where ϕ is the total energy dissipated and A_{ac} is the total cross-sectional area of the system, assumed a constant.

482

Given Eqn. 9, the expression for σ in Eqn. 8 with the appropriate absolute temperature profile (obtained from heat and mass transfer relations) can be substituted in Eqn. 10. The resulting equation can be integrated over the volume of the bin and over a specified length of time to obtain the total system energy dissipation.

Now, define a dimensionless energy dissipation index (EDI), ξ, such that

$$\xi = \frac{\phi}{P_i A_{ac} u_i t} \tag{11}$$

where P_i is the internal pressure, A_{ac} is the cross-sectional area available for air flow, u_i is the interstitial velocity and t is the elapsed time. From a force balance, the internal pressure is related to the known external atmospheric pressure, P_a, by

$$P_i = \frac{P_a}{\varepsilon} \tag{12}$$

where ε is the porosity of the medium.

Equation 11 is the ratio of the energy dissipated through entropy production and the energy due to the motion of the ventilation air. This approach normalizes the energy dissipation function and thus allows direct comparisons to be made between different ventilation rates.

RESULTS AND DISCUSSIONS

Based on the experimental set-up of Misener (1973) for the ventilation of potatoes, Eqn. 11 was solved for four different inlet air temperature conditions. Three of the conditions are hypothetical. The four conditions used are inlet ventilation air temperatures of 3°C (37.4°F), 6.7°C (44.1°F) (the temperature of the ventilation air for Misener's data), 10°C (50°F) and a sinusoidal inlet temperature that satisfies the equation

$$\theta = 6.0 + 6.0 \sin \frac{\pi t}{12} \qquad (13)$$

where t is the elapsed time in hours. Eqn. 13 describes an inlet temperature oscillating between 0° C (32 ° F) and 12°C (53.6 °F), with a period of 24 hours.

Equation 11 was solved numerically with the temperature profile obtained from the heat and mass transfer relations developed by Ofoli and Burgess (1985). The results, for the four inlet temperature conditions listed above, are plotted in Figure 2. The optimum ventilation rate based on the energy dissipation index for Misener's (1973) experimental conditions is 22 m^3 $m^{-2} h^{-1}$(72.1 ft^3 ft^{-2} hr^{-1}). Given the size of the experimental storage volume and the high porosity this is an acceptable rate. The zone of optimum ventilation is, approximately, 20 to 25 m^3 m^{-2} h^{-1} (65.6 ft^3 ft^{-2} hr^{-1} to 81.9 ft^3 ft^{-2} hr^{-1}). The optimum ventilation rates for the 3° C (37.4°F), 10 °C (44.1° F) and sinusoidal conditions are 17, 28 and 22 m^3 m^{-2} h^{-1} (55.7, 91.8 and 72.1 ft^3 ft^{-2} hr^{-1}), respectively.

The fact that the EDI curve for the sinusoidal condition is essentially the same as the one for the 6.7 °C (44.1°F) entry condition is to be expected, since the mean temperature for the sinusoidal condition is 6°C (42.8°F). This is significant, however, because the result implies that the optimization procedure can be based on the mean temperature, thus avoiding the task of having to continuously vary the inlet air temperature during the computer runs.

The optimization procedure was also performed on a commercial processing potato storage facility, based on the data collected by Cargill and Price (1982-83). The results, for three temperature conditions, is plotted in Figure 3. The EDI profiles are essentially the same as those resulting from Misener's laboratory experiment, although the optimum ventilation rates (as would be expected) are much

higher. If the ventilation system is run on a continuous basis, the optimum rates are 150, 165 and 172
$m^3 m^{-2} hr^{-1}$ (491, 541 and 564 $ft^3 ft^{-2} hr^{-1}$) for 5, 10 and
15 °C (41,50 and 59°F), respectively.

These results strongly suggest that, from at
least a heat transfer point of view, the EDI can be
effectively used to optimize the ventilation rate.
It must be pointed out that these results are viewed
only from the point of view of energy dissipation.
Another important factor that must be considered is
the effect of the ventilation rate on product
quality. The quality factor, however, was not
considered in this paper because of the inherent
difficulties in characterizing "quality" mathematically.

The parameters used in the optimization program
are listed in Table 1.

CONCLUSIONS

A model for entropy production and energy
dissipation in the storage environment of
agricultural products has been presented and analyzed
using the principles of the thermodynamics of
irreversible processes. The model leads to a scheme
for optimizing the ventilation rate by minimizing
production of entropy in the system.

The optimization scheme is based on the energy
dissipation index (EDI), defined as the ratio of the
total energy dissipated by the system to the energy
due to the motion of the ventilation air. The
maximum efficiency occurs at the minimum value of the
EDI. Simulation results indicate that this parameter
may provide a useful tool for optimizing the
ventilation rate.

REFERENCES

Bejan, A. 1982. Entropy Generation Through Heat and
    Fluid Flow. John Wiley, New York.

Bennett, C.O. and J.E. Meyers. 1974. Momentum, Heat
    and Mass Transfer. McGraw-Hill, New York.

Briedis, D. 1981. Energy and entropy flows in living systems. Ph.D. thesis, Iowa State Univ., Ames, Iowa.

Brugger, M.F. 1979. A two-dimensional finite diffrence model of the transient enviornment within a potato pile. Ph.D. thesis, University of Wisconsin, Madison, Wisconsin.

Cargill, B.F. and K.C. Price. 1982-83. Michigan State University, East Lansing, Michigan. Personal communication on potato ventilation data.

Ergun, S. 1952. Fluid flow through packed columns. Chem. Engr. Progress, 48(2):89-94.

Fortes, M. and M.R. Okos. 1981a. A non-equilibrium thermodynamics approach to transport phenomena in capillary-porous media. Transactions of ASAE 24(3):756-760.

Fortes, M. and M.R. Okos. 1981b. Non-equilibrium thermodynamics approach to heat and mass transfer in corn kernels. Transactions of ASAE, 24(3):761-769.

Hunter, J.H. 1976. An engineering analysis and computer simulation of the potato in storage. Ph.D. thesis. University of Mass.

Lerew, L.E. and F.W. Bakker-Arkema. 1977. The effect of ventilation schemes on the storage of potatoes. ASAE Paper 77-3534.

Misener, G.C. 1973. Simulated cooling of potatoes. Ph.D. Thesis, University of Illinois, Champagne. Illinois.

Ofoli, R.Y. 1984. Entropy production by biological products in storage. Ph.D. thesis. Department of Agricultural Engineering, Michigan State University, East Lansing, Michigan.

Ofoli, R.Y. and G.J. Burgess. A thermodynamic approach to heat and mass transport in agricultural storage media. Submitted to J Food Engineering, April, 1985.

NOMENCLATURE

A	affinity of chemical reaction,	J/kg
A_T	total system cross-sectional area,	m^2
D	diameter of bin,	m
D_{AB}	binary diffusivity,	m^2/h
D^T	modified thermal diffusion coefficient,	$kg\ m^{-1}\ h^{-1}\ K^{-1}$
f_p	friction factor,	dimensionless
g	gravitational acceleration,	m/sec^2
h	heat transfer coefficient,	$J\ m^{-2}\ h^{-1}\ C^{-1}$
h_D	mass transfer coefficient,	m/h
J_{ch}	velocity of chemical reaction,	$kg\ h^{-1}\ m^{-3}$
J_s	entropy current flux,	$J\ m^{-2}\ h^{-1}\ K^{-1}$
L	characteristic length,	m
L_{ch}	phenomenological coeff. of chemical reaction,	$kg\ h\ m^{-5}$
L_{KK}	modified convective flux coefficient,	$kg\ h\ m^{-1}$
L_{KQ}	modified cross-kinetic coefficient,	$kg\ m^{-2}\ h^{-1}$
L_{QQ}	modified heat flux coefficient,	$J\ m^{-2}\ h^{-1}$
p	pressure,	$N\ m^{-2}$
R	universal gas constant,	$m^2\ h^{-2}\ K^{-1}$
S_v	entropy density,	$J\ m^{-3}\ K^{-1}$
t	time,	h
T	absolute temperature,	K
T_p	product temperature,	K
u_i	interstitial velocity,	m/h
u_s	superficial velocity,	m/h
V	volume of storage medium,	m^3

Greek Symbols

Γ	dissipation function,	$J\ m^{-3}\ h^{-1}$
δ	partial differential	
ϵ	porosity of the porous medium,	dimensionless
ξ	energy dissipation index,	dimensionless
ρ	density,	$kg\ m^{-3}$
σ	local volumetric entropy production,	$J\ m^{-3}\ hr^{-1}\ K^{-1}$
τ_{rz}	shear stress,	$kg\ m^{-1}\ hr^{-2}$
ϕ	total energy dissipation,	J

Table 1. Parameters used in optimization program

Initial storage temperature, C (F)	15.5 (57.9)	16.0 (60.8)
Outside air temperature, C (F)	6.7 (44.1)	5.0-15.0 (41-59)
Outside air relative humidity, %	60.0	80.0-95.0
Porosity of medium, dimensionless	0.64	0.4
Bulk density of potatoes, kg/m³ (16/ft³)	1085 (67.5)	1085 (67.5)
Initial potato moisture content, %	80	80
Bin capacity, 1000 kg. (cwt)	0.36 (7.92)	400.0 (8800)
Pile height, m (ft)	2.40 (7.88)	3.67 (12.0)

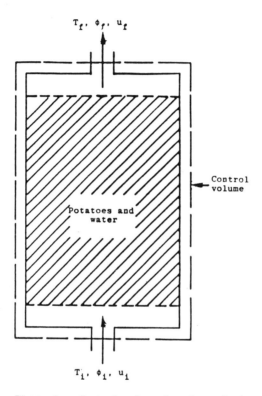

T_f, ϕ_f, u_f

Control
volume

Potatoes and
water

T_i, ϕ_i, u_i

Figure 1   Control volume for the analysis
of total entropy production (actual calculations
were based on twelve subdivisions of the above
control volume.)

489

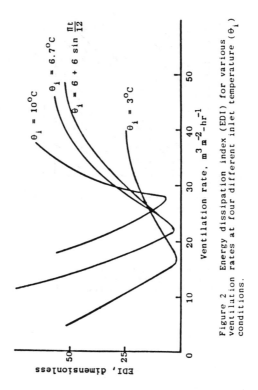

Figure 2   Energy dissipation index (EDI) for various ventilation rates at four different inlet temperature (θ_i) conditions.

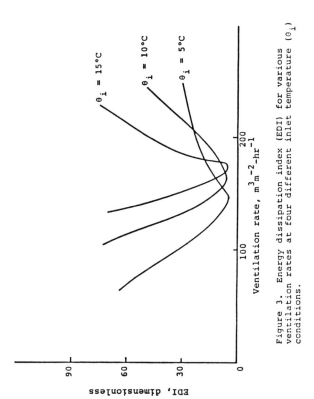

Figure 3. Energy dissipation index (EDI) for various ventilation rates at four different inlet temperature (θ_i) conditions.

491

V. STORAGE AND AIR HANDLING

Control of Temperature in Larger Storages for
    Process Potatoes in the Northwest –
    Nathan H. Gellert

Heat of Respiration and Weight Loss From
    Potatoes in Storage – James H. Hunter

Storage Management Influences Potato Quality
    in the Dutch Polders Region – Jan C.
    Hesen

Ventilation System Performance in Michigan Bulk
    Potato Storages – B.F. Cargill

Mathematical Expressions for Lateral Potato
    Pressures – L.A. Schaper

Carbon Dioxide and Wind Monitoring in the
    Commercial Potato Storage – J.L. Varns

Comparison of Potato Pile Pressures on Vertical
    and Inclined Walls – Earl C. Yaeger

CONTROL OF TEMPERATURE IN LARGER STORAGES
FOR PROCESS POTATOES IN THE NORTHWEST

by

Nathan H. Gellert, President, The Gellert Company,
Boise, Idaho

ABSTRACT

French fry processors require accuracy of $\pm.28°C$ ($\pm.05 °F$) in plenum temperature, but will accept higher temperature variance in the pile. Respondents were evenly divided on preference for differential temperature control vs. outdoor air sensing only. Operating programs vary widely, pointing to desirability of control systems with multiple operating modes.

ASAE Paper No. 85-4034

INTRODUCTION

Improvement in the quality of processed potatoes over the past ten years has been accompanied by a tightening of temperature tolerances in raw product storage facilities. Particularly in French-fry plants where fry color is a measure of acceptability of raw product, Field Department Managers have become insistent about the maintenance of specific storage temperatures and intolerant of wide deviations.

In a letter to a ventilation equipment supplier, the Raw Product Manager of a major northwest French-fry processing plant writes, "Controlling the temperature of the air going under the pile is the most important function of the air system..."

Control of temperature requires the transfer of heat in a precise manner from the potatoes to a a stream of cooler air (A). In order to insure that only cooler air can enter the pile, a device (B) for sensing the temperature of the outdoor air is required. This can be differential temperature control or an outdoor air control. Using cool air from out-of-doors and warmer air from the pile, an accurate temperature controller (C) signals a group of control motors (D) to operate dampers or louvers (E), blending the two air streams to hold a constant temperature in the supply air plenum.

A.   A cool stream of air ...

The temperature controller, that operates the louver in an atmospheric cooling system, has no way of knowing whether the outdoor air is cooler or warmer than the potatoes. Its sensor is in the supply air plenum. In fact, it is connected into the control circuit in such a way that it assumes that the outdoor air is always cooler. Therefore, another temperature control device must tell it otherwise.

B.   A device for sensing the temperature of the outdoor air...

This control may be a differential temperature control with sensors in the pile and out of doors, or a single-sensor control that senses only the outdoor temperature. The differential control or the outdoor air control gives to the main temperature controller the ability to operate the louvers when the outdoor air is cooler than the potato pile and takes away that ability when the outdoor air is warmer than the potato pile. It may also start and stop the fans, depending on the position of a selector switch on the control panel.

Most control systems in large processor storages in the northwest are equipped with solid-state differential temperature controls having two to four individually selectable indoor sensors, and one outdoor sensor. Contacts close when the outdoor temperature drops about $1.5\,°C$ $(2.7\,°\,F)$ below the temperature of the indoor sensor that has been selected for reference, and open when the outdoor temperature rises to within about $1\,°C$ $(1.8°\,F)$ of the temperature of the indoor sensor.

Indoor sensors are commonly mounted on the "potato side" of the plenum wall about five feet above the floor and can properly be referred to as "pile sensors."

Recently a decline in preference for the differential temperature control has been noticed. Responses from eight Storage Managers to question no. 1 in a recent questionnaire were evenly divided in their preference for differential control vs. the outdoor air control. Therefore it seems worthwhile to list some of the claimed advantages of and objections to each.

ADVANTAGES OF THE DIFFERENTIAL TEMPERATURE CONTROL

1. No manual adjustment is required.

2. The maximum available hours of cooling can be utilized because of the constant sensing of piling temperature and outdoor air temperature.

3. Outdoor air that is warmer than pile temperature is automatically excluded.

OBJECTIONS TO THE DIFFERENTIAL TEMPERATURE CONTROL

1. The human operator has no control over the decision whether to admit outdoor air of a particular temperature.

2. The indoor sensors may not be at locations that sense the coolest part of the pile, and therefore may permit the entry of air that is warmer than the coolest potatoes.

3. Because calibration of the control requires the use of special instruments, the control is not always accurate, and may either admit undesirable warm air, or may exclude air that is cool enough to be used.

4. Even though the indoor sensors are firmly mounted, they can be torn loose, and depending on the nature of the differential control, a loose wire on an indoor sensor will either permit the entry of outdoor air, no matter how warm, or will exclude all outdoor air.

ADVANTAGES OF THE OUTDOOR AIR CONTROL

1. The human operator makes the decision what temperature air is to be admitted or excluded. (Whether this is an advantage or a disadvantage depends on one's confidence in the human operator.)

2. Calibration of the control is simple. Its set point is merely checked with a test thermometer.

3. The control can be set several degrees lower than the temperature, thus limiting the ratio of outdoor air to indoor air in the air supply, and raising the humidity of the air in the supply plenum.

4. The control can be set at a temperature that is very close to the pile temperature, thus utilizing the maximum number of cooling hours that are available.

OBJECTIONS TO THE OUTDOOR AIR CONTROL

1. The control can easily be set higher than the
    pile temperature, thus risking the warming of
    potatoes that have already been cooled.

2. Daily monitoring and frequent readjustment of
    the control are required in the fall as the
    pile is gradually cooled. Failure to readjust
    will result in repeated cooling and reheating
    of the pile.

3. In the absence of refrigeration, the control
    must be closely monitored and readjusted in
    the spring, for as pile temperatures
    increase, failure to increase the setting on
    the Outdoor Air Control will deprive the
    storage of much needed cool air.

C. An accurate temperature controller...

Responses from Storage Managers to question no. 2
in the previously mentioned questionnaire show a
strong preference for temperature controllers
that can maintain supply air temperature within
$\pm.28$ °C ($\pm 1/2$ °F). This close tolerance can be
achieved by solid-state industrial temperature
controllers having both proportional and reset
functions.

The proportional band is that number of degrees
that the temperature must change in order for the
controller to drive the louver motors from their
counterclockwise limit to their clockwise limit.
For example, if the calibration point of a
controller is the temperature which just barely
causes the fresh air inlet louvers to open, the
proportional band is the number of degrees that
the temperature must rise in order for the
controller to open the fresh air inlet louvers
fully.

A popular model of a 135 ohm electro-mechanical
temperature controller has a minimum
proportioning band of 1.7 ° C (3 °F). This
controller has no reset function and therefore
can suffer an offset as much as 1.7 °C (3°F) if it

is required to drive the fresh air inlet louvers to the wide open position to satisfy its temperature setting.

The reset function in an industrial temperature controller is a circuit which senses temperature deviation from set point and automatically decreases it to near zero. For example, if the proportional band of a controller lacking the reset function is, say 4°C, and the fresh air louver motor has settled at the half-stroke position, the supply air temperature will have risen 2 above setting, (half the proportional band). A controller having a reset circuit would be aware of this offset, and in a series of timed impulses, would open the fresh air inlet louvers sufficiently to bring the supply air temperature down to within .28°C (.5°F) of the set-point, or even closer.

Input Signals

The temperature signal to a 135 ohm electro-mechanical temperature controller is hydraulic pressure in a bulb-and-capillary system. We will not refer to this type of controller in the discussion to follow.

In the industrial, solid-state temperature controller the input signal is one of the following: millivolts from a thermocouple, change in resistance in a wire-wound sensor, or change in resistance in a thermister.

All three types of sensors may be found in control systems in the northwest, but the wire-wound sensor and the thermister dominate.

Output Signals

Output from earlier models of temperature controllers was "position-proportioning," utilizing two relays and a null position to cause the louver motors to move clockwise, counter-clockwise or to remain at rest. Later control systems have temperature controllers with "current output." These generate a 4 to 20 milliampere signal in a direct ratio to an increase in the cooling requirement.

500

Evaporative Cooling Effect

Controlling the temperature of the air going under the pile is the job of the temperature controller, whose sensor is in the air supply plenum, but the humidifier may affect the temperature of the air in the plenum in a manner beyond the influence of the temperature controller.

Installation instructions for potato storage ventilation equipment specify that the sensor for the main temperature controller be located in the plenum DOWNSTREAM of any humidification equipment. This is required so that the evaporative cooling effect of the humidifier will be felt by the main control sensor. If the sensor is placed upstream of the humidifier, it will be dry, and the air temperture in the plenum will be lower than the controller setting whenever the relative humidity of the air passing the sensor is lower than 100 percent. On the other hand, when the sensor is downstream of a fog-type humidifier, it remains wet. If the wet-bulb effect on the sensor is not the same as the wet bulb effect on the air stream, the controller will be inaccurate to the extent of that difference. In the northwest, this inaccuracy may be noticed soon after harvest, when large amounts of dry outdoor air are required for cooling. The effect fortunately diminishes as the pile temperature drops, as less outdoor air is taken in and the humidity of the supply air approaches 100 percent.

In ventilation systems with air washers, or cell-type air coolers, such as are widely used in eastern Washington and northeastern Oregon, inaccuracies due to operation of humidification equipment are not encountered, since air leaves the evaporative coolers carrying no visible fog.

It can easily be deduced that the practice of some installers of spotting fog nozzles at intervals along the length of the air plenum would confuse the temperature controller, since it would have no way of knowing the evaporative

501

effect of the nozzles at any point downstream of
its sensor. Fortunately, this arrangement is not
popular in large processor storages in the
northwest.

D. A group of control motors...

The signal from the temperature controller is
accepted by one or more of the louver control
motors. If the circuit is designated so that one
motor accepts the 4-20 mA signal, the control
panel may contain a "manual-automatic" louver
switch and a louver-positioning potentiometer for
operating the louver motors manually, if desired.
In these systems, the louver motor accepting the
signal retransmits its position to the other
motors in the group by means of an electro-
mechanical circuit.

Alternately, the 4-20 mA signal can be made to
travel through all of the louver motors in
series. Manual louver-positioning potentiometers
are usually not found in control circuits of this
type.

E. To operate dampers or louvers...

Processor storages in the northwest are large.
Single bins or zones of 6,000 metric tons (6,600
tons) are not uncommon; and they require large
air flows: 35 to 52 M^3/sec. (75,000 to 110,000
CFM) or more.

All currently-supplied potato storage ventilation
systems in the northwest (of which the writer is
aware) are capable of taking 100 percent of their
fan capacity as outdoor fresh air. Therefore,
the fresh air inlet louvers and the exhaust
dampers, as well as the return air louvers, must
be large enough to pass the full capacity of the
fans with a reasonable pressure drop. Typical
louver and damper areas for a 47 M^3/sec. (100,000
CFM) air system are as follows:

	M^2	Sq. Ft.	Number of Sections
Fresh air inlet louvers	7.2	77	6
Return air louvers	6.6	71	6
Exhaust dampers	7.4	80	8

502

The motor-driven fresh air and return air louvers, sized for 100 percent of the fan capacity, are oversized for the normal winter cooling load. Oversized louvers, like oversized valves, are difficult to control at low rates of flow. There is a tendency for the louver or valve to open slightly at the command of the temperature controller, then correct by going fully closed. In other words, modulating control is hard to achieve when even a little cold air is too much.

This problem was observed and corrected as many as 20 years ago in processor storages in Idaho. As currently practiced by at least two of the ventilation system suppliers in the northwest, the correction consists of splitting the linkage of the fresh air inlet louver so that the upper one-third of the blades are separately controlled. The main temperature controller's signal is first felt by the motors serving the upper section of the fresh air inlet louver and the return air louver. If the controller is satisfied with a partial opening of the fresh air inlet louver and a partial pinch back of the return air louver, no further action takes place. However, if more outdoor air is required to satisfy the controller, its heavier signal is sent directly or indirectly, to the motor serving the lower section of the fresh air inlet louver, which can open fully if required. A full opening of the upper and lower sections of the fresh air inlet louver is accompanied by complete closure of the return air louver.

In addition, to the sequential opening of the fresh air inlet louvers just described, some control systems have a switching circuit that can be manually operated to hold the lower section of the fresh air inlet louver closed, regardless of the strengh of the signal from the temperature controller.

PLENUM DESIGN

The main temperature controller, with its sensor in the plenum, can control the temperature of the air at one point. Beyond that point, if the air

503

temperature should rise or fall, there is nothing that even the most accurate temperature controller can do about it.

A typical large storage building in the northwest might have a center plenum with a catwalk on top. This plenum will neither gain or lose heat once the pile is brought to a uniform temperature. The air temperature can be expected to remain constant throughout the length of the plenum. There are, however, many large storages with side-wall plenums. These plenums can be expected to lose heat in cold weather and gain heat in warm weather, thus decreasing or increasing the temperature of the air that was carefully controlled as it entered the plenum. The amount of change in temperature is affected, of course, not only by the difference in temperature between the plenum and the out-of-doors, but also by the length of the plenum and the value of the insulation material in its exposed wall.

PILE TEMPERATURE VARIANCE

Question no. 2 in the questionnaire asked the respondent to check a box corresponding to the acceptable deviation of plenum temperature from set point of the main temperature controller. Most of the eight who responded checked the 1/2°F box (.28° C). Question no. 3 then asked the respondent to fill in the number of degrees F that represented the maximum difference in temperature that he would consider acceptable between the bottom and top of the pile of potatoes. One respondent wrote in "1/2 ° F" (.28°C). Other responses ranged upward to as high as 3°F (1.67°C).

Assuming proper air distribution system design, differences in temperature between the bottom and top of the potato pile are the result of the following factors:

1. Air flow per unit mass of potatoes

2. Height of the pile

3. Running time of the ventilation equipment

and, while the potatoes are being cooled after harvest

504

4.   The rate at which the temperature of the
      pile is lowered.

AIR FLOW RATE

Air flow rate is a function of the original
design of the ventilation system. Air flow rates in
processor storages are generally in the range of 24-
32 M /hr./ton (13-17 CFM per ton) depending on their
geographical location. Obviously, the higher the
air flow rate, other things being equal, the lower
the difference in temperature between the bottom and
top of the pile.

HEIGHT OF THE PILE

Pile heights range from 5.5 to 7.3 M (18 to 24
ft.). The height of the pile is determined by the
height of the building and the policy of the
processor, so this factor, though it affects the
temperature difference between the bottom and top of
the pile, is not susceptible to changes in the field.

RUNNING TIME

Running time accounts for the differences in top
to bottom pile temperatures among the various
processors in the northwest. Question no. 4 of the
Survey form asked the Storage Managers how they
preferred to operate their fans at various times in
the storage season. Taking the winter season as the
time when pile temperatures are the most uniform, our
survey found that, in general, processors who keep
the minimum temperature difference also run their
fans the longest. Following is a sample of their
responses:

Respondent	Maximum Difference in Temperature Permitted after Pile has been brought to "Storage Temperature"		Preferred Fan Operation (See Appendix i)	
	°F	°C		
I	½	.28	F,G	Continuous
III	1	.55	A	Whenever cooling air is available
V	1½	.83	C	On the timer, whether cooling air is available or not. Use refrigeration when cooling air is not available.
VII	3	1.67	B	On the timer, but only when cooling air is available.

THE RATE OF LOWERING OF THE PILE TEMPERATURE AFTER HARVEST

Potato processors in the northwest are sensitive to the necessity of lowering pile temperatures very slowly after harvest. Nevertheless, when cooling a pile of warm potatoes, those at the bottom of the pile will give up their heat first. Those near the top must wait. The gradual lowering of plenum air temperature over the first several weeks of the storage season keeps the pile temperature difference within the desired range.

AIR DISTRIBUTION DESIGN

Finally, uniformity of temperature throughout the pile, whether from top to bottom, from end to end, or from side to side, depends on air distribution system design. Duct spacing, previously standardized at 3M (10 ft.) has gradually been supplanted by 2.43M (8 ft.) spacing, partially as a result of higher air flows and wider bins, but also as a means of minimizing the size of the "dead triangle" which may exist between the ducts from the floor upward several feet. The proper duct outlet area is extremely important. There have been several

506

instances of improper punching of duct holes in large storages in the northwest, resulting in uneven temperatures in the pile, and requiring running times longer than would have been necessary otherwise.

SUMMARY

Seven of eight Storage Managers responding to a questionnaire require plenum temperature accuracy within $\pm.28$ °C (1/2 °F) of control setting. This is achievable with industrial solid-state temperature controllers having proportional and reset functions.

Half of the respondents do not want the temperature of the warmest potatoes to exceed the temperature of the coldest potatoes in storage by more than .56 °C (1 °F) once the pile has been brought to the desired storage temperature.

Storage Managers are evenly divided on the benefits of the automatic differential temperature control vs. the semi-automatic outdoor air control.

Suppliers of automatic ventilation systems are well advised to continue to offer multi-mode control panels, since there is a wide diversity of practice in the operation of these systems among Storage Managers in the northwest. Furthermore, operation of ventilation systems by storage operators corresponds only lightly to typical operating instructions published by the suppliers of the equipment. (See appendix i, question no. 4.

Respondent	QUESTION NO. 1 Preference for differential temperature control (DTC) or outdoor air control (OAC)		QUESTION NO. 2 Plenum temperature acceptable deviation from setpoint	QUESTION NO. 3 Maximum temperature difference in pile permitted after pile has been brought to storage temperature	QUESTION NO. 4 Preferred operation (SEE LETTER REFERENCES)			
	DTC	OAC			FALL	WINTER	SPRING	SUMMER
I		X	±.28°C (±½°F)	.28°C (½°F)	B	F,G	B	B
II	X		±.28°C (±½°F)	.42°C (3/4°F)	A,C,D	A,B	A	A,G
III		X	±.28°C (±½°F)	.56°C (1°F)	A	A	A,E	A,E
IV	X		±.14°C (±¼°F)	.56°C (1°F)	A	A	A	A
V	X		±.14°C (±¼°F)	.83°C (1½°F)	A	C	E	E
VI	X		+.56°C (+1°F)	1.11°C (2°F)	A,B,E	C,E	A,B,E	A,B,E
VII		X	±.28°C (±½°F)	1.67°C (3°F)	A	B	B	A,E
VIII		X	±.28°C (±½°F)	1.67°C (3°F)	D	C	A	A,E

Letter references pertaining to QUESTION NO. 4

A. Whenever cooling air is available

B. On a timer but only when cooling air is available

C. On a timer, whether cooling air is available or not

D. Whenever cooling air is available, plus a daily timed run whether cooling air is available or not

E. On a timer, with refrigeration

F. Continuously without refrigeration

G. Continuously with refrigeration

QUESTION NO. 4

Typical operating instruction, equipment supplier's manual

FALL	WINTER	SPRING	SUMMER
A,G	B,F	D,E	E

RESPONSES FROM 8 STORAGE MANAGERS

SURVEY FORM for "CONTROL OF TEMPERATURE IN LARGE STORAGES FOR PROCESS POTATOES IN THE NORTHWEST"

1. Most control systems in potato storage buildings incorporate a solid state differential temperature control which simultaneously senses indoor (pile) temperature and outdoor temperature. This control excludes outdoor air that is warmer than the indoor sensor.

   Recently, some otherwise sophisticated control panels have been built in which the differential temperature control is replaced by a manually adjustable outdoor air control. This control excludes outdoor air that is warmer than its setting. Which control do you prefer?

   The differential temperature control . . [4]

   The outdoor air control . . . . [4]

2. A temperature controller in your control panel operates fresh-air and return-air louvers to hold a "constant" temperature in the air plenum. What deviation from set-point is acceptable on a hour-to-hour, day-to-day basis, (ignoring short periods of offset such as may occur when fans start)? (Please check one box.)

±.14°C	±¼°F	[2]		+1½°F	[ ]
±.28°C	±½°F	[5]		+2°F	[ ]
+.56°C	+1°F	[1]		+3°F	[ ]

3. What is the maximum difference in temperature that you aim to hold in your storages, bottom to top of pile, after the pile has been brought to "storage temperature"?

Temperature °C	.28°	.42°	.56°	.83°	1.11°	1.67°
°F	¼°	3/4°	1°	1½°	2°	3°
Number of Respondents	1	1	2	1	1	2

(continued)

509

4. In the management of your storages, how do you prefer to operate the fans? (Check only those boxes which apply).

	SEASON			
	Fall	Winter	Spring	Summer
A. Whenever cooling air is available	[6]	[3]	[5]	[6]
B. On a timer but only when cooling air is available	[2]	[1]	[3]	[2]
C. On a timer, whether cooling air is available or not	[1]	[3]	[ ]	[ ]
D. Whenever cooling air is available, plus a daily timed run whether cooling air is available or not	[2]	[ ]	[ ]	[ ]
E. On a timer, with refrigeration	[1]	[1]	[3]	[5]
F. Continuously without refrigeration	[ ]	[1]	[ ]	[ ]
G. Continuously with refrigeration	[ ]	[1]	[ ]	[1]
TOTAL RESPONSES	12	10	11	14
TOTAL RESPONDENTS	8	8	8	8

510

HEAT OF RESPIRATION AND WEIGHT LOSS FROM POTATOES IN STORAGE

by

James H. Hunter, Associate Professor of Agricultural
Engineering, University of Maine at Orono,Maine
Agricultural Experiment Station, Presque Isle,
Maine

ABSTRACT

Weight losses and respiration rates were
measured for potatoes of several varieties, mature
and immature and sprout inhibited and non-sprout
inhibited, over a period of several years. Data were
fitted to exponential type curves. Results are
presented in both graphic and tabular form. Methods
of estimating respiration and weight loss rates are
presented as well as suggestions for minimizing
losses in storage.

ASAE Paper No. 85-4035

511

INTRODUCTION

For the four most recent years for which statistics are available (1980-83) the fall potato crop in the United States has had a production of about 13.2 million metric tons with a value of about 1.4 billion dollars (Anonymous, 1983). Most of the fall crop is placed in storage and marketed throughout the fall, winter, spring and sometimes summer seasons. Evaporative weight losses are in the order of 3-10 percent of the harvested weight (Sparks and Summers, 1974). The amount of loss in a particular case depends on variety, maturity, storage conditions and time in storage. Minimizing losses however, offers the potential for savings in the order of 6-7 percent or in value, about 91 million dollars to the producers. Further, portions of the crop may be rendered unsalable due to pressure flattening, sprouting or other storage related disorders.

Respiration rates and evaporative loss rates are important in considering the design and management of potato storages. The rate of respiratory heat production at various times of the storage season must be known in order to determine the level of insulation and the rate of air circulation required. As will be shown in further detail, the rate of respiration and the rate of evaporative weight loss are inter-related. Moreover, the rate of evaporative loss determines what portion of the respiratory heat which is produced is available as sensible heat to offset the conductive and convective heat losses from a storage building. Heat which is lost to the evaporative process is subsequently available only if condensation takes place (Hunter, 1983). Condensation is usually most undesirable, especially on ceiling surfaces, since dripping which often occurs may result in soft rot infection and subsequent wet breakdown of stored tubers. Often large portions of bins break down as a result.

EQUIPMENT AND METHODS

Weight losses were determined on a weekly basis using the type of apparatus shown in Figure 1. Each sample consisted of approximately 11.4 kg of potatoes placed in trays fabricated of expanded steel mesh.

Four samples of each treatment were used. The
apparatus was placed in refrigerated compartments at
temperatures of 3.33 ° C, 7.22 °C and 10.0°C or 12.77
° C. These temperatures correspond respectively to
the usual seed and table stock temperature, the
normal par-fry (partially cooked french fries)
temperature or the temperatures normally used for
holding chip stock.

The refrigerated compartments were humidified to
levels of 93-95 percent RH. Air was supplied at a
velocity rate of 15 meters per minute.

Respiration rates were determined by the method
of carbon dioxide evolution using an MSA LIRA carbon
dioxide analyzer. The apparatus is shown in Figures
2 and 3. Potatoes were held and tested in glass jars
of 3.785 liter liquid capacity holding about 2 kg of
tubers. Testing was done weekly or monthly as
required. Samples were held in the refrigerated
compartments mentioned above at temperatures
corresponding to those used for weight loss studies.

When the studies were begun in 1973, two
varieties: Russet Burbank and Kennebec were used.
These were tested at two maturity levels: mature and
immature. "Mature" treatments were produced by the
use of chemical vine killers applied 2-3 weeks prior
to harvest. "Immature" treatments were harvested
without artificial vine kill. Also, treatments were
further subdivided by "sprout inhibited" or "non-
sprout inhibited." Foliar application of Maleic
Hydrazide (MH 30) was used for sprout inhibition.
When these series of studies were completed (1976)
another series of studies were begun using newly
named varieties and advanced selections from the
Maine Potato Breeding Program compared with standard
varieties. Data from the earlier study and from the
last two seasons (1983-84 and 1984-85) of the later
study are presented.

RESPIRATION AND WEIGHT LOSS - THE INTER-RELATIONSHIP

Potato tubers stored in large piles are almost
totally cooled by transfer of sensible and
respiratory heat to the surrounding air in the
interstitial spaces. Respiratory heat is transferred

513

to the air by either of two means. It may either cause the air temperature to rise (sensible heat) or it may result in the evaporation of water from stored tubers (latent heat).

If a large vapor pressure deficit (VPD) exists, the transfer will be mainly in the form of latent heat. If the VPD is small (i.e. the relative humidity of 97-98%) heat transfer will take place in proportion to the ratio of sensible to latent heat at the temperature specified. Thus for these conditions, at any given respiration rate there is a corresponding evaporative weight loss rate as shown in Table I (Hunter, 1983).

The concept of "critical" relative humidity is illustrated in Figure 3 and 4. Figure 3 shows the effect of air velocity on weight loss rates at various relative humidity levels. Note that under these conditions of heat generation rate and skin permeability, there is essentially no velocity effect at 97.8 percent R.H. At higher humidity levels, lower losses occur at high velocity levels. Figure 4 shows those concepts in another way. In this case, the critical relative humidity value (97.8%) is that at which the relative humidity tends to stabilize as air moves through a bin. As discussed in a previous paper, (Hunter, 1983) the actual value of the critical relative humidity level is a function of the heat generation and skin permeability factor.

This would lead to the conclusion that weight loss rate is a function of respiration of rate, provided that high input relative humidity is used. That this is the case is shown by experimental data in several ways. First, minimum measured weight loss rates are found to be in the order of .08 to .10 percent per week regardless of ambient relative humidity or air flow rate. These loss rates correspond to heat production values of about 6.5 to 8.0 watts per metric ton (1-1.25 BTU per cwt hour). These are the estimated values for heat production based on measured carbon dioxide evolution. Secondly, as will be noted from experimental results presented later, the shape of respiration and weight loss rate curves is very similar.

RESULTS

A sample of raw weight loss data is shown in Figure 5. Raw respiration data is shown in Figure 6. It can be noted that these data, especially the weight loss data have the form for a curve of rate = $Ae^{-KT}+C$ in the falling rate period. It was found that these data can be fitted to such a curve with only small errors. Totals for a time period can be found by integration and are found to be: $A/K(1-e^{-KT})+CT$ For the rising period (after dormancy ends), rate = $A(e^{KT}-1)+C$ and total $=A/K(e^{KT}-1)+CT$. This results in a rate of C at time T = 0 and a total of 0 at T = 0.

It can be noted in Figure 6 that respiration rates at 3.33 and 7.22°C do not drop steadily, but in several steps initially, with periods of rebound, especially at 33.33 ℃. The initial drop apparently is a chemical rate effect induced by temperature. However, under stress, living tubers apparently react with an increased respiration rate as would an animal under similar stress.

Figure 7 to 26 represent composits of two years data for respiration and weight loss. (The weight loss data are all presented on the basis of 1 mm Hg vapor pressure deficit.) Figures 7 to 11 compare respiration levels for two pre-storage treatments and two varieties. In Figure 7 note that respiration at 3.33 ° C falls and rises the most slowly. At 7.22 ° C the values are intermediate and at 12.8°C the rates of decrease and the subsequent rise are most rapid. Figure 8 shows the same variety, Kennebec, with no sprout inhibitor used. Note that at 12.8 dormancy is ended early, and that following the end of dormancy, the rise in respiration is much more rapid than when sprout inhibitor was used. The effect at 7.22 ℃ is not as pronounced.

In Figure 9 and 10 results for the variety Russet Burbank are shown. Figure 9 shows data for stock treatment with sprout inhibitor and Figure 10 without sprout inhibitor. The values in Figure 9 for temperatures 7.22 and 12.8°C are somewhat lower than for the Kennebec (Figure 7). In Figure 10 it can be seen that although dormancy is broken earlier at 7.22 than at 3.33 °C (140 days versus 175 days), the respiration rate is lower at 7.22 during the entire storage period. This is a consequence of the fact that the Russet Burbank, unlike most varieties, will not break dormancy or sprout early when stored at 7.22°C (45°F). It has a dormant period of 140–175 days at 7.22°C compared to about 98–112 days for most round whites.

Data for the means of several round white varieties for the seasons 1983–84 and 1984–85 are shown in Figure 11. Initial rates are somewhat higher than in the previous figures, reflecting relative immaturity for the year 1984, the result of a late season drought. Domancy was broken at 16 weeks at 7.22°C and at 12 weeks at 10°C. However, rates of rise for the two temperatures are similar. Similar data for the variety Russet Burbank are shown in Figure 12. Note again the longer dormant period at 7.22 ° C (45°F) and the lower respiration rate at 7.22 C. Figure 13 shows data for the newly released variety, Gold Rus. Note the early end of dormancy and rapid increase in respiration at 10 °C.

Three types of potatoes are compared for respiration at the three storage temperatures in Figure 14–16 at 3.33°C. Gold Rus shows a lower respiration rate much of the season at 3.33° C (Figure 14). Although Gold Rus shows an earlier more rapid drop in respiration than does Russet Burbank at 7.22 °C, it breaks dormancy earlier (112 days versus 175 days), rising then essentially at the same rate as the round whites (Figure 15). Figure 16 shows the relatively greater tolerance of the 10°C temperature by the Russet Brubank with 147 days of dormancy as compared to 84 days for round whites and 49 days for the Gold Rus.

Weight loss rates for mature Kennebecs treated with sprout inhibitor are shown in Figure 17. Figure 18 shows immature Kennebecs with sprout inhibitor. Figures 19 and 20 show the data for Russet Burbank with the same treatments. Total losses for the 36 week season are less in each case for the "immature" tubers, those from vines not sprayed with vine killer. This would indicate that in both varieties, these potatoes from vines which matured naturally were actually more physiologically mature. This observation is also borne out by comparison of the respective initial rates and the "constant" rates.

Weight loss rates for round whites at 3.33, 7.22
and 10°C are shown in Figure 21.   The lowest weight
loss is shown to be at 7.22 °C until dormancy is
broken at 112 days.   The initial loss rate is higher
at 10°C but declines more rapidly until dormancy is
broken at 84 days. Data for Russet Burbank are shown
in Figure 22.   These again refect the ability of this
variety to tolerate a storage temperature of 7.22 ° C
with a rising rate of loss shown only after 168 days
and the lowest rate produced at that temperature
until the end of dormancy.   Figure 23 shows losses
for the variety Gold Rus and reflects a rate nearly
double that of most round white varieties, and more
than double that of Russet Burbank.

Weight loss comparisons of varieties at the
same temperatures are made in Figure 24 to 26.
Figure 24 shows that the round whites and Russet
Burbank do not differ much at 3.33° C but the rate for
Gold Rus is much higher.   At 7.22° C (Figure 25), the
rate for Russet Burbank is lower during the later
part of the season and dormancy lasts much longer
than for round whites (168 days versus 112 days).
Gold Rus again has a much higher rate and breaks
dormancy about two weeks earlier than round whites.
Dormancy for the Russet Burbank also lasts longer at
10°C (Figure 26).   The rate of weight loss increase
after break of dormancy is also less, reflecting a
slower rate of sprout growth.   Table II and III list
the values used in plotting the curves of Figures 7
to 16.   Tables IV and V list the values for Figures
17 to 26.

DISCUSSION

Weight loss in potatoes is not entirely the
result of evaporative water loss.   A portion of the
loss is a direct dry matter loss resulting from the
loss of carbon in carbon dioxide in respiration of
carbohydrate.   For example, on a seasonal basis the
total carbon dioxide loss can be calculated from the
rate equation by integration.   Using the prediction
equation for round whites stored at 33.3 ° C, the
seasonal loss of carbon dioxide is 17.576 grams per
kilogram of fresh weight.   However, the oxygen in the
carbon dioxide is balanced by intake of atmospheric
oxygen.   Thus only carbon is actually lost in the
respiration process.   The actual weight loss is only

517

12/44 (the ratio of the atomic weight of carbon to the molecular weight of CO_2 x 17.576 or 4.793 grams per Kg of fresh weight or 0.48 on a percentage basis. This is approximately 4.65 percent of the total predicted weight loss of 10.535 percent for a 36-week storage season. The loss of the original dry matter would be in the order of 1.17 percent, provided that the original dry matter percentage was about 20.0 by weight.

Since the data for weight loss in Figures 17-26 are presented on the basis of a 1.0 mm Hg VPD, the actual weight loss rates and the total seasonal losses would be less at higher humidities or lower VPD values. For example the rates at 95 percent RH would be adjusted as follows:

For temperature = 3.33°C, VPD = 5%/17.17% = 2.91 mm Hg. From (Hunter, 1976) the adjusted weight loss = sqrt (VPD) x loss at 1.0 mm Hg. or loss = loss at 1 mm Hg x sqrt (.291) = .5394 x 1 mm Hg loss.

Values for the adjustment for various temperatures are as follows:

     3.33°C - .5395
     7.22°C - .6175
    10.0 °C - .6784
   12.78°C - .7439

(Weight loss is not directly proportional to the existing VPD but is more nearly proportional to (VPD) to the nth power, where n = 0.4-0.6).

Energy released by respiration is approximately 2.55 Kilocalories per gram of carbon dioxide produced (Burton, 1948). This translates to about 2.959 watts per metric ton per mg per Kg hour of carbon dioxide production or about 0.46 BTU per cwt hour.

The data for weight loss represents values for tubers directly exposed to air and not for tubers stored on a bulk basis. In the case of bulk storage, the effects of pile depth, air velocity and heat rate on relative humidity must be accounted for (see Figures 3 and 4). In general relative humidity will tend to increase with bin depth.

The values for A, K and C were originally found by curve fitting by the method of least squares. The data were first linearized and the best fit value of the constant, C was determined by trial and error using a simple computer program. Theoretically there should be one exact curve which best fits the data. In the case of weight loss, this is somewhat simplified, since an accumulated value for weight loss is available. The curves are fitted in two parts, first for the falling rate period and then for the rising rate period. The first period is assumed to end when the lowest rate of weight loss is measured. This minimum value is also assumed to be the "C" value or constant. The initial rate for time = zero is assumed to be the "A" value for the falling rate period. The total weight loss for the falling rate period is $A/K (1-e^{-KT})$ + CT. All values except K are known, so K can be computed directly.

Similarly, for the rising rate period, the total loss is equal to $A/K (e^{KT}-1)$ +CT and the rate is equal to $A(e^{KT}-1)$+C after time, T. A and K are two unknowns with two equations, thus:

$$K = (rate-C)/(loss-CT)$$

$$\text{and } A = (rate-C)/e^{KT}-1$$

A problem may arise if the value of (e^{-KT}) does not approach zero in the rising rate period. In this case the values of A and C must be adjusted so that the value of C for the rising period is equal to $A(e^{-KT})$+C for the falling rate period at time, T.

Similar computations can be done for respiration data. In that case, however, some method of estimating the total respiration must be used. Curve fitting and integration can be used for this purpose or it can be assumed that the rate measured at any time is the mean rate for the period represented, such as one week, two weeks or a month. The total values are then computed and summed for the falling rate periods in question.

The value, K, reflects the rate of fall or rise of the exponential curve and is also the slope of the line for the linearized data (log values). Since A/K = total variable loss for the complete curve in the falling rate period, and $A/K (e^{KT}-1)$ +CT = total loss for the rising rate period, then:

K = initial rate/total loss (falling rate
    period

and K = final rate/total loss (rising rate
      period

CONCLUSIONS

1. Respiration rate in storage is determined by variety, maturity, preharvest treatment such as damage, disease, sprout inhibitor, curing regimen and storage temperature. The direct effect of temperature on respiration in potatoes is of relatively short duration (7-10 days). In general, respiration rate decline is more rapid at higher temperatures during the falling rate period and rate increase more rapid during the rising rate period after the end of dominancy. On a longer term basis, respiration is often minimized at 7.22 °C (45 °F).

2. Respiration rate determines weight loss rate to a large extent, especially at high ambient relative humidity levels or low vapor pressure deficit.

3. Maturity is indicated by both respiration rate and initial weight loss rate at time of harvest.

4. Both respiration and weight loss rate can be expressed by exponential type curves. For the falling rate period the rate is:

$$A(e^{-KT})+C$$

For the rising rate period the rate is: $A(e^{KT-1})+C$

5. Weight loss rates are determined by variety, preharvest treatment, curing regimen, storage temperature and vapor pressure deficit in the storage. Loss rates are high early in the season, drop off to a fairly low level and then increase after the break of dormancy. Weight loss is especially rapid after serious sprouting develops.

6. The effect of vapor pressure deficit on weight loss is not in direct proportion to the level of VPD. At higher levels of VPD, liquid diffusion

within the tuber apparently becomes a factor. In general, the effect is proportional to (VPD) to the nth power. In this case "n" may vary from 0.4-0.6.

   7. If tubers are mature at harvest, well cured and kept at high relative humidity levels, it should be possible to retain weight loss levels to the range of 3.0 to 4.0 percent for a storage period of 180 days for most varieties. The initial rate might be in the order of 0.5 percent per week dropping rapidly to 0.08 to 0.10 percent per week.

   8. A respiration rate of four mg per kg hour of carbon dioxide at time of harvest indicates relatively mature tubers. This rate is found by mid September in most early and medium maturing varieties under Main conditions. Late varieties such as Russet Burbank are not mature until about September 30 or later. The time of maximum maturity varies from year to year and depends on growing conditions and soil temperature and moisture conditions which exist as harvest time approaches.

REFERENCES

Anonymous. 1983. Potato Statistical Yearbook for 1983. The National Potato Council, Denver, Colorado.

Burton, W.G. 1948. The Potato, London: Chapman and Hal Ltd., p. 254.

Hunter, James H. 1976. "Variation in Respiration Rates and Moisture Loss Rates as Affected by Time, Temperature and Vapor Pressure Deficit." ASAE Paper No. 76-4504.

_____. 1977. "Prediction of Weight Losses in Stored Potatoes by Computer Simulation," ASAE Paper No. 77-4063.

_____. 1983. "External Heat and Moisture Balance for Potato Storage." ASAE Paper No. 83-4081.

Sparks, Walter C. and Larry V. Summers. 1974. Potato Weight Losses, Quality Changes and Cost Relationships During Storage. Idaho Agr. Exp. Sta.

Table I

Percentage of Generated Heat Used for Evaporation
Together with Weight Loss Rates at a Respiration Rate of
6.45 Watts per Metric Ton at Critical Humidity Levels.

Temp. deg.		% heat to	% wt. loss
C.	F.	evaporation	per week
3.33	38	45.90	0.0719
7.22	45	52.21	0.0821
10.00	50	56.07	0.0884
12.78	55	60.34	0.0954
15.56	60	64.36	0.1020
18.33	65	66.05	0.1081
21.11	70	71.53	0.1140

Table II

Seasonal Respiration Predictions (1974-76)
For the Equation Rate=Ae^{-KT}+C or A=(e^{KT}-1)+C

Variety	Temp. deg. C.	A	K	C	weeks	A	K	C	weeks
Treatment	3.33	3.315	-.168	1.530	26	1.0169	.0506	1.530	10
Kennebec	7.22	3.868	-.109	1.250	14	.1434	.1186	1.250	22
MH-Mature	12.78	4.252	-.513	1.372	12	.259	.111	1.372	24
Russet	3.33	5.285	-.198	1.464	24	.853	.039	1.464	12
Burbank	7.22	3.666	-.179	1.0168	19	.057	.193	1.139	17
MH Mature	12.97	3.236	-.442	1.139	14	.097	.171	1.336	22
Kennebec	3.33	4.248	-.115	.8964	21	1.302	.034	1.276	15
No MH	9.22	3.344	-.144	.4536	14	.245	.119	.899	22
Mature	12.78	5.788	-.489	1.239	11	.398	.151	1.239	17
Russet	3.33	4.752	-.128	.9723	25	.203	.246	1.166	11
Burbank	7.22	3.090	-.152	.754	20	.110	.191	.901	16
No MH	12.78	4.518	-.331	1.026	11	.399	.136	1.157	18
Mature									

Note:MH=MH-30 Applied
     Mature=Vines Killed

Table III

Seasonal Respiration Predictions (1983-85)
For the Equation Rate=Ae-KT+C or A(e^{KT}-1)+C

Variety	Temp. deg. C.	Fall				Spring			
		A	K	C	weeks	A	K	C	weeks
Round	3.33	5.284	-.219	2.153	25	.121	.136	2.153	11
whites	7.22	6.438	-.267	1.632	16	.323	.172	1.722	20
(means)	10.00	6.515	-.257	1.946	12	.4815	.146	2.244	24
Russet	3.33	5.602	-.2173	1.890	25	.3416	.083	1.89	11
Burbank	7.22	6.372	-.258	1.462	25	.101	.223	1.462	11
	10.00	6.032	-.366	1.725	21	.228	.235	1.725	15
Gold Rus	3.33	7.698	-.328	1.577	25	.241	.144	1.577	11
	7.22	7.850	-.396	1.530	16	.221	.170	1.530	20
	10.00	8.963	-.507	1.880	7	.205	.214	2.138	29

Table IV

Seasonal Weight Loss Prediction (1974-76)
For the Equation Rate=Ae^{-KT}+C or A(e^{KT}-1)+C (spring)
Adjusted to a 1 mm. Hg VPD Basis

		Falling Rate				Rising Rate			
Variety	Temp. deg. C.	A	K	C	weeks	A	K	C	weeks
Treatment	3.33	.392	-.121	.107	36				
Kennebec	7.22	.246	-.122	.095	36				
MH Mature	12.78	.550	-.346	.172	14	.214	.040	.172	22
Russet	3.33	.423	-.141	.116	36				
Burbank	7.22	.221	-.099	.103	36				
MH Mature	12.78	.694	-.354	.182	14	.247	.0325	.182	22
Kennebec	3.33	.394	-.157	.087	36				
No MH	7.22	.203	-.114	.080	36				
Mature	12.78	.723	-.262	.104	14	.0353	.142	.104	22
Russet	3.33	.303	-.147	.090	36				
Burbank	7.22	.233	-.118	.086	36				
No MH Mature	12.78	.980	-.319	.111	14	.0191	.1839	.111	22

Note:MH=MH-30 Applied
Mature= Vines Killed

Table V

Seasonal Weight Loss Predictions (1983-85)
For the Equation Rate=Ae^{-KT}+C or A(e^{KT}-1)+C (spring)
Adjusted to a 1 mm. Hg VPD Basis

		Falling Rate				Rising Rate			
Variety	Temp. deg. C.	A	K	C	weeks	A	K	C	weeks
Round	3.33	.952	-.339	.175	25	.0353	.201	.175	11
Whites	7.22	.542	-.482	.180	16	.0404	.210	.180	20
(means)	10.00	.660	-.522	.243	12	.0438	.266	.243	24
Russet	3.33	.825	-.230	.131	25	.0200	.2915	.131	11
Burbank	7.22	.633	-.215	.121	24	.0192	.375	.121	12
	10.00	.945	-.182	.089	14	.0463	.208	.159	22
Gold Rus	3.33	1.293	-.302	.348	24	.0379	.257	.348	12
	7.22	.691	-.331	.330	16	.0456	.225	.330	20
	10.00	1.147	-.150	.1854	12	.1094	.217	.375	24

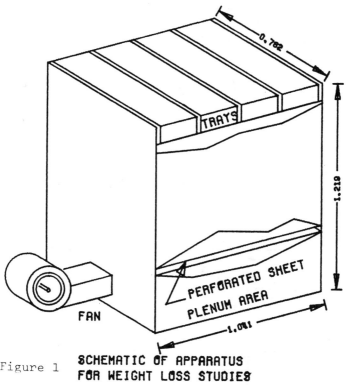

Figure 1   SCHEMATIC OF APPARATUS FOR WEIGHT LOSS STUDIES

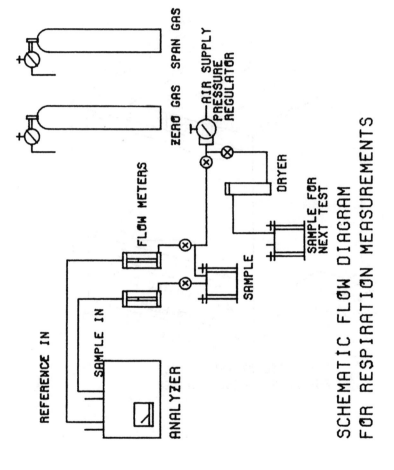

SCHEMATIC FLOW DIAGRAM
FOR RESPIRATION MEASUREMENTS

Figure 2

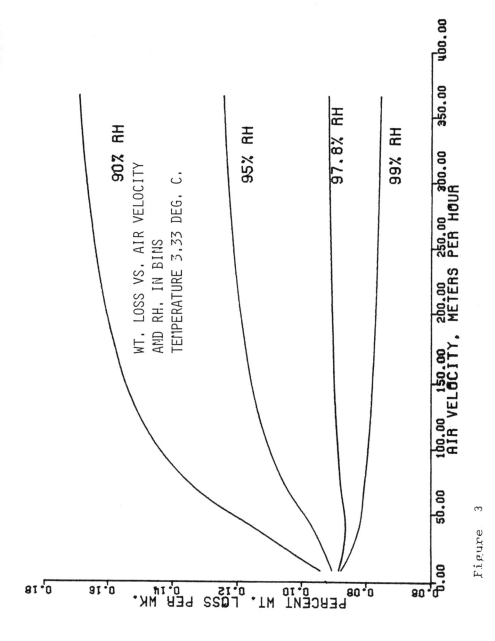

Figure 3

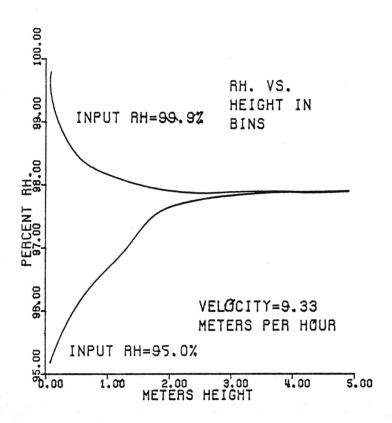

Figure 4

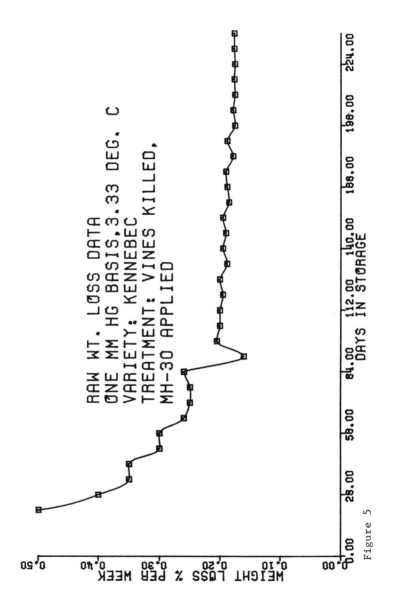

RAW WT. LOSS DATA
ONE MM HG BASIS,3.33 DEG. C
VARIETY: KENNEBEC
TREATMENT: VINES KILLED,
MH-30 APPLIED

Figure 5

529

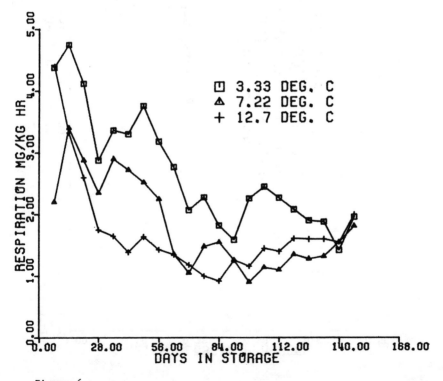

Figure 6

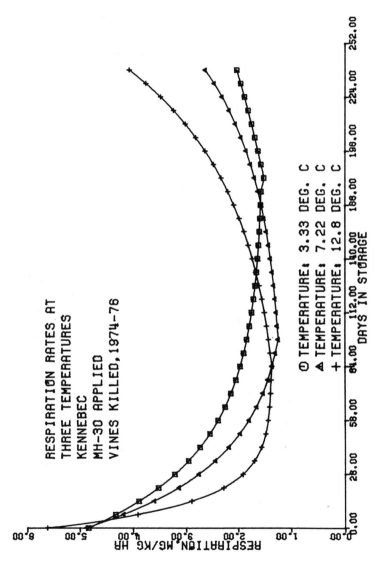

RESPIRATION RATES AT
THREE TEMPERATURES
KENNEBEC
MH-30 APPLIED
VINES KILLED,1974-76

⊙ TEMPERATURE: 3.33 DEG. C
▲ TEMPERATURE: 7.22 DEG. C
+ TEMPERATURE: 12.8 DEG. C

Figure 7

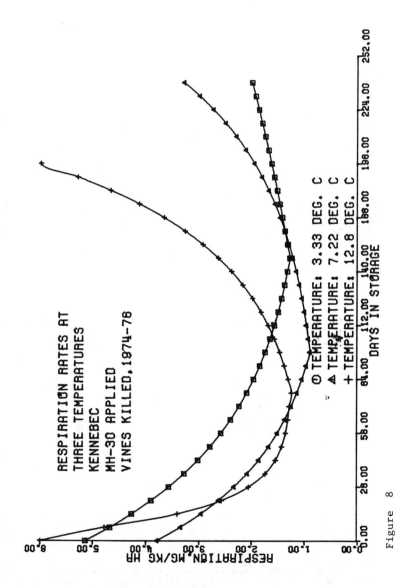

RESPIRATION RATES AT
THREE TEMPERATURES
KENNEBEC
MH-30 APPLIED
VINES KILLED, 1974-78

⊕ TEMPERATURE: 3.33 DEG. C
▲ TEMPERATURE: 7.22 DEG. C
+ TEMPERATURE: 12.8 DEG. C

Figure 8

532

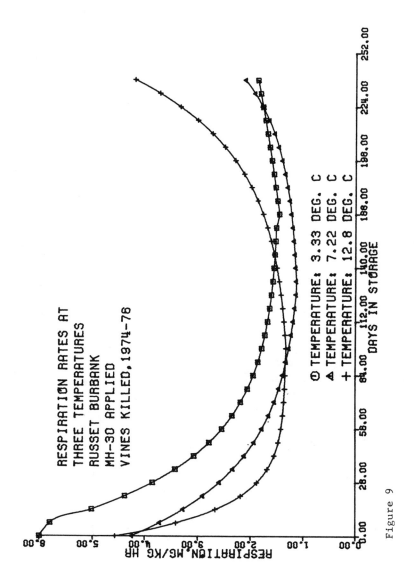

Figure 9

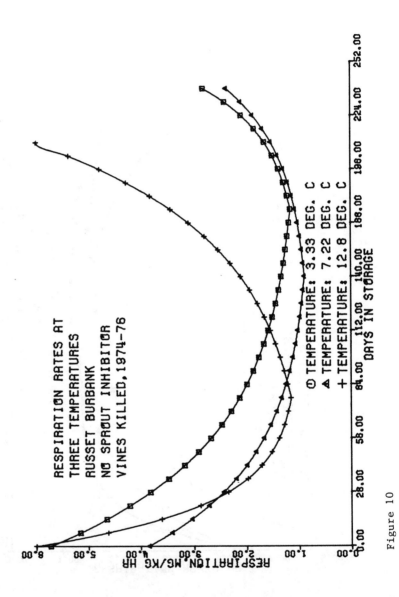

Figure 10

534

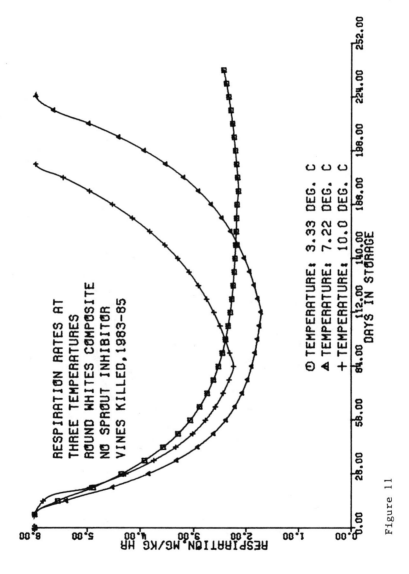

RESPIRATION RATES AT
THREE TEMPERATURES
ROUND WHITES COMPOSITE
NO SPROUT INHIBITOR
VINES KILLED,1983-85

⊙ TEMPERATURE: 3.33 DEG. C
▲ TEMPERATURE: 7.22 DEG. C
+ TEMPERATURE: 10.0 DEG. C

Figure 11

535

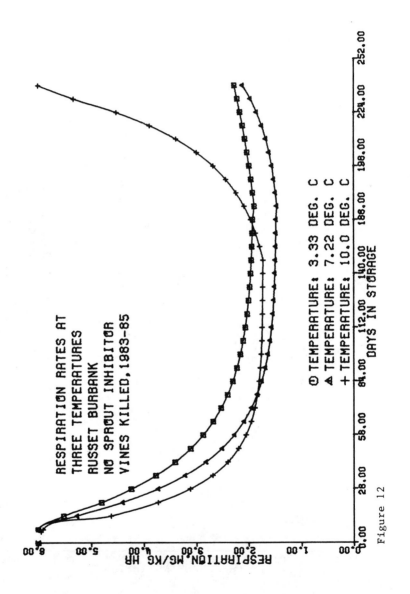

RESPIRATION RATES AT
THREE TEMPERATURES
RUSSET BURBANK
NO SPROUT INHIBITOR
VINES KILLED,1983-85

⊕ TEMPERATURE: 3.33 DEG. C
▲ TEMPERATURE: 7.22 DEG. C
+ TEMPERATURE: 10.0 DEG. C

DAYS IN STORAGE

RESPIRATION,MG/KG HR

Figure 12

536

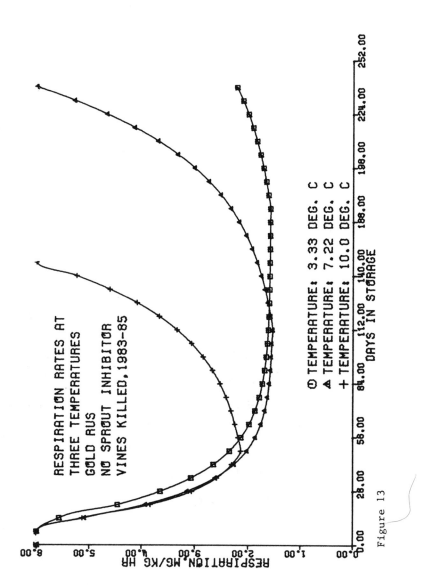

Figure 13

537

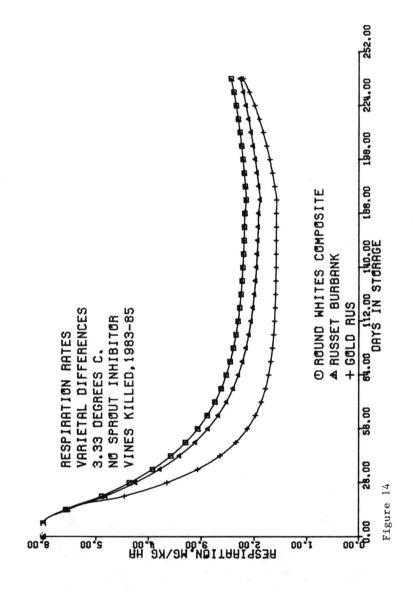

Figure 14

538

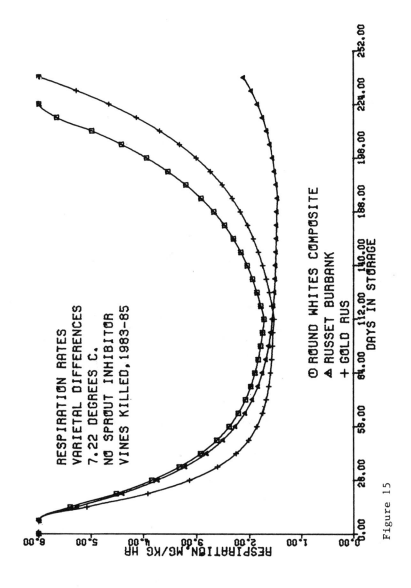

RESPIRATION RATES
VARIETAL DIFFERENCES
7.22 DEGREES C.
NO SPROUT INHIBITOR
VINES KILLED,1983-85

⊙ ROUND WHITES COMPOSITE
▲ RUSSET BURBANK
+ GOLD RUS

Figure 15

539

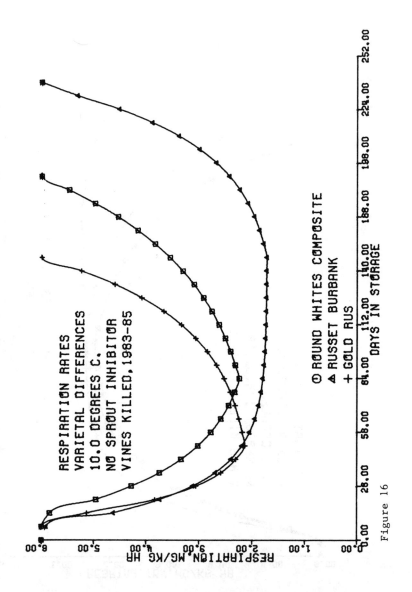

RESPIRATION RATES
VARIETAL DIFFERENCES
10.0 DEGREES C.
NO SPROUT INHIBITOR
VINES KILLED, 1983-85

⊙ ROUND WHITES COMPOSITE
▲ RUSSET BURBANK
+ GOLD RUS

Figure 16

540

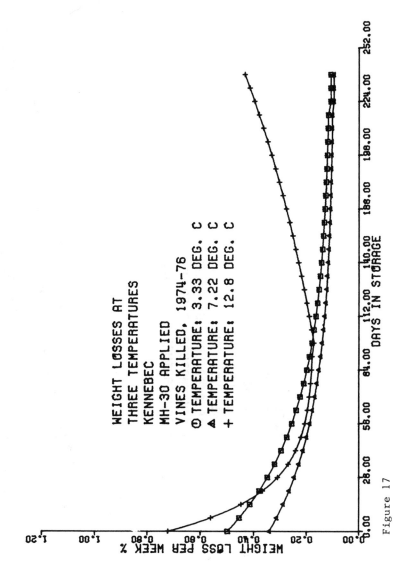

WEIGHT LOSSES AT
THREE TEMPERATURES
KENNEBEC
MH-30 APPLIED
VINES KILLED, 1974-76
⊙ TEMPERATURE: 3.33 DEG. C
▲ TEMPERATURE: 7.22 DEG. C
+ TEMPERATURE: 12.8 DEG. C

Figure 17

541

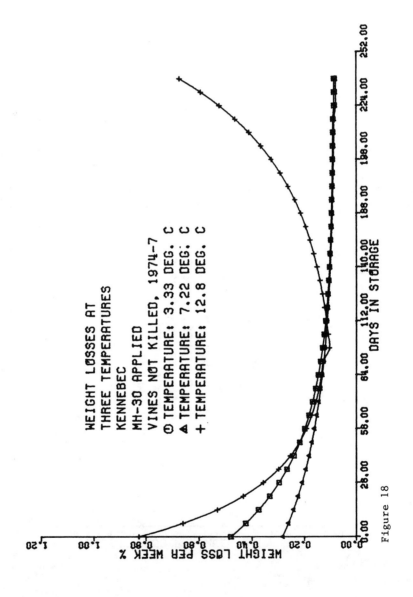

Figure 18

542

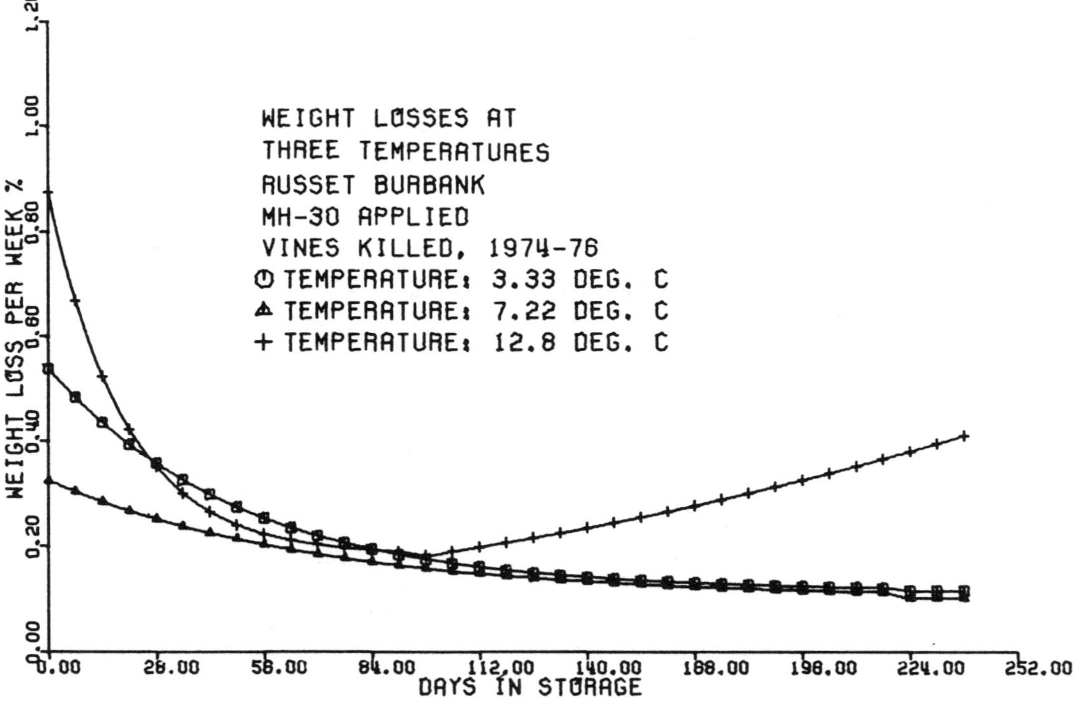

WEIGHT LOSSES AT
THREE TEMPERATURES
RUSSET BURBANK
MH-30 APPLIED
VINES KILLED, 1974-76
⊙ TEMPERATURE: 3.33 DEG. C
▲ TEMPERATURE: 7.22 DEG. C
+ TEMPERATURE: 12.8 DEG. C

Figure 19

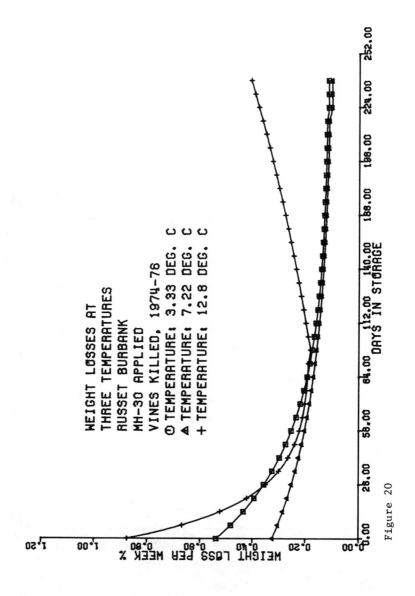

Figure 20

544

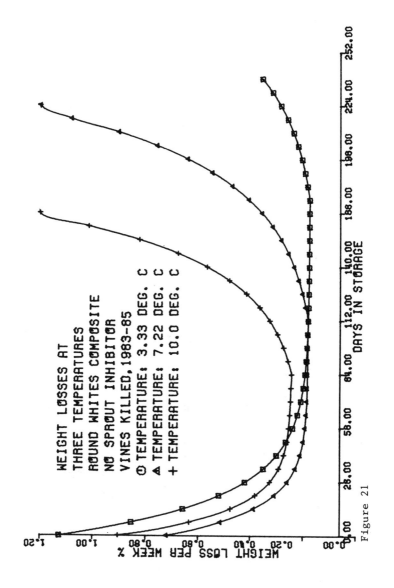

Figure 21

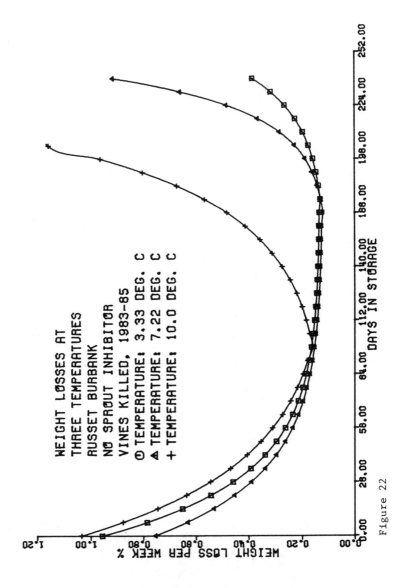

WEIGHT LOSSES AT
THREE TEMPERATURES
RUSSET BURBANK
NO SPROUT INHIBITOR
VINES KILLED, 1983-85
⊙ TEMPERATURE; 3.33 DEG. C
▲ TEMPERATURE; 7.22 DEG. C
+ TEMPERATURE; 10.0 DEG. C

Figure 22

546

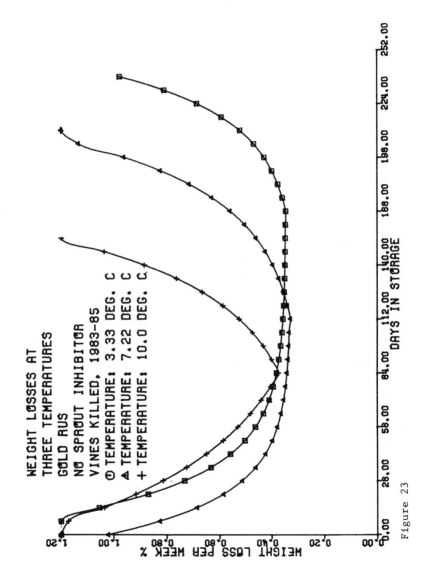

Figure 23

547

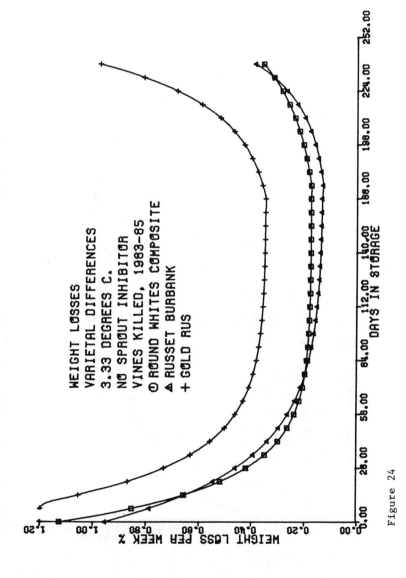

WEIGHT LOSSES
VARIETAL DIFFERENCES
3.33 DEGREES C.
NO SPROUT INHIBITOR
VINES KILLED, 1983-85
⊙ ROUND WHITES COMPOSITE
▲ RUSSET BURBANK
+ GOLD RUS

Figure 24

548

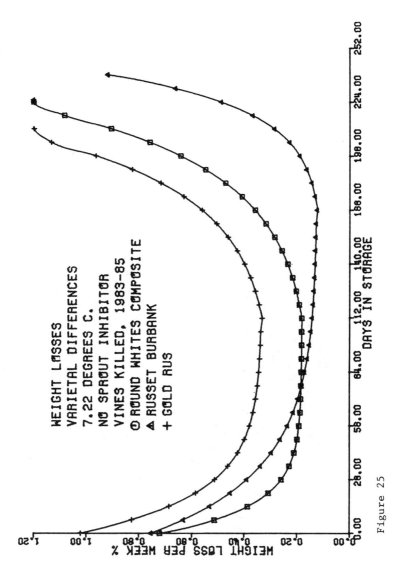

WEIGHT LOSSES
VARIETAL DIFFERENCES
7.22 DEGREES C.
NO SPROUT INHIBITOR
VINES KILLED, 1983-85
⊙ ROUND WHITES COMPOSITE
▲ RUSSET BURBANK
+ GOLD RUS

Figure 25

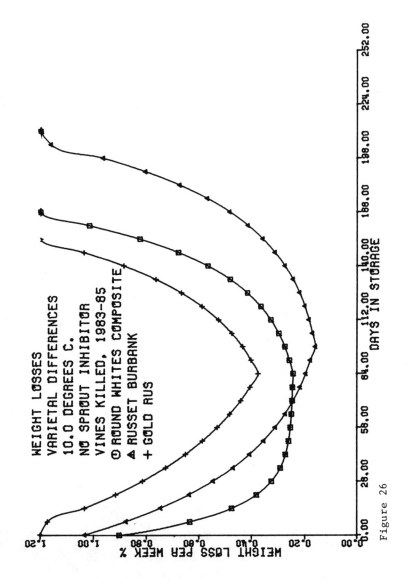

WEIGHT LOSSES
VARIETAL DIFFERENCES
10.0 DEGREES C.
NO SPROUT INHIBITOR
VINES KILLED, 1983-85
⊙ ROUND WHITES COMPOSITE
▲ RUSSET BURBANK
+ GOLD RUS

DAYS IN STORAGE

WEIGHT LOSS PER WEEK %

Figure 26

550

STORAGE MANAGEMENT INFLUENCES POTATO QUALITY
IN THE DUTCH POLDERS REGION

by

Jan C. Hesen, Institute for Storage and Processing
of Agricultural Produce, IBVL, P.O. Box 18
Wageningen, the Netherlands

ABSTRACT

     With   23   percent of the arable land   cultivated
with   potatoes   this crop is most   important   in   the
Netherlands.   Growing,   storing,   processing   and
marketing   are   well developed and as a   result   more
than   2/3   of   the   entire   Dutch   potatoes   crop   of
approximately   6,500,00 metric tons (7,150,000   short
tons) is exported.   After harvest, potatoes have to be
stored   for varying periods up to 10 months·in   order
to   supply the (international) market throughout   the
year   with potatoes for direct human consumption   and
processing industry.   Seed potatoes have to be stored
till   the   next   planting   season   and   for   export
purposes.   In   view   of the high demands   on   potato
quality,   it   is   important that potatoes are   stored

ASAE Paper No. 85-4036

under optimal conditions with adequate storage/management. With the applied storage system and storage management the quality of potatoes is retained during a period up to 8-9 months and losses are limited to 4.5-5.0 percent during this period.

INTRODUCTION

Potatoes are grown in the Netherlands on 160,000 ha (384,000 ac) (23% of the arable land) with a yearly production of 6,500,000 metric tons of which more than 2/3 are exported (Table 1).

In the Netherlands, as in most parts of Europe, there is one potato crop a year. Although harvest of potatoes may be spread over three months, the main crop is harvested in autumn within a period of three months. After harvest, potatoes have to be stored for a shorter or longer period in order to supply the (international) market throughout the year with potatoes for direct human consumption and processing industry. Seed potatoes have to be stored till the next planting season and for export purposes. In veiw of the high demand on potato quality, it is of importance that the crop is stored under optimal conditions with an adequate storage management. Storage research was started in the Netherlands more than 35 years ago (I.B.V.L.) and today practically all potatoes are stored in ventilated storages. Approximately 80 percent of all potatoes are stored on farms and the rest in central stores.

STORAGE CONDITIONS AND MANAGEMENTS

The physiological, physical and pathological processes during storage are determined by the potato itself (variety, damages, disease infection, etc.) and by the storage conditions, where humidity, and in particular, temperature are of importance. Good storage conditions and management are necessary in order to minimize losses in weight and quality after harvest.

Drying Wet Potatoes

It is generally known that potatoes are very difficult to keep under wet harvest conditions.

552

Potatoes that have been rained on are practically impossible to store due to the development of extensive rotting. After loading the store both tubers and adhering soil should be dried as soon as possible. To ensure quick drying, forced ventilation with a high air rate (150 m^3 air/m^3 potatoes/hour [5.95 cfm/cwt]) preferably at temperatures lower than the potatoes (but >10 °C or 50° F) is most effective. Drying wet lots can be promoted by artifically warming up the air, especially when much soil is brought in, and in late autumn this should be considered. Ventilation is stopped as soon as the soil is dry and this normally will be the case after one or only a few days.

Curing

When the potatoes have been dried or brought in the store under dry conditions it is necessary to "cure" the product for one to two weeks at a temperature of about 15 °C (59 °F) and a relative humidity of the air of >90 percent. Under these conditions, wound periderm is formed and suberization taken place. Well suberized potatoes will evaporate less water during further storage and moreover the potato tubers are better protected against infection by microorganisms. The environmental conditions favoring suberization also promotes several diseases to develop. In cases of known diseased potatoes it is even preferred not to cure potatoes but start immediately with ventilation to control a further spreading of diseases (plan to move these potatoes early in the marketing plan). During the curing period practically no ventilation is applied but when the temperature rises too much (>20 °C) or when the potatoes become humid several hours of ventilation are necessary.

Cooling

In cooling of potatoes there are two distinct periods: 1) lowering the pulp temperature to the designed storage temperature and 2) holding the designed temperature during the rest of the storage period. Since approximately 3600 kJ (3396 btu) per ton of potatoes must be removed to lower the temperature 1° C (1.8 °F), and the product may generate

4200 kJ/day (3962 btu/day) or more in respiration, a high cooling capacity is needed during lowering the temperature. Once the potatoes have been cooled to the storage temperature, potatoes generate only 1000 kJ per ton (943 btu) of potatoes per day. Besides the heat load of potatoes there is also a heat gain in the storage environment caused by heat transfer through walls, floor and ceiling, and heat generated by fans, etc.

The cooling rate of potatoes is proportional to the difference in temperature between potatoes and air and the velocity of air or rate of air flow around the tubers respectively. The following are the recommended temperatures for optimal storage results:

seed potatoes	2-4°C (36-39°F)
table stock	4-6°C (39-43°F)
processing	6-8°C (43-46°F)
chip industry	8-12°C (46-54°F)

It is well known that low storage temperatures (3 to 5°C) give the least problems. But because of sugar build up potatoes for the processing industry have to be stored at higher temperatures. To control the temperature, potatoes have to be ventilated with cooler air resulting in evaporation losses. Water loss due to evaporation represents about 90 percent of the overall loss in weight of healthy tubers and it can cause quality deterioration of the stored product (shrivelling, blackspot). Evaporation is a physical process, the rate being affected mainly by the condition of the air (T. and R.H.) and permability of the tuber skin. Immature, damaged or sprouted potatoes have a high evaporation rate. Water loss by evaporation can be reduced by ventilating with air of high humidity and reducing the time of ventilation. Therefore storage management should maintain the desired storage temperature with as few ventilation hours as possible and/or humidification of the ventilating air.

In Holland and most other European countries a high ventilation rate (150 m^3 air/ton potatoes/hr [4 cfm/cwt]) is used to minimize the time of ventilation. Under Dutch climatical conditions it is

possible to store potatoes up to May/June with
outside air cooling, ventilating only 200-300 hours
per season. The average weight loss in this period
is 4.5 to 5.0 percent when the cooling air is not
humidified (normal practice) and 3.8 to 4.3 percent
with artificial humidification.

To level out temperature differences in the
potato pile, the air is recirculated at regular
intervals of several hours per week (internal
ventilation). Recirculation of the air in the potato
storage also is practiced to reduce condensation
problems on the ceiling of the storage and provide
oxygen. For preventing of dripping condensation from
roofs or ceilings of the storages in winter there is
usually another ventilation system on top on the
potato pile (over pile circulation).

Sprout Inhibiting

Potatoes will sprout eventually when stored at
temperatures over 4 to 5°C (39-41° F). There are
several chemicals known to suppress sprouting, MH30,
IPC/CIPC, DMN, Tecnazene, Nonylalcohol. IPC/CIPC is
generally used on commercial practice because it is
effective, inexpensive, easy to apply, and doesn't
cause deviations in the potato tubers (taste, color).

This sprout suppressant can be applied as a dust
mostly with one percent active agent or as a liquid
containing 20-30 percent active agent. Application
of dust is only possible when loading the store and
this causes problems when the tubers are damaged or
not well suberized (skin irritation). Most of the
potatoes, therefore, are treated with IPC-CIPC after
the suberization and cooling down period by applying
an aerosol (swing-fog a.o.) which is evenly
distributed through the pile of potatoes by the
ventilation system. In Holland, a maximum dose of 20
ppm is permitted and often this amount is applied two
or three times during the storage season. The
allowed residue level is in most countries 5 ppm.

To achieve a good sprout inhibiting effect the
following points are of importance:

1. The first dose (usually 10 ppm) is applied
two to four weeks after harvesting.

2.   The   treatment is repeated before sprouting starts, e.g., each two to three months.

3.   The dose is sufficient, a total of 66 ml/ton (2 oz/ton) of a 30 percent compound per season or 80 ml (2.4 oz/ton) of a 25 percent compound.

4.   The   agent is well distributed through the potato pile (adequate ventilation system, no soil cones).

5.   After each treatment internal recirculation should be continued about 15 minutes until the fog has disappeared.

6.   No ventilation with outside air' for a period of two days after treatment to give the compound the chance to settle on the tubers.

If   these   precautions   are   not   sufficiently observed,   it will be difficult to suppress sprouting especially   at   high   storage   temperatures   (chip industry).   In spring time some problems may occur in connection   with internal sprouting.   It   is   obvious that seed   potatoes may not be treated with sprout inhibitors.   It   is   also common practice that   seed potatoes   are   not stored in buildings   where   sprout inhibitors   are used.   To control   storage   diseases (Fusarium,   Phoma,   Silver   scab)   most of   the   seed potatoes   are treated with fungicides (benzimidazole a.o.) preferably when loading the storages.

Reconditioning

Before   unloading   the storage, the potatoes   are generally warmed up to about 15° C (59 °F) in order   to reduce bruising.   If the reducing sugar content has increased too much during storage,   which is   usually due   to too low storage temperatures,   one can try to reduce   these   sugars   by   reconditioning   at   higher temperatures   (20 ° C   or   68 ° F).   During   the reconditioning   process,   which lasts several   weeks, the   reducing   sugars are converted into   80   percent starch   and 20 percent is lost in   respiration.   The results   of reconditioning,   however,   vary and it is often not possible to reach a sufficient low level of reducing sugars.

Immature harvested potatoes are harder to recondition than mature potatoes. It also is known that, as soon as potatoes are unloaded from the storage the reducing sugar content may rise very rapidly certainly at low temperatures. Therefore, it is recommended to process potatoes as soon as possible after unloading the storage (within 2 days or even better within 24 hours). The problem which arises after prolonged storage of potatoes is that reducing sugars are accumulated in the potatoes which cannot be removed by reconditioning. This is called "senescent sweetening," a phenomena related to the physiological age of the tuber. Although senescent sweetening is mainly determined by the variety, also growing and storage conditions influence this phenomena and more research is needed to solve this problem. For long term storage (eight months and more) a somewhat lower storage temperature for processing could be recommended (6-7°C, 43-45°F).

STORAGE SYSTEMS

Good storage facilities should have an insulated structure; equipment for efficient cooling, drying and heating of potatoes; and the necessary controls.

Storage Design

Ware or fresh market potatoes are usually stored in bulk and the size of these storage bins vary from 500-800 metric tons (11,000-17,600 cwt) of potatoes at farms and up to several thousands of tons in commercial and cooperative stores. Sometimes pallet boxes containing 1000 kg (2200 lbs.) of potatoes are used for storage of seed potatoes and incidentally also for storage of chip potatoes.

Piles of potatoes are usually 3.5 - 4 m high (11.6 -13.2 ft.) (potatoes piled deeper than 5 m [16.5 ft.] pressure bruise). The overall heat transfer coefficient for walls is usually 0.35 W/m^2 K (0.06 btu/hr sq. ft F) and for roof or ceiling 0.3 W/m^2 °k, (0.05 btu/hr.sq ft. °F), viz. the mean maximum heat flow through walls and roof does not exceed 4 W/m^2 (1.3 btu/hr.sq ft.). Polystyrene and polyurethane are mostly used for insulation and only incidentally glasswool or rockwool.

557

Paved and non-insulated floors are customary. Most common structural materials are galvanized steel, concrete, aluminum, timber and asbestos-cement. The units (bins) in which potatoes are stored depend on the number of stored varieties (seed potatoes), difference in quality of the various lots, variation in required storage conditions and the rate of filling and unloading the store (1-2 weeks).

Ventilation Systems

To control the environmental conditions in a potato storage, forced ventilation with outside air is generally applied. Relatively few potato storages are equipped with mechanical cooling, mainly for seed potatoes and for long term storage of potatoes for the processing industry. Due to climatical conditions in the Netherlands, high ventilating rates of 70-100 m^3 air/m^3 potatoes/hour (2.87-3.97 cfm/cwt) are used for cooling and for drying of wet potatoes. Generally axial-flow fans with a static pressure Pa = 150 Pa (.6 in. H_2O) are used. Both underfloor and above-floor air ducts are used in potato stores. The air distribution depends solely on the duct spacing (maximum 75-80% top height of pile) and the air distribution through each duct. The highest air velocity in tapered lateral ducts should not exceed 6-8 m/s (1200-1580 ft/min) and in ducts of equal size the air velocity is limited to 4-6 m/s (790-1200 ft/min).

For prevention of dripping condensation from roofs or ceilings in winter there is usually an additional over pile ventilation system.

For efficient air movement under the roof either special fans hanging under the roof (ceiling) are used or the air is circulated by means of the main ventilation system.

Control of Ventilation

Ventilation for drying of wet potatoes is usually controlled manually. Sensors for detecting free moisture on the surface of potato tubers, which can control the drying process, are being tested. Ventilation for cooling of the potatoes with fresh outside air is usually controlled automatically.

Cooling is monitored by the following parameters; temperature of the potatoes, temperature of outside ambient and temperature of the air flow in the plenum.

Average time of ventilation during storage from October to June with the present rate of ventilation does not exceed 200 to 300 total hours per season. If the ambient conditions do not allow for ventilation with fresh air during prolonged periods, internal circulation of air will be switched on at regular intervals in order to prevent forming large temperature gradients within the pile. The energy consumption for ventilating during the storage season is approximately 2.8 to 3.3 KW/t (0.127 to 1.5 KW/cwt) of potatoes and the energy cost 0.70 to 0.82 (U.S. $0.18 to $0.21) per ton of potatoes. The average weight loss of potatoes during the storage season is 4.5 to 5.0 percent when the cooling air is not humidified and 3.8 to 4.3 percent with artifically humidified air.

Table 1. Dutch potato production and export of potatoes and potato products

	Production Metric Tons	Export of potatoes and potato products in tonnage of potatoes Metric Tons
Seed potatoes	850,000	500,000 (to 70 countries)
Consumption potatoes (fresh market)	2,300,000	1,300,000 (for direct human consumption and processing)
Processed potatoes	1,000,000	750,000 (mainly french fries)
Starch potatoes	2,400,000	1,900,000 (starch and starch derivitives)
TOTAL	6,650,000	4,450,000

VENTILATION SYSTEM PERFORMANCE IN
MICHIGAN BULK POTATO STORAGES

by

B.F. Cargill, Professor and K.C. Price, Specialist,
Department of Agricultural Engineering,
Michigan State University,
East Lansing, Michigan

ABSTRACT

In 1981 a program was initiated to analyze and
make modification recommendations in Michigan potato
storages. General ventilation problems encountered
are discussed and basic fluid flow principles and the
results of previous research are applied to obtain
solutions. A set of criteria to evaluate the
ventilation systems and general techniques to obtain
near uniform air distribution are estabished.

ASAE Paper No. 85-4037

561

INTRODUCTION

The marketable quality of stored potatoes is greatly influenced by the environmental conditions of the storage. Many potato disorders and losses in storage are the result of a lack of control of the storage environment.

A properly designed ventilation system which provides uniform[1] air distribution is necessary in order to properly control the storage environment (Statham, 1983). Studies by Schaper et al. (1976) on the "smoothwall" ducts of the Red River Valley discovered severe problems with uniformity of air distribution.

In 1981, a program called "bin balancing" was initiated to analyze and redesign the air distribution systems in Michigan potato storages. Since 1981, over 100 Michigan storages have been redesigned to achieve uniform air distribution. This paper reports on the general observations and results of this program in light of potato storage ventilation design.

VENTILATION SYSTEM CRITERIA

The results by Cloud and Morey (1980) on smooth-wall ducts in the Red River Valley provided useful information for the analysis of the side main and lateral storages. These results, the basic fluid flow equation from ASHRAE (1972 and 1981), and the ventilation rates[2] and storage environments of Cargill (1976), helped to form a general set of criteria with which to evaluate the air distribution systems. These criteria are:

----

[1]Near uniform air distribution is a more accurate description, but for simplicity only the term "uniform" will be used in this paper.

[2]Recommended ventilation rates vary widely from source to source (Lerew and Bakker-Arkema, 1978).

1. A pressure differential across the fan of 1/2 inch of water (125 Pa) or less was desired in order to optimize the fan efficiency.

2. Return air systems with a minimum dynamic loss coefficient and a calculated mean velocity of less than 850 ft/min (259 m/min) were also necesssary to optimize the fan efficiency.

3. A calculated mean plenum entrance velocity which is less than 850 ft/min (259 m/min).

4. A calculated mean lateral entrance velocity which is 850 ft/min (259/m min). The ratio of the lateral opening to the cross-sectional area of the plenum must be a value between 0.75 and 1.0.

5. A calculated effective slot velocity of 1000 ft/min (305 m/min). The ratio of the effective slot area to the cross-sectional area of the lateral must be a value between 0.75 and 1.0.

6. A ratio of actual slot area to effective slot area of 3 to 4:1. The actual slot area is the available slot area in an empty storage. The effective slot area is the available discharge area in a full storage. The effective slot area is approximately 25-35% of the actual slot area and depends upon the shape, size, and foreign material content of the product in storage. See Figure 1.

7. Ventilation rates of 0.6-1.2 cfm/cwt (0.25-0.5 m^3 air/min/m^3 potatoes) for seed and table stock and 1.5-1.8 cfm/cwt (0.64-0.77 m^3air/min/m^3 potatoes) for chip and processing potatoes.

Field Analysis

The field analysis of the storage involved the following:

1. A general sketch of the storage and air distribution system (such as location, above or below ground laterals, etc.) was made. Dimensions were taken to size the storage and the air system.

2. Fan performance was calculated by measuring the pressure differential across the fan and the respective fan performance curve.

3. Bin capacity was calculated using the calculated storage volume and a crop density of 0.42 cwt/ft^3 (674 kg of potatoes/m^3 of storage).

4. The ventilation rate (cfm/cwt or m^3 air/min/m^3 of potatoes) was calculated from the fan performance and bin capacity. From the fan performance and calculated areas the air velocities for the return air system, plenum, lateral and effective slot were calculated.

The results of this initial field analysis were evaluated according to the criteria established in Ventiliation System Criteria section. Design recommendations and modifications were made. Following the completion of the modifications, a second analysis was made in order to determine the effect of the modifications.

The second analysis consisted of simulating full storage conditions by covering approximately 75 percent of the distribution slots with carpet padding (reducing the actual slot area to the effective slot area). The slot velocities were measured using an Alnor velometer. Static pressures were measured with an inclined manometer. The storage was then divided into a number of equal floor area sections. The number of floor sections is determined by multiplying the number of laterals by three. (See Figure 2) The average of the measured slot velocities and required ventilation (ventilation rate is cfm/cwt multiplied by the section capacity in cwt) were calculated and compared to the other sections. This comparison determined whether further modifications of the storage were necessary.

RESULTS AND DISCUSSION

The results and observations of the Michigan "bin balancing" program will be discussed as follows: 1) return air system, 2) air distribution in the plenum; and 3) air distribution in the laterals.

Return Air System

Schaper et al. (1976) reported that the return air system typically contributes a high percentage of the total pressure loss in the ventilation system. This was also true in Michigan storages as over 90 percent of the storages had return air system pressure losses that exceeded the pressure losses of the other components of the system. In most cases the return air pressure losses accounted for more than 50 percent of the total pressure drop in the entire ventilation system. These excessive pressure losses were the result of high dynamic loss coefficients and high air velocity.

Typically, the dynamic loss coefficients[3] for the return air system ranged from $C = 0.5$ to $C = 4.0$ ($C = 0.5$ for straight entance; $C = 1.0$ for 90° mitered corners and $C = 2.5$ for square edged orifice entrance leading into a plenum). Velocities in nearly every system exceeded 1000 ft/min (305 m/min) with many of the systems having velocities over 1500 ft/min (457 m/min).

Most of the modifications to the return air system centered on the square edged orifice entrance because the pressure losses could be reduced with relatively quick and inexpensive modifications when compared to modifying other components of the return air system. An increase in the orifice opening has a twofold effect: 1) it lowers the dynamic loss coefficient, and 2) it lowers the entrance velocity head.

Air Distribution in the Plenum

Cloud and Morey (1980) stated that the common problem in "smoothwall" ducts is that of higher

----

[3]Values for the dynamic loss coefficient can be found in Chapter 25 of ASHRAE 1972 or Chapter 33 of ASHRAE 1981.

airflows at the distal end, which is the result of static pressure regain. The conversion of velocity head into static head in the plenum was caused by airflow diversion and the changing cross-sectional area of the airstream.

Whenever a portion of the airstream of a constant cross-section duct is diverted, a static regain will result as discussed in the Ventilation System Criteria section of this paper. The static regain can become a concern when a significant portion of an airstream is diverted as is the case in the side plenum and lateral storages commonly found in Michigan.

Since the velocity head moves with the square of the velocity, higher velocity airstreams are more susceptible to problems with static regain. For example: two systems are identical in design except for the initial plenum velocity. System 1 has an initial plenum velocity of 1500 ft/min (457 m/min) and system 2 has an initial plenum velocity of 1000 ft/min (305 m/min). The difference in velocity head between these two systems is 0.078 in. of water (19.5 Pa). Assuming that the velocity head is totally converted into static head by the distal end of the duct and using a static regain coefficient of 0.75. System 1 will have a difference in static pressure from entrance to distal end of 0.105 in. of water (26.3 Pa). System 2 will have a difference in static pressure from entrance to distal end of 0.047 in. of water (11.7 Pa). The higher velocity system has a greater variation of static pressure and thus it will have a greater variation in airflow.

Higher velocities resulting in excessive static pressure regain were found in nearly every storage analyzed in the Michigan "bin balancing" program. Plenum velocities were nearly always in excess of 1000 ft/min (305 m/min), with velocities in the 1500 ft/min (457 m/min) range being commonplace. Lower air velocities and increased frictional losses are two possible methods to reduce static regain. In Michigan, modifications to reduce air velocities (enlarging the effective cross-sectional area of the plenum) were used almost exclusively to reduce static

regain. Increasing the friction of the duct will
reduce the efficiency of the fan and is difficult to
implement in an existing storage, thus it was rarely
used.

A static pressure regain is also associated with
a changing cross-sectional area of the airstream.
The static regain is the result of flow development
of the fan discharge airstream. Figures 3 and 4 show
two typical fan locations and flow patterns found in
Michigan storages.

To achieve uniform air distribution it is
important to keep the length of duct required to
develop the airstream into the plenum to a minimum.
The length of duct required for the development of
the plenum airstream is unique to each system.
However, it was found that an increase in the cross-
sectional area of the plenum reduces the length of
duct required to develop the airstream.[4] This is the
result of a more rapid air entrainment into and
expansion of the airstream. For fans discharging
down the plenum (Figure 3), "scoops" or dampers were
sometimes necessary to help distribute air into the
laterals close to the fan. For fans discharging
perpendicular to the plenum (Figure 4), a "jump" (See
Figure 5) was sometimes used to help the airstream
more rapidly develop into the full cross-sectional
area of the duct.

Besides reducing air velocities to help obtain
uniform air distribution, two other methods, as
proposed by Cloud and Morey (1980), were used. The
first, reduces the ratio of effective discharge area
(lateral opening) to the cross-sectional area of the
duct (plenum). Cloud and Morey's research showed
that reducing this ratio to a value less than one
greatly improves the uniformity of air distribution.
While, reducing this ratio to less than 0.75 results
in an increased system pressure requirement. Most

----

[4] Development of the flow into the full cross-
   sectional area of the duct not developed flow
   as in a constant velocity profile.

567

of the Michigan storage have lateral opening to plenum cross-sectional area ratios of less than one. The improvement in the uniformity of air distribution was often overshadowed by the factors discussed earlier. Varying the discharge area (lateral opening) along the length of the duct will also improve the uniformity of air distribution. This method proved effective where fans discharged directy down the plenum and limitations on modifications prevented plenum velocities from being lowered below 1000 ft/min (305 m/min).

Air Distribution in the Lateral

The common problem with air distribution in the laterals of Michigan storages is that of higher airflows at the distal end which is caused by static regain. This is the result of flow diversion and development.

Although the flow diversion of a lateral is more gradual than that of a plenum, the static regain becomes a problem when velocities begin to exceed 1000 ft/min (305 m/min). Therefore it is necessary to keep the entrance velocities of the lateral under 1000 ft/min (305 m/min). The discussion of static regain in relationship to flow diversion in the lateral is similar to that of the plenum. See Air Distribtion in the Plenum section.

Duct ˑ entrance affects, such as flow separation during a 90 turn, or a vena contracta reduce the effective cross-sectional area of the airstream. This results in an increased air velocity and a corresponding increase in a velocity head. As flow develops into the duct, the velocity head caused by the duct entrance affects will be converted into static pressure, and thus a static regain occurs.

The lateral velocity of the majority of the Michigan storages exceeded 1200 ft/min (372 m/min). These high velocities combined with the duct entrance effects caused severe air distribution problems near the lateral entrance. In many instances, negative static pressures occurred near the lateral entrance which resulted in airflow from the potato pile into the duct. The reversed airflow can cause serious disorders in the potato pile.

Increasing the lateral cross-sectional area lowers the air velocities and reduces the length required for the flow to adequately develop into the duct. The discussion here is the same as with the air distribution in the plenum, Air Distribution in the Plenum section.

Air Distribution in the Slot

Reducing the ratio of effective discharge area (effective slot area) to the duct (lateral) cross-sectional area to less than one, greatly improves the unformity of air distribution. For the effective slot-lateral ratio, Coud and Morey (1980) proposed two reasons to keep this ratio above 0.75. First, it results in increased pressure requirements. Second, the effective slot area will change as the properties of the crop (shape, size, foreign material content) change. Also, not much is known about the blockage affect of the potatoes and reducing the effective slot-lateral cross-section ratio below 0.75 may lead to additional ventilation problems.

One method used in the Michigan "bin balancing" program to eliminate the design problem involved with the changing effective slot area and lack of information on the blockage affects of the potato was the "guarded slot." In the "guarded slot design," two types of distribution slot were used. The "guarded slot" was the control slot, located on the ventilation system side of the lateral duct and was designed to the effective slot area. The "guarder slot" was the distribution slot located on the pile side of the lateral duct and was designed with an area greater than or equal to four times the "guarded slot" area. With this design, the "guarded slot: area or effective slot area is constant and will not vary with crop properties. (See Figure 6)

The problem common to every Michigan storage was that a ratio of effect slot area to lateral cross-sectional areas greater than one. Many of the storages had ratios exceeding a value of three.

Varying the discharge area (effective slot area) along the length of the lateral also proved to be very effective in improving the uniformity of air distribution. This method was most effective when lateral entrance velocities exceed 1000 ft/min (305 m/min) and were not easily changed.

Field Example

An analysis, as described in the Ventiliation System Criteria section of this paper, that was performed on a refrigerated potato storage at Wayne J. Lennard & Son's, Samaria, Michigan yielded these results:

1. Bin capacity = 12,230 cwt (865.8 m^3 of potatoes)

2. Fan capacity = 20, 200 cfm (572.0 m^3 air/ min)

3. Ventilation rate = 1.65 cfm/cwt (0.66 m^3 air/min/m^3 potatoes)

4. Pressure differential across fan = 0.62 in. of water (77.5 Pa)

5. Initial plenum velocity = 773 ft.min (236 m/min)

6. Initial lateral velocity = 900 ft/min (274/ m/min)

7. Effective slot velocity = 772 ft/min (267 m/min)

8. A ratio of lateral opening to plenum cross-sectional area of 0.86

9. A ratio of effective slot area to lateral cross-sectional area of 1.17

It was important to note that there were 12 laterals, 8 ft. (2.44 m) on center, with the fan located at the first lateral opening and discharging directly down the plenum. See Table 1 for the static pressure measurements in the storage.

From this information it can be seen that several modifications were necessary to improve the ventilation system. First, the pressure differential across the fan was greater than 1/2 in. of water (125

Pa). But, the design of the return air system could not be altered due to the location of the refrigeration coils. Since the fan discharged directly down the plenum, it was decided to vary the cross-sectional area of the lateral opening down the length of the plenum. Figure 6 shows the length along the plenum versus the lateral cross-sectional area. Although "scoops" are often used when a fan discharge is located near the lateral opening, a "scoop" was only needed for the first lateral as the fan rotation and geometry of the storage caused a "natural" funneling of the air into the first few laterals.

Figures 7 and 8 compare the static pressures in the plenum and laterals before and after the modifications respectively.

CONCLUSIONS

The following conclusions can be drawn from the Michigan "bin balancing" program:

1. Return air systems contributed a high percentage of the total pressure requirements for the system. Typically the return air systems were plagued by high velocities and high dynamic loss coefficients.

2. Higher airflows, caused by static regain, were found at the distal end of the distribution ducts. The static regain was the result of diverging and developing airflow.

3. High distribution duct air velocities, over 1000 ft/min (305 m/min) which contributes to the static regain, were found in most Michigan storages.

4. Duct discharge area to duct cross-sectional area ratios were normally found to be between 0.75 and 1.0 for the lateral opening plenum ratio.

5. The effective slot, lateral cross-sectional area ratios were typically over one with many storages having ratios exceeding a value of three.

The design of the ventilation systems in potato storages varies. Each system can have a problem unique to its particular design. Since the Michigan

"bin balancing" program concentrated on existing
ventilation systems, the techniques used to "balance"
the air flow in the storages may change from one
system to the next. However, a general set of
modifications were used in most storages:

1. Reduce air velocities below 850 ft/min (259
m/min)

2. The ratio of effective duct discharge area to
distribution duct cross-sectional area should be
between 0.75 and 1.0.

3. "Guarded slots" should be used whenever possible.

4. Vary the effective duct discharge area along the
duct length where duct velocities exceed 1000 ft/min
(305 m/min) or where fans discharge directly down the
plenum or lateral cross-sections cannot be increased.

All other modifications to the design of the
ventilation system should fall within the criteria
established in the Ventilation System Criteria
section.

REFERENCES

Anon. 1972. ASHRAE Handbook of Fundamentals. Amer-
    ican.Society of Heating, Refrigerating, and Air
    Conditioning Engineers. NY., NY.

Anon. 1981. ASHRAE Handbook of Fundamentals. Amer-
    ican Society of Heating Refrigerating, and Air
    Conditioning Engineers. NY., NY.

Cargill, B.F., et al. 1976. The Potato Storage.
    Michigan State University, East Lansing, MI.

Cloud, H.A. and R.V. Morey. 1980. Distribution duct
    performance for through ventilation of stored
    potatoes. Trans. ASAE V. 23, 1213-1218.

Lerew, L.E. and F.W. Bakkar-Arkema. 1978. Storage
    of potatoes-A simulation model. Paper No. 78-
    4059. American Society of Agricultural
    Engineers. St. Joseph, MI.

Schaper, L.A., H. Cloud and D. Lundstrom. 1976. An engineering evaluation of potato storage ventilation system performance. Trans. ASAE V. 19, 584-590.

Statham, O.J.H. 1983. Better Storage Design. The Agricultural Engineer V. 38:46-48. Institute of Agricultural Engineers. Silsoe, Beford, England.

FIGURE 1. Blockage of the distribution slot
by the potatoes. The effective slot
area is 25-35% of the actual slot area.

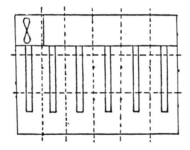

Figure 2. Example of the equal floor area divisions used for analysis of the
storages in the Michigan "bin balancing" program.

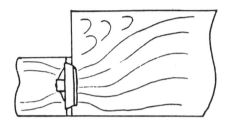

FIGURE 3. Flow patterns for a fan discharging
directly down the plenum.

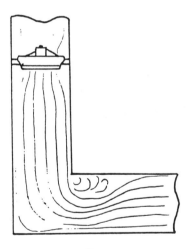

FIGURE 4. Flow patterns for a fan discharging
perpendicular and directly into a plenum.

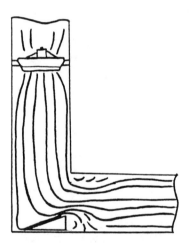

FIGURE 5. Flow patterns for a "jump" that's used
when a fan discharges perdendicular to
the plenum.

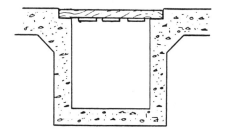

FIGURE 6. Example of a "guarded slot" in a below floor
lateral. The "guarder slot" area is designed
to be greater than or equal to four times the
"guarded slot" area.

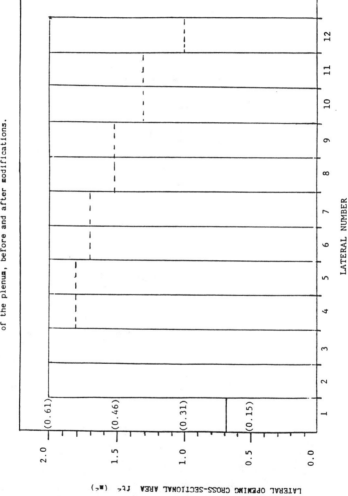

FIGURE 7. Lateral opening (discharge area) along the length of the plenum, before and after modifications.

FIGURE 8. Comparisons of the static pressures in the plenum before and after modifications.

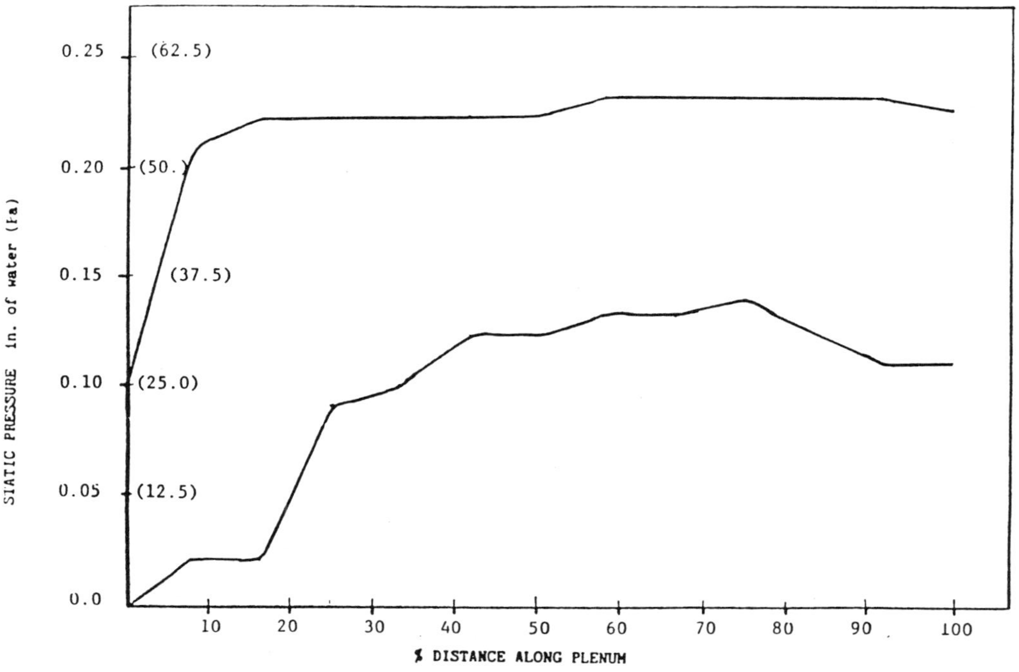

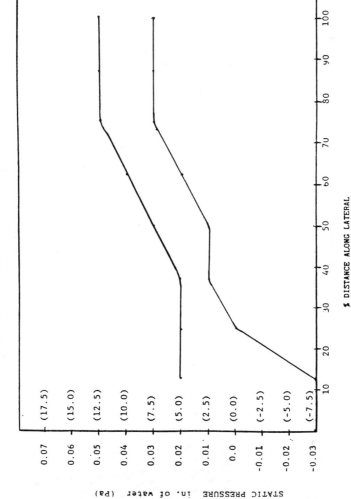

Figure 9. Comparisons of the static pressures in the laterals before and after modifications.

580

MATHEMATICAL EXPRESSIONS FOR LATERAL
POTATO PRESSURES

by

L.A. Schaper, Agricultural Engineer and P.H. Orr,
USDA-ARS-NSA, Red River Valley Potato Research
Laboratory, East Grand Forks, Minnesota; E. C.
Yaeger, Agricultural Engineer, USDA-ARS-MA, Nursery
Crops Research Laboratory, Delaware, Ohio; and
K.G. Janardan, Statistician, Mathematical Science
Department, North Dakota State University, Fargo,
North Dakota

ABSTRACT

The relationship ln pressure = a + B (distance
above floor)$^{3.5}$ was developed to accurately estimate
lateral pressures for Irish potatoes with wet or dry
surfaces for a 5.3 m (17.5 ft.) pile height. When
dry surface conditions existed, this relationship
more accurately predicted reactions and bending
moments for simply supported beam conditions than the

ASAE Paper No. 85-4038

equivalent fluid density analogy. When wet surface
conditions existed, there were no major differences
in predicted reactions and moments for either method
of representing lateral pressures.

INTRODUCTION

In prior work, equivalent fluid density, EFD,
was used to approximate the lateral unit pressure of
potatoes on a vertical wall (Schaper and Yaeger,
1983). For simply supported beam conditions, sill
and plate reactions and bending moments were
calculated using EFD approximations and then compared
to these same parameters calculated from the actual
measured pressure curve.

Since a triangular-shaped load distribution
occurs with the EFD analogy, designers frequently use
the center-of-force at one third of the pile height,
h/3. Results from the above study indicated good
agreement between the EFD analogy and results with
actual measured pressures for a 3.5 m (11.5 ft.) pile
height. For a 5.3 m (17.5 ft.) pile height, the
center of force had to be selected at h/3.3 for
bending moment values and h/3.5 for sill and plate
reactions in order to yield agreement between
predicted results and those calculated from actual
pressure data.

Since h/3 is the mathematically derived center
of force for a triangular load distribution, it was
used with various incremental values of EFD to find
reactions and bending moments that were consistent
with those obtained from actual pressure data. With
this center of force when an EFD was chosen that gave
satisfactory sill reactions, the plate reactions and
bending moments were over estimated by 10 to 30
percent.

The objective of the research reported here was
to develop a better mathematical model for lateral
pressure than EFD by developing and comparing various
algebraic lateral pressure and pile height functions
and testing for more accurate design reactions and
moments than those given by the EFD analogy.

PROCEDURES

Type of Potato and Storage Conditions

The data used in these analyses were the maximum total pressure curves for a vertical wall storage bin for each respective year during the six year duration of this study. Norchip variety potatoes were used for five years. In 1974, 1975, and 1976 they were placed in storage with a dry potato skin surface. In 1977 and 1978 a water-fungicide solution at the rate of 1/ton was applied to the potatoes with mist-type spray nozzles resulting in a lower internal coefficient of friction than in prior years. In 1979, Russet Burbank variety potatoes, also sprayed with the water-fungicide solution, were used. The potatoes in all the tests were cooled to 8 °C (46 °F) and stored at greater than 90 percent RH.

Curve Fitting Procedures

A linear regression program was used to fit the algebraic functions, shown in Table 1, to the actual pressure data (SAS, 1979). The coefficient of determination, r^2, was used as the criterion for selecting the best type of function.

Evaluation of Accuracy of Curves for Design Calculations

Sill and plate reactions and bending moments were calculated based on best fit mathematical expressions. These reactions and bending moments were compared to the results from both the EFD analogy and the recorded pressure data. A spline, curve-fitting program was used to plot the original pressure data (Schaper and Yaeger, 1983). Iteration procedures were used to determine the reactions and bending moments for the statistically developed expressions and the plot of the recorded pressure data.

The difference between a predicted value from a selected equation and that derived from the actual pressure data curve was considered to be the relative error and was expressed as:

$$\text{Relative Error} = \frac{P_{EQ} - P_{DATA}}{P_{DATA}} \qquad [1]$$

RESULTS AND DISCUSSION

Curve Fit to Data

Preliminary trials using the various algebraic functions in Table 1 indicated that the combined exponential and power function

$$p = Ae^{B(h)^C} \qquad [2]$$

was the only one that showed any potential for fitting the actual recorded pressure data. This equation was transformed to semi-logarithmic form

$$\ln p = a + B(h)^C \qquad [3]$$

The coefficient A shown in Table 1 is the same as e . In this semi-logarithmic form, with C being a constant, linear regression analyses were run for the various sets of data. The exponent C was assigned values from 0.5 to 4.5 in increments of 0.5 and then 0.25 as the optimum range was isolated. A value of 3.5 for C was eventually selected. After C was determined, linear regressions were again run for each year to determine the a and B coefficients.

584

Coefficients resulting from these runs are shown in Table 2.

An analysis of variance procedure was utilized to determine if the respective regression coefficients in Table 2 were significantly different for each year. At $p \geq .025$ significance level, no statistically significant differences could be found between pairs of slopes, B, for 1974, 1975 and 1976. Also no significant differences could be found between pairs of slopes for 1977, 1978 and 1979. However, the slopes for 1974, 1975 and 1976 were significantly different from the slopes for 1977, 1978 and 1979. At $p \geq .025$ signficance level, the intercept, a, was significantly different for each year.

Figure 1 shows the actual maximum pressure curve, the equivalent fluid density line for this curve and the regression curve for 1976. This was the year that maximum total pressure occurred for Norchip potatoes with dry skin surfaces. Figure 2 shows the same relationships for Norchip with wet skin surfaces. Figure 3 shows the same relationship for Russet Burbank with wet skin sufaces.

Accuracy of Curves for Design Parameters

Table 3 indicates the relative error of the least square linear regression fit for design parameters predicted with eq. [3] when compared to design parameters determined from the actual pressure data curve for each respective year. The results of this comparison indicate that the respective yearly least square linear regression curves consistently underestimate the sill reaction. There is an inverse pattern between the sill reaction and center of force. The more the center of force is overestimated, estimated higher above the floor than it actually is, the more the sill reaction is underestimated. Figure 1 graphically indicates the rapid rate of increase of the lateral pressures that can occur below one third of the pile height under certain conditions.

As was previously done with EFD analogy (Schaper and Yaeger, 1983), adjustments were made in linear regression coefficients a and B in an attempt to get positive relative error values. Data for 1976, 1978 and 1979 are used as the basis for comparisons since those three years reflect the effect of surface conditions and/or varietal factors. Tables 4 and 5 indicate the relative error for arbitrarily selected linear regression coefficients and EFD's. Center of force in the EFD analogy was assumed at one third of the pile height.

The rationale for selecting values of up to 2.3 (5.4) for the coefficient a, as shown in Tables 4 and 5, was to obtain representative values for the large unit lateral pressures at h equal zero, while still retaining reasonable values for the errors in calculated reactions and moments. If 2.3 (5.4) is converted back to unit lateral pressure, p, using eq. [3] with h equal to zero, p equals 10.0 kPa (221 lb/ft). Equation [3] then has 10.0 kPa (221 lb/ft^2) as a limit. The maximum unit pressure in 1976 ws 12.9 kPa (270 lb/ft^2) and in 1978 12.3 kPa (256 lb/ft^2).

Figure 1 indicates the possible extreme skewness of the pressure patterns that may occur with dry potatoes. Since these data appeared nonlinear they were also evaluated for possible design parameter relative errors using the linear regression analysis results and an EFD analogy. These results are also shown in Tables 4 and 5 and should indicate the greatest relative error that might occur with linear type approximations.

Effect of Surface Condition of the Potato

Visual comparison of the pressure curves in Figures 1 and 2 indicate a definite nonlinear trend of pressure for the dry potato surface condition. As indicated in Table 2 and our analysis of variance tests, there is a statistically significant shift in the regression coefficient B for the transformed data, eq. [3], based on the two potato surface conditions. In essence, there are three parallel relationships for the dry condition that are significantly different from the three parallel relationships for the wet condition.

As seen in Figures 2 and 3, potatoes with a wet surface exhibit a fairly linear trend in the undulating pressure curve throughout the 5.3 m (17.5 ft) pile depth. In Figure 1, there appears to be two fairly linear segments to the undulating pressure curve. As mentioned earlier (Schaper and Yaeger, 1982), the noticeable change in the trend line seemed to occur at a pile depth of about 3.5 m (11.5 ft). Apparently, when this approximate depth is exceeded, consolidation occurs in the bottom portion of the pile if the potatoes have a dry surface. Possibly the overpressure of 3.5 m (11.5 ft) of potatoes is sufficient to partially overcome the static coefficient of friction between the dry potato surfaces in the lower portion of the pile. When potatoes have a wet surface, the coefficient of friction between potatoes may be low enough that the vertical force in all portions of the pile is sufficient to larely overcome the static coefficient of friction and a fairly uniform lateral pressure trend results.

Results of Potato and Skin Texture

As indicated in Figures 2 and 3, the Russet Burbank variety did not develop nearly as large a unit lateral pressure as the Norchip variety. In Table 2, the EFD values and the coefficient a also bear this out. This noticeable difference in levels of pressure between the Russet Burbank and Norchip varieties may be due to shape, surface contour and surface texture. The Russet Burbank is relatively long potato with a length-to-major diameter ratio of approximately 2 and a rather irregular surface contour. The Norchip has a length-to-major diameter ratio of approximately 1.25 and a smoother surface contour than the Russet Burbank. The Russet Burbank has a "netted" surface texture which is relatively rough while the Norchip has a smooth surface texture. Due to these differences in characteristics, the Russet Burbank potatoes in bulk piles would not be expected to slide as readily as Norchip potatoes, hence would exhibit a lower lateral pressure.

Effect of Distance Reference Location

As mentioned earlier, eq. [3] has a limit e if distance h is measured with respect to the floor. Since this precludes any form of extrapolation, a more "open ended" type function which used distance from the top of the pile as the independent variable was tried. When this independent variable was used in eq. [3], the coefficient of determination, r^2, was reduced by about one-half.

Effect of System of Units on Regression

Due to the original data being a nonmonotonic sequence, slope regression coefficients determined using customary units could not be transformed to the SI unit system by using appropriate unit conversion factors. If the original data does not have a consistent trend line, as was the case for the dry Norchips in 1976, changing the system of units resulted in two distinctly different linear regression curves, see Figure 1. Since unit conversions could not be made for all coefficients, all results are given in both customary units and SI units.

Comparison of Nonlinear Equation and EFD Analogy

Eq. [3] with C equal to 3.5 gave a good least square fit of the lateral pressure data, see Table 2. However, as indicated in Table 3, there was a consistent tendency to underestimate the sill reaction relative effort, the plate reaction and bending moment are inflated as shown in Tables 4 and 5.

For wet potatoes (1978 and 1979), it appears that the EFD analogy estimates the design parameters as well as or better then the nonlinear equation, see Table 4 and 5. For dry potatoes (1976), which tend to show a "bulge" in the pressure curve near the bottom of the pile, the nonlinear relationship appears to better predict design parameters.

If eq. [2] is used to represent pressure, numerical iteration procedures must be used to integrate this relationship in order to obtain shear and moment values. There is no analytical solution for the integral of a function of this form.

CONCLUSIONS

Based on regression analyses of measured lateral potato pressure data obtained in bulk potato piles greater than 3.5 m (11.5 ft) deep, the following conclusions have been reached.

1. The nonlinear relationship $\ln p = a + B$ (distance above floor)$^{3.5}$ can be used to represent lateral pressures for both wet and dry surface potatoes.

2. There is a different lateral pressure distribution for wet surface than for dry surface potatoes.

3. For wet surface potatoes, which have a more uniform pressure pattern than dry surface potatoes, the EFD analogy represents the pressure curve as satisfactorily as the nonlinear relationship.

ACKNOWLEDGEMENTS

The authors wish to thank Marilyn Nelson, Engineering Technician, USDA-ARS, Red River Valley Potato Research Laboratory, E. Grand Forks, MN for assistance in processing the data.

REFERENCES

Schaper, Lewis A. and Earl C. Yaeger. 1982. Horizontal and vertical pressure patterns of stored potatoes. Transactions of the ASAE, 25(3):179-724.

Schaper, Lewis A. and Earl C. Yaeger. 1983. Accuracy of equivalent fluid density for potato storage wall design. Transactions of the ASAE 26(1):179-184, 187.

SAS User's Guide, 1979 Edition. 1979. SAS Institute, Inc., Post Office Box 10066, Raleigh, NC 27605.

NOMENCLATURE

a $\doteq$ intercept value for least square linear regression fit for transformed data

A $\doteq$ intercept value for least square linear regression fit for original data

B $\doteq$ slope for least square linear regression fit

C $\doteq$ constant, which is power term in algebraic relationships

EFD $\doteq$ equivalent fluid density, kg/m^3 (lb/ft^3)

ft $\doteq$ feet

h $\doteq$ pile height with respect to floor, m (ft)

kg $\doteq$ kilograms

lb $\doteq$ pound

m $\doteq$ meter

N $\doteq$ Newton, $kg\text{-}m/sec^2$

p $\doteq$ unit pressure at selected location, Pa (lb/ft^2)

Pa $\doteq$ Pascal, N/m^2

P_{EQ} $\doteq$ parameter calculated with an assumed loading condition

P_{DATA} $\doteq$ parameter determined from actual data

r^2 $\doteq$ coefficient of determination indicating proportion of change in pressure that can be related to change in pile height.

TABLE 1. ALGEBRAIC FUNCTIONS CONSIDERED FOR RELATING LATERAL POTATO PRESSURE (p)
AND HEIGHT ABOVE FLOOR (h)

LINEAR	EXPONENTIAL	POWER	COMBINATION EXPONENTIAL AND POWER
$p = A + Bh$	$p = \exp(Bh)$	$p = Ah^B$	$p = \exp(Ah^B)$
$p = h / (Ah + B)$	$p = \exp(A \exp Bh)$		$p = A \exp(Bh^C)$
$p = 1 / (A + Bh)$			$p = A \exp(B / h^C)$
$p = A + (B / h)$			$p = A \exp(B\sqrt{h})$
			$p = A \exp(B / \sqrt{h})$

TABLE 2. EQUIVALENT FLUID DENSITIES FROM PRESSURE DATA AND RESULTS OF LINEAR REGRESSION ANALYSIS OF
THE FUNCTION ln PRESSURE = a + B (DIST. FROM FLOOR)^3.5 FOR 5.3 m (17.5 ft) PILE HEIGHT.

YEAR	VARIETY	POTATO SURFACE CONDITION	SI UNITS				CUSTOMARY UNITS			
			EFD (kg/m^3)	a	Bx10^-4	r^2	EFD (lb/ft^3)	a	Bx10^-4	r^2
1974	NORCHIP	DRY	150	1.7945	−157.89	0.88	9.5	5.1184	−4.0090	0.90
1975	NORCHIP	DRY	155	1.8327	−162.58	0.86	9.5	5.0910	−3.4694	0.92
1976	NORCHIP	DRY	180	1.9869	−153.77	0.93	11.0	5.2453	−3.3316	0.92
1977	NORCHIP	WET	185	1.9209	−118.10	0.80	11.5	4.9600	−1.8463	0.80
1978	NORCHIP	WET	195	2.0809	−114.34	0.94	12.5	5.1200	−1.7875	0.94
1979	RUSSET BURBANK	WET	135	1.6380	−87.67	0.80	8.5	4.6770	−1.3705	0.80

TABLE 3. RELATIVE ERRORS* IN DESIGN PARAMETERS DERIVED FROM LEAST SQUARE LINEAR REGRESSION EQUATIONS (TABLE 2) WHEN COMPARED TO DESIGN PARAMETERS FROM ACTUAL DATA CURVE FOR 5.3 m (17.5 ft) PILE HEIGHT AND 5.8 m (19.0 ft) WALL HEIGHT.

YEAR	VARIETY	POTATO SURFACE CONDITION	SILL REACTION		PLATE REACTION		BENDING MOMENT		CENTER OF FORCE	
			DATA VALUE	RELATIVE ERROR	DATA VALUE	RELATIVE ERROR	DATA VALUE	RELATIVE ERROR	DATA VALUE	RELATIVE ERROR
			kN/m		kN/m		kN m/m		m	
1974	NORCHIP	DRY	16.0	-0.22	5.0	0.00	13.0	0.08	1.35	0.19
1975	NORCHIP	DRY	16.0	-0.19	5.0	0.00	15.0	-0.07	1.45	0.10
1976	NORCHIP	DRY	19.0	-0.18	5.5	0.09	16.0	0.06	1.30	0.27
1977	NORCHIP	WET	19.0	-0.21	6.5	-0.08	18.0	-0.06	1.45	0.17
1978	NORCHIP	WET	20.0	-0.10	7.5	0.07	19.0	0.05	1.60	0.09
1979	RUSSET BURBANK	WET	13.0	-0.08	6.0	0.00	15.0	-0.07	1.80	0.06
			lb/ft		lb/ft		ft-lb/ft		ft	
1974	NORCHIP	DRY	1100	-0.03	350	0.02	3000	0.14	4.5	0.04
1975	NORCHIP	DRY	1100	-0.03	350	0.01	3500	0.03	4.7	0.03
1976	NORCHIP	DRY	1300	-0.05	400	0.14	3500	0.18	4.3	0.15
1977	NORCHIP	WET	1300	-0.21	450	0.03	4000	-0.02	4.8	0.21
1978	NORCHIP	WET	1350	-0.10	500	0.06	4500	0.06	5.2	0.12
1979	RUSSET BURBANK	WET	900	-0.05	400	-0.06	3500	-0.04	5.9	0.06

* RELATIVE ERROR = (Peq - Pdata)/Pdata

TABLE 4. RELATIVE ERRORS* IN DESIGN PARAMETERS (IN SI UNITS) DERIVED FROM THE EQUATION ln PRESSURE = a + B (DIST. ABOVE FLOOR)^3.5 AND FROM EFD ANALOGY FOR A 5.3 m PILE DEPTH FOR SELECTED YEARS.

				RELATIVE ERROR		
YEAR	SELECTED COEFFICIENTS AND EQUIVALENT FLUID DENSITIES			SILL REACTION	PLATE REACTION	BENDING MOMENT	CENTER OF FORCE
1976	a	B					
	2.0	-153.77E-04		-0.18	0.09	0.06	0.27
	2.3	-250.00E-04		0.02	0.15	0.19	0.10
	2.3	-240.00E-04		0.03	0.18	0.23	0.11
	EFD (kg/m^3)						
	180 (ANALYTICAL FIT)			-0.05	0.45	0.19	0.38
	190			-0.03	0.45	0.25	0.38
	200			0.03	0.54	0.31	0.38
1978	a	B					
	2.1	-114.34E-04		-0.10	0.07	0.05	0.09
	2.3	-200.00E-04		0.01	-0.04	0.11	-0.05
	2.3	-180.00E-04		0.03	0.02	0.26	-0.03
	EFD (kg/m^3)						
	195 (ANALYTICAL FIT)			-0.05	0.07	0.05	0.13
	200			-0.03	0.13	0.11	0.13
	205			0.00	0.20	0.16	0.13
1979	a	B					
	1.6	-87.67E-04		-0.08	0.00	-0.07	0.06
	1.8	-100.00E-04		0.01	0.01	0.14	0.02
	1.8	-90.00E-04		0.03	0.07	0.29	0.04
	EFD (kg/m^3)						
	135 (ANALYTICAL FIT)			0.00	0.00	-0.07	0.00
	145			0.08	0.00	0.00	0.00
	150			0.12	0.08	0.07	0.00

* RELATIVE ERROR=(Peq - Pdata)/Pdata

TABLE 5. RELATIVE ERRORS* IN DESIGN PARAMETERS (CUST. UNITS) DERIVED FROM THE EQUATION ln PRESSURE = a + B (DIST. ABOVE FLOOR)^3.5 AND FROM EFD ANALOGY FOR A 17.5 ft PILE DEPTH FOR SELECTED YEARS.

YEAR	SELECTED COEFFICIENTS AND EQUIVALENT FLUID DENSITIES		RELATIVE ERROR			
			SILL REACTION	PLATE REACTION	BENDING MOMENT	CENTER OF FORCE
1976	a	B				
	5.2	-3.3316E-04	-0.05	0.14	0.18	0.15
	5.4	-4.0000E-04	0.07	0.20	0.29	-0.02
	5.4	-3.5000E-04	0.10	0.29	0.35	0.22
	EFD (lb/ft^3)					
	11.0 (ANALYTICAL FIT)		-0.23	0.25	0.14	0.35
	11.5		-0.08	0.38	0.29	0.35
	12.0		-0.04	0.38	0.29	0.35
	12.5		0.04	0.50	0.29	0.35
1978	a	B				
	5.1	-1.7875E-04	-0.10	0.06	0.06	0.12
	5.2	-1.5000E-04	0.01	0.26	0.21	0.17
	5.4	-3.0000E-04	0.10	0.05	0.18	-0.03
	EFD (lb/ft^3)					
	12.0		-0.07	0.10	0.00	0.12
	12.5 (ANALYTICAL FIT)		0.00	0.20	0.00	0.12
	13.0		0.04	0.20	0.11	0.12
1979	a	B				
	4.7	-1.3705E-04	-0.05	-0.06	-0.04	0.06
	5.0	-2.0000E-04	0.20	0.14	0.19	-0.01
	5.0	-1.5000E-04	0.25	0.32	0.29	0.03
	EFD (lb/ft^3)					
	8.5 (ANALYTICAL FIT)		0.00	0.00	-0.14	-0.02
	9.0		0.06	0.00	0.00	-0.02
	9.5		0.11	0.13	0.00	-0.02

* RELATIVE ERROR=(Peq - Pdata)/Pdata

594

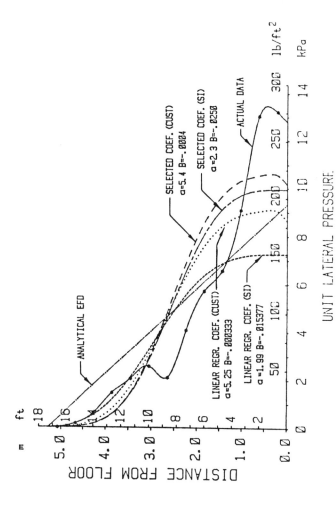

FIG. 1. Actual data for dry, Norchip variety for 1976, analytically determined EFD, and curves for various coefficients for the equation $\ln p = a + B(h)^{3.5}$ for SI and customary units.

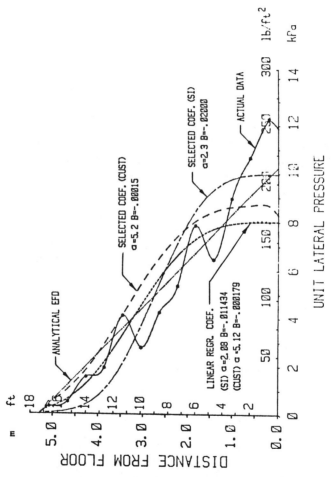

FIG. 2. Actual data for wet, Norchip variety for 1978, analytically determined EFD, and curves for various coefficients for the equation ln $p=a+B(h)^{3.5}$ for SI and customary units.

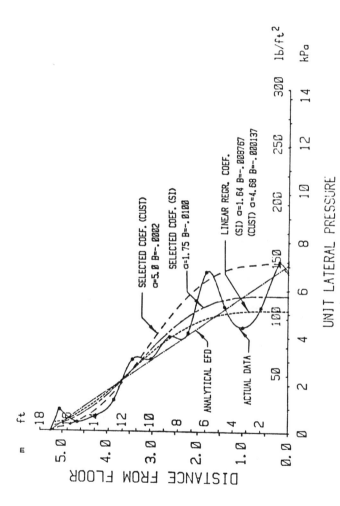

FIG. 3. Actual data for wet, Russet Burbank variety for 1979, analytically determined EFD, and curves for various coefficients for the equation ln p=a+B(h)$^{3.5}$ for SI and customary units.

597

CARBON DIOXIDE AND WIND MONITORING
IN A COMMERCIAL POTATO STORAGE

by

J.L. Varns, Research Biochemist and L.A. Schaper,
Research Argricultural Engineer, USDA-ARS; M.T.
Glynn, Research Specialist, North Dakota State
University; Red River Valley Potato Research
Laboratory, USDA-ARS-Northern State Area,
E. Grand Forks, North Dakota 58201

ABSTRACT

A prototype volatile monitoring system was
installed in a commercial potato storage containing
eight chipping bins. A personal computer controlled
the modular system that remotely sampled up to 60 bin
locations. One task in the system shakedown was to
measure the influence of the wind upon bin
atmospheres (CO_2 concentrations) during suberization.
Two bins, with similar composite pulp temperatures at
bin fill, average CO_2 atmospheres of 1.23-1.35
percent CO_2 over a one-week period when subjected to
average wind speeds that ranged 1.69-2.35

ASAE Paper No. 85-4039

meters/seconds (3.77-5.25 miles/hour). However, actual CO_2 and wind plots for these bins indicated CO_2 concentrations exceeded 4-6 percent during calm intervals; such high CO_2 atmospheres were rapidly removed when wind exceeded 4.5 m/s (>10 mph). The effect of wind upon the storeability of such typically constructed storages is discussed.

INTRODUCTION

The potato processing industry requires quality raw product availability on a nearly year-round basis. Such storage conditions for processing quality, i.e., other higher holding temperatures, relative humidities, and ventilation rates than those used by fresh market suppliers, frequently create a greater hazard for disease, earlier sprouting, pressure bruising, and irreversible increases in reducing sugar content.

After harvest the process of suberization and "wound healing" are vitally important to the success of extended storage (Pisarczyk 1982). The formation of the suberin layer, which results in a decrease in water permeability (Kolattukudy and Dean 1974; Rastovksi and van Es 1981), retards the turgor loss in potatoes piled to 4.8-5.5 m (16-18 ft.) depths and also creates a pathogenic barrier. Unless the tubers are extremely warm after harvest, it is a common practice to suberize them for 7-10 days in a nonventilated mode. During this period the storer normally watches for the bin to "go through a sweat" which is considered a favorable observation. In actuality this "sweat" is an indicator of the delayed respiratory response to prior handling stresses. When this response occurs, a water film visually forms because the water generated by accelerated respiration exceeds the rate of evaporation from the tuber surface.

This practice during suberization also promotes a rapid unobserved accumulation of CO_2 and the associated conditions that are favorable for attack by anaerobic bacteria. The current method for controlling bacterial decay is to use increased air flows of relatively dry air. Simulation studies by Hunter (1979) indicate that air flow rates need to be four times normal 78 m^3/hr/metric ton (2.1 cfm/cwt) to contain soft rot decay in deep bins.[1] Such a ventilation rate to control disease is far beyond the fan specifications suggested for current storage design. Because of these ventilation limitations the proper management during suberization is again emphasized. Various amounts of ventilation are used during suberization depending upon storage design and geographical location. Locally changing harvest conditions during the filling of a multiple-bin storage routinely cause bin-to-bin variation.

Varns (1984) reported both the speed and direction of the wind could uniformly change the internal atmosphere of a tightly sealed research bin. These changes in bin atmosphere by the wind becomes a factor in the development of sampling procedures that link the quantity of key volatiles to disease detection (Varns 1979; Waterer and Pritchard 1984) and physiological changes in storage (Day et al., 1978; Varns 1982). Information concerning mathematical relationships between the wind and structural design and its orientation are available in several reviews (ASHRAE 10985; Buffington et al., 1983). Banks et al. (1983) have recently reported on wind-induced pressure distributions in grain storages. However, such data are not yet linked to any physiological responses.

The overall objective of this research was to evaluate a prototype volatile monitoring system under commercial storage conditions. The specific objectives were to:

1. measure the differences in bin atmosphere (via CO_2 concentrations) within bins and between bins during suberization.

2. record wind speed and direction effects upon bin CO_2 concentrations.

3. test the reliability of the various monitoring components when exposed to both environmental and handling operations for storage.

----

[1]Hunter states normal at approximately 0.6 cfm/cwt to about 2.4 cfm/cwt in his 1979 paper.

MATERIALS AND METHODS

Layout of Commercial Storage

The 64.0 m long x 26.8 m (210 x 89 ft) wide flat roof storage (Figure 1) contains eight bins (6.6 x 27.4 m each [21.6 x 90 ft.]; 550 metric ton [12,000 cwt]). Bin access for shipping is provided by a centralized alleyway. Ventilation is provided by three parallel ducts (1-center trench; 2-removable, triangular side wall [leaner ducts] which are commonly connected to a plenum chamber that houses a two-speed fan (Buffington et al., 1983). The terrain surrounding the storage was flat and shelter from the wind was not present.

Design of Monitoring System

The system as described by Schaper and Varns (1984) utilized a personal computer that was programmed to control a 16 port rotary valve for remote air sampling (Figure 1, top half). The PC referenced and logged analog data via an A/D interface from the various sensors and an infrared CO_2 analyzer[2] (Anarad Model AR-411, 0-1.0/10% ranges, Anarad, Inc., Santa Barbara, CA). Sensors were as follows: anemometric (Model 5103, wind speed/azimuth, 0-5V linear output, R.M. Young Co., Traverse City, MI, positioned 3.5 m (11.5 ft.) above roofline); bin air temperature (8 RTDs, type TD4A, water resistant, Micro Switch, Freeport, IL, positioned 0.3 m (1 ft.) above bin pile surface); fan operation (8-Model S688A sail switches, on/off, Honeywell, located proximate to each fan housing).

The initial monitoring system was expanded to permit bin air to be pumped to the monitor room from 60 locations via 6.3 mm (1/4 in.) OD heavywall nylon tubing. Tubing was strong near the alleyway ceiling and seven tubes per bin were run thorugh the leaner ducts to their respective sampling points. Steel spring reinforced tubing (SSRTs, 4.0 mm (5/32 in.)

----

[2] The mention of firm or trade products does not imply that they are endorsed or recommended by the U.S. Department of Agriculture over other firms of similar products not mentioned.

ID, Newage Industries, Inc., Willow Grove, PA) was then attached at the bin sampling point (Figure 2A) and could be uncoiled and placed into the pile during bin fill (Figure 2B). Clogging of sample tubes and analytical contamination were controlled by inserting glass wool in the SSRT ends and by the placement of fritted brass air filters (Model F10-10, 35 micron porosity, Industrial Specialities, Inc., Englewood, CO) in all nylon sampling tubes. The seven sample locations in each bin were (1) alley end, floor level, left and right sides 24 m (78.7 ft.) from fan, (2) pile center, 2.4 m (7.87 ft.) up from floor, left and right sides 12 m (39.3 ft.) from fan, (3) fan end, floor level, left and right sides 2.4 m (7.87 ft.) from fan, and (4) pile surface, 7.6 m (25.0 ft.) from alley. One of the 16 tubes on the 16 port rotary valve was placed outside the storage to act as a reference standard for the CO_2 infrared analyzer.

Each of the 60 nylon tubes were connected to a normally closed solenoid valve (Minimatic ET-2MLP, 12 VDC Clippard Instrument Lab, Inc., Cincinnati, Ohio) and then ganged to 15 manifolds that housed four solenoid valves each (Figure 1). The manifolds were then connected to the 15 lines from the rotary valve. The tubing-manifold configuration could be programmed to monitor any number of bins during the harvest-bin filling period. The BASIC programming for the solenoid operation was cross-checked by an · LED display that indicated which solenoid valves were activated during a test period. The sixteen lines on the rotary valve (5 slm/min maximum total flow) and their accessed portion of the 60 locations were continuously purged by a chemically-inert diaphragm pump (Model 279, Air Dimensions Inc., Kulpsville, PA).

A two minute purge of the CO_2 analyzer cell, using the next line to be sampled, was operated between sample readings to insure complete displacement of the previous sample. Sample flow conditions were monitored for (1) total continous flow entering the rotary valve (15 lines) and (2) the selected sample flow exiting from rotary valve to the CO_2 analyzer.

Data Acquisition

The BASIC program was set to recognize the time for a sampling cycle as equal to the selected cycle of sampling locations selected times a three minute sampling duration per sample. During harvest this cycle would get progressively longer as the number of filled bins (sampling locations) increased. The average of the last three of five CO_2 readings was recorded for each sample location. Data from the additional sensing equipment were recorded during the two minute system purge between CO_2 sampling locations. The number of sample locations per cycle and the number of cycles per day could be changed by the operator. All raw data were recorded on diskettes for later use. The operator was able to visually monitor all sensor data by CRT or by printout in a summarized format for each bin. Graphic results were prepared by the following software: Fast Graphs (Innovative Softare, Inc., Overland, KS) or BPS Business Graphics (Business & Professional Software, Inc., Cambridge, MA).

Storage Operations

Bins were filled to a 4.8-5.4 m (15.7-17.7 ft.) depth. A complete bin fill usually required 1-2 days. Pulp temperatures of each load were recorded by the cooperator. The composite pulp averages for the bin ranged from 6.3 to 17.0°C (43.3 to 62.6 °F). The amount of ventilation selected for each bin, as indicated by the storer, depended upon such factors as pulp temperature, outside air temperature, and harvest damage. An internal bin wall failure permitted only four bins to be monitored; bin #3 was uniformly half filled (2.4-3.0 m [7.87-9.8 ft.] depth) because of a crop shortage.

Test data and related cooperator-storage information were collected under the guidelines that storage management decisions were not to be influenced by observed test data.

RESULTS AND DISCUSSION

Effect of Wind on Storage (CO_2) Environment

The wind and CO_2 profiles for the first seven days of suberization are shown for bin #2 (Figure 3A) and bin #4 (Figure 3B). Similarities between these two included (a) filled capacity, (b) location, ie., north side of facility, (c) harvesting conditions (dry), and (d) sub-optimum temperatures for suberization. It was the practice of the storer to treat such bins (<10 C) with little or no ventilation for the first week after bin fill to permit a warming of the bulk pile for improved suberization. This time period permitted us to monitor the expected high concentrations of CO_2 that could be attained' during the high respiratory period following harvest (Schippers 1977) and to note the wind effect upon the respective CO environment.

Figure 3A (bin #2) shows rapid decreases (valleys) in the CO_2 plot (foreground, shaded) which correspond to increases (peaks) in the wind plot. This inverse relationship between CO_2 and wind is again demonstrated in Figure 3B when the wind plot (foreground; shaded) is presented. Generally speaking, the wind-driven rate of CO_2 removal in Figure 3A was similar to the rate of CO_2 generation (valley bottoms of 1-1.5% CO_2) when the wind speed was 2.2-4.5 m/s (5-10 mph). These actual data plotted in Figure 3A are similar to the bin #2 summary data in Table 1; bin 2 averaged 1.23 percent CO_2 over a seven day period when the corresponding wind speed averaged 2.35 m/s (5.26 mph). However, such averages in Table 1 do not reflect the ability of the CO_2 concentration in bin #2 to increase two-fold in less than 24 hours under low wind conditions.

A bin wall failure in another partially filled bin forced the relocation of those potatoes into the last one-third of bin #4 as monitored in Figure 3B. Consequently, these potatoes were handled twice. Higher CO_2 concentrations were measured in this portion of bin #4 than in bin #2, at times over 6 percent, but it is not known whether the higher CO_2 in Figure 3B was the result of increased handling or that the pulp temperature was higher in this bin region. The concentration of accumulated CO_2 would also depend on the time interval between wind speeds that cause CO_2 removal (>4.5 m/s or >10 mph). Fans were turned on in bin #4 after a 147 hour period of nonventilation (Figure 3B) because the storer experienced labored breathing while in the #4 fan plenum. Bin #4 repeatedly demonstrated a pattern of 2-3 fold increases in CO_2 if low wind conditions (2.2-4.5 m/s) persisted for half-day periods. Winds usually diminish at night along with a decrease in air temperature. Therefore an effort to cool down a bin of hot harvested potatoes (>18 ° C) could also prevent the greatest potential accumulation of CO_2.

Bin #6 exhibited a 6.19 percent CO_2 concentration within a 34-hour period following bin closure (Table 1), a CO_2 value similar to that reached in bin #4 (Figure 3B). These data suggest that such 6-7 percent CO_2 accumulation are not uncommon and greater concentrations would be expected in warmer bins, especially under milder wind conditions.

The data summary in Table 1 suggests that bins of this construction can yield similar CO_2 information if factors such as pulp temperature and wind conditions do not differ greatly. For example, bins #4 and #2 maintained means of 1.03 percent CO_2 and 1.35 percent CO_2 for six and seven days, respectively, under similar wind speed averages and pulp temperatures. Bin #3 was uniformly half-filled, and consequently, maintained approximately one-half the seven-day mean of the completely filled bins (0.55% CO_2).

Variation Within a Single Bin

Table 1 indicates the temperature range of harvest loads (> 5 °C) may cause different rates of respiration, i.e., different rates of CO_2 generation and accumulation, to be operating in a filled bin. Any ability of the monitor system to pick up such respiratory differences was quickly diminished when the magnitude of the wind effect was measured. Figure 4 shows the average percent CO_2 at six locations in bin #2 from 3-10 days following bin fill. Generally speaking, the highest average CO_2 concentrations were measured at the pile centers (locations R12 or L12) because each bin end had access doors which were not air tight. The greatest wind effect upon the outside doors (locations R2.4 or L2.4) are indicated by the lowest average CO_2 concentrations.

The ranking of actual CO_2 concentrations by sampling location were sometimes observed to switch as shown in Figure 5. At time points A and B in the upper graph of Figure 5, the three monitored locations on the left side of bin #3 exhibited a concentration spread exceeding one percent CO_2 ; however, the order of CO_2 ranking switched from 12>2.4>24 m to 2.4>24>12 m for time values A and B, respectively. Such reversals were not expected since the CO_2 peaks correspond to the low regions (A and B) of the wind profile in the lower graph of Figure 5. The corresponding plot of the wind direction (azimuth, 360 degrees ÷ 100 ; shaded) measured for the wind speed profile permitted a comparison of wind direction for points A and B. Wind direction was approximately northeast for both points; therefore it is suggested that unknown change(s) in storage operation, as well as the wind effect, can cause disruptive changes in bin environment.

Commercial Considerations

The marketing advantage of comparable quality between potato bins after extended storage dictates a goal to minimize the differences in bin environments during wound healing and suberization. The storer wishes to provide adequate ventilation for harvest recovery, but an inflexible ventilation program for a multi-bin facility does not compensate for (a) the variation in harvested tubers entering the storage, e.g., different amounts of harvest damage or pulp temperatures because of weather changes, and (b) the changing ventilation needs of filled bins as the storage continues to load towards its capacity. The wind effect reported herein further complicates any effort to normalize the raw product prior to preparation for long term storage. It is likely that fan operation on a windy day would serve only to remove excessive water from the potatoes, a situation to be avoided if tissue turgor is to be retained to minimize pressure bruising.

606

The manager of the commercial storage indicated sensor data for each bin should be periodically compiled and be available in graphic format. It is expected that any controlling function added to a computerized monitoring system, such as ventilation, would strengthne the quest by the opertor to be provided with decision-making graphics. The described layout for bin sampling did not interfere with normal storing and shipping operations and the air filtering precautions against dust contamination were adequate for a storage season.

It is suggested the manpower limitations in smaller storage operations will necessitate the automation of routine ventilation decisions if the manager is to minimize harvest and early storage variables. Fan operation regulated by monitored CO_2 limits (via decision software) is one approach to normalizing the bin environment. This approach compensates for (a) respiratory and stress changes in the raw product and (b) external changes such as wind speed and direction. Environmental normalization may also be favorable for extended periods of storage since elevated CO_2 concentrations are reported to stimulate respiration (Perez-Trejo et al., 1981), aid in breaking dormancy (Reust and Gugerli 1984), and alter the respiratory quotient (Isherwood and Burton 1974).

SUMMARY

The following observations are drawn from this study:

1. The tested bins, of typical construction for chipping requirements, provide similar gaseous environments if bin fill, pulp temperature and wind conditions are also comparable.

2. Unwanted CO_2 concentrations exceeding six percent can be reached in bins containing suberizing potatoes having pulp temperatures below 10 °C; however high CO_2 concentrations were rapidly reduced to <2% if winds speeds averaged 4.5 m/s (approximately 10 mph). This suggests the differences in ventilation that are argued for optimum suberization may, in part, be explained by geographical wind differences.

607

3. The storer can minimize the stress of water
loss by linking ventilation control with monitored CO_2
concentration limits. Unless cooling is required,
fan operation would not be necessary with a
prevailing wind effect. Likewise, ventilation would
be triggered during calm periods when an undesirable
upper CO_2 limit is exceeded.

4. This wind effect would decrease the
detection sensitivity of a disease monitoring system
that is based upon quantitation of specific stress
volatiles. This emphasizes the need to normalize any
stress quantitation with a ventilation reference such
as CO_2.

ACKNOWLEDGEMENT

This research study was made possible by the
cooperation and extensive facilities provided by R.D.
Moen and Sons located at Reynolds, ND.

REFERENCES

ASHRAE. 1985. Natural ventilation and infiltration
    in Handbook of fundamentals, Chapter 22,
    American Society of Heating, Refrigeration and
    Air-conditioning Engineers, Atlanta, GA 30329.

Banks, H.J., R.A. Longstaff, M.R. Raupach and J.J.
    Finnigan. 1983. Wind-induced pressure distri-
    bution on a large grain storage shed: predic-
    tion of wind-driven ventilation rates. J. of
    Stored Products Research, 19:181-188.

Buffington, D.C., L.D. Albright, S.K. Sastry, L.A.
    Schaper and R.B. Furry. 1983. Ventilation for
    horticultural crop storage in Ventilation of
    agricultural structures, ASAE monograph No. 6,
    ASAE, St. Joseph, MI 49085, pp. 303-332.

Day, D.A., G.P. Arron, R.E. Christoffersen, and G.G.
    Laties. 1978. Effect of ethylene and carbon
    dioxide on potato metabolism. Plant Physiol.
    62:820-825.

Hunter, J.H. 1979. Simulation studies for control of tuber decay in potato storage. Presentation at ASAE meetings, New Orleans, LA. Dec. 11-14, ASAE Paper No. 79-4535.

Isherwood, F.A. and W.G. Burton. 1974. The effect of senescence, handling and chemical sprout suppression upon the respiratory quotient of stored potato tubers. Potato Res. 18:98-104.

Kolattukudy, P.E. and B.B. Dean. 1974. Structure, gas chromatographic measurement, and function of suberin synthesized by potato tuber tissue slices. Plant Physiol. 54:116-121.

Perez-Trejo, M.S., W.J. Janes, and C. Frenkel. 1981. Mobilization of respiratory metabolism in potato tubers by carbon dioxide. Plant Physiol. 67: 514-517.

Pisarczyk, J.M. 1982. Field harvest damage affects potato tuber respiration and sugar content. Amer. Potato J. 59:205-211.

Rastovksi, A. and A. van Es et al. 1981. Storage of potatoes, Center for Agricultural Publishing and Documentation, Wageningen, the Netherlands, pp. 129-137.

Reust, W. and P. Gugerli. 1984. Oxygen and carbon dioxide treatment to break potato tuber dormancy for reliable detection of potato virus Y (PVY) by enzyme-linked immunosorbent assay (ELISA). Potato Res. 27:435-439.

Schaper, L.A., J.L. Varns, M.T. Glynn and J.D. Hilley. 1984. A computerized gas sampling and analysis system for potato storages. Presentattion at ASAE meetings, New Orleans, LA, Dec. 11-14, ASAE Paper No. 84-5532.

Schippers, P.A. 1977. The rate of respiration of potato tubers during storage 1. Review of literature. Potato Res 20:173-188.

Varns, J.L. and M.T. Glynn. 1979. Detection of disease in stored potatoes by volatile monitoring. Amer. Potato J. 56:185-197.

Varns, J.L. 1982. The release of methyl chloride from potato tubers. Amer. Potato J. 59:593-604.

Varns, J.L. 1984. CO_2 and Storage. Proceedings, Meetings of the Prairie Potato Council, Feb. 5-9, Saskatoon, Sack., Canada, pp. 150-152.

Waterer, D.R. and M.K. Pritchard. 1984. Volatile monitoring as a technique for differentiating between E. carotovora and C. sepedonicum infections in stored potatoes. Amer. Potato J. 61:345-353.

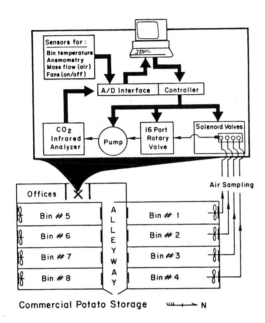

Fig. 1 Schematic diagram of a multiple-bin storage and the major components of the remote gas monitoring system (location X). The paths for air sampling (→) and interactive data transfer (➡) are shown.

Fig. 2 Sample tubing at a bin floor location (A) before leaner duct installation, and (B) during bin fill.

612

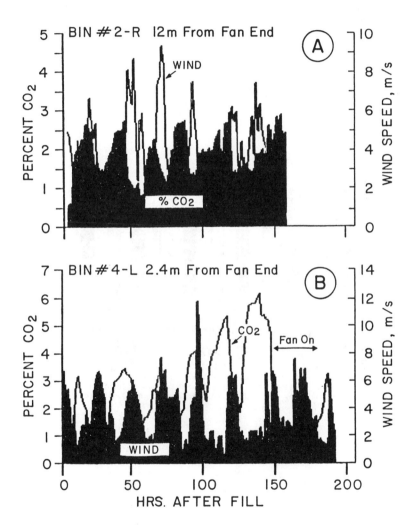

Fig. 3 Relationship between bin CO_2 concentration and wind speed
during the first week after bin fill: (A) bin #2 - right 12 m
sampling location (% CO_2, shaded foreground) and (**B**) bin #4 -
left 2.4 m sampling location (wind speed, shaded foreground).

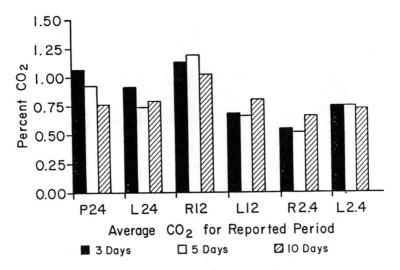

Fig. 4 Changes in averaged CO_2 concentrations at different sampling
locations within suberizing potato pile (bin #2 locations
designated by meters from fan end, (r)ight and (l)eft sides.

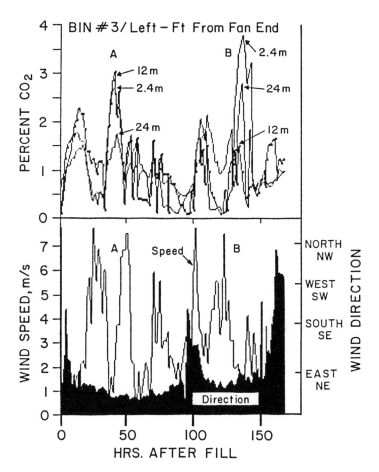

Fig. 5   Shifts in CO_2 accumulations at different levels within a suberizing potato pile (regions A & B, upper) and their corresponding profiles (regions A & B, lower) of wind speed (background) and wind direction (shaded foreground).

COMPARISON OF POTATO PILE PRESSURES
ON VERTICAL AND INCLINED WALLS

by

Earl C. Yaeger,[1] Agricultural Engineer, Nursery
Crops Research Laboratory, Midwest Area, Delaware,
Ohio; Lewis A. Schaper[2] and Paul H. Orr,[2] Research
Laboratory, Northern States Area, East Grand Forks,
Minnesota

ABSTRACT

Inclined and vertical wall pressure data are
compared and equated by a trigonometric
approximation. Plate reaction (PR), sill reaction
(RS) and bending moment (MB) based on EFD analysis
procedure and on data values are shown for a vertical
wall and inclined wall angle of 5, 10, 15, 20 and 25
degrees.

ASAE Paper No. 84-701

INTRODUCTION

Storage structures with vertical and inclined walls are commonly used to store potatoes. Lateral potato pressures on vertical walls have been investigated and reported for different periods of time between 1950 and 1979, (Edgar, 1960; Willson, 1968, Powell et al., 1980; Schaper and Yaeger, 1982). Yaeger and Schaper (1984) report significant reduction of the normal and vertical pile pressure as the inclined wall more closely approaches the natural angle of repose of the potato pile.

The objectives of this study are to (1) directly compare vertical and inclined wall pressure data and wall design parameter values for a single commercial size potato bin: (2) determine the relationship between potato pressures on a vertical wall and inclined walls.

PROCEDURES

Experimental Conditions and Data Collection

Twelve pressure panels and transducers were installed in the sloped end wall of a prototype, commercial size, experimental storage bin located at the Red River Valley Potato Research Laboratory. This bin was 7.3 m (24 ft.) wide and 24.4 m (80 ft.)

----

[1]Agricultural Engineer at the Nursery Crops Research Laboratory, USDA-ARS, Delaware, Ohio. (Formerly at the Red River Valley Potato Research Laboratory).

[2]Agricultural Engineers at the Red River Valley Potato Research Laboratory. This laboratory is cooperatively operated by the Northern States Area, Agricultural Research Service--USDA; the Minnesota Agricultural Experiment Station; the North Dakota Agricultural Experiment Station; and the Red River Valley Potato Growers Association.

*This paper was prepared on official Government time and reports research paid for by U.S. taxpayers. The article and the research information, therefore, are in the public domain and cannot be copyrighted.

long. Initially, pile depths (heights) of 5.3 m
(17.5 ft.) were used for wall inclination angles of 0
and 25 (recorded day after filling). Due to
requirements of a companion project, the pile depth
(height) was reduced to 4.9 m (16.0 ft.) for all
other angles of inclination. The panels were 305 mm
by 305 mm (12 in. by 12 in.) and mounted in a
continuous row from the top of the pile to the floor
at the center line of the end wall. For this series
of tests, 25 from the vertical was selected as the
initial inclination angle of the wall, then each
successive test year the angle was decreased by 5 ° .
This range of angles closely approximates the 15 to
30 incination angles commonly used in commercial
buildings (Roepke et al., 1980). To attain the
desired inclination of the test bin wall, the main
frame containing the wall pressure panels was tilted
into the storage bin the desired angle and then
welded into place.

Potato harvesting and bin filling were done in a
manner typical of commercial practices. As the
potatoes were conveyed into the bin, they were
sprayed with a water-fungicide solution from mist
type spray nozzles 1 gallon/ton or 3.79 liter/20 cwt
The potatoes were stored at 8° C 46° F) and the bin
relative humidity was maintained at 90 percent or
higher. The cultivar, Norchip, was used for all
tests. For further information on instrumentation
and bin conditions see Yaeger and Pratt (1977) and
Schaper and Yaeger (1982).

Initial pressure readings were taken after the
first 6.1 m (20 ft.) of bin length was filled level
full with potatoes. Readings were taken daily
throughout the storage season, but were analyzed for
Monday of each week. The one day data that indicated
maximum total force for each year was then used for
further analysis.

It is important to note that the bin pressure
referred to in this study is always that pressure
measured perpendicular to the wall. The pressure was
measured by panels installed parallel to the plane of
the wall for all wall incline angles tested.

Calculations and Error Analysis

The vertical wall and the 25 inclined wall data,

618

recorded for a 5.3 m (17.5 ft.) pile depth were
adjusted to a 4.95 m (16.2 ft.) pile depth and 5.3 m
(17.5 ft.) wall height so that comparisons with
values of the remaining inclinations could be made.
The adjustment was accomplished by deleting the
bottom panel, pressure reading for the vertical and
25° inclined wall and then proceeding with the
analysis. This allows for a direct comparison of the
results.

Inclined walls were considered a special case of
a vertical wall, and ways of relating vertical and
inclined wall pressures were compared. We selected
equivalent fluid density (EFD) as the parameter for
comparing vertical and inclined wall results because:
1) The raw data pressure patterns were too irregular
for direct comparison at incline angles from 15
through 25 from vertical, and 2) equivalent fluid
density analogy is often used in design.

Equivalent fluid density may be described as the
apparent liquid specific density of a semi-fluid
material that relates unit lateral pressures linearly
to depth. Various EFD values were tried for each
pressure curve until an EFD value was found that
caused the area under the triangular EFD load
distribution to equal the area under the actual
pressure curve distribution (Schaper and Yaeger,
1983).

An error analysis was performed to estimate the
accuracy of all parameters calculated from the
original measured data (Ku, 1967). An estimate of
the design error due to calculation of various wall
and moment reactions using a range of selected EFD's
for inclined walls, was done as detailed earlier for
vertical wall data (Schaper and Yaeger, 1983).

Inclined/Vertical Wall Relationships

The following approaches were considered for
relating the pressure normal to a wall as the wall is
inclined from vertical:

1. Since EFD equals active pressure coefficient
(K_A) time product density, equations for K using
various combinations of sine and cosine functions for
appropriate parameters were tried according to
Merritt (1983).

619

2. Various powers of the cosine of the angle of incline were tried.

3. Reimbert and Reimbert (1974) present a trigonometric approximation that incorporates the wall angle (θ) and angle of repose (α) of the stored product. This approximation reduces the lateral pressure for inclined walls. This relationship is as follows:

$$\frac{(90° - \theta)^- \alpha}{90° - \alpha}$$

The dependent variable in our analyses was K_A (inclined wall) divided by K_A (vertical wall) or EFD (inclined wall) divided by EFD (vertical wall).

RESULTS AND DISCUSSION

Accuracy of Physical Measurements

Measurement of pile depth was determined through experimental and statistical analyses to be within $\pm$ 0.03 m (0.1 ft.) for these tests. Total force (TF) was found to be accurage to 1 percent (Schaper and Yaeger, 1982). Measurement of wall height was within $\pm$0.06 m (0.2 ft.). Since the wall was carefully adjusted to and securely anchored at the required inclination each season, the accuracy of the inclination angle was $\pm$ 0.5 .

Accuracy of Calculated Parameters

Figure 1 (vertical wall) and Figure 2 through 6 (inclined walls) illustrate the patterns of the maximum unit normal pressure data and the resulting equivalent fluid densities. For the five seasons of inclined wall tests (Figure 2 through 6), the unit normal pressure curves showed patterns consistent with the vertical wall lateral pressure patterns (Figure 1) reported by Schaper and Yaeger (1982). The magnitude of the total force decreased as the wall angle increased from vertical.

Except for the season with the 15 ° inclined wall, all unit normal pressure curves showed some additional increase in pressure after initial filling

620

of the storage (zero elapsed days). The lack of increase in pressure for the 15° season is likely due to relatively less initial moisture on the surface of the potatoes which affected the surface coefficient of friction .

The values in Table 1 (Table 2) were calculated according to the procedure reported in Schaper and Yaeger (1982). These were derived by first fitting a spline function curve to the pressure data. Numerical integration of the resulting curve gave the total force (TF). Center of the force (C) was also determined using a numerical integration procedure. Reactions were calculated assuming simple supported beam conditions. Bending moments were obtained by numercial integration of the shear curve for the potato pile pressure.

All calculated parameters of Table 1 (Table 2) reflect the relationship of perpendicularity to the plane of the wall for all given incline angles. All total force values in Table 1 (Table 2) are those that occurred on the day that measured normal pressures resulted in maximum total force during a given storage season. From the error analysis procedure, the following rounding was applied to the data of Table 1 (Table 2).

Parameter	Round to Nearest	
	SI Units*	Customary Units*
TF	0.5 kN/m	50 lb/ft
C	0.05 m	0.2 ft
EFD	5.0 kg/m^3	0.5 lb/ft^3
RP,RS	0.5 kN/m	50 lb/ft
MB	1.0 kN·m/m	500 ft-lb/ft

*See Nomenclature for definition of terms.

The plate reaction (RP), as calculated using EFD values, tends to overestimate the data RP value at the 0°, 5°, 15° and 20° wall inclination. The sill reaction (RS) values based on EFD tend to underestimate the actual data RS for all wall inclinations except 25°.

Bending moment (MB) based on EFD closely estimate values based on actual pressures at 0°, 10°, and 25° and overestimate at 5° and 15°.

Errors in Various Inclined Wall Design Parameters With Selected EFD's

Table 3 (Table 4) is an error table comparing RS, RF, and MB for EFD and data values. The EFD values are compared at 5 or 10 kg/m^3 (± 0.5 lb/ft^3) intervals. For wall inclinations of 0°, 5°, and 10°, the error in most cases is between −10 to 2 percent. However, as the wall is inclined from 15° to 25°, error estimates, based on actual data values, are as high as 150 percent. These high error values can be misleading because they are based on small actual values with high rounding intervals. Error at the 15 incline may have been the result of potatoes being loaded into the storage during an extremely dry harvest season resulting in an uneven loading pattern.

Relationship between Inclined and Vertical Wall Normal Pressure

Figure 7 is a plot of the ratio of the EFD for the inclined wall to the EFD for the vertical wall versus incline angle. A number of algebraic and trigonometric relationships were evaluated for relating the results shown in this figure.

The results of various least square fit algebraic relationships are shown in Table 5. These algebraic relationships contain only the angle of wall incline as an independent variable.

Tests with trigonometric equations, which incorporate several independent variables, for K_A for soils did not prove satisfactory in relating vertical and inclined wall potato pressures (Merritt,

1983). Similar results occurred with powers of the cosine of the angle of inclination with respect to vertical.

The trigonometric correction factor as proposed by Reimbert and Reimbert (1974) did not adequately relate our results for inclined walls. However, when their suggestion function was cubed a viable correction vertical wall data for inclined wall conditions is:

$$\frac{EFD \; Incline}{EFD \; Vertical} = \left| \frac{(90° - \theta) - \alpha}{90° - \alpha} \right|^3$$

To evaluate the goodness of fit of this equation, a multivariable regression analysis was run. The angle of repose and the incline angle were the two independent variables. The results are included in Table 5. Curves for this function with an angle of repose of 28 ° and 35° , respectively, are shown in Figure 7. The angle of repose for potatoes has been determined to be between 28 ° and 35° (Yaeger, 1985).

As indicated in Table 5 both algebraic and trigonometric functions will predict the reduction in potato pressure normal to a bin wall due to increasing inclination of the wall. Since the trigonometric function includes more physical variables and better predicts conditions at 20 and 25 inclines, it may be the most applicable function for determining changes in wall pressures as walls are inclined from vertical. The ratio, "EFD of Inclined Wall/EFD of Vertical Wall" is to be applied as a multiplier to the vertical (0 °) wall EFD value to obtain the applicable EFD value for any given wall incline between 0° and 25 ° from the vertical.

CONCLUSIONS

Based on a single year's data obtained for each of 5 ° , 10 ° , 15 ° , 20° and 35 ° wall inclinations, we concluded.

1. Inclining the storage bin wall is an effective way of reducing the normal potato bin wall pressures.

2. Inclined wall, normal pressures can be estimated by applying the trigonometric correction factor.

$$\left| \frac{(90 - \theta) - \alpha}{90 - \alpha} \right|^3$$

to vertical wall pressure data.

ACKNOWLEDGEMENTS

The authors wish to thank Marilyn Nelson, Engineering Technician, USDA-ARS, Red River Valley Potato Research Laboratory, East Grand Forks, MN for assistance in obtaining and processing data and R.D. J. Gill, and K.G. Janardan, Statisticians, North Dakota State University, Fargo, ND for statistical advice.

REFERENCES

Edgar, Alfred D. 1960. Potato pressures on walls of storage bins. USDA, Agr. Marketing Ser. AMS-401.

Ku, Harry H. 1967. Statistical concepts in metrology. Handbook of Industrial Metrology, Am. Soc. of Tool and Manufacturing Engineers. Prentice-Hall, Inc. New York, New York.

Merritt, Frederick A. 1983. Standard handbook for civil engineers, 3rd ed. McGraw-Hill Book Co. New York, New York.

Powell, Albert E., C. Alan Pettibone and M. Reza T Torabi. 1980. Pressure exerted on the walls of large bins by stored potatoes. Transactions of the ASEA 23 (3); 685-687.

Reimbert, Marcel L. and Andrew M. Reimbert. 1974. Retaining walls: Anchorages and sheet piling. Theory and practice, vol. I, 274 p. Trans Tech Publications, Bay Village, Ohio.

Roepke, Warren L. and Richard Patterson. Butler Manufacturing Co., Agri. products Division, Kansas City, Missouri, 1980 Personal Communication, 5/18/80.

Schaper, Lewis A. and E.C. Yaeger. 1982. Horizontal and vertical pressure patterns of stored potatoes. Transactions of the ASAE 25(3):719-724.

Schaper, Lewis A. and Earl C. Yaeger. 1983. Accuracy of equivalent fluid density for potato storage wall design. Transactions of the ASAE 26(1):179-184, 187.

Willson, G.B. 1968. Lateral pressures on walls of potato storage bins. USDA, Agr. Res. Ser. ARS 52-32.

Yaeger, E.C. and G.L. Pratt. 1977. Instrumentation for measurement of lateral and vertical pressures in potato storages. Transactions of the ASAE 20(6):1180-1184.

Yaeger, E.C. and Lewis A. Schaper. 1984. Pressure patterns of stored potatoes on sloped wall structures. ASAE Paper 84-4002, University of Tennessee, Knoxville, Tennesse, June 24-27.

Yaeger, Earl C. 1985. Unpublished data. Red River Valley Potato Research Laboratory.

NOMENCLATURE

C   –Center of force with respect to the bottom of the pile, m(ft)

EFD –Equivalent fluid density, $kg/m^3(lb/ft^3)$

ft   –Foot (or feet)

K_A –Active pressure coefficient (ratio of the lateral pressure to the vertical pressure)

kg   –Kilogram

lb   –pound

m   –meter

MB   –Bending Moment, kN·m/m(ft-lb/ft)

N   –Newton, $kg·m/sec^2$

P   –Unit pressure at selected location, $Pa(lb/ft^2)$

Pa   –Pascal, N/m^2

RS   –Sill reaction, kN/m(lb/ft)

RP   –Plate reaction, kN/m(lb/ft)

TF   –Total force per unit wall length, kN/m(lb/ft)

α –Angle of repose, degrees

θ –Angle of wall incline from vertical, degrees

626

TABLE 1. MEASURED DATA AND CALCULATED DESIGN PARAMETERS FOR POTATO BIN PRESSURE*

WALL INCLINE Deg	MAX. TF DATA kN/m	EFD DATA kg/m³	CENTER OF FORCE		PLATE REACTION		SILL REACTION		BENDING MOMENT	
			C DATA m	C EFD m	Rp DATA kN/m	Rp EFD kN/m	Rs DATA kN/m	Rs EFD kN/m	MB DATA kN·m/m	MB EFD kN·m/m
0	21.0	180	1.40	1.60	5.5	6.5	15.5	14.5	14	15
5	15.5	125	1.30	1.60	4.0	5.0	12.0	11.0	9	11
10	13.0	110	1.35	1.60	3.5	4.0	9.5	9.0	8	9
15	8.0	65	0.85	1.60	1.0	2.5	6.5	5.5	3	5
20	6.5	55	1.35	1.60	1.5	2.0	5.0	4.5	4	5
25	3.5	30	1.85	1.60	1.0	1.0	2.0	2.0	2	2

* All values occurred on day of maximum total force during storage season and are perpendicular to bin wall.
All measured data and calculated parameters at the 0° and 25° inclinations were adjusted to 4.9m pile depth.
5.3m wall height.

TABLE 2. MEASURED DATA AND CALCULATED DESIGN PARAMETERS FOR POTATO BIN PRESSURE*

WALL INCLINE Deg	MAX. TF DATA lb/ft	EFD DATA lb/ft³	CENTER OF FORCE		PLATE REACTION		SILL REACTION		BENDING MOMENT	
			DATA C ft	EFD C ft	DATA R_p lb/ft	EFD R_p lb/ft	DATA R_3 lb/ft	EFD R_3 lb/ft	DATA MB ft-lb/ft	EFD MB ft-lb/ft
0	1450	11.5	4.6	5.4	400	450	1050	1000	3000	3000
5	1050	7.5	4.4	5.4	250	350	800	750	2000	2500
10	900	7.0	4.4	5.4	250	250	650	600	2000	2000
15	550	4.0	2.9	5.4	100	150	450	350	500	1000
20	450	3.5	4.6	5.4	100	150	350	300	1000	1000
25	250	2.0	6.0	5.4	100	50	150	150	500	500

* All values occurred on day of maximum total force during storage season and are perpendicular to bin wall. All measured data and calculated parameters at the 0° and 25° inclinations were adjusted to 16.0 ft pile depth, 17.5 ft wall height.

628

Table 3. ERROR* ANALYSIS FOR SELECTED EFD'S WITH CENTER OF FORCE AT ONE THIRD OF PILE DEPTH**

WALL INCLINE DEG	EFD VALUE kg/m³	SILL REACTION			PLATE REACTION			BENDING MOMENT		
		ACTUAL DATA VALUE R_S kN/m	EFD BASED VALUE R_S kN/m	PERCENT ERROR %	ACTUAL DATA VALUE R_P kN/m	EFD BASED VALUE R_P kN/m	PERCENT ERROR %	ACTUAL DATA VALUE M_R kN·m/m	EFD BASED VALUE M_R kN·m/m	PERCENT ERROR %
0°	190	15.5	15.5	0	5.5	7.0	27	14.0	16.0	14
	185	15.5	15.0	-3	5.5	6.5	18	14.0	15.0	7
	175	15.5	14.5	-6	5.5	6.5	18	14.0	14.0	0
5°	145	12.0	11.5	-4	4.0	5.0	25	9.0	12.0	33
	135	12.0	11.0	-8	4.0	5.0	25	9.0	11.0	22
	130	12.0	10.5	-13	4.0	4.5	13	9.0	10.0	11
10°	120	9.5	9.5	0	3.5	4.5	29	8.0	10.0	25
	110	9.5	9.0	-5	3.5	4.0	14	8.0	9.0	13
	105	9.5	8.9	-11	3.5	3.5	0	8.0	8.0	0
15°	70	6.5	6.0	-8	1.0	2.5	150	3.0	6.0	100
	65	6.5	5.0	-23	1.0	2.5	150	3.0	5.0	67
	55	6.5	4.5	-31	1.0	2.0	100	3.0	4.0	33
20°	65	5.0	5.0	0	1.5	2.5	67	4.0	5.0	25
	55	5.0	4.5	-10	1.5	2.0	33	4.0	4.0	0
	50	5.0	4.0	-20	1.5	1.5	0	4.0	4.0	0
25°	40	2.0	3.0	50	1.0	1.5	50	2.0	3.0	50
	30	2.0	2.5	25	1.0	1.0	0	2.0	3.0	50
	25	2.0	2.0	0	1.0	1.0	0	2.0	2.0	0

* Error = $\dfrac{\text{EFD value} - \text{Data value}}{\text{Data value}}$ X 100

**All measured data and calculated parameters at the 0° and 25° inclinations were adjusted to 4.9m pile depth, 5.3m wall height

Table 4. ERROR* ANALYSIS FOR SELECTED EFD'S WITH CENTER OF FORCE AT ONE THIRD OF PILE DEPTH**

WALL INCLINE DEG	EFD VALUE lb/ft³	SILL REACTION			PLATE REACTION			BENDING MOMENT		
		ACTUAL DATA VALUE R_S lb/ft	EFD BASED VALUE R_S lb/ft	PERCENT ERROR %	ACTUAL DATA VALUE R_P lb/ft	EFD BASED VALUE R_P lb/ft	PERCENT ERROR %	ACTUAL DATA VALUE M_R ft-lb/ft	EFD BASED VALUE M_R ft-lb/ft	PERCENT ERROR %
0°	12.0	1050	1050	0	400	450	13	3000	3500	17
	11.5	1050	1000	-5	400	450	13	3000	3500	17
	11.0	1050	1000	-5	400	450	13	3000	3000	0
5°	9.0	800	800	0	350	250	40	2000	2500	25
	8.5	800	750	-6	350	250	40	2000	2500	25
	8.0	800	700	-13	350	250	20	2000	2500	25
10°	7.5	650	650	0	250	300	20	2000	2000	0
	7.0	650	600	-8	250	250	0	2000	2000	0
	6.5	650	600	-8	250	250	0	2000	2000	0
15°	4.5	450	400	-11	100	200	100	500	1500	200
	4.0	450	350	-22	100	150	50	500	1000	100
	3.5	450	300	-33	100	150	50	500	1000	100
20°	4.0	350	350	0	100	150	50	1000	1000	0
	3.5	350	300	-14	100	150	50	1000	1000	0
	3.0	350	250	-29	100	100	50	1000	1000	0
25°	2.5	150	200	33	100	100	0	500	500	0
	2.0	150	200	33	100	100	0	500	500	0
	1.5	150	150	0	100	50	-50	500	500	0

Error = $\dfrac{\text{EFD Value} - \text{Data Value}}{\text{Data Value}}$ X 100

*All measured data and calculated parameters at the 0° and 25° inclinations were adjusted to 16.0 ft. pile depth, 17.5 ft wall height.

TABLE 5. FUNCTIONAL RELATIONS OF EFD INCLINE/EFD VERTICAL TO ANGLE OF
INCLINE FROM VERTICAL (θ) FOR WALL NORMAL PRESSURES OF POTATOES.

REGRESSION FUNCTION	PROB > F (Significance Probability Level)	COEFFICIENT OF DETERMINATION (R^2)
$EFD_i/EFD_v = .9114 - .0317\theta$	.0008	0.95
$EFD_i/EFD_v = 1.0329 \exp. (-.0678\theta)$	.0003	0.97
$EFD_i/EFD_v = \left\| \dfrac{(90 - \theta) - \alpha}{90 - \alpha} \right\|^3$	.0009	0.99

Prob > F = .0008 indicates a .08 percent probability that the assumption
of the regression coefficients being zero is correct.

631

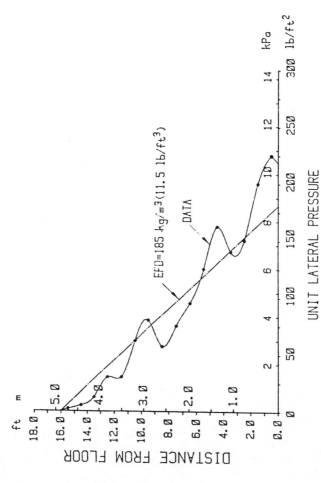

Fig. 1. Wall pressures and calculated EFD on day of maximum total force for vertical wall. (Largest value of maximum total force for five seasons of storage).

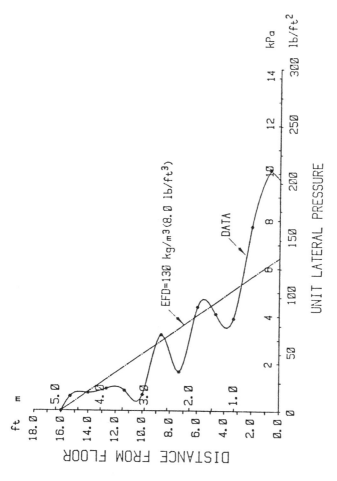

Fig. 2. Wall pressures and calculated EFD on day of maximum total force for 5" inclined wall.

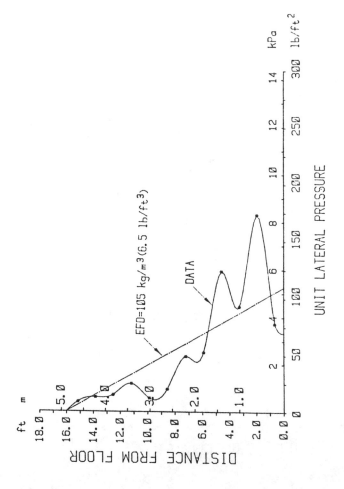

Fig. 3. Wall pressures and calculated EFD on day of maximum total force for 10° inclined wall.

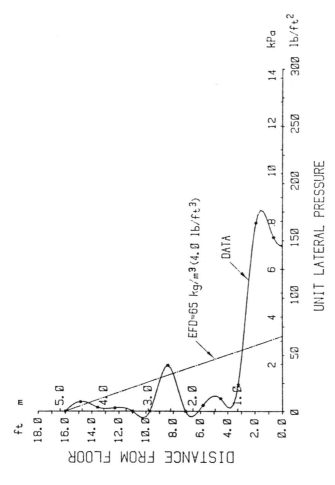

Fig. 4. Wall pressures and calculated EFD on the day of maximum total force for 15° inclined wall.

635

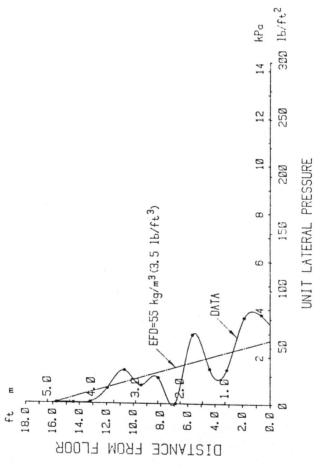

Figure 5. Wall pressures and calculated EFD on day of maximum total force for 20° incline wall.

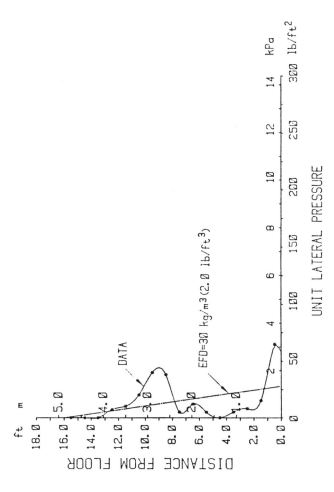

Fig. 6. Wall pressures and calculated EFD on day of maximum total force for 25° inclined wall.

637

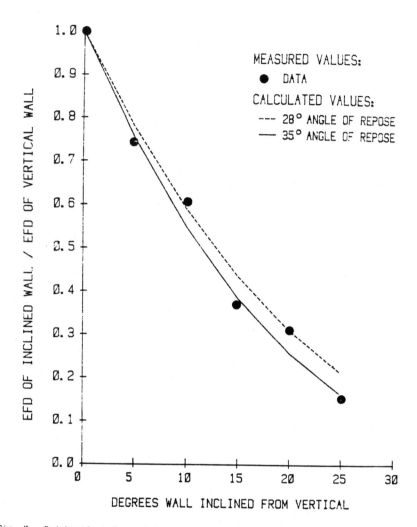

Fig. 7. Reimbert's trigonmetric approximation raised to the third power

$$\frac{\text{EFD Incline}}{\text{EFD Vertical}} = \left[\frac{(90° - \text{Wall Angle}) - \text{Angle of Repose}}{90° - \text{Angle of Repose}}\right]^3$$

and measured data values

638

Figure 8. Remaining wall after failure during bin filling.

Figure 9. Interior view of vertical end wall and bin instrumented with pressure panels.

APPENDIX

ENGLISH TO METRIC CONVERSION FOR THE POTATO INDUSTRY

ENGLISH TO METRIC CONVERSIONS FOR THE POTATO INDUSTRY

Length:

```
1 inch = 2.54 cm
1 foot = 0.305 m
1 mile = 1.61 km
1 inch = 25.4 mm
```

Area:

```
1 square inch = 6.45 sq. cm
1 square foot = 0.093 m²
1 acre       = 0.405 ha
```

Mass:

```
1 ounce (oz) = 28.3 grams (g)
1 pound (lb) = 0.454 kilograms (kg)
1 pound (lb) = 454 grams (g)
1 short ton  = 0.907 metric tons (t)
1 hundred weight (cwt) = 0.0454 metric tons (t)
```

Volume:

```
1 fluid ounce (fl.oz.) = 29.6 milliliters(ml)
1 cubic ft (ft³)       = 0.028 cubic meters (m³)
1 quart (qt)           = 0.946 Liters (l)
1 gallon (gal)         = 3.79 Liters (l)
1 liter (l)            = 0.264 gallon (gal)
```

Temperature:

```
1 degree Fahrenheit (F) = 0.556 degree celsius
    (°C)
To convert:
    0.556 (°F - 32) = °C
```

Density:

```
2.38 cubic feet per hundred weight (ft³/cwt) =
    1.49 cubic meters per metric ton (m³/t)
```

Miscellaneous:

1 ft/s	= 0.305 m/s
1 mile per hour mph	= 1.61 km/hr
1 BTU	= 1.055 kJ
1 BTU/lb	= 2.33 kJ/kg
1 cwt/a	= 0.112 t/ha
1 fl. oz./ton	= 32.6 ml/t
1 fl. oz./a	= 73 ml/ha
1 gal/a	= 9.36 l/ha
1 cfm	= 0.0284 m^3/min
1 cfm/cwt	= 0.624 m^3air/min. ton
1 cfm/cwt	= 0.4167 m^3air/min/m^3 potatoes
1 in. S.P.	= 0.00246 atm.

Abbreviations:

ft	= foot	lb	= pound
in	= inch	kg	= kilogram
m	= meter	t	= metric ton
km	= kilometer	fl oz	= fluid ounce
s	= second	ml	= milliliters
hr	= hour	ton	= short ton

BTU = British Thermal Unit
kJ = Kilojoule